How to Enter China

How to Enter China

Choices and Lessons

Yadong Luo

Ann Arbor

THE UNIVERSITY OF MICHIGAN PRESS

2003   2002   2001   4   3   2   1

A CIP catalog record for this book is available from the British Library.

Library of Congress Cataloging-in-Publication Data

Luo, Yadong.
    How to enter China : choices and lessons / Yadong Luo.
        p.   cm.
    Includes bibliographical references and index.
    ISBN 0-472-11188-4 (cloth : alk. paper)
    1. International business enterprises — China.   2. Investments,
Foreign — China.   3. China — Economic conditions — 1976–
I. Title.

HD2910 .L86   2000
658.1'149'0951 — dc21   00-049096

Contents

Tables

Figures

Preface

This book is designed to cast some light on how China, the largest emerging market in the world, can be entered by multinational corporations (MNCs) seeking preemptive opportunities and long-term competitive positions abroad. Specifically, it aims to (1) present China's investment environment at the turn of the new century, (2) outline the impact of China's World Trade Organization (WTO) membership on MNCs, (3) discuss the logic and pattern of evolutionary expansion by most MNCs, (4) articulate each entry mode choice available to MNCs, (5) analyze various factors underlying entry mode selection and equity ownership arrangements, and (6) provide insight into entry mode selection through case studies. It also synthesizes literature on entry modes and the Chinese business environment, offers managerial lessons and practical guidance regarding entry strategies, and illustrates both the Chinese government's views and its expectations of MNCs.

This book is written for students taking a "Doing Business in China" course, executives interested in foreign investment, and scholars interested in international expansion. The dynamic Chinese economy is now encouraging the use of more diverse and creative investment modes and expansion strategies for MNCs. China's WTO membership creates even more choices for MNCs in selecting an appropriate entry mode that can generate maximum risk-adjusted net returns. In China's complex and dynamic environment, the entry mode decision has a strong influence on investment success and business development since this decision is associated with an investor's resource commitment, organizational control, and risk taking. By choosing an appropriate entry mode that fits organizational capabilities, strategic objectives, and environmental contingencies, MNCs can accomplish their strategic goals, prevent uncompensated exposure of proprietary knowledge, and mitigate transactional hazards that may be precipitated during resource allocation and local operations.

This book is divided into three parts. The first provides background on MNCs in China and their opportunities and challenges in the coming years. Specifically, it reviews MNCs in China over the past two decades (chap. 1), illuminates the Chinese economic environment at the turn of the new century and the effect of WTO membership on MNCs (chap. 2), and elaborates the evolutionary path of MNCs over the years (chap. 3).

The primary focus of this book is in part 2, which illuminates entry mode choices, decisions, and strategies for MNCs. This part describes all entry modes available presently, analyzes the advantages and disadvantages of each, and discusses the governmental policies involved (chap. 4). It further articulates various factors at the country, industry, firm, and project levels that affect the entry mode decision and illustrates how the decision should be configured with these external or internal dynamics (chap. 5). Finally, it outlines the contingencies and consequences of equity ownership arrangements and highlights the control implications of arrangements involved in cooperative entry modes (chap. 6). Each chapter includes several mini-cases that illustrate the entry experiences of these MNCs.

Part 3 presents 11 case studies that offer some insights into how major MNCs such as Nokia, Hewlett Packard, IBM, Motorola, General Motors, Ford, General Electric, and Procter & Gamble successfully entered the Chinese market. Apart from the entry mode strategy, other strategic and operational issues are introduced and analyzed. Each case study details a company's background, its external and internal environments, and its entry, cooperative, and operational strategies. Managers can learn more about competitors' activities, the Chinese environment, and international expansion from these case studies. These cases, together with most of the mini-cases, were prepared by the author based on publicly available information. They are included solely for the purposes of class discussion and are not intended to imply the effective or ineffective handling of an administrative situation.

In the course of writing this book, I have benefited from the comments of my former colleagues in the Ministry of Foreign Economic Relations and Trade, China, and two anonymous reviewers. I also wish to thank my family for their continuing selfless support.

PART 1
Multinational Corporations in China

Situation, Environment, and Evolution

CHAPTER 1

Multinational Corporations in China: An Overview

This chapter provides background on foreign direct investment in China. The discussion is divided into five sections. The first provides an overview of foreign direct investment in the world. This is followed by an introduction to some of the characteristics of foreign direct investment in China. The third section is a historical review of such investment from 1979 to 1996. The fourth section addresses current developments, especially with respect to recently emerging policy changes. The last section speculates on the future of foreign investment in China.

MNCs and Worldwide Investment

The 1990s was the era of globalization, when the rapid growth of international trade, financial flows, and foreign direct investment (FDI) affected more and more economies in deeper and deeper ways. The benefits of financial globalization in particular have been many, but the world economy has periodically been buffeted by international financial shocks, the latest of which has been the most severe. It can be regarded as having begun when the Thai baht collapsed on July 2, 1997, after which it spread to other Asian economies and has since touched countries on every continent in one way or another.

Global FDI flows on a balance of payments basis reached record levels in 1997. Both outward and inward investment broke through the U.S.$400 billion mark for the first time, with outward investment up 27.0 percent in 1996 (U.S.$423.7 billion) and inward investment up 18.6 percent (U.S.$400.5 billion). Outward FDI, despite a year-on-year decline in 1996, picked up in 1997 due to greater investment by developed nations. Growth in both FDI inflows and outflows in 1997 was driven mainly by the United States and the United Kingdom, with the United States contributing 12.2 and 4.7 points and the United Kingdom contributing 7.9 and 3.6 points to growth in outflows and inflows, respectively. Much of the increase in outward FDI by the United States was directed at Dutch and British holding companies. U.S. investment in the Netherlands was targeted ultimately at investment in Asia via that country. According to U.S. statistics, in recent years the reinvestment of profits by overseas subsidiaries has accounted for nearly 50 percent of U.S. FDI and a large proportion of the equity capital comprising new investments has taken the form of mergers and acquisitions. Stock for stock transactions, developed in the United States as a means of acquiring companies, have been widely used for cross-border mergers and acquisitions.

FDI received by developing countries in 1997 was 14.7 percent higher than that received in the previous year. Inflows of FDI into Latin America rose sharply thanks to strong growth in investment in Brazil and Mexico. In Brazil, foreign firms were attracted by large-scale privatization in the electricity and telecommunications sectors. This was a result of the Brazilian government policy of attracting foreign capital to improve its infrastructure, and more than 80 percent of inward FDI was in Brazil's nonmanufacturing sector in 1997. Within East Asia, investment grew in China, the Republic of Korea (ROK), Singapore, Taiwan, and Thailand but fell in Indonesia and the Philippines. Inflows entering the four member countries of the Association of Southeast Asian Nations (ASEAN) continued to decline, but this accounted for only a small proportion of global FDI. The United Nations Conference on Trade and Development (UNCTAD) estimated that global FDI outflows in 1998 would reach $430 to $440 billion, higher than in 1997.

International production by multinational corporations (MNCs) has continuously grown in recent years. As table 1.1 shows, all major indicators related to MNC activities demonstrated high rates of growth. Specifically, worldwide FDI stock, which constitutes the capital base for MNC corporations, rose over 10 percent annually in the 1990s. It is held

TABLE 1.1.   Major Indicators of FDI, 1986–97

Item	Global Annual Growth Rate (%)			
	1986–90	1991–95	1996	1997
FDI inflows	23.6	20.1	1.9	18.6
FDI outflows	27.1	15.1	−0.5	27.1
FDI inward stock	18.2	9.7	12.2	12.7
FDI outward stock	21.0	10.3	11.5	13.7
Cross-border mergers and acquisitions	21.0	30.2	15.5	45.2
Foreign affiliate sales	16.3	13.4	6.0	7.3
Foreign affiliate assets	18.3	24.4	12.0	13.0

Source: Adapted from UNCTAD 1998, 2.

by a minimum of 53,000 MNCs, large and small (UNCTAD 1998). The regional distribution of outward FDI stock is heavily skewed toward developed countries, indicating that in the past most FDI originated and stayed in developed countries, although there have been some noticeable recent increases in the stock of developing countries. The share of South, East, and Southeast Asia in world inward FDI nearly doubled during the 1990s. Table 1.2 lists the world's largest host and home economies for FDI flows. It shows that China has the second-largest FDI inflow in the world, surpassed only by the United States.

There are at least 448,000 foreign affiliates in the world (UNCTAD 1998). The role that they play in host countries has become more and more important. Total assets held by all foreign affiliates in 1997 were 3.5 times as large as FDI stocks. These assets imply the capacity of foreign affiliates to produce goods and services. The average size of assets owned by foreign affiliates worldwide in the mid-1990s was about $28 million. Sales of goods and services by foreign affiliates, which were about $9.5 trillion in 1997, grew faster than worldwide exports, which amounted to $6.4 trillion in the same year. This suggests that MNCs use FDI more than they use exports—by a factor of 1.5—to service foreign markets. Foreign affiliates worldwide also generated more than $2 trillion in value added in 1997. They accounted for an increasing share in the world's gross domestic production (GDP): close to 7 percent in 1997, compared to 5 percent in the mid-1980s. Moreover, MNC affiliates accounted for some one-third of world exports in 1995, compared to about one-quarter during the latter half of the 1980s. Since the mid-1980s, the export propensity of MNC affiliates (i.e., the ratio of exports

TABLE 1.2.   The World's Top Host and Home Nations for FDI, 1996

	FDI Inflows ($bil)		FDI Outflows ($bil)	
Rank	Economy	Value	Economy	Value
1	United States	76.5	United States	74.8
2	China	40.8	United Kingdom	34.1
3	United Kingdom	26.0	France	30.4
4	France	22.0	Germany	29.5
5	Belgium and Luxembourg	14.1	Hong Kong, China	26.4
6	Brazil	11.1	Japan	23.4
7	Singapore	9.4	Netherlands	23.1
8	Mexico	8.2	Switzerland	11.6
9	Netherlands	7.8	Canada	8.5
10	Spain	6.5	Belgium and Luxembourg	8.4

Source: Adapted from UNCTAD 1998, 11.

to total sales) has remained close to one-quarter. Since 1980, the ratio of FDI stock to GDP for the world as a whole has increased steadily and at a much faster rate than the ratio of world trade to GDP, suggesting that global integration seems to have proceeded faster through FDI than through trade.

As a function of the extent to which a firm's activities take place abroad, the transnationality of MNCs has remained at a high level in recent years. The value of this index, measured by a composite of foreign assets/total assets, foreign sales/total sales, and foreign employment/total employment, for the top 100 MNCs was 55 percent in 1996, representing an increase of 4 percentage points over 1995. The growing internationalization of assets has contributed the most to the increase in the transnationality index. For the top 100 MNCs as a whole, this index ranged from 97 percent for Seagram, a Canadian beverage company with interests increasingly geared toward the entertainment and publishing industries, to 16 percent for GTE in 1996; this is quite similar to 1990, when the range was 97 for Nestle to 15 for General Electric (GE). Table 1.3 suggests that the 10 MNCs with the highest transnationality show values between 85 and 97 percent.

The table suggests that firms with the highest transnationality index, such as Asea Brown Boveri (ABB), Nestle, Solvay, Electrolux, Unilever, and Roche, come from small industrial countries. Over the 1990–96 period, the average transnationality of the top 10 firms from small countries increased from an already high 77 percent to an even higher 79 percent. During the same period, the average transnationality of the top 10 firms located in larger countries remained around 50 percent. Food and beverages, chemicals and pharmaceuticals, electronics

TABLE 1.3. The Top 10 MNCs in Terms of Transnationality, 1996

Rank	MNCs	Country	Industry	Transnationality Index
1	Seagram Co.	Canada	Beverages	97.3
2	Asea Brown Boveri	Switzerland	Electrical equipment	96.1
3	Nestle SA	Switzerland	Food	95.3
4	Thomson Corp.	Canada	Printing/publishing	94.9
5	Solvay SA	Belgium	Chemicals/pharmaceuticals	92.2
6	Holderbank	Switzerland	Construction	89.8
7	Electrolux AB	Sweden	Electrical appliances	88.7
8	Unilever	Netherlands	Food	87.1
9	Roche Holding AG	Switzerland	Pharmaceuticals	87.0
10	Michelin	France	Rubber/plastic	84.9

Source: Adapted from UNCTAD 1998, 45.

and electrical equipment, oil and petroleum, and telecommunications are among the leading industries in terms of averages in transnationality.

Cross-border mergers and acquisitions have fundamentally increased in recent years, accounting for about one-quarter of all mergers and acquisitions worldwide. These transactions amounted to $342 billion in 1997. Their value in relation to total FDI inflows rose from 49 percent in 1996 to 58 percent in 1997, representing the highest share attained in the 1990s.

Repeated episodes of financial turmoil have focused international attention on the problem of the volatility of private foreign capital flows and the extent to which such volatility creates an unstable environment detrimental to economic development, particularly in developing and transition economies. In most cases, while foreign portfolio investment shows high volatility, FDI does not. For instance, when portfolio investment fell sharply in Mexico in 1994–95 during the peso crisis, FDI was very much sustained. MNCs are normally more interested in longer-term profits from the production of goods and services, whereas portfolio investors are normally more interested in quick financial returns. Thus, FDI is less prone to reversals in response to adverse situations if these are perceived to be short term. Moreover, divestment and reversibility are more difficult for FDI than for portfolio investment, which can be disposed of easily by selling in financial markets. Portfolio investors' strategies, combined with the problems of asymmetrical information and the inherent volatility of emerging markets, make portfolio investment more prone to herd behavior and more easily affected by the short-term fluctuations in financial markets that influence investors' expectations of capital gains.

MNCs and FDI Flows to Asia

Despite the financial crisis affecting a number of Asian economies, FDI in Asia rose by about 8 percent to about $87 billion in 1997, led primarily by increased flows to China. The region accounted for 57 percent of flows into all developing countries and over half of their FDI stock. An overwhelming proportion of the region's inward FDI was directed to East and Southeast Asia in the 1990s. China, Taiwan, and Singapore are leading FDI destinations in this subregion. Even in the five Asian economies most affected by the crisis (Indonesia, South Korea, Malaysia, the Philippines, and Thailand), overall inflows remained at a level similar to that a year before the crisis. This suggests that foreign direct investment in Asia launched by MNCs was not significantly affected by the financial crisis that erupted in July 1997. Thus, FDI was much less variable than portfolio capital flows and commercial leading, both of which declined sharply as a result of the crisis. The share of FDI in total resource flows to East and Southeast Asia has increased remarkably in recent years, from 10 percent in 1990 to 53 percent in 1997. Indeed, FDI has become the single most important source of private development financing for the region, and it is likely to be particularly important for the economies most affected by the crisis.

China is the front-runner, with new record inflows of $45 billion in 1997, which accounted for over half of the flows into Asia and 11 percent of the world total. The country continued to maintain its position as the second-largest FDI recipient in the world and the single largest among developing countries.

The four minidragons (Hong Kong, Singapore, South Korea, and Taiwan) achieved a modest combined FDI growth of 6 percent in 1997. Flows into these economies taken together reached a record $17 billion in 1997, twice as much as FDI flows to the entire African continent. Singapore remained the single largest recipient among the four economies and ranked at the top of Asian countries in terms of the ratio of FDI stock to GDP.

Total flows into the ASEAN countries (Indonesia, Malaysia, the Philippines, Thailand, and Vietnam) remained at a level similar to that of 1996 despite the crisis. FDI flows to South Asia rose to another record level of about $4.4 billion in 1997, compared to $3.3 billion in 1996, mostly reflecting an increase of about 37 percent in flows into India. FDI flows into the eight Central Asian economies also increased for a fifth consecutive year, reaching $2.4 million in 1997. Finally, flows into Western Asia increased by a multiple of six, from a level of some $300 million in 1996 to 1.9 billion in 1997. Table 1.4 indicates FDI inflows in selected Asian countries, especially those affected by the financial crisis.

Receipts of FDI in 1997 by South Korea and ASEAN, according to

TABLE 1.4.   FDI Inflows into Selected Asian Countries (in billions of dollars)

Country	1990	1991	1992	1993	1994	1995	1996	1997
China	3.5	4.4	11.2	27.5	33.8	35.8	40.8	45.3
Indonesia	1.1	1.5	1.8	2.0	2.1	4.3	6.2	5.4
South Korea	0.8	1.2	0.7	0.6	0.8	1.8	2.3	2.3
Malaysia	2.3	4.0	5.2	5.0	4.3	4.1	4.7	3.8
Philippines	0.5	0.5	0.2	1.2	1.6	1.5	1.5	1.3
Thailand	7.2	9.2	10.0	10.6	10.2	13.7	16.9	16.4

Source: Adapted from UNCTAD 1998, 201.

each country's own statistics, showed no sign of being affected by the currency and economic crises, and with the exception of Malaysia it rose in all cases (although growth rates varied from country to country). In 1998, however, receipts of FDI fell across the board. This was due to (1) a decline in investor confidence caused by serious slumps in domestic production and the wider economic malaise caused by the crisis and (2) sudden drops in investment from Japan due to the prolonged economic recession there. Other factors related to the currency and economic crises also played a major role, such as the tendency of firms to postpone new investments in Indonesia because of the political unrest. Vietnam, meanwhile, suffered sharp reductions in investment in 1997 and the first six months of 1998 due to declining investment from other ASEAN countries.

In South Asia, the currency and economic crises had relatively little impact on the real economy. Investment in India in 1997 was up 150 percent over the previous year due mainly to growth in investment in the electricity industry, and Bangladesh saw FDI rise by 500 percent in fiscal 1997 (July 1997 to June 1998) due mainly to investment in social infrastructure and utilities. In the Pacific, investment in Australia was up 2.3 percent in fiscal 1996–97 (July 1996 to June 1997) as a result of greater investment in manufacturing, but in New Zealand there was a 24.1 percent drop as sales of state-owned enterprises to foreign firms came to a halt.

The financial crisis led to a sharp decrease in private capital flows to some Asian developing countries. Net private foreign bank lending and portfolio equity investment turned negative in 1997 for the group of countries most affected by the crisis. However, while large amounts of short-term capital left these countries, FDI inflows remained positive and continued to add to the existing FDI stock. The behavior of these two types of investment flows to the Asian economies most influenced by the crisis is reminiscent of their behavior during the crisis that struck Mexico in 1994–95. At that time, total portfolio investment in Mexico fell by nearly 40 percent, from $12 billion in 1994 to $7.5 billion, with portfolio equity investment falling by almost 90 percent, from $4.5 to $0.5 billion. FDI flows, in contrast, which had more than doubled in 1994, fell by only 13 percent in 1995.

Even though FDI is more stable than portfolio investment, it is not insensitive to crises and especially to changes in the determinants of investment induced by a crisis. Some MNCs may consider increasing FDI in the short or medium term because of the decrease in the costs of establishing and expanding production facilities in crisis-affected countries. The decrease is the result of exchange rate depreciation, lower property prices, and more company assets offered for sale, given the heavy indebtedness of domestic firms and their reduced access to liquidity. Export-oriented FDI may also benefit more from currency devaluations, even though inflation could eventually eliminate the advantage. The impact of the crisis may therefore be mitigated somewhat for the affected Asian economies because international integration at the level of production allows MNCs to compensate for declining local sales through increased exports spurred by devaluation. The downturn in domestic demand in Asia, however, has had adverse consequences for host-market–oriented FDI. Reduced demand and slower growth led to cancellation, scaling down, or postponement of some FDI in these countries.

The financial crisis has also affected FDI regulations enacted by governments. Some countries have further liberalized their FDI regimes. In addition to unilateral measures and measures implemented in pursuit of multilateral commitments, liberalization measures have been taken in the context of the adjustment programs linked to the package of financial support from the International Monetary Fund (IMF). Recent moves by the crisis-affected countries include opening industries like banking and other financial services to FDI and relaxing rules with respect to ownership, mode of entry, and financing. While these new policies create more favorable conditions for FDI, they can lead to market distortions and intensify incentive competition in the region.

Overall, controls on foreign capital have been more liberalized. Recognizing that since the eruption of the currency and economic crises in July 1997 the introduction of foreign capital has been essential to economic recovery, Thailand, Malaysia, Indonesia, the Philippines, and South Korea have rushed to loosen their controls on foreign investment. In Thailand, the government allowed 100 percent foreign equity ownership of currently approved enterprises eligible for investment incentives in December 1997; then, in May 1998, 100 percent ownership was allowed in the case of nonapproved enterprises in industries covered by measures intended to encourage investment. In August, cabinet approval was given for the abolition of ceilings on foreign equity ownership in 30 of the 68 sectors, such as the retail sector, covered by the Foreign Enterprise Control Act. Meanwhile, in August 1998 Malaysia announced the abolition of controls on foreign equity ownership in most areas of manufacturing until the end of 2000. In July 1998, Indonesia, too, amended its "negative list" of sectors subject to controls on foreign investment to allow 100 percent foreign capital participation, under certain conditions, in the wholesale and retail sectors. In October 1998, the Philippines amended its negative list to allow 100 percent foreign capital participation in the construction industry. In South Korea, the Foreign Direct Investment and Foreign Capital Inducement Act was revised and renamed the Foreign Investment Promotion Act in November 1998, thus allowing investment in 21 sectors such as the securities exchange business.

The crisis does have several important policy implications. First, given that sudden, massive, short-term capital flows brought about the currency and economic crises in Asia, international rules need to be established for monitoring short-term capital movements to prevent a recurrence of such crises. Second, the Asian currency and economic crises have prompted developing countries to reaffirm the importance of FDI inflow. The resulting relaxation and abolition of regulations on FDI is improving the investment environments in these countries. In the future, industrial bases must also be improved. More specifically, this includes not only infrastructure, such as roads, ports, and electricity, but also the development of financial systems and human resources and the stabilization of labor-management relations. Doing so will require the technical and financial support of developed nations, including official development assistance. Third, local authorities seeking to attract foreign investment must provide information that is more detailed and has a wider scope. So far, information has concerned mainly industrial estates and the level of development of local infrastructures. In the future, greater emphasis will have to be placed on information of specific interest to foreign firms such as residential environments and the growth prospects of local economies, industries, and markets. Comprehensive information will have to be provided via channels such as electronic media.

FDI in China, 1979–98

China officially opened its doors to foreign investment in 1979 with the promulgation of a joint venture law. Through the end of 1998, Chinese authorities had approved the establishment of over 300,000 foreign invested enterprises (FIEs) involving $522.4 billion in foreign capital. Of these, over 150,000 FIEs representing $221.04 billion in investment had commenced operations by the end of 1997 (table 1.5).

Foreign investors are generally free to choose their mode of entry into deregulated Chinese industries. Table 1.6 depicts the recent pattern of foreign investment, including both FDI and foreign loans. FDI dominated in foreign capital inflows, representing about 90 percent of the nation's total in 1996. Among FDIs in 1997, equity joint ventures accounted for 40.64 percent while wholly foreign owned enterprise represented 34.62 percent and contractual joint ventures 23.66 percent. Longitudinally, the ratio of wholly foreign owned ventures has been growing

TABLE 1.5. Actual Value of FDI in China, 1979–97 (in hundreds of millions of dollars)

Year	Total Foreign Investment	Foreign Direct Investment	Other Foreign Investment[a]
1979–83	26.83	18.02	8.81
1984	14.19	12.58	1.61
1985	19.59	16.61	2.98
1986	22.44	18.74	3.70
1987	26.47	23.14	3.33
1988	37.39	31.94	5.45
1989	37.73	33.92	3.81
1990	37.55	34.87	2.68
1991	46.66	43.66	3.00
1992	112.91	110.07	2.84
1993	277.71	275.15	2.56
1994	339.46	337.67	1.79
1995	378.06	375.21	2.85
1996	421.35	417.26	4.09
1997	456.50	452.60	3.90
Total	2,254.84	2,201.44	53.4

Sources: For 1979–96: *China Statistical Yearbook* 1997, 605; for 1997: UNCTAD 1998, 204.

[a]Other foreign investments include international leasing, compensation trade, and processing and assembling.

TABLE 1.6. Approved Foreign Investment in China by Form (in millions of dollars)

Investment Form	1995	1996	1997
Foreign direct investment	91,282	73,276	51,003
Equity joint ventures	39,741	31,876	20,726
Contractual joint ventures	17,825	14,297	12,066
Wholly foreign owned	33,658	26,810	17,658
Joint exploration	57	293	402
Shared enterprise			151
Other foreign investment	635	371	4,183
International lease	42	33	289
Compensation trade	404	129	124
Processing and assembling	189	209	1,696
Stock/bond issuance			2,074
Foreign loans	11,288	7,962	5,872
Government loans	4,754	4,203	754
Loans from international organizations	3,680	1,682	3,732
Commercial/export loans	2,854	2,077	1,386
Total	103,205	81,610	61,058

Source: China Statistical Yearbook 1997 (605), 1998 (602).

in recent years (it was only 7 percent prior to 1990). Nevertheless, the equity joint venture remains the primary entry mode used by MNCs to expand into the Chinese market.

FDI has experienced three phases in China. Phase 1 (1979–85) was the initial stage of foreign investment, starting with the promulgation of the Joint Venture Law by the Chinese government in 1979 and the establishment of four special economic zones (SEZs) in Guangdong and Fujian Provinces where preferential economic policies were pursued. In 1984, 14 coastal cities were opened to foreign investment, which resulted in the spread of FDI from the SEZs to other coastal regions and led to the first FDI boom in 1984–85. However, the initial boom ended in late 1995 due to high inflation and a lack of legal clarity regarding FDI. During this stage, foreign investments were concentrated in small-scale assembling and processing for export.

In phase 2 (1986–89), in response to a decline in FDI, the Chinese government published its "Provisions for the Encouragement of Foreign Investment" (October 1986), which was followed by a set of central regulations intended to implement them and a flurry of provincial and municipal-level regulations. These provisions and regulations clarified the legal environment for FDI and also provided solutions to some major problems, such as foreign exchange imbalances, facing foreign invested enterprises. To encourage foreign investment in high-technology industries, all the open coastal cities set up economic and technical development zones where extra tax breaks and other incentives were offered. The improved investment environment promoted a quick recovery of FDI after 1986. In contrast to the prior structure, over 70 percent of FDI projects were involved in manufacturing industries in this period. The new investment boom ended in mid-1989 as a result of worsening economic and political conditions.

During phase 3 (1990–97), in recognition of the negative reaction of foreign investors to the worsening investment climate, the Chinese government issued amendments to the Joint Venture Law (April 1990). These amendments codified several rules designed to encourage investment. In 1991, the Income Tax Law for Enterprises with Foreign Capital and Foreign Enterprises standardized income tax rates for different types of FIEs. In 1992, the Chinese government adopted a "socialist market economy" strategy and sped up market-oriented reforms. A set of commercial laws and regulations was passed to improve the legal framework and policy settings in which foreign business operates. As a result, foreign investment surged after 1992. Since 1994, foreign investment in China has entered a new stage of adjustment and consolidation, which has exhibited some new features. The average size of foreign investment projects has increased, with the main focus on large infrastructure and manufacturing projects. The growth rate of FDI has fallen back to a sustainable level from one that was unusually high.

FIEs have played a major role in the modernization of the Chinese economy. As shown in table 1.7, the share of total industrial output in China made by FIEs reached 18.6 percent in 1997. The share of total national export volume made by FIEs climbed to 41 percent in the same year. The tax contribution as a share of the nation's total was 13.2 percent. FDI already accounted for 17 percent of total gross domestic investment in 1996. A total of 17.5 million Chinese were employed in FIEs in 1997, 12.7 million more than six years before.

FDI can affect a local economy at both the macro- and microlevels. At the microlevel, FDI may influence the technological and managerial efficiency of joint ventures and local firms through technology transfer, labor training, and spillover effects. At the macrolevel, FDI may affect both "real" macroeconomic variables (e.g., domestic investment, economic growth, employment, exports, and imports) and "financial" variables (e.g., interest rates, exchange rates, and inflation). The macroeconomic impact of FDI in China is primarily reflected in its effects on real economic variables, as financial variables are essentially controlled by the government.

Recently, several studies have found that FDI significantly promoted the economic growth of China during the 1979–96 period by contributing to domestic capital formation, increasing exports, and creating new employment. Moreover, FDI has improved the productive and resource allocation efficiency of Chinese domestic sectors by transferring technology and facilitating interregional and intersector flows of

TABLE 1.7.   Contributions of FDI to China's Economy, 1991–97

Item	1991	1992	1993	1994	1995	1996	1997
FDI inflows ($bil)	4.4	11.2	27.5	33.8	35.8	40.8	45.3
Average amount per project ($mil)	0.9	1.2	1.3	1.8	2.5	na	na
FDI/gross domestic investment (%)	3.9	7.4	12.7	17.3	15.1	17.0	14.8
FDI stock/GDP (%)	5.6	7.1	10.2	17.6	18.8	24.7	na
FIE exports ($bil)	12.0	17.4	25.2	34.7	46.9	61.5	75.0
FIE exports/national exports (%)	17.0	20.4	27.5	28.7	31.3	41.0	41.0
FIE output/national output (%)	5.0	6.0	9.0	11.0	13.0	na	18.6
Number of employees (mil)	4.8	6.0	10.0	14.0	16.0	17.0	17.5
Tax contribution as share of total	na	4.1	na	na	10.0	na	13.2

Source: Adapted from UNCTAD 1996 (198), 1998 (204).

labor and capital. While recognizing these benefits, some side effects must be acknowledged as well. These include worsening environmental degradation as a result of shifting polluting industries to China and income loss for the host state and firms as a result of transfer pricing among foreign affiliates by MNCs.

FIEs have diverse foreign sources. Table 1.8 lists the top 10 countries or regions of origin for FDI in China during the period 1995–97. The top 10 sources together constitute 82.18 percent of China's total FDI in 1997. Among them, Hong Kong and Macau took the lead in direct investment on the mainland, contributing $21.46 billion, or 51.43 percent of the national total in 1996. They were followed by Japan (8.85 percent), Taiwan (8.34 percent), the United States (8.25 percent), Singapore (5.39 percent), South Korea (3.60 percent), and the United Kingdom (3.12 percent).

Interestingly, of the top 10 foreign sources, five come from Asian developing countries or regions. They collectively undertook about 70 percent of the total actual FDI in China in 1996, whereas their counterparts from Japan, the United States, the United Kingdom, and Germany accounted for only 21.46 percent (table 1.8). The accumulated amount of FDI by the end of 1996 also suggests that FDI in China launched by developing country businesses has been more than three times that of developed country firms over the last 17 years.

Although Hong Kong and Taiwan are the top two investment sources, in a broad sense, they are simply moving relatively labor-intensive activities into China in an attempt to escape rising labor costs and space constraints at home. Moreover, the average size of investment

TABLE 1.8.   FDI in China of the Top 10 Countries or Regions, 1995–97 (in millions of dollars)

Rank	Country/Region	1995	1996	1997	Percentage in 1997
1	Hong Kong/Macao	20,625	21,458	21,954	41.91
2	Japan	3,212	3,692	4,390	8.38
3	United States	3,084	3,444	3,461	6.61
4	Taiwan	3,165	3,482	3,342	6.38
5	Singapore	1,861	2,247	2,607	4.98
6	Republic of Korea	1,047	1,504	2,228	4.25
7	United Kingdom	915	1,302	1,860	3.55
8	Virgin Islands	304	539	1,717	3.28
9	Germany	391	519	1,009	1.93
10	France	287	425	476	0.91

Source: China Statistical Yearbook 1997 (606–7), 1998 (603–4).

from these two sources is relatively small. For instance, the average equity pledged by U.S. investors is nearly twice as high as that of FDI from Hong Kong and about 50 percent higher than the average FDI project from Taiwan and Southeast Asian countries.

While Hong Kong and Taiwan investors emphasize labor-intensive and simple industrial processing for light industrial and textile goods aimed at the international market, U.S. and European firms tend to place their emphasis on capital- or technology-intensive manufacturing sectors in an effort to gain access to the growing Chinese domestic market. Japanese investors, while also interested in China's domestic market, have placed less emphasis on manufacturing and have instead become more involved in various forms of property development.

FDI in China has been active in a variety of industries. Table 1.9 presents industrial patterns in 1996, when the industrial sector accounted for 68.90 percent of total FDI, leading all other sectors in influencing the economy. The real estate and utility sector follows, with $12.85 billion in investments or 17.54 percent of the total. Commercial and food services, construction, transportation and telecommunications services, and agriculture are also important sectors, ranking from third to sixth.

Different sectors have idiosyncratic patterns of FDI growth. FDI in agriculture, industry, transportation and telecommunications services, and health care and social welfare services has boomed, growing from 12 to 75 percent between 1993 and 1995. FDI in other sectors, especially real estate and construction, has slowed. For instance, foreign invest-

TABLE 1.9.   Approved FDI in China by Sector, 1996

Sector	Number of Projects	Value ($mil)
Agriculture	812	1,139
Industry	18,280	50,486
Construction	387	2,001
Transportation and telecommunications	196	1,599
Commerce and food services	1,655	2,347
Real estate and utilities	1,961	12,851
(Tourist hotels)	(81)	(291)
Health care and sports	128	354
Education, culture, and the arts	63	171
Scientific research	124	175
Other	950	2,154
Total	24,556	73,277

Source: China Statistical Yearbook 1997, 611.

ment in the hotel and construction sectors decreased by 55.35 and 102 percent, respectively, during the same period. This reflects structural changes in Chinese FDI policies over the past few years.

FDI in China occurs throughout the country. Table 1.10 shows that it has been present in almost every province in recent years. However, its obviously uneven geographical distribution within various regions in China is a critical issue. For example, in 1996, the total value of FDI in 18 central and western provinces or autonomous regions was $4.8 billion, only 11.40 percent of nationwide FDI. The number of registered FIEs in all central and western provinces or autonomous regions as of

TABLE 1.10.   Realized FDI in China by Location (in millions of dollars)

Rank	Region	1994	1995	1996	1997
1	Guandong	9,463	10,260	11,754	11,711
2	Jiangsu	3,763	5,191	5,210	5,435
3	Fujian	3,713	4,044	4,085	4,197
4	Shanghai	2,473	2,893	3,941	4,225
5	Shandong	2,552	2,689	2,634	2,493
6	Tianjin	1,015	1,521	2,153	2,511
7	Liaoning	1,440	1,425	1,738	2,205
8	Beijing	1,372	1,080	1,553	1,593
9	Zhejiang	1,150	1,258	1,521	1,503
10	Hebei	523	547	830	1,101
11	Hainan	918	1,062	789	706
12	Hunan	331	508	745	917
13	Hubei	602	625	681	790
14	Guangxi	838	673	663	880
15	Heilongjiang	48	517	567	735
16	Henan	387	479	524	692
17	Anhui	370	483	507	434
18	Jilin	242	408	452	402
19	Sichuan	922	542	441	635
20	Shaanxi	239	324	326	628
21	Jiangxi	262	289	301	478
22	Shanxi	32	64	138	266
23	Gansu	88	64	90	41
24	Inner Mongolia	40	58	72	73
25	Yunnan	65	98	65	166
26	Xinjiang	48	55	64	25
27	Guizhou	64	57	31	50
28	Ningxia	7	4	6	7
29	Qinghai	2	2	1	2
30	Tibet	0	0	0	0
	Total	33,268	37,215	42,135	45,257

Source: China Statistical Yearbook 1997, 608.

1995 was 44,875, or just 23.78 percent of the number in eastern regions. Meanwhile, the portion of registered foreign capital in the central and western regions by the end of 1995 was $40,249 million, constituting only 15.67 percent of the nation's total. Although over the last few years the Chinese government has called for an increase of FDI in the central and western regions, the flow of foreign investment to these areas still lags far behind that directed toward the eastern region.

Present Challenge and Future Outlook

China has experienced a boom in FDI inflows, which reached $45 billion in 1997. The boom has been fueled by various factors, including the country's large and continuously growing domestic market, its export-oriented strategy and successful penetration of the world markets, the liberalization of its inward-industrial upgrading in neighboring economies — the so-called flying-geese pattern — and the low level of FDI stock relative to the size of the economy until recently. However, the rate of growth of FDI inflows has slowed, from an average of 165 percent in 1992–93 to 17 percent in 1994–95 and 11 percent in 1997. This slowdown raises the question of whether the FDI boom in China is nearing its end. The relevance of this question is twofold. First, considering the position of FDI in both gross fixed capital formation and GDP in China (among the highest in the world), a major change in FDI inflows may have wide-ranging consequences for the Chinese economy. Second, developments with respect to FDI in China will have a sizable impact on FDI trends in Asia and the developing world generally since China has become the single largest FDI recipient among developing countries and the second-largest recipient worldwide.

To the extent that FDI approvals are indicative, they do suggest that actual flows may decline in the coming years, as approvals have been declining for some years, falling from $111 billion in 1993 to $52 billion in 1997. Experience suggests that the decline in approvals may be followed by a decline in actual inflows in the short-to-medium term. Various developments in pull and push factors for inward FDI in China suggest that such a prediction is plausible.

Slowdown in economic growth. FDI tends to be positively correlated with GDP growth. Hence, reduced economic growth in China can be expected to have a negative impact on FDI inflows. Although GDP growth has remained high in China (at 8.8 percent in 1997), it is below the double-digit growth of earlier years. More importantly, real GDP growth showed a further slowdown, to 7.2 percent in 1998. Market-seeking FDI, in particular, would be depressed by weaker demand in China.

Excess capacity. FDI in China's industrial sector will be the first to be affected by worsening demand. It may turn out that the massive foreign and domestic investment of the recent past has resulted in excess capacity in a number of industries, such as some consumer electrical and electronics products, textiles and clothing, and other light industrial products. The capacity of such industries to absorb further FDI inflows may thus be limited in the next few years. This is true especially of industries in the coastal area, in which FDI has been concentrated. Competition in the coastal areas for sales in the domestic market is becoming more intense, and, in addition to foreign enterprises, a few domestic firms are emerging as strong competitors. This suggests that the "gold rush" by investors into certain manufacturing industries in China may be coming to an end. The pressure on profit rates stemming from excess capacity and increased competition could reduce the incentive for latecomers among MNCs to undertake new FDI. At the same time, established MNCs are likely to postpone sequential FDI unless a reasonable balance between demand and supply is restored.

Declining locational advantages for efficiency-seeking FDI. When China emerged as a major host country for FDI, most investment went into labor-intensive, export-processing operations. Several factors have played a role in creating a new set of conditions. First, wage increases, particularly in China's coastal areas, where FDI is concentrated, are eroding incentives for MNCs to establish labor-intensive export-processing operations. Second, despite special efforts by the government, MNCs' relocation of investment from China's coastal regions to the interior has not been significant. MNCs have preferred, rather, to move to other low-income countries where transportation costs are lower and the infrastructure is more advanced than in China's interior provinces. Third, for certain labor-intensive products, even though they remain internationally competitive, the potential of exporting from China is constrained by trade barriers in major export markets (import quotas, antidumping provisions, and so on). In addition, the demand for labor-intensive products in these markets is likely to decline if expectations of an economic slowdown in the world economy turn out to be correct. The recession in Japan is of particular relevance here. Fourth, China's price competitiveness in international markets has been reduced vis-à-vis that of a number of Southeast Asian countries that recently devalued their currencies. This could break the flying-geese pattern of industrialization in Asia from which labor-intensive industries in China have benefited in the past.

These problems not only might discourage efficiency-seeking FDI in China but they could also affect the country's impressive export performance. In the short run, export growth is indeed likely to slow down, especially to the Southeast Asian countries currently affected by the financial crisis. With regard to total exports, a decline in annual growth from 20 percent in 1997 to 3 percent in 1998 and 1999 has been forecast.

Reduced outward FDI from Asian neighbors. FDI in China has mainly come from within the Asian region. Hong Kong, China; Taiwan Province of China; Singapore; Japan; the Republic of Korea; Thailand; and Malaysia rank among the top investors, accounting for 80 percent of China's inward FDI stock. The share of these countries in approved FDI in China in 1996–97 was also high. It is questionable, however, to what extent the approvals in 1996–97 will be realized, given the current constraints on outward investment facing some of these countries. A significant decline in flows from other Asian economies to China can thus be expected between 1998 and 2000.

To sum up, FDI in China will probably decline in the short run. Although the financial crisis in Asia has not directly affected China, its indirect repercussions are as yet unclear. If they are serious, and if the country's economic growth slows down considerably, various structural weaknesses may come to the surface and erode investors' confidence in the short and medium term. It should be noted, however, that FDI flows are an incremental measure, representing additions to a stock of assets for production; it cannot be expected that they will grow forever at the same rate, even if a host country continues to have a relatively high rate of economic growth. As long as flows fluctuate at a relatively high level, they contribute, other things being equal, to the increase in stocks and play an important role in the host economy.

The Chinese central government has introduced measures to prevent speculative investment (e.g., in real estate) and has forced some "phantom" foreign affiliates to terminate operations. It also strengthened monitoring by setting up administrative procedures for appraising foreign invested property in early 1994. The appraisals aim to prevent speculative investments or the use of inferior capital equipment. China has also become more selective in screening FDI projects to ensure compliance with economic development objectives. This is reflected in newly adopted FDI guidelines that are in line with the national development plan and the country's industrial policies. Moreover, the nation is targeting large MNC investments. This is reflected in the incentives aimed at attracting large MNCs to technologically advanced or capital-intensive projects.

China is moving toward national treatment — an effort to level the playing field for domestic and foreign firms and facilitate its entry into the World Trade Organization. Policy measures since 1994 have been aimed at eliminating those preferences for foreign investors that have distorted markets and led to a bias against domestic firms. Such measures include unification of the tax system and elimination of the exemption on import duties granted to FIEs.

To be more specific, in the tax reform undertaken in 1994, the turnover tax and individual income tax regimes were unified. As a result, both domestic and foreign firms are now governed by a unified set of rules on value-added, consumption, business operations, and individual income taxation. A notable exception, however, is the corporate income tax regime, under which foreign investors still enjoy preferential treatment.

In April 1996, China substantially reduced the average general tariff level from 35.9 to 23.0 percent, covering nearly 5,000 tariff lines with an average reduction margin of 36.0 percent. At the 1996 Asia-Pacific Economic Cooperation (APEC) meeting, China again announced that it would reduce the average general tariff level to 15 percent by the year 2000. China is phasing out nontariff measures and has submitted a timetable for the gradual elimination of the remaining measures, which apply to around 400 tariff lines. FIEs have faced the same duties and import-related taxes that domestic firms do on all imported equipment, materials, and other items since April 1996. Although overall tariff rates had already been lowered considerably at the beginning of 1996, the abolition of the preferential import duties awarded to FIEs is important, given that nearly 70 percent of China's FDI is in the form of imported capital equipment or raw materials.

In 1996, China incorporated FIEs into the system of buying and selling foreign exchange through banks and realized the convertibility of the renminbi (RMB) under current account on December 1 of the same year. At the same time, China keeps the foreign exchange swap center as a source of procurement and settlement of foreign exchange. Nevertheless, more and more FIEs are likely to choose designated banks through which to buy or sell foreign exchange because the new scheme offers much greater benefits. RMB convertibility under current account will help improve the investment and operating environment for foreigners. It provides a more adequate institutional guarantee of the legitimate revenues of foreign investors, minimizes the risks involved in the remittance of profits, and gives a stronger sense of security to foreign investors. Meanwhile, the removal of restrictions on the payment and transfer of foreign exchange helps streamline the procedures for examination and approval, which will in turn increase the turnover rate of capital, thus improving business performance.

China is now experimenting with Sino-foreign joint venture trading companies in Pudong, Shanghai. A pilot registration system for granting trading rights to production enterprises in the five special economic zones has been introduced. Foreign banks have begun to engage in local currency business in Pudong on a trial basis.

Although compared to 1996 the value of investments implemented in China in 1997 rose 8.5 percent, to reach a record $45.26 billion, the value of contracts fell 30.4 percent to $51.04 billion. This decline appears to have been the result of the emergence of problems surrounding policies on foreign capital (such as the problem of the value-added tax [VAT] on exports and the scrapping of a tax exemption for imported plants and equipment) and the shift of foreign capital from new investments to the operation and maintenance of existing facilities.

The value of investments implemented posted a slight decline of 0.6 percent in the first nine months of 1998, but the value of contracts bounced back with a year-on-year increase of 2.4 percent. While the value of investment from Asia generally stagnated in terms of both investments implemented and investment contracts, the active role played by Western firms helped push investment up overall. Japanese investment registered negative year-on-year growth of 18.5 percent in terms of contract value and −25.4 percent on an investments implemented basis.

The combination of the Asian financial crisis and China's restrictive investment environment continued to hamper FDI in 1998. Contracted FDI was up only 2.5 percent through the third quarter over the same period of the previous year, to $53.58 billion. Utilized investment for the period was down 0.6 percent, to $31.4 billion. The composition of FDI in China is also changing. Although Asian investment still constitutes the majority of FDI, its share slipped in the first three quarters of 1998, when it accounted for 74 percent of projects (down 3 percent from 1997), 53 percent of contracted investment (down 9 percent), and 70 percent of utilized investment (down 4 percent). Despite a 36 percent increase in Singaporean investment over the period, utilized investment from Asia dropped by more than 10 percent. Investment from Hong Kong, which had constituted 43 percent of utilized FDI, fell almost 11 percent. As capital flows from other parts of Asia slow, the share of FDI from the United States and Europe is growing. Utilized investment from the United States and Europe was up 45 and 20 percent, respectively, over the same period in 1997. The most dramatic increase in FDI came from the Virgin Islands, which showed an increase of 198 percent.

Foreign companies continue to prefer strong management control and have taken advantage of China's 1996 move allowing greater flexibility in establishing wholly foreign owned enterprises (WFOEs). These have become the favored investment vehicle for FDI and made up 50 percent of all projects through the first nine months of 1999. While 7,395 WFOEs were approved, up almost 9 percent from the previous year, only 5,841 equity joint ventures were approved, down almost 11 percent. Most contracted FDI went into WFOEs, which accounted for roughly 43 percent of total FDI, compared to 34 percent for equity joint ventures (EJVs). Nevertheless, EJVs still make up the lion's share of utilized investment, perhaps reflecting past commitments. Only about a third of utilized investment went into WFOEs.

The decline in foreign investment appears to have attracted the Chinese government's attention. Recent moves, including the reinstatement of certain capital equipment duty exemptions, accelerated approval procedures, and attempts to abolish illicit fees, are aimed at increasing FDI. The government is now planning for the opening of China's service industries to foreign investment, promoting investment in Central and Western China, and increasing investment incentives for multinational corporations. Problems for foreign investors persist, however. New administrative procedures for obtaining foreign exchange are complicating bilateral trade, causing costly delays in current account transactions, and restricting capital account transactions. Reevaluation of both locally approved retail ventures and the so-called Chinese-Chinese-foreign telecom investment structure, as well as the ban on direct selling, calls into question the security of investments in China. Although overall investment flows for 1998 are likely to approximate the previous year's total of $45 billion, they could drop in 1999 unless China takes concrete measures to improve a deteriorating investment environment.

Recent policy changes are expected to have an impact on FDI over the next few years. The movement toward national treatment discourages "round-tripping" (i.e., capital outflows that are repatriated back to China disguised as FDI, taking advantage of tax and regulatory incentives to FIEs) and "phantom" foreign ventures. Tighter screening and monitoring of FDI projects may significantly reduce the overvaluation of FDI that takes place through incorrect invoicing of imported equipment. In addition, tight monetary policies (likely to continue to be pursued by the government in the near future to curb inflation and cool the overheated economy) will have a bearing on FDI. This is because FDI projects usually must be coupled with domestic capital (an entry requirement for FDI in some industries). More expensive domestic capital discourages domestic investment and hence diminishes the ability of foreign investors to find joint venture partners.

China's attractiveness to foreign investors, however, remains strong. First, China's growth performance is outstanding. With an average annual GDP growth of 12 percent in 1991–96, China is one of the fastest growing economies in the world. This trend is expected to continue. Second, the liberalization of FDI policies is still under way. Some industries that had been off-limits to foreign investors, including air transport, general aviation, retail trade, foreign trade, banking, insurance, accounting, auditing, legal services, the mining and smelting of precious metals, and the prospecting, extracting, and processing of diamonds and other precious nonmetal minerals, are gradually being opened. Third, there is also a significant potential for FDI participation in infrastructure. Several build-operate-transfer (BOT) schemes have already been concluded. Foreign investors are now allowed to acquire state-owned firms. Fourth, to the extent that Chinese currency becomes convertible profit repatriation will be easier, making it more attractive to invest in China. Last, according to the Ministry of Foreign Trade and Economic Cooperation (MOFTEC), the following tax policies will guide FDI in the future.

1. General preferential rate. For manufacturing businesses, a preferential income tax rate of 33 percent will apply.
2. Reduced tax rate extended to special areas. For FIEs located in the SEZs or manufacturing businesses in the economic and technological development zones (ETDZs), a 15 percent income tax will apply. The income tax rate of 24 percent will apply for foreign-invested manufacturing enterprises located in the old town of a city located in the coastal economic open areas, SEZs, or ETDZs.
3. Reduced tax rate extended to special sectors. For Sino-foreign joint ventures that meet certain qualifications and engage in energy, transportation, or port or pier construction, a 15 percent income tax rate will apply.
4. Preferential rate extended to special businesses. The flow of FDI to high-tech or export-oriented businesses will continuously be encouraged. Once confirmed as this type of business, they will be granted special tax incentives.
5. Manufacturing FIEs in operation for more than 10 years will be continuously granted tax exemptions for two years, starting in the profit-making year, and given a half rate for three years afterward.
6. If foreign investors make additional investments with profits made from the FIEs, they will receive a refund of 40 percent of the income tax already paid.

As a result of this, the already great importance of FDI to China's economy is likely to grow. Thus, while FDI inflows to China might fall below $30 billion in the next few years, there is reason to believe that this will be a temporary adjustment rather than a response to a change in general economic factors. One strong piece of evidence supporting this speculation is that the top 12 MNCs from the United States that already have the biggest stakes in China are maintaining their commitment through ongoing construction and investment. Thus, China should remain one of the top FDI destinations in the world marketplace.

CHAPTER 2

The Economic Environment at the Turn of the New Century

China's strong growth over the past two decades should continue well into the next century, as the momentum of reform continues in the post-Deng era. Markets now allocate most resources in China, while state planning plays a small and shrinking role. However, China is now entering the more difficult phase of its reforms, that of developing the legal, administrative, and regulatory framework that supports a modern economy. Until this is complete, China will be a challenging and sometimes difficult environment for MNCs. This chapter reviews China's economic environment at the turn of a new century, presents recent economic policies that may affect MNC operations, and elaborates managerial implications for foreign companies that are active in the Chinese market today.

Overview of the Chinese Economy

China is a huge economic success story. The past two decades have brought big increases in every imaginable indicator of economic performance. China is in the throes of two transitions today: from a command economy to a market-based one and from a rural, agricultural society to an urban, industrial one. So far, both transitions have been reasonably successful. China is the fastest-growing economy in the world, with per capita income more than quadrupling since 1978. Economic reforms have advanced China's integration into the world economy, maintained a strong external payments position, essentially privatized farming, liberalized markets for many goods and services, intensified competition in industry, and introduced modern macroeconomic management. In two generations, it has achieved what took other countries centuries. For a country whose population exceeds that of sub-Saharan Africa and Latin America combined, this has been a remarkable development.

China's growth has been outstanding in the second half of this century (see table 2.1). It began in 1978, when China officially opened

TABLE 2.1. Major Economic Indicators of the Chinese Economy, 1966–98

	1966–73		1974–90		1991–96		1997		1998	
	China	World	China	World	China	World	China	World	China	World
Real GDP growth	9.0	5.1	9.0	2.8	11.8	2.3	9.1	3.2	7.2	1.8
GDP per capita growth	6.2	2.9	7.5	1.1	10.6	0.8	8.1	1.8	6.2	0.3
Inflation	−1.7	5.4	3.8	7.8	11.2	4.4	2.3	2.8	1.7	2.9
Current account balance (% of GDP)	−0.4	−0.1	0.1	−0.4	1.0	−0.1	2.1	0.2	2.6	0.0

Source: World Bank, *Global Economic Prospects*, 194–97.

the door to the outside world. Between 1978 and 1995, annual per capita real GDP growth in China averaged 8 percent while it was only 1.5 percent in the United States. This growth makes China the fastest-growing economy in the world over the past two decades. Starting from a position of near autarky, China has been catching up rapidly in integrating itself in the global economy. Increased integration and openness have paid rich dividends in rapid growth despite much room for progress. China's economic growth accelerated after reforms were introduced in 1979. Remarkably, the record growth was achieved entirely by means of improvements in total factor productivity growth — between 3.6 and 4.1 percentage points. Market-based transactions now dominate the Chinese economy, with over 90 percent of retail prices and 80 percent of producer and agricultural prices determined by the market. Tables 2.2–2.5 illustrate major economic indicators in 1997 from economic growth, consumer price inflation, and foreign reserves to origins and outlays of GDP and import and export patterns.

China's effort to engineer industrial growth has included measures designed to gradually introduce market competition, encourage mergers and acquisitions, and foster the expansion of collective enterprises. As a result of industrial reform, firms have had increasing autonomy in determining how and with whom they will conduct business. From methods of production to decisions about hiring and firing workers, Chinese business organizations are becoming less and less dependent on central authority.

TABLE 2.2. Geographic and Economic Indicators, 1993–97

Economic Indicators	1993	1994	1995	1996	1997
GDP at current market prices					
(in billions of yuan)	3,450.1	4,711.1	5,940.5	6,936.6	7,607.7
Real GDP growth (%)	13.5	12.6	10.5	9.7	8.8
Consumer price inflation					
(avg. %)	14.7	24.1	17.1	8.3	2.8
Population (mil)	1,178	1,192	1,205	1,218	1,230
Merchandise exports fob ($bil)	75.7	102.6	128.1	151.1	182.7
Merchandise imports fob ($bil)	86.3	95.3	110.1	131.5	136.4
Current account balance ($bil)	−11.6	6.9	1.6	7.2	29.7
Total debt, including undisbursed					
($bil)	86.3	103.7	130.2	141.5	150.9
Reserves, excluding gold (year					
end; $bil)	22.4	52.9	75.4	107.0	142.8
Exchange rate (avg.; yuan:$)	5.8	8.6	8.4	8.3	8.3

Source: EIU Country Report 1998, 6.
Note: On November 20, 1998, Rmb 8.28 equaled one U.S. dollar.

TABLE 2.3. Origins and Components of GDP, 1997

Origins of GDP 1997	Percentage of Total	Components of GDP 1997	Percentage of Total
Primary industry	18.7	Private consumption	47.5
Secondary industry	49.2	Government consumption	11.4
Tertiary industry	32.1	Gross fixed investment	33.8
Total	100.0	Exports of goods and services	24.5
		Imports of goods and services	−20.9
		Total, including others	100.0

Source: EIU Country Report 1998, 6.

TABLE 2.4. Imports and Exports, 1997

Principal Exports 1997	$ Billion	Principal Imports 1997	$ Billion
Textiles and clothing	45.6	Machinery and electrical equipment	46.7
Machinery and electrical equipment	38.3	Textiles and textile articles	17.2
Garments and accessories	31.8	Chemicals and chemical products	10.3
Textiles, yarn, and fabric	13.8	Mineral fuels	10.3
Foodstuffs, beverages, and tobacco	12.1	Iron and steel	6.7
Footwear, headgear, and umbrellas	10.2		
Chemicals and chemical products	9.4		
Mineral fuels and electricity	7.0		

Source: EIU Country Report 1998, 6.

TABLE 2.5. Regional Patterns of Imports and Exports, 1997

Main Destinations of Exports	Percentage of Total	Main Origins of Imports	Percentage of Total
Hong Kong	24.0	Japan	20.4
United States	17.9	Taiwan	11.5
Japan	17.4	United States	11.4
South Korea	5.0	South Korea	10.5
Germany	3.6	Hong Kong	4.9
Netherlands	2.4	Germany	4.4
Singapore	2.4	Singapore	3.2
Taiwan	1.9	Russia	2.9

Source: EIU Country Report 1998, 6.

Managers have more responsibility for finding productive inputs, determining appropriate production and inventory levels, and locating markets for their products. Bankruptcy and unemployment, unheard of in the past, have also increased in recent years, demonstrating that poor firm performance may result in failure for the firm and unemployment for its managers.

Three features of China's rapid growth since 1978 are especially noteworthy. First, the benefits of growth have been widely shared among China's country-sized provincial economies. Although the coastal provinces grew faster than the average, at 9.7 percent a year, the other provinces also fared well. In fact, if China's 30 provinces were counted as individual economies, the 20 fastest-growing economies in the world would have been Chinese. Second, Chinese economic development has been coupled with the sharp cyclical pattern of economic growth. The growth cycles have been accompanied by similar fluctuations in the rate of inflation, revealing fault lines in macroeconomic management stemming from partially completed reforms in the fiscal, enterprise, and banking systems. Third, China's growth has been less dependent on volume increases in inputs of capital and labor than on productivity growth, relative to other emerging economies. This suggests that factors other than capital accumulation have been important determinants of China's GDP growth.

China's rapid growth since 1978 has been driven by several factors. The first is a high savings rate, which has supported vigorous rates of investment and capital accumulation. China's savings rate averaged 37 percent of GDP between 1978 and 1995, in sharp contrast to the collapse of savings in the transition economies of Eastern Europe and the former Soviet Union. Accounting for half of total savings, household savings exploded from about 1 percent as a share of income before reforms to 21 percent since then. Second, structural change has been both a cause and effect of growth. This change has given a significant boost to China's growth over the past two decades. Since a large portion of the agricultural labor force was underemployed, productivity leaped as workers moved from low-productivity agriculture to more productive employment in industry and services. This process contributes about 1 percentage point per year to GDP growth. The changing pattern of ownership also contributes about 0.5 percentage point per year to growth, as employment has shifted to the collective and private sectors where productivity is higher. Third, pragmatic reforms were well suited to China's unusual circumstances and enjoyed broad support. China's economic reforms in 1978 were triggered by neither economic crisis nor ideological epiphany. Reform measures were introduced incrementally and involved decentralizing authority over capital spending. A favored approach was for the central authorities to experiment with new policies in selected provinces, prefectures, countries, and even firms. If the experiments worked, they were quickly replicated. This approach, or what is called "crossing the river by groping for stepping-stones," has been a systematic component of Chinese reforms. Pragmatism and incrementalism were also behind the government's evolving objectives (see table 2.6). Finally, economic conditions in 1978 were especially receptive to reform. Contrary to the popular perception, planning was less entrenched in China than it was in other transition economies. China's economy could be described as a dry prairie, parched by years of planning, awaiting the first sprinklings of market reform.

Interactive reform is the basic mechanism of China's transition. The profit motive is everywhere. Even large state-owned enterprises (SOEs) have found themselves pushed toward adopting the culture of the market. Despite the continuation of various forms of subsidy, agents throughout China's economy are increasingly forced to live with market-generated financial outcomes. Domestic industries, formerly insulated from international market trends, find themselves buffeted by global as well as domestic market forces. Instructional arrangements bend in the face of external pressures. These developments continue to reshape individual attitudes, expectations, and behavior at every level of Chinese society. Early reform efforts were partial and tentative. The current objective of creating a "socialist market economy" is itself an outcome of the reform processes that emerged only in the 1990s. Until recently, reform policies have consistently focused on enabling measures (profit sharing and market opening) rather than compulsion (privatization and bankruptcy). Despite their limited scope, these enabling measures served to erode entry barriers, intensify competition, reduce profit rates, and undermine the growth of public revenue, especially at the

TABLE 2.6. Evolving Objectives of Economic Reform

Period	Objectives
1978–79	A planned economy started with the "open door policy"
1979–84	A planned economy supplemented by market regulation
1984–87	A planned commodity economy
1987–89	An economy in which the state regulates the market and the market regulates enterprises
1989–91	An economy with organic integration of a planned economy and market regulation
1993–present	A socialist market economy with Chinese characteristics

Source: World Bank 1997, 9.

national level. The resulting financial pressures continue to push enterprises and policymakers in the direction of innovation, cost reduction, and further market-leaning policy shifts.

In China, reform is not a sequence of events in which the state makes decisions to which businesses and individuals react. Reform unfolds as an extended process replete with interaction and feedback among government administrations, enterprises, workers, and consumers. Erosion of governmental power is both an unintended consequence and a powerful engine of China's reform. The most difficult reform task is to force state enterprises and their employees from comfortably protected niches into the hurly-burly of market competition. The declining revenue share of the state and the emergence of fierce economic competition among China's provinces and localities are essential in motivating serious efforts to attain this unpalatable objective.

Semimarket systems can generate growth spurts. As critics rail about insecure property rights, the absence of commercial law, internal trade barriers, corruption, and many other difficulties, China's crude semimarket system continues to deliver massive gains. Achievement of a full market system is not a prerequisite for accelerated economic growth, structural change, and technological development. Economic reforms are built on large numbers of complex and intricately connected institutions. Western-style economic policies may turn out to be the best long-run option for China but not necessarily the best now.

The Chinese economy is still only about halfway through its transition from a centrally planned to a market economy. Difficult reforms are ongoing, in particular the development of the legal, administrative, and regulatory framework that supports a modern economy. As reform rolls on, a seemingly endless array of gaps, obstacles, shortcomings, and problems comes to the surface. Swift growth and structural change, while resolving many problems, have created new challenges: employment insecurity, growing inequality, stubborn poverty, mounting environmental pressures, and periods of macroeconomic instability stemming from incomplete reforms. Unmet, these challenges could undermine the sustainability of growth and China's promise could fade.

Lack of progress in reforming SOEs is a major bottleneck hampering reform in China. The delay in SOE reform is largely responsible for delays in fiscal, financial, and trading system reform. A bankruptcy law introduced in the late 1980s has had a minimal effect, as until recently it was rarely used because of fear of the social consequences. State banks still cannot refuse to extend loans to unprofitable SOEs if the authorities request it. Liberalization of bank interest rates and trade protection have been slow because of fear of the consequences for cash-strapped

SOEs. Wage pressures sometimes divert earnings away from much needed long-term investments. Government supervisory agencies continue to interfere with shareholding firms' management. It is still too early for shareholders to gauge firm performance through the two stock markets, which have had their share of insider trading and stock manipulation. Moreover, most SOEs will be restructured, at least in the medium term, into limited liability companies rather than limited liability stock companies. Bank credit, therefore, rather than share issues, likely will be the dominant source of financing for most SOEs. However, the deeply troubled state banking sector is not yet capable of imposing financial discipline on SOEs. The most daunting challenge still to be met is how to manage state assets efficiently and by whom. Currently, the State Asset Management Commissions at various levels are the major management authority representing the state. It is well recognized that asset management by these commissions is ineffective due to the lack of professional knowledge, organizational responsibility, and managerial incentive. It is easy to change the SOE ownership structure but difficult, if not impossible, to manage state assets effectively and maximize their value when the government still controls the ownership of these assets. As unprofitable SOEs continue to demand soft loans, the success of banking, taxation, and social welfare reforms is affected by the pace and pattern of SOE reforms in productive sectors.

Current Situations and Challenges

The Asian crisis has plunged several of the fastest-growing economies in the world into a severe recession and slowed the growth of world output and trade. Individual countries in crisis are facing steep social costs, which may be long-lasting, and difficult recoveries from their depressed economic conditions. The crisis showed that one of the most competitive markets in the world, the international market for financial assets, can fail in a major way. Economic growth in China slowed in 1997, but was still almost 9 percent, as the country continued its soft-landing strategy of reducing inflation without delivering a major shock to economic growth. The softening of growth in consumption, combined with a slow pace of restructuring in the state sector, exacerbated losses incurred by SOEs as inventories of unsold goods rose. Losses of SOEs reached about 10 percent of GDP in 1997. SOEs continued to lag behind the nonstate industrial sector in growth rates of output, exemplifying a trend that has been maintained since the mid-1980s; but growth also decelerated in the nonstate sector recently, owing to slowing demand and probably a need for small and medium-sized collective and private businesses to upgrade their managerial and technological skills.

Weakening domestic demand has been counterbalanced by strong external demand. Exports grew almost 21 percent in 1997, rebounding from the slowdown of 1996, while imports increased by only 2.5 percent. Inflation continued to moderate as a result of the slower growth of domestic demand, aided by the effect of good harvests on prices. Consequently, the rate of inflation in 1997 was only 2.8 percent, the lowest since 1985. In order to strengthen the national economy, the government has relaxed monetary policy further by cutting interest rates and lowering the required reserve ratio while increasing public spending in support of infrastructure development. Because the fallout from the Asian financial crisis slowed China's export growth, the impetus for growth is largely reliant on domestic development, bolstered by more expansionary macroeconomic policies.

The Chinese yuan renminbi largely escaped the contagion effect of the Asian financial crisis, thanks to a sizable foreign exchange reserve (over $140 billion at the end of 1997) and controls over the capital account. The Asian crisis nevertheless highlighted the urgency of economic reform, particularly regarding the development of the financial and enterprise sectors and market institutions in China. In the next three years (1998–2000), unprofitable enterprises will be closed down or merged into profitable ones or firms that are deemed inherently viable but sinking under an unsupportable debt burden may receive a measure of debt relief. The coverage of the experiment, ongoing since 1991, whose aim is to convert SOEs into joint stock companies, has been broadened, as the number of firms and cities under the scheme has doubled. China is now also reforming its civil service by merging 40 government ministries into 29 new ones and reducing its staff by half, or by four million persons.

Financial sector reform has progressed as well with measures to boost the independence of the central bank and to develop a market-oriented commercial banking sector. These measures include the administrative streamlining of regional branches of the central bank to reduce the political influence of local governments on their operations. Top-down credit quota allocation has been replaced with guidelines for capital-to-loan ratios and regulations governing prudential supervision of commercial banks. These measures are intended to increase operational autonomy in the banking sector while strengthening bank supervision.

The implementation of a public, in lieu of a firm-based, social welfare system is necessary to mitigate the impact of unemployment resulting from large-scale SOE restructuring. China is gradually expanding city-based experimentation in public pension funds and health and unemployment insurance schemes. Although these welfare reforms lessen the financial burden on enterprises, which used to provide such benefits, they do require support from the government budget, which may result in tax increases. In addition, accelerated housing reform is envisioned by the government as a means of stimulating domestic demand in the near term. Although commercialization of housing has been carried out on an experimental basis in some cities, housing subsidies for employees are still a major responsibility of SOEs and government agencies. The elimination of such subsidies and the commercialization of residential housing will free up public resources, thus lessening the financial burdens of SOEs and the pressure on the public budget. Conversion to private ownership of housing will also stimulate investments in renovations and expenditures on household appliances. Nevertheless, the concurrent implementation of these major reforms and the initiation of new ones launched by Premier Zhu Rongqi will be more challenging as economic growth deccelerates, the social environment destabilizes, and/or the political climate becomes more conservative.

The government sought to boost growth during 1998. The marked slowdown in the first half of the year, when both domestic and external demand were constrained, caused serious concern. The government, worried that GDP growth would fall below the official target of 8 percent, embarked on a program of accelerated spending. It also relied on its remaining administrative mechanisms to order the resumption of active lending by state banks to the sectors the state wants supported— selected large SOEs, small and medium-sized enterprises (SMEs), and exporters.

Interest rates have been lowered on several occasions. Further reductions will only be made if the government believes such cuts will not undermine public confidence in the ability of the government to maintain the exchange rate at Rmb 8.3 to $1.00. Looser monetary policy has therefore also taken the form of allowing and encouraging greater volumes of lending by state-owned banks.

At the same time, there has been a large increase in central government spending directed mainly at infrastructure projects and targeted in particular toward the central and western areas, which experienced slower growth in the 1990s. Spending was also stimulated by the massive resource deployment effort made necessary by the flood emergencies of mid-1998. In the first nine months of 1998, government expenditures rose by 17.5 percent, compared to a budgeted target of 10.3 percent for the year as a whole, while revenue rose by 10.4 percent compared to a budgeted rise of 12.1 percent.

The additional spending, and the increased budget deficit that resulted, is being financed by additional debt, which is mainly domestic owing to the difficulty of raising funds abroad. By mid-October, Rmb 220 billion ($26.50 billion) had been issued in state bonds over and above the Rmb 100 billion in bonds issued to finance infrastructure spending. The state is also monetizing its broader deficit—which includes policy lending by the People's Bank of China (PBC, the central bank) to SOEs—by expanding the money supply so that state banks can support state-owned industries.

Pressure to boost the export competitiveness that was lost as a result of the large-scale devaluation of the currencies of many other emerging markets has been exerted by some industry sectors but has been resisted by the government. The official calculus still reckons that the gains would outweigh the costs of devaluation—political loss of face, more expensive imports for export-oriented and import-intensive industries, the risk of higher inflation at a time of economic stimulus, more expensive debt-service costs for some shaky Chinese borrowers, and a generally heightened sense of instability as a result of the government's reversal of policy on an issue on which it has previously been adamant. The gains would include an enhanced ability to compete on price without denting margins or being accused of dumping as well as deterring cheap imports. But many export markets, especially in Asia, are regarded as being too severely depressed to respond to a devaluation of the renminbi on any scale that has occurred previously.

Meanwhile, China is acting to deter imports by administrative means, including what may be a rather liberal interpretation of the concept of smuggling. Exports are being supported by increased tax rebates on value-added tax (VAT) and increased export credits. Western trading partners regard current Chinese moves as lessening the country's eligibility for WTO membership, and it must be concluded that the Chinese government has decided that WTO membership is not at the top of the policy agenda, at least not while the current weakness and instability of the world economy persists.

The overriding goal of economic policy is now the maintenance of stability. This, the government believes, means that growth must accelerate. However, the longer-term problems of industrial enterprise and financial sector reform and the urgent need to raise the productivity of agriculture and combat environmental degradation have not disappeared and will need to be tackled sooner rather than later.

Although a certain amount of restructuring of the SOE sector has continued this year, the process of enterprise reform is not proceeding at the pace envisaged by Mr. Zhu when he made bold commitments to accelerated reforms in early 1998. The recapitalization of the state-owned banks, in particular, has been set back by their deployment, once more, as channels of working capital to allow SOEs to continue to produce during the current economic downturn. There is virtually complete agreement within China that state enterprise reform is of the highest priority. State enterprises absorb a disproportionately large share of the country's resources; they have also become a drag on growth and employment creation.

The government's enterprise reform program operates at two levels: improving economic performance through stricter market discipline and developing better governance within firms to improve productivity. State-owned enterprises are being disciplined by the market through tough competition created by trade liberalization and the proliferation of nonstate enterprises. At the same time, financial support for state enterprises is being cut back. The combination of these two pressures is encouraging enterprise restructuring, especially at the provincial and municipal levels.

The stated policy of the government is to strengthen state enterprises and maintain their position as the mainstay of the economy. To focus its efforts, the central government recently selected 1,000 large state enterprises as priority targets of reform and development. For the other state enterprises, various approaches to reform are under way in the form of experiments at the provincial and municipal levels.

Looking ahead, the task of improving the efficiency and competitiveness of China's state enterprises is expected to be complex and difficult. The Chinese government may move in several directions in advancing SOE reform. First, it could implement programs to improve internal governance, diversify ownership, and lower budgetary and financial subsidies. A first priority would be to implement a new accounting system, set clear commercial objectives, streamline asset management bureaus, clarify representation of the government on boards of directors, and transfer autonomous management rights to enterprises. Second, it could accelerate the transfer of pension, health, and education obligations from state-owned enterprises to government authorities. It would be difficult to liquidate, sell, merge, or restructure enterprises if they were still required to make these social expenditures. Pilot programs to transfer such expenditures to municipal authorities need to be accelerated. At an appropriate point, these could be merged with the national pension and health programs. Third, the government could promote competition to encourage greater efficiency in state enterprises. Of some importance would be the reduction of interprovincial and international trade and investment barriers. Lower foreign trade and investment barriers

would have the added advantage of strengthening China's case for joining the WTO.

In implementing these policies, the government will need to consider
the specific needs and circumstances of different groups of state enterprises. Implementation could proceed, first, by using competition and
governance policies, not subsidies, to foster the efficient development of
the central government's priority in 1,000 large state enterprises. These
state enterprises and enterprise groups are expected to eventually form
the core of China's modern enterprise system. An appropriate way to
improve their efficiency would be to provide these enterprises with
greater management autonomy and better governance structures, expose
them gradually to domestic and international competition, diversify their
sources of finance, and apply better regulations. In cases in which the
government feels compelled to provide subsidies, these should be limited,
time-bound, and channeled through the budget rather than the financial
system. Second, the government could improve the efficiency of 14,000
large and medium-sized industrial enterprises by diversifying ownership,
reconfiguring operations, restructuring debt, encouraging mergers and
consolidations, and, when necessary, liquidating. Marginally unprofitable firms that are inherently viable financially could be restructured by
shedding labor, investing in new equipment, and restructuring their fi-
nances. Debt restructuring should occur only when a corporate strategy is
agreed upon by the bank, the (local) government, and the enterprise's
management on the strict understanding that there will be no future
bailouts. Heavy losers with dim futures would need to be closed down,
while highly profitable enterprises could be corporatized. Finally, the
government could systematically develop and implement a program to
transfer the remaining 90,000 small industrial state enterprises to the
nonstate sector through sales, leases, or mergers. The government's proposed policy for such enterprises is to loosen controls on leasing, mergers,
sales, restructurings, and bankruptcies. But it should go further and systematically facilitate the transfer of these enterprises to the nonstate sector. A first phase could include the transfer of 10,000 to 20,000 state
enterprises in the 18 reform cities over two years.

Over the past 25 years, China's GDP growth has averaged 10 percent a year and its share of world trade has tripled to about 3 percent.
The strength of the Chinese economy over the past two decades, however, does not guarantee that China will continue to grow rapidly in the
future. Nevertheless, China has some real advantages that can bolster its
economy. Its high saving rate, large domestic market, and record of
reform bode well for future growth. China's five-year plan for 1996–
2000 targeted GDP growth of 8 percent a year. To achieve the target by

2000, China will need to grow by an average of 7.6 percent a year over the next two years. By the standards of recent years, such growth does not seem unduly ambitious.

Even so, the future will be challenging and probably increasingly so. Rapid economic growth is not the government's sole objective nor should it be. It is very likely that the pace of reform will slow if social instability intensifies as a result of income disparity, bureaucratic corruption, and hyper-underemployment. Obstacles to future growth also include incomplete foundations upon which to impose reforms. China is midstream in its transition to a market economy. The government's role in laying the institutional, social, physical, and legal foundations for market development will be crucial in completing the transition. Although China is now restructuring and downsizing its governments at various levels, it remains to be seen to what extent, and for how long, it can fulfill its goal of establishing an efficient and clean governmental system.

The bracing effects of competition are accompanied by increased risks, especially to employment and income. As China grows richer, it will require policies and institutions that ensure a caring yet competitive system to help manage these risks and promote human potential in all dimensions. This will require the creation of entirely new social structures for the next century. Changing employment patterns and foreseeable shifts in the age structure of China's population call for a fresh look at the policies and institutions affecting labor markets, the welfare of the poor, the financial security of the elderly, and equal access for all to jobs, health care, and education.

Whether or not China can meet these challenges and sustain rapid growth depends largely on continuing its reforms. First, the spread of market forces must be encouraged, especially through the reform of state enterprises, the financial system, grain and labor markets, and the pricing of natural resources. Second, the government must begin serving markets by building the legal, social, physical, and institutional infrastructure needed for their rapid growth. Finally, integration with the world economy must be deepened by lowering import barriers, increasing the transparency and predictability of the trade regime, and gradually integrating the country into international financial markets.

In balance, China's role in the world economy in the next century should increase further, although its pace of economic growth is expected to slow to more sustainable levels. According to one World Bank forecast (World Bank 1997), China's share in world trade will more than triple by 2020 (to about 10 percent), and it is expected to become a leading trading nation, second only to the United States. China will account for some 40 percent of the increase in all developing country imports between 1992 and 2020 and will serve as an engine of growth for world trade.

The Economic Environment and Entry Choice

Despite uncertainties, the growth of China's consumer market is drawing MNCs from all over the globe. Those that entered China in the mid-1980s have the benefit of perspective, which is serving them well in the current climate of stiff competition and decreasing tax benefits. Facing China's current economic environment, most foreign companies choose to make a further commitment to this market, although many firms have adopted a more cautious attitude than they had when they first arrived, tempered by the realization that the market itself is in flux.

Despite the fact that not all of the original ventures have been successful, many firms that entered the market in the early days of China's opening to the global economy achieved profitability within a reasonable time frame. The question for newcomers now is not "Is it worthwhile to be in China?" but rather "How can we make it worthwhile in China?" In an effort to create payoffs under the aforementioned economic environment, investments in China require commitment, patience, and planning. For instance, Johnson & Johnson has boosted its presence from one equity joint venture to three EJVs, two wholly owned subsidiaries, and a representative office. Eastman Kodak, which initially transferred technology for color film and paper, has seen its presence grow to one cooperative joint venture, which manufactures optical lenses; two EJVs in document management; two wholly owned subsidiaries, one for electric flash units and the other manufacturing minilabs; and 10 representative offices nationwide. In March 1998, Kodak announced that it would invest more than $1 billion over several years to produce Kodak branded world-class products in China. Ingersoll-Rand has also increased its total number of EJVs from one to five. The company now has ventures manufacturing rock drills and accessories, bearings, pneumatic tools, compressors, and road machinery. It also set up a holding company in 1996 in Shanghai. Aiming to capture 50 percent of the market share in China, the Air Bus Company established the Sino-Europe Aviation Training and Aid Center in 1997 to enhance its efforts to expand into the Chinese market.

Among all the factors that contribute to MNC success in China, the entry mode decision is most critical. Each entry mode (e.g., equity joint venture, contractual joint venture, or wholly foreign owned enterprise) has implications for the level of control the MNC will enjoy over its foreign operations, the amount of investment required, and the degree of risk the firm will face in operations in China. Moreover, this decision is linked to the MNC's core competency contributions, control over subsidiaries, parent-subsidiary relations, and vulnerability to external changes in the host country. By choosing an appropriate entry mode that fits their internal capabilities, strategic goals, and environmental contingencies, MNCs can prevent the exposure of distinctive technologies, mitigate transactional hazards that may be precipitated during resource dispersal or interactions with contextual forces, and boost economic rents earned from productive knowledge. Daimler Benz, for instance, abandoned its plans to produce luxury cars in China through an equity joint venture because of market uncertainties and the difficulties of finding an appropriate local partner. Similarly, Nissan has not developed any major plans for establishing an equity or contractual joint venture in China, which consequently has kept the market share of Nissan automobiles declining in this market. The major reason behind this is that Nissan's strategic goal is to standardize the operation of its existing production enterprises abroad (such as those in Mexico, America, and Europe) before making other large-scale investments outside Japan. Globalstar, ICO Global Communications, and Iridium, the world's three major satellite telephone companies, however, are eager to use the contractual joint venture or licensing mode. This is because they must rely upon local service providers such as China Telecom or other firms owned by the Ministry of Information Industry (MII) to reach Chinese consumers. Recently, MII allowed China Telecom to administer land-based operations for the satellite telephone network nationwide. In conclusion, the entry mode decision is not only fundamental to every foreign company that plans to enter China but contingent on both organizational and environmental dynamics that are specific to different firms.

WTO Entry and Its Impact on MNCs

On November 15, 1999, the United States and China signed the bilateral WTO agreement in Beijing. This agreement, described as the "deal of the century" by some critics, was a full 13 years in the making. It is a big step for China toward its WTO membership. Since the United States has so much clout, this agreement will spur China's negotiations with those WTO members yet to clinch bilateral deals (notably the European Union).

From the Chinese perspective, WTO entry will legitimize its standing as a global power and stimulate export growth. As a member, China would be entitled to take advantage of the free trade commitments made by the 135 members of the WTO — covering over 90 percent of the world's trade. This would result in a substantial benefit to China's export trade — particularly low- to midtechnology, labor-intensive industries such as clothing, footwear, textiles, toys, and consumer electronics. For example, following the Uruguay Round of trade negotiations, average tariff levels among the WTO's developed countries dropped from 6.3 to 3.8 percent.

A key principle underlying the WTO is the most favored nation (MFN) principle. This means that a WTO member must ensure that its commitments apply equally to all WTO members without discrimination or exception. If a member grants a new concession to one of its trading partners in the WTO, it must extend the concession to all members. This assurance of nondiscrimination would increase the certainty and stability of the export environment for China's exporters and also free the government from the threat that a trading partner might use economic sanctions to further a political goal. The prime example of this is the U.S. linkage of MFN status with its evaluation of China's human rights policy. In addition, China will have the power to help draft the most important trading rules in the world when it becomes a member. A truly global power is not only subject to regulations that dictate global conduct, but it is an actual part of the apparatus making said decisions, regulations, and policies.

The main disadvantage of membership is the potential effect of China's trade liberalization commitments on its burgeoning local industries, many of which are in the infancy stage and clearly uncompetitive on the global stage. The price China must pay for membership is a broad array of tariff, market access, and other trade concessions. One of the key principles underlying the WTO is that of national treatment. This means that once a WTO member's goods or services have entered another WTO member country, they must be accorded the same treatment as the destination country's domestic goods and services. While it is generally considered a benefit of WTO membership, the principle of national treatment would work to the overall disadvantage of China. It would prohibit the granting of special advantages to local firms and the requirements to "buy local." Such measures to boost local industry are commonly employed by the Chinese government at present.

The immediate economic effect of joining the WTO would be a reduction of China's tax revenues. The longer term effect may be a loss of market share or even market exit by China's farmers and domestic enterprises in the face of more competitive foreign imports. This effect would be compounded by the fact that China will also remove long-standing prohibitions on foreign firms against engaging in the import-export business and the distribution of goods within China. Opinions are mixed as to whether the increase in competition will be beneficial in the long run or will cause so much short-term pain as to cripple the development of Chinese industries. As a general rule, the threat of foreign competition is considered to be a healthy influence spurring domestic enterprises to improve their performance. On the other hand, infant industries may need a degree of protection before being exposed to highly competitive foreign firms.

The effects of increased competition will vary from industry to industry. The reduction of tariffs on imported automobiles from 80 to 100 percent to 25 percent by 2006 will have a great impact on the market share of China's domestic automobile industry. Domestic companies such as Haier, Guangdong Kelon, and Legend have learned from competition and achieved dominant positions in their respective industries. The computer manufacturer Legend even seized a 5.4 percent share of the Asia-Pacific market (excluding Japan) in 1998.

Participation in the WTO will make Chinese SOEs more competitive due to the pressure of competition not only with domestic non-SOEs but also with foreign enterprises. This sounds good for China, but reform of SOEs is not so easy. The most important task for China now is how to maintain social stability while introducing competition. Although obtaining membership in WTO might promote a certain level of SOE reform, the Chinese government will find a way to prevent too much social instability caused by closing unprofitable SOEs or laying off more workers.

China's expected entry into the WTO will eliminate the policy attraction of special economic zones. This is due to the "national treatment" clause, a key WTO principle that restricts member countries from treating foreign and domestic companies differently. This rule will remove the preferential tax rates and other exemptions for foreigners that currently are SEZ core attractions.

However, even after these policy incentives disappear, systemic incentives such as superior power supply, telecommunications, and other advanced infrastructure will remain a key attraction. This will be obvious especially among the SEZs built by the central government or richer provinces in the coastal areas thanks to their higher infrastructure investment per square foot ($96 to $120 million in Pudong) compared to SEZs set up by provinces and major cities (averaging $24 million) or lower-level zones (averaging $1.2 million). Considering these infrastructure incentives together with the higher quality of the work force and adoption of more international standards, some of the major SEZs will remain leading economic powers while minor enterprises will gradually fade away if they do not have systemic incentives other than those of policy.

China's WTO entry will bring changes to almost all MNCs in most industries in the country. The overall tariff will fall to 17 percent. Most quotas and other nontariff barriers will be eliminated within five years; some will be phased out in two to three years. Tariffs on all industrial products will fall to an average of 9.4 percent (compared to 24.6 percent in 1997) by 2005. By opening previously closed sectors to foreign investment and promising established investors easier operating conditions, China should see a revival of foreign investor interest, especially in the following areas.

1. Agriculture. Tariffs on "U.S. priority" products (beef, grapes, wine, cheese, poultry, and pork) will be reduced from the current 31.5 to 14.5 percent by January 2004. China will not provide subsidies on crops, including cotton and rice.

2. Industrial products. Import tariffs on automobiles will gradually be reduced from about 90 percent at present to 25 percent by July 1, 2006. Foreign banks and nonbank financial institutions will be allowed to finance automobile purchases upon China's accession to the WTO. Tariffs on information technology (IT) products such as computers, telecommunications equipment, semiconductors, computer equipment, and other high-technology products stipulated in the Information Technology Agreement (ITA) will be eliminated by 2005. Tariffs on U.S. listed priority industrial products such as wool, paper, and medical equipment will fall to an average of 7.1 percent by the year 2003. Finally, tariffs on chemicals will be reduced to zero to 6.5 percent.

3. Trading rights and distribution. Trading rights and distribution are the major priority of the manufacturing sector. At present, China severely restricts trading rights (the right to import and export) and distribution (wholesaling, retailing, direct selling, maintenance and repair, transportation, etc.). In China today, for instance, MNCs have no right to distribute products other than those they make in China or to own or manage distribution networks, wholesaling outlets, or warehouses. After entry, China for the first time will provide trading rights and distribution rights to MNCs. Trading rights will be progressively phased in over three years. Distribution rights will be provided even for China's most restricted distribution sectors such as wholesale,

transportation, maintenance, and repair. Furthermore, MNCs will be able to directly handle services auxiliary to distribution, including rental and leasing, air courier, freight forwarding, storage and warehousing, advertising, technical testing and analysis, and packaging services. All restrictions will be phased out in three to four years, at which time U.S. service suppliers will be able to establish 100 percent wholly owned subsidiaries.

4. Banking. Foreign banks will be allowed to conduct renminbi business with Chinese companies two years after China's accession to the WTO and with Chinese individuals five years after accession. Both geographic and customer restrictions on foreign banks' operations will be lifted five years after accession. Foreign banks will have the same rights (national treatment) as Chinese banks within designated geographic areas.

5. Securities. Upon China's accession to the WTO, MNCs will be able to invest in joint venture fund management companies. The ceiling on foreign ownership will be 33 percent initially, rising to 49 percent three years after accession. Foreign-invested joint ventures in this sector will be allowed to underwrite domestic securities issues and foreign currency-denominated securities (debt and equity). The ceiling on foreign ownership will be held at 33 percent.

6. Insurance. MNCs in this sector are now allowed to operate only in Shanghai and Guangzhou. After accession, China will permit foreign property and casualty firms to insure large-scale risks nationwide immediately upon accession and will eliminate all geographic limitations in three years. China will expand the scope of activity for foreign insurers to include group, health, and pension lines of insurance, which represent about 85 percent of total premiums, phased in over five years. Moreover, China has agreed to award licenses solely on the basis of prudential criteria, with no economic needs test or quantitative limits on the number of licenses issued. Finally, China has agreed to allow 50 percent ownership for life insurance companies. Life insurers may now choose their own joint venture partners. For nonlife, China will allow branching or 51 percent ownership on accession and the establishment of wholly owned subsidiaries in two years. Reinsurance will be completely open upon accession (100 percent with no restrictions).

7. Telecommunications. China will allow 49 percent foreign ownership in all services, including the Internet sector, upon accession; 50 percent ownership in value-added paging services two

years after accession; 50 percent foreign ownership in mobile telecommunications in five years; and 49 percent foreign ownership of international and domestic services in six years. In addition, China will phase out all geographic restrictions on paging and value-added services in two years, mobile/cellular in five years, and domestic wireline services in six years. China's key telecommunications services corridor in Beijing, Shanghai, and Guangzhou, which represents approximately 75 percent of all domestic traffic, will open immediately on accession in all telecommunications services. Finally, China has agreed to implement the pro-competitive regulatory principles embodied in the Basic Telecommunications Agreement (including cost-based pricing, interconnection rights, and independent regulatory authority) and technology-neutral scheduling, which means that foreign suppliers will be allowed use any technology they choose to provide telecommunications services.

8. Professional services. In professional services, China currently tightly restricts the operation of foreign law and accounting firms. After China's accession, MNCs involved in such enterprises as legal, accountancy, taxation, management consultancy, architecture, engineering, urban planning, medical and dental, and computer and related services will have a much broader scope. China will permit foreign majority control except for the practice of Chinese law (an exception common among many WTO members). For accountancy, China has agreed to eliminate a mandatory localization requirement and allow unrestricted access to its market to licensed professionals and to follow transparent procedures.

9. Audiovisual. China's commitments cover the right to distribute video and sound recordings and cinema ownership and operation. For video and sound recordings, China will allow 49 percent foreign participation in joint ventures engaged in the distribution of these products. China has also agreed to import 40 films after accession and 50 films in three years, of which 20 will be subject to revenue sharing in each of the three years.

10. Travel and tourism. China will allow unrestricted access to the Chinese market for hotel operators with the ability to set up 100 percent foreign-owned hotels in three years, with majority ownership allowed upon accession. Foreign travel operators will be able to provide a full range of travel agency services. Travel agents will have access to government resorts as well as services in Beijing, Shanghai, Guangzhou, and Xian.

11. Protocol provisions. China has agreed to eliminate or cease enforcing trade and foreign exchange balancing requirements and local content rules. These provisions will help protect MNCs against forced technology transfers, as China has also agreed that upon accession it will not base investment approvals, import licenses, or any other import approval process on performance requirements of any kind such as local content requirements, offsets, transfers of technology, or requirements to conduct research and development in China.

China's joining the WTO should create tremendous new opportunities for MNCs in various industries, no matter whether they export or are already invested there. The influences of China's WTO membership on MNCs' entry mode choice are threefold. First, MNCs will have more freedom to opt for entry mode choices. In the past, foreign companies were generally limited to the minority equity joint venture mode in entering emerging yet regulated industries such as the automobile and computer sectors. This restriction will be removed after China's accession. MNCs will be able to use other choices such as the wholly owned subsidiary, majority equity joint venture, cooperative joint venture, and acquisition. These new choices may be superior to the minority joint venture in implementing organizational control, resource exploitation and exploration, and knowledge protection. Second, MNCs will be more free to determine the geographical regions, local partner selection, and investment strategies that are associated with a particular entry mode. In most restricted sectors, China has agreed to lift geographical restrictions against foreign investors. As the Chinese market is highly geographically segmented, this removal implies enormous opportunities for MNCs that move early into newly opened territories. Meanwhile, MNCs will be allowed to partner with those non-state-owned enterprises that have dominated the local market. Third, MNCs will not have to consider governmentally instituted constraints such as foreign exchange balance, local content requirements, ownership restrictions, and distribution limitations in the process of entry mode selection. The removal of these constraints will create more entry mode choices for MNCs.

The global economy is a system of both dramatic change and dramatic possibilities. It is estimated that the size of the global economy could double by the year 2020. This potential has been generated by increased technology, communications, and social progress, which makes various nations more interdependent and international businesses more globalized. What is at stake is not simply China's formal entry into a global trading arena but future global economic conditions. With the conclusion of the cold war, we are now standing at the threshold of a new era of possible global cooperation. Issues surrounding China's entry into the WTO seem to exemplify this circumstance in a real, concrete, and observable manner. Without joining the WTO, China will face more difficulties in continuing its economic reforms and integrating itself into the outside world. Without China as part of the formal, global economic trading apparatus, the greatest potential for the economic advancement of all nations will be constrained. As front-runners in the economic integration of the world economy, MNCs play a very important role in shaping the path and pattern of globalization on the one hand and the benefits of such globalization on the other.

CHAPTER 3

Entering China: An Evolutionary Path

During the past two decades, both the contextual environment and corporate investment strategies have drastically changed. FDI in China is undergoing fundamental structural changes in such areas as entry modes, industry selection, project location, investment size, and operational phase. The assessment of macrolevel data demonstrates that foreign investors are following an evolutionary approach by incrementally increasing their resource and financial commitments to local operations and gradually heightening their proactiveness and risk taking in the Chinese market. This chapter articulates the economic rationality underlying an evolutionary approach, presents evidence about the evolutionary pattern, and outlines implications for MNCs active or interested in China.

Why Evolutionary?

When companies invest in transitional economies characterized by economic transformation, an imperfect market structure, and poorly protected property rights, the evolutionary effect is likely to be magnified (Child and Markoczy 1993). Building upon the behavioral theory of the firm, Johanson and Vahlne (1977) developed the international expansion process model. Also known as the Uppsala process model, this theory maintains that transnational investors incrementally increase their investment commitments to foreign territories as they gain accumulated knowledge and experience in the host market. In other words, this model sees international expansion as a process involving a series of step-by-step decisions. The basic assumption of the model is that lack of knowledge is an obstacle to the development of international operations that can be overcome through experience over time. Accumulated knowledge about country-specific markets, practices, and environments helps firms increase their local commitment, reduce operational uncertainty, and enhance economic efficiency (Davidson 1980; Welch and Luostarinen 1988).

Country-specific information about task and institutional environ-ments drives international expansion because such knowledge cannot be easily acquired in factor markets. This knowledge is thus considered an owner-specific advantage in the MNC theory. Buckley (1983), Caves (1971), and Hennart (1982) reinterpreted this view, identifying country-specific knowledge as a source of rent-generating intangible assets and monopolistic power. Previous studies have confirmed the positive corre-lation between ownership-specific assets and international expansion success (Kogut and Chang 1991). In a similar vein, organizational learn-ing theory maintains that time-related learning is imperative for the evolution of rent-generating capabilities that are created over time through complex interactions among resources (Butler 1995; Levitt and March 1988). Information flowing into the organization is continuously primed by external message sources and timekeeping devices. Routini-zation of activities constitutes the most important form of storage of an organization's specific operational knowledge. Therefore, organiza-tional learning is progressively accumulated over time through routine exercise and organizational evolution is a continuous learning process spurred by the difference between expectations and experience. Pra-halad and Hamel (1990) propose that learning can occur as a firm acquires new complementary competencies. This possibility does not emerge directly from resource utilization but rather from knowledge accumulation over time. Freeman, Carroll, and Hannan (1983) main-tain that an organization's "liability of newness" will be reduced as it gains more external legitimacy, experience, and ties. Because of this external legitimacy, firms with different levels of time-based experience will perform differently (Singh, Tucker, and House 1986). Zaheer (1995) argues that the intrinsic disadvantages derived from the "liability of foreignness" will be substantially diminished over time as an investor's capabilities improve through an incremental increase in organizational learning. This has been further supported by Wilson (1980), Yu (1991), Hennart and Park (1994), and Chang (1995).

Both the international expansion process model and organizational learning theory suggest that country-specific knowledge and experience are acquired over time. Knowledge is typically accumulated through a process of learning by doing, which is a positive function of the length of a firm's presence in the host country (Levitt and March 1988). The develop-ment of knowledge about a foreign market is a sequential, evolutionary process (Chang 1995). According to the organizational learning theory, learning, change, and development involve adaptive processes that prog-ress over time (Glaser and Bassok 1989; March 1991). Moreover, the institutionalization of learning takes place through organizational codes, procedures, and routines that embed inferences about past successes and failures. This is a dynamic process in which internal changes also occur over time. When a firm operates internationally, autonomous learning becomes even more dependent on length of time because the firm confronts a variety of indigenous contingencies that vary greatly from those usually encountered in the home country.

After being isolated from the rest of the world for many decades, emerging economies are currently making political and economic transitions toward more market-based systems. These markets are characterized by many potential opportunities and new markets, on the one hand, and a tremendous amount of uncertainty and difficulty on the other. In transitional economics, the time-related learning curve is treated explicitly as an important exogenous variable for performance variance (Jefferson and Rawski 1993). Markoczy (1993) demonstrated that managerial and organizational learning effects in Western-funded enterprises in Eastern Europe are fundamentally greater than in local companies. Also drawing upon organizational learning theory, Shenkar and Nyaw (1995) suggest that transnational investors coming from individualistic cultures take a considerably longer time to achieve satisfactory performance in China than do those from collective cultures. This is because societal differences in work attitudes, motivational structures, interpersonal norms, and negotiation patterns result in more interpartner conflicts and higher learning costs, which in turn lead to low performance. Analogously, Sharma (1995) and McCarthy, Puffer, and Simmonds (1993) have shown that time has an amplified influence on foreign investors' local operations in the former Soviet Union because it is difficult for them to construct environment-stabilizing devices and reduce contextual uncertainties. Child and Markoczy (1993) observed that the ways of foreign investors and local governments in emerging economies (e.g., China) both take some time to learn; the latter's trial and error policies add more challenges to the former's ability to learn.

China is, and will long remain, a difficult and uncertain operating environment for MNCs. The long-term economic opportunities, however, are so remarkable that international investors are simply not willing to lose the opportunity to preempt or participate. According to the survey results of McKinsey (Shaw and Meier 1994), all of the sample MNCs that took an evolutionary investment approach in China have been successful. More than half are now earning a return on sales of 10 percent or more from their China-based businesses; another third are achieving returns of 6 to 10 percent. Many pioneering MNC subunits have been purposefully and incrementally increasing their commitment to and investments in local operations. Most Western companies are not in China just to take advantage of low labor costs and then jump to another country when development drives those costs up. They are there for the long haul. As a result of accumulated knowledge about the Chinese market, these companies have learned how to make profits and sustain them over time and are now working to lock out late entrants (Shaw and Meier 1994).

Operational Features

Most foreign companies gradually increase their commitment to the Chinese market in three phases: as an opportunistic experimenter, then a strategic investor, and finally a dominant local player. These operating phases are essentially on a continuum. The early phase involves a very low level of corporate commitment. The major objective of FDI is to establish a small local presence, learn how to operate and manage a business in the Chinese market, and assess the risks and potential rewards of making additional investments. During this experimental stage, foreign investors generally begin with one or two ventures, with little financial commitment, scale, or exposure, as a way of putting an opportunistic toe in the water. These few, small ventures are usually an extension of previous trading operations. The underlying aims are primarily to experiment with localization, business system design, and partnerships.

With increased familiarity, foreign investors may move to the second stage of investment, as "strategic investors," by making a much higher corporate commitment to the local market than during the earlier stage. Today the majority of foreign companies are in this phase. They have begun to build a broader multiregional or national presence through marketing or by establishing more facilities. They seek to preempt a competitive advantage by seizing early-mover benefits and market opportunities as well as developing local management. As a consequence, these companies have multiple strategic business units (SBUs) in various locations under umbrella management (a head office of interorganizational network in China). Their scope has substantially expanded from basic manufacturing into marketing, service, product design, and the like. In order to enhance their competitive position in the market, these investors also increase the scale of production and operations, scan for possible business opportunities, track progress relative to major rivals, and heighten exposure to the local market via increased sales and asset commitment.

Later, foreign investors may step up to the next, perhaps the last, stage as "dominant local players." Some well-known early-mover MNCs such as Motorola and Volkswagen have already entered this phase, accompanied by an extremely high level of corporate commitment to investment and operations in China. For instance, Motorola recently made a $1.2 billion commitment to the development of several new ventures and an additional $560 million for a semiconductor water fabrication plant, all in Tianjing. Coca-Cola, which already had a $500 million stake in China as the producer of Coke, Fanta, Sprite, and Hi C at 16 locations, recently opened seven more facilities. MNCs at this stage aim to secure the dominant share of the market within an industry sector. They plan to shape the industrial structure and its norms to achieve sustained superior efficiency. Operations during this phase are characterized by highly localized management, leading the market in their respective industries, becoming true local players as perceived by customers and suppliers, and acting as long-term partners in boosting local economic growth as that is defined by the Chinese government.

Industrial Participation

In the earliest stage of investment, foreign companies invest and operate primarily in less capital- and technology-intensive industries such as foods, electronics, construction materials, textiles, toys, and other light industries. Most projects in these areas have been an extension of previous import and export businesses with Chinese partners. These were viewed as having less risk, and accordingly a lower commitment to local production and marketing was required. With increased experience in the market and accumulated knowledge about the industrial structure, foreign companies have extended their scope into infrastructure facility construction, energy, transportation, telecommunications, high-tech and capital-intensive machinery and equipment, automobiles, and other Chinese "pillar" industries. These newly developed industries provide relatively less competitive and more preemptive opportunities. At the same time, risks are greater, as they require more technological input, higher startup costs, and a larger operational commitment. This strategic move seems to be ongoing. For example, from January to May 1997 foreign investors invested $1.72 billion in technology or capital-intensive manufacturing projects. This was a 370 percent increase over the amount invested during the same period the previous year. These changes are particularly prominent in special economic zones such as Shengzhen, Zhuhai, Shantou, and Xiamen and in coastal regions such as Shanghai, Guangzhou, Dalian, and Tianjing.

Table 3.1 illustrates the industrial patterns of foreign direct investment in China in 1993, 1995, and 1997. In 1997, the industrial sector accounted for 61.64 percent of total FDI, leading all other sectors in

TABLE 3.1.   Evolutionary Patterns in Industrial Participation (approved investments in millions of dollars)

Sector	1993		1995		1997	
	Number of Projects	Value	Number of Projects	Value	Number of Projects	Value
Agriculture	1,704	1,191	903	1,736	814	1,065
Industry	56,549	51,174	27,687	61,648	15,840	31,438
Construction	3,167	3,878	944	1,918	455	3,119
Transportation and telecommunications services	915	1,490	268	1,697	279	2,622
Commerce and food services	4,842	4,606	1,851	3,427	1,198	1,839
Real estate and utilities	11,322	43,771	3,279	17,835	2,262	8,891
Tourism and hotel	(806)	(1,482)	(171)	(954)	(87)	(200)
Health care, sports, and social welfare	206	477	174	837	38	143
Education, culture, and the arts	458	452	162	345	34	70
Scientific research	881	588	275	278	56	138
Other	3,393	3,808	1,468	1,560	839	1,678
Total	83,437	111,435	37,011	91,281	21,001	51,004

influencing the economy. The real estate and utilities sector follows, involving $8,891 million in investments or 17.43 percent of the total. Construction, infrastructure, commercial and food services, and agriculture are also important sectors, ranking from third to sixth, respectively.

The table reflects some of the evolutionary changes in industries in which foreign investors participate. The proportion of FDI in agriculture, industry, transportation and telecommunications services, and construction has increased drastically, while FDI in the real estate and tourism sectors has decreased. For instance, foreign investment in real estate reached $43.77 billion in 1993 but dropped to $8.89 billion in 1997.

Project Location

FDI is now to be found throughout China. In the early period, however, there were very few foreign investment projects in the inland provinces. The levels of economic development and the stages of reform are not the same in different regions across China. The open coastal cities and economic regions have historically been more developed economically and contain better infrastructure (transportation, communications, production, business services, etc.) for foreign businesses than do the inland provinces. The open areas have enjoyed greater autonomy and authority in conducting their economic affairs. Furthermore, they provide more Western-style business facilities and a more familiar cultural atmosphere. The inland provinces, by contrast, were considered to be more hostile, unstable, and risky investment locations. As a result, there were only 333 FIEs registered in the central and western provinces in 1990. However, as a result of more experience and better knowledge about Chinese business practices, governmental policies, market conditions, and sociocultural factors, foreign direct investment in the inland provinces has been steadily rising. The number of registered FIEs in these areas increased to 44,971 as of 1996. A progressively increasing commitment to the relatively uncharted territories of inland markets, coming with the accumulation of experience, can promote the overall market power and competitive position of foreign investors in China.

As table 3.2 shows, actual FDI in the inland provinces (the central and western regions) was only $215 million in 1990 but reached $7,185 million in 1997, 33.42 times the former figure. Similarly, the number of registered FIEs as of 1995 was more than triple the 1992 number. Both the total amount of investment and registered capital have been steadily increasing over the years, with average annual growth of over 50 percent from 1990 to 1997. This evidence supports the notion that foreign companies heighten their commitment in a relatively uncertain and risky environment in an evolutionary manner as a result of increased familiarity with that environment. In general, they first locate within an economically well-developed, culturally congenial area. With accumulated

TABLE 3.2. Evolutionary Patterns in Project Location: FDI in the Inland Provinces

	Central and Western Regions (18 provinces)[a]			
Year	Actual FDI ($mil)	Number of FIEs (year end)	Total Investment ($mil)	Registered Capital ($mil)
1990	215	na	na	na
1991	371	na	na	na
1992	1,110	11,459	20,574	14,746
1993	4,656	31,614	63,900	45,090
1994	4,829	39,664	80,286	56,223
1995	4,867	44,875	96,760	66,818
1996	5,413	44,971	109,020	65,071
1997	7,185	43,937	104,637	77,762

[a]These provinces include Hebei, Shanxi, Inner Mongolia, Guangxi, Jiangxi, Henan, Hubei, Hunan, Anhui, Sichuan, Guizhou, Yunnan, Tibet, Shaanxi, Gansu, Qinghai, Ningxia, and Xinjiang.

knowledge of the host country environment, they tend to gradually shift to, or increase their participation in, less-developed, uncertain regions where market potentials have been largely unexplored.

Entry Mode

Foreign investors are generally free to choose their mode of entry into the Chinese market. According to the Chinese government's classifications, these modes include the following.

1. Equity joint ventures, which accounted for 37.56 percent of the total contractual amount of FDI in 1997. An EJV involves the creation of limited liability companies with equity and management shared in negotiated proportions by foreign and Chinese partners.
2. Wholly foreign owned enterprises, which represented 32 percent of the total value of FDI in 1997. According to China's Law on Wholly Foreign Owned Enterprises, promulgated in April 1986, the WFOE is organized by a foreign company using its own capital, technology, and management. The enterprise manages its operations independently and is responsible for all risks, gains, and losses.
3. Contractual (or cooperative) joint ventures (CJVs), which constituted about 21.86 percent of FDI in 1997. The CJV encompasses a variety of arrangements and is a looser association of partners (although they may still involve establishment of a limited liability company) who agree to pursue a joint undertaking. The Chinese and foreign partner cooperate in joint projects or other business activities according to the terms and conditions stipulated in a venture agreement. Technology transfer and long-term licensing agreements are also included in this mode.
4. Joint exploration projects (e.g., offshore oil exploration consortia), which represented 0.73 percent of the total amount of FDI in 1997. Under these arrangements, the exploration costs are borne by the foreign partner, with development costs later shared by a Chinese entity. Although such explorations allow the foreign firm to manage specific projects, this type of FDI does not result in the establishment of new limited liability enterprises.
5. Other forms of FDI, which constituted 7.58 percent of total FDI in 1997. These include (1) processing and assembling agreements in which foreign firms provide Chinese manufacturers with raw

materials or semiprocessed products with which to produce manufactured goods to be directly distributed in international markets;
(2) compensation trade agreements, under which foreign firms
provide Chinese partners with inputs with which to manufacture
products to be sold in either the domestic or the international
market; (3) international leasing agreements, whereby the foreign party retains ownership (and therefore the equity and risk) of
the equipment used in China throughout the period of the lease;
and (4) stock and bond issuance.

As shown in table 3.3, the ratio of wholly foreign owned ventures
has been substantially and steadily growing in recent years, although
equity joint ventures are still the dominant entry mode. In 1985, wholly
owned foreign subsidiaries accounted for less than 1 percent of the total
contractual value of FDI projects. This percentage increased to 7.75 in
1988, 29.52 in 1991, and 36.30 in 1996. In the first half of 1997, the
number of newly approved wholly foreign owned projects (45 percent of
total FDI) surpassed the number of equity joint ventures (43 percent of
the total). A major factor underlying this change is that an increasing
number of pioneering investors already in China have employed wholly
owned ventures as a form of reinvestment. It is also likely that those new
investors who have gained experience and knowledge from early entrants will consider using wholly foreign owned subsidiaries as an entry
mode. Those without experience, either direct or indirect, still need to
opt for a joint venture.

In the FDI literature, it is recognized that a wholly foreign owned
subsidiary involves higher operational risks, greater financial costs, and
more organizational commitment in the host country environment than
any other entry mode (Beamish and Banks 1987). The risks and costs of
the wholly foreign owned mode are further magnified when firms invest
and operate in transitional economies such as that of China because foreign investors encounter greater contextual uncertainty, institutional hostility, and contractual risks (Shan 1991). Thus, a steady and incremental
increase in the utilization of wholly foreign owned subsidiaries as an entry
mode implies that foreign businesses have improved their ability to reduce contextual risks and mitigate operational uncertainties in gradual
steps as a result of learning and experience over time. Once a firm is
equipped with these capabilities, the wholly owned entry mode is deemed
superior because it can enhance organizational control over local operations, dispel the costs of interpartner mistrust and opportunism, and protect the company's tacit knowledge or technologies in an environment
where intellectual property rights systems may not be well established.

TABLE 3.3. Evolutionary Patterns in Entry Modes (contractual value in millions of dollars)

Entry Mode	1985	1988	1991	1992	1993	1994	1995	1996	1997
EJVs	2,030	3,134	6,080	29,128	55,175	39,355	38,839	31,876	20,726
CJVs	3,496	1,624	2,138	13,255	25,499	20,347	17,791	14,297	12,066
WFOEs	45	480	3,667	15,696	30,456	21,472	33,601	26,810	17,658
Joint exploration	360	59	92	43	304	232	57	293	402
Other FDI	402	894	445	612	531	565	679	371	4,182
International leasing	–	156	30	77	65	17	42	33	289
Compensation trade	260	532	266	415	271	203	531	129	124
Production/assembly	142	205	148	120	195	345	106	209	1,696
Stock issuance									2,074
Total	6,333	6,191	12,422	58,735	111,966	81,971	90,967	73,647	55,186

Investment Size

Throughout the 1980s, the average value of FDI contracts in China was less than 1 million U.S. dollars. Table 3.4 shows, for example, that the average value of FDI was $0.89 million in 1988 and $0.97 million in 1989. This amount has grown gradually since 1990, with a steady increase of 22 percent per year. Of 167,000 FIEs at the end of 1993, medium and small projects, each with less than $5 million invested, accounted for only 12 percent of the national total. There were more than 6,000, each with over $10 million in investment, in 1992–93. This number doubled the combined total of the previous 12 years, from 1980 through the end of 1991. In 1996, the average value per FDI contract reached $3.02 million, a 23.27 percent increase compared to the number in 1995. Although the average contractual value per project was smaller in 1997 than in 1996, the number of projects valued at more than $100 million was larger in 1997 than in 1996.

This evidence suggests that financial commitments are circumspect overall but incrementally increase over time along with the accumulation of China-specific experience. Organizational learning is inherently incremental (Cohen and Levinthal 1990). When a firm expands abroad, learning is transmitted via institutionalized organizational practices such as decision-making procedures and corporate policies, through which firms progressively acquire site-specific knowledge (Pennings, Barkema, and Douma 1994). This knowledge, gained over time, enables them to reduce operational costs and uncertainty, enhance the effectiveness and efficiency of local operations, and boost their organizational and product

TABLE 3.4. Evolutionary
Patterns in Investment Size (in
millions of dollars)

Year	Average Contractual Amount per Project
1988	0.89
1989	0.97
1990	0.91
1991	0.92
1992	1.16
1993	1.33
1994	1.71
1995	2.45
1996	3.02
1997	2.43

images (Benito and Gripsrud 1992). Since the predominant motivation of most MNCs entering China is to obtain long-term economic rents through business preemption and market expansion, the more site-specific experience a FIE has accumulated the more likely it is that it will increase its resource and financial commitment to the local environment (Chang 1995; Kogut 1983).

Site-specific knowledge can only be obtained through an actual presence and the conduct of operations in the market, not by means of "objective" information gained through market research (Johanson and Vahlne 1977). Davidson (1980) reported that less-experienced firms often overstate risks, understate returns, and consequently shy away from undertaking significant resource contributions and making commitments to the local market. This in turn lessens the potential for the firm's growth, leading to low financial and market performance. With increasing experience, however, firms acquire more knowledge of the foreign market, perceive less uncertainty, and acquire more confidence in their ability to correctly estimate risks and returns and manage foreign operations (Erramilli 1991). As a result, pioneering firms continuously reinvest their distinctive resources and increase their commitments to local markets over time (Anderson and Gatignon 1986). Meanwhile, new entrants are also likely to make greater financial commitments to the host market because they face greater competitive pressure and benefit from the experience of earlier movers.

Conclusion

Overall, the macrolevel evidence suggests that the key notions of the international expansion process model and organizational learning theory are generally applicable to foreign direct investment in China. Foreign businesses take an evolutionary approach in developing their presence and participation in the Chinese market. They began their investments in the early 1980s as "opportunistic experimenters" by setting up one or two small, mostly joint ventures in less risky sectors and in more economically and culturally developed locations. They used this circumspect approach as a way of testing the riskiness of an uncharted new territory.

As a result of more experience in China's industrial and institutional environment, accumulated over time, foreign companies gradually became "strategic investors" in the late 1980s and early 1990s. During this period, foreign companies incrementally increased their commitments to local operations in terms of both investment size and production scale, used a larger number of wholly foreign owned subsidiaries as an entry mode, entered more and more capital- or technology-intensive indus-tries, and located more projects in less-developed inland provinces. Some large pioneering firms established multiple subunits in various geo-graphical or product domains, pursuing greater market power and supe-rior competitive positions nationwide. A large and growing number of foreign companies are now operating at this stage.

With the accumulation of tremendous diversified experience in China's macroenvironment, some world class early entrants (e.g., Mo-torola, Atlantic Richfield, Coca-Cola, Lucent Technologies, United Technologies) have moved in recent years to the stage of "dominant local player." They secured dominant market shares in particular indus-tries and began to generate above-average financial returns in those industries. They are viewed by the host country government and custom-ers as "local" players not only because they rely on indigenous produc-tion, materials purchasing, and parts and components but also because they make considerable use of local management and demonstrate a continuous commitment to China's consumers. These companies are committed to pursuing ambitious investment programs and building dominant, nationwide market positions and global businesses. As table 3.5 shows, the top 12 multinationals from the United States that have the biggest stakes in China are maintaining their commitment through ongo-ing construction and investment.

For pioneering firms, however, translating commitment into reality in China takes far more than a blank check, a good product, and a careful strategy. For one thing, it demands that MNCs understand and deal effectively with the complex, often confusing web of government entities that approve and facilitate business development — especially in such highly regulated sectors as telecommunications, energy, and auto-mobiles. Internally, MNCs face the equally daunting task of coordinat-ing multiple subunits and supporting units to realize synergies, maximize impact, and contain cost duplication. Moreover, enormous amounts of time and energy are needed to manage multiple joint ventures with local partners that typically lack the product and market knowledge, distribu-tion reach, and financial resources to match MNCs' aspirations. Skilled local managers and experienced expatriates capable of taking the initia-tive in China are woefully scarce.

Indeed, China's unique opportunities and challenges are prompting many multinational pioneers to rethink their established ways of building businesses in new markets as they seek to increase the pace and payoff of their Chinese investments. As illustrated earlier, these structural changes include multiple market presences (e.g., moving inland), multiple entry modes (e.g., more wholly owned), multiple unit operations, and multiple

TABLE 3.5.   Ongoing Commitments by the Top 12 U.S. Companies with the Biggest Stakes in China

Rank	Company
1	Motorola: $1.2 billion. The company's recent commitments include several joint ventures and a $560 million semiconductor wafer fabrication plant in Tianjing.
2	Atlantic Richfield: $625 million. ARCO has completed China's largest offshore natural gas project, a $1.13 billion pipeline half owned by the Chinese government.
3	Coca-Cola: $500 million. Coke, Fanta, Sprite, and Hi C are bottled at 16 locations. Seven more facilities are being constructed.
4	Amoco: $350 million. Amoco started producing oil in March 1995 from a development project in the South China Sea.
5	Ford: $250 million. Ford has three factories making auto components, light trucks, and vans; two other plants are under construction.
6	United Technologies: $250 million. The company's Otis subsidiary makes elevators and escalators; Carrier manufactures air-conditioning equipment.
7	Pepsico: $200 million. Pepsi has 12 bottling plants, two joint ventures producing Cheetos, 62 KFC franchises, and 19 Pizza Huts.
8	Lucent Technologies: $150 million. This AT&T spinoff is involved in seven joint ventures, including a $70 million project to provide digital private line service to Beijing.
9	General Electric: $150 million. GE is a partner in 14 joint ventures, including ones that make X-ray and other medical systems. It owns 80 percent of the largest lighting manufacturer in China.
10	General Motors: $130 million. Delphi, a subsidiary, is a partner in three auto parts facilities. Not counted, because the money is not yet committed, is GM's 50 percent partnership in a $1 billion project to build cars in Shanghai.
11	Hewlett Packard: $100 million. HP has been investing in China for 12 years and now manufactures computers, medical systems products, and analytical chemical equipment.
12	IBM: $100 million. IBM has six joint ventures producing computers, electronic cards, advanced workstations for the banking industry, and software.

industry investments. A growing number of firms are using innovative organizational approaches to improve the coordination and control of business development by cutting across traditional global business-unit boundaries, centralizing key functions, and developing local structures and staff that will allow MNCs to better shape their own destinies in China. For pioneering "strategic" or "dominant" investors, it is critical today to (1) gain control of inherently weak joint ventures by maintaining majority equity stakes, deploying expatriates in key management positions, and providing outside support; (2) coordinate multiple subunits by providing focused management leadership while sharing services and product expertise across ventures; (3) attain effective coordination of external relationships and investment decisions by establishing a strong corporate center in China with a clear mandate to take the lead in strategy development and implementation; and (4) strengthen local human resources by bringing in expatriate managers or trainers while investing heavily in training local staff, establishing career paths for them, and instilling corporate values.

For late entrants or those remaining in the "opportunistic experiment" stage, being left behind has become a real and urgent risk. If China is indeed of strategic importance, such companies must act quickly by drawing on the lessons learned by more aggressive players in the Chinese market. Today late foreign entrants are competing not only with early foreign investors but with local firms. In China, an increasing number of firms, especially township and village enterprises, have mushroomed in every economic sector. As a result of structural reform and industrial deregulation, these local businesses are much more strategically flexible, organizationally autonomous, and technologically proactive and innovative than Chinese companies under the old regime. Therefore, the later the entry into this market the more competitive pressure the entrant will encounter.

China's rich market potential and rapid economic reforms have made the country a prime target for multinational companies. Despite daunting challenges, China's attractiveness to foreign investors remains bright. China's growth performance is outstanding. With an average annual GDP growth of 12 percent in 1991–96, it has one of the fastest growing economies in the world. This trend is expected to continue. In addition, the liberalization of FDI policies is still under way. Some industries that were once off limits to foreign investors, including air transport, general aviation, retail trade, foreign trade, banking, insurance, accounting, auditing, legal services, the mining and smelting of precious metals, and the prospecting, extracting, and processing of diamonds and other precious nonmetal minerals, are gradually being opened. Moreover, there is also a significant potential for FDI participation in the infrastructure. Several build-operate-transfer schemes have already been implemented. Foreign investors are now allowed to acquire state-owned firms. Further, to the extent that the Chinese currency becomes convertible, profit repatriation will be easier, making it more attractive to invest in China. As a result, the already great importance of FDI to China's economy is likely to grow. Thus, while FDI inflow to China might fall below $30 billion in the next few years, there is reason to believe that this will be a temporary adjustment rather than a response to a change in general economic factors. China will remain one of the top FDI destinations in the world marketplace.

PART 2
Entering China
Entry Mode Choices, Decisions, and Strategies

CHAPTER 4

How to Enter China: Entry Mode Choices

The dynamic Chinese economy is now encouraging the use of more diverse and creative entry modes for international investors. This chapter illustrates various entry modes of foreign direct investment available at present to foreign companies entering China. These entry modes include equity joint ventures, wholly foreign owned subsidiaries, contractual joint ventures, umbrella companies, acquisitions, representative offices, branches, build-operate-transfers, licensing, and franchising. The merits and limitations of each entry mode are discussed. Some practical advice on entry strategies for international executives active in the Chinese market is also highlighted.

The growing Chinese economy has lured many foreign companies to commence operations there. China's special economic, cultural, and political context is, however, unfamiliar territory to many executives. The rules of the game are often dissimilar to those in market economies. Choosing the right entry mode is therefore crucial to the success of the joint venture.

For both the new investor beginning to explore the Chinese market and incumbents with multiple investments in China, the choice of entry modes has expanded in recent years. Entry modes available to international trading businesses include conventional import and export, flexible trade (i.e., processing imported materials or foreign samples and assembling imported parts and components), international leasing, and countertrade (i.e., barter, counterpurchase, offset, switch trading, compensation trade, or buybacks).

Two prominent characteristics of entry mode selection have been emerging in the country. First, several new investment vehicles such as umbrella companies, acquisitions of Chinese enterprises, and build-operate-transfers have been created and employed. Second, the use of conventional entry modes such as equity joint ventures and wholly foreign owned subsidiaries is undergoing fundamental structural changes. For example, wholly foreign owned ventures accounted for less than 1 percent of the total contractual value of FDI in 1985; this had increased to 43 percent by the first half of 1997. Understanding the advantages and disadvantages of each entry mode choice is a prerequisite for foreign firms in formulating their entry strategies.

In general, foreign investors are free to choose from several entry modes. These include the following.

1. Equity joint ventures, the most favored mode in the past, which accounted for 49.97 percent of the total amount of FDI in 1996. An EJV is a limited liability company with equity and management shared in negotiated proportions by foreign and Chinese partners.
2. Wholly foreign owned enterprises, which represented 29.85 percent of the total value of FDI in 1996. According to China's Law on Wholly Foreign Owned Enterprises, promulgated in April 1986, a WFOE is a foreign company using its own capital, technology, and management while operating in China. The enterprise manages its operations independently and is responsible for all risks, gains, and losses.
3. Contractual (or cooperative) joint ventures (CJVs), which constituted about 20.81 percent of actual FDI in 1994. The CJV refers to a variety of arrangements and a loose association of partners that agree to pursue a joint undertaking (which may include a limited liability company). The Chinese and foreign partner cooperate in joint projects or other business activities according to the terms and conditions stipulated in the venture agreement.
4. Other options, including the establishment of representative offices, branch offices, and umbrella companies; the acquisition of existing firms; licensing and franchising; and BOT operations.

A detailed discussion of these entry modes follows.

Entry Mode 1: Equity Joint Ventures

The most common entry mode for MNCs in the Chinese market is the EJV. To set up an EJV, each partner contributes cash, facilities, equipment, materials, intellectual property rights, labor, or land-use rights. According to the EJV law, a foreign investor's share must be at least 25 percent of total equity. Generally, there is no upward limit in most deregulated industries. However, in governmentally controlled or institutionally restricted sectors, such as automobiles and telecommunications, foreign investors are often more confined with respect to equity arrangements. According to the Interim Provisions on the Term of Joint Ventures of Sino-Foreign Equity Joint Ventures, approved by the State Council in September 1990, there is no maximum term of operation for EJVs, although most are granted as many as 50 years. This time frame can be extended at any time, depending upon the agreement of the partners. Chinese approval authorities generally encourage these extensions.

As an alternative to either full integration or simple market exchange, the EJV facilitates interfirm learning and the transfer of intangible assets while mitigating incentives for opportunism by creating interdependence between the transacting parties (Luo 1997). If the benefits derived from joint efforts, minus the transaction costs specific to the formation and operation of an EJV, are greater than the sum of benefits obtained from exploiting firm-specific advantages separately, an EJV creates synergies that enhance economic rents to the partners. These synergies can be the result of risk reduction, economies of scale and scope, production rationalization, convergence of technologies, or improved local acceptance (Beamish and Banks 1987).

The EJV form provides foreign companies with long-term connections to the Chinese market. The EJV's ability to sell through the local partner's established marketing channels seems especially attractive to manufacturers hoping to penetrate the domestic market. The Chinese government normally favors this mode because it often involves significant technology transfer to the Chinese partner. When EJVs enter industries in compliance with governmental plans, they are more likely to receive special access to utilities and critical input than those utilizing other entry modes such as WFOEs.

EJVs are, however, notoriously hard to sustain even in the relatively stable environments of the United States and Europe (Harrigan 1985; Osborn and Hagedorn 1997). Investment in China is even more difficult because the country is vast and varied, its culture and traditions are profoundly different from those of the West, and its social, governmental, and economic systems are particularly complex. Today foreign investors must contend with several additional factors when considering EJVs in China.

First, the marketplace in China is rapidly evolving, fragmenting, and becoming more competitive as more foreign companies commence operations there. Many new entrants are vying for first-mover advantages. Top-level players in some of the most promising industries (e.g.,

consumer packaged goods, infrastructure, construction, chemicals, pharmaceuticals, and electronics) are pursuing aggressive growth strategies
with a focus on gaining market share. Some companies are willing to
sustain losses in order to establish beachheads in China, be they in the
form of manufacturing plants, distribution networks, or consumer awareness of their products.

Second, the distribution system in China is quite chaotic and undergoing fundamental changes. The traditional three-tiered (national, provincial, and local) distribution system in China is crumbling, giving way
to various parallel channels that charge different fees and provide different services in every geographic area. These changes indicate that getting a product into the Chinese market can be daunting. Expanding the
scope of operations can be even more so. Every Chinese company be-
longs to and operates under some combination of local, provincial, and
central government authority, each with its own agenda. Hence, there
are many conflicting interpretations of rules and regulations. If an EJV
partner tries to do business outside its authorized territory, it is apt to
run into trouble.

Third, negotiations on the joint venture contract can be lengthy and
complicated, with a tendency to negotiate in a style described by one
veteran China trader as "a blend of the Byzantine and evangelical"
(Tateisi 1996). Chinese negotiators often frustrate Western businesspeo-
ple unused to their tactics. They may attempt to control meeting locations and schedules, take advantage of perceived weaknesses, use shame
tactics, pit competitors against each other, feign anger, rehash old issues,
and manipulate expectations. Often negotiation continues even after the
signing of the joint venture contract. Therefore, a foreign company
should choose effective negotiators, prepare for time-consuming meetings, and develop a sophisticated strategy before opening negotiations.

Fourth, foreign companies often find themselves in a dilemma when
the Chinese partners demand technology that is "state of the art." Chinese negotiators routinely request the most advanced technology from
foreign suppliers during initial negotiations, though they may lack sufficient foreign exchange and an adequate infrastructure to utilize complex
technology and trained personnel. To ensure a better chance of success,
foreign companies are strongly advised to provide the most appropriate,
price-competitive technology.

Finally, it is often difficult to decide on the contribution to be made
by each partner. The Chinese side normally prefers to contribute non-
cash items such as land use and existing buildings and construction materials, all of which are easy for the Chinese to overvalue due to the
difficulty of assessing prices accurately. In order to avoid such complica-

tions, foreign investors should have assessments made by independent professional consulting or accounting firms.

Entry Mode 2: Wholly Foreign Owned Enterprises

The WFOE form offers foreign investors increased flexibility and control. Within the constraints of the Chinese system, WFOEs allow managers to expand as quickly as they want and where they want without the burden of an uncooperative partner. WFOEs also allow foreign investors to set up and protect their own processes and procedures, which leads to more careful strategic and operational oversight. Moreover, they can be established more quickly than EJVs, for local Chinese authorities are required to respond to initial project proposals within 30 days.

WFOEs offer hope for a more effective way to work in China. But in any competitive market, turning dreams into reality is challenging. China's complexities double that challenge. However, foreign investors who can let go of the conventional wisdom that joint ventures are the only way to do business in China have a new way to take advantage of the country's vast opportunities. For companies willing to accept the challenge, WFOEs may be ideal.

WFOEs have traditionally been viewed by the Chinese government as offering little in the way of technology transfer or other benefits to the Chinese economy (Vanhonacker 1997). Although governmental support of WFOEs trails behind that of EJVs, the attractiveness of this entry mode to the government has gradually increased. It helps stimulate economic growth, generate foreign exchange earnings, and reduce the unemployment rate. When domestic credit is tight, WFOEs provide China with a means of attracting foreign capital.

WFOEs today operate in many areas where EJVs are currently approved. In some sectors, such as the automotive and telecommunications industries, heavy regulations apply, which implies that EJVs are a safer choice. Exceptions always abound in China, however, as Motorola proved in Tianjing and General Motors in Guangzhou. From the Chinese government's perspective, the form of the investment is negotiable; WFOEs are possible even in regulated industries. The real key to the entry mode regulation is not what the rule book says but whether or not a foreign company will bring something of value to the Chinese government.

Some notes of caution should be stated. First, WFOEs must still handle *guanxi* relations (i.e., interpersonal connections). Many foreign investors need to rely on Chinese agents to make liaisons on their behalf and to help procure land, materials, and services. WFOEs should identify exactly which connections will help and who has them and then engage as advisers those Chinese individuals and organizations that have access to the relevant decision-making authorities.

Second, WFOEs are not allowed to invest and operate in certain industries that are vital to the Chinese economy. Nevertheless, the Chinese regulatory environment is evolving; more industries, including some service sectors, are opening up to foreign investment. Although it will be a gradual opening, China will eventually grant WFOE investment access to more industries.

Third, as WFOEs operate without the control of a Chinese partner, investment approval authorities often hold them to higher standards, including stricter foreign exchange balance requirements. If a WFOE is profitable, the Chinese government may encourage it to find a Chinese partner in the hope of getting the foreign party to share its profits and pass along technological and management know-how. Alternatively, a Chinese business may try to form an EJV with another foreign party to produce similar goods in competition with the existing WFOE.

Finally, WFOEs are more vulnerable to criticism relating to cultural and economic sovereignty. Naturally, the Chinese do not want foreign companies taking advantage of their country, and WFOE managers should recognize and address this concern. One way to do so is to localize production, that is, to buy as many parts and components as possible from local Chinese suppliers. Another way is to hire Chinese managers. Motorola, for example, employs only Chinese managers, very few of whom hold U.S. passports. Foreign companies can also be active in socially responsible projects such as financing schools, sports events, the arts, public safety, or other community service projects. They can also nurture local brands. Coca-Cola, for example, recently transferred the trademark of its new Tian Yu Di fruit drink to a local producer, the Tianjin Jinmei Beverage Co. This move was warmly received as an example of the company's sensitivity to the Chinese notion of reciprocity.

Entry Mode 3: Contractual Joint Ventures

Unlike an EJV, in which profit distributions and management of the venture are determined by the proportion of total registered capital contributed by each partner, the CJV (as governed by the Law of the People's Republic of China on Sino-Foreign Cooperative Enterprises, adopted by the National People's Congress on April 13, 1988) is an investment vehicle in which profits and other responsibilities are assigned to each party according to the joint venture contract. These are not necessarily in accordance with the percentage of each partner's share of total investment. A CJV is a business partnership in which each party cooperates as a separate legal entity and bears its own liabilities. The two firms entering into a CJV have the option of forming a limited liability entity with legal independence status, similar to that of an EJV.

In China, joint exploration projects (e.g., offshore oil exploration consortia) are a special type of CJV. Under these arrangements, the exploration costs are borne by the foreign partner, with development costs later shared by a Chinese entity. Although such explorations allow the foreign firm to manage specific projects, this type of FDI does not necessarily result in the establishment of new limited liability enterprises. The major features of CJVs are as follows.

1. Liability. A CJV is allowed to adopt nonlegal person status. The liability of investors in a venture with nonlegal person status is unlimited, while the liability of investors in a joint venture with legal person status is limited to the amounts they have invested. Legal person status is automatic for EJVs, but CJVs may elect either status. Investors in CJVs may be able to use the unlimited liability conferred by nonlegal person status in the tax structure for their Chinese venture.

2. Capital requirements. Foreign investors in CJVs with legal person status are required to contribute 25 percent or more of the venture's total registered capital. This requirement does not apply to CJVs that adopt nonlegal person status. In practice, 25 percent was generally assumed to be the minimum amount that a foreign investor could contribute to a CJV with nonlegal person status.

3. Import tax exemptions. Like EJVs, CJVs are exempt from paying transfer taxes and duties on imported equipment used as part of the foreign partner's investment in the enterprise, provided the equipment is required for the operation of the joint venture and is valued at no more than the total investment amount specified in the CJV contract.

4. Strategic flexibility. There are no limits on the duration of the contract or prohibitions on the withdrawal of registered capital during the contracted term. A CJV has great freedom to structure assets, organize production processes, and manage operations. This flexibility can be highly attractive for a foreign investor

interested in property development, resource exploration, and other production projects in which the foreign party incurs substantial up-front development costs (Randall and Telesio 1995). A CJV, for example, can build an accelerated return on its share of investment into the contract to allow it to recoup its equity share by the end of the term. Further, CJVs can be developed quickly to take advantage of short-term business opportunities and can be dissolved when they complete their assigned tasks.

CJVs differ from EJVs in several ways. First, profit distributions among parties to a CJV need not be in strict proportion to their registered capital contributions. The foreign party may recover its investment earlier than the Chinese partner upon meeting certain conditions, including reversion of all fixed assets to the Chinese partner. In contrast, the parties to an EJV can distribute profits only in strict proportion to their contributions to the EJV's total registered capital. Moreover, a CJV may distribute profits both in cash and in venture output, while an EJV is restricted to making cash distributions. Second, as noted earlier, the CJV's ability to adopt nonlegal person status also distinguishes it from an EJV. Besides affecting the liability of the joint venture partner, nonlegal person status may allow foreign CJV partners to contribute less than 25 percent of the total registered capital of the joint venture. Foreign partners in an EJV must contribute a combined minimum of 25 percent of a venture's registered capital. Finally, CJVs are not required to survey Chinese sources before importing supplies or raw materials from abroad, while EJVs must give first priority to Chinese suppliers.

Because of their ability to provide foreign investors with returns in excess of their proportional contributions to the venture's total registered capital, CJVs have been the vehicles of choice for build-operate-transfer infrastructure projects. The CJV option is expected to continue to be useful in BOT projects and, as a result of the new regulations, will become a more popular option for other types of ventures as well, especially those in which foreign investors seek a preferential return.

Entry Mode 4: Umbrella Companies

Many foreign companies are now seeking greater flexibility of operation in China's market. A growing number of firms are interested in establishing fully integrated companies that can combine sales, procurement, subsidiary investment, manufacturing, and maintenance for a broad range of products. Foreign investors interested in the concept include those new to China as well as established firms seeking to unite various existing investments under a parent company. The growing complexity of operations of many MNCs in China and the need to more closely coordinate numerous joint ventures and/or wholly owned subsidiaries have led several firms to set up holding companies in recent years. The umbrella enterprise, also known as an "investment company" (*touzi gongsi*) or "holding company" (*konggu gongsi*), has emerged for this purpose.

In contrast to joint ventures, which can manufacture and market only approved product lines, a holding company is able to unite existing investments under one umbrella to combine sales, procurement, manufacturing, and maintenance. It can also help balance foreign exchange reserves between joint ventures, act as a clearing house for intragroup RMB financing, and help in the establishment of new enterprises.

Du Pont was an early convert to the holding company format in the late 1980s, although Philips is credited with starting the concept — apparently after the company's chief operating officer (CEO) met with Li Peng in 1989 and received the premier's endorsement. By the end of 1998, the Chinese government had approved more than 25 holding companies, both in wholly owned and joint venture form, involving foreign multinationals. One of the MNCs that set up a holding company in China is CIBA, the Swiss pharmaceutical and chemical giant. The group's wholly owned umbrella company, CIBA China, employs approximately 30 people in its Beijing office and has branches in Shanghai and Qingdao. It was founded in 1993 and is now capitalized at U.S.$30 million. In total, CIBA boasts 15 equity joint ventures in China, has a handful of nonequity ventures and one wholly owned subsidiary, and has $260 million worth of investments in the country.

The umbrella model is especially useful for companies that are multidivisional, where each division adopts different entry modes and is run independently while the holding company coordinates them. This also suits the way the company is run worldwide, preferring individual businesses so as to avoid building up reserves that would limit the volume of cash that can be cycled on a global basis. With a holding company in China, profits can be more easily transferred among different strategic business units (SBUs) and taken out of the country.

A foreign investor may consider establishing an umbrella enterprise to achieve some or all of the following objectives.

1. Investing in subsidiary projects.
2. Manufacturing products.
3. Facilitating foreign exchange balances for all China activities.

4. Centralizing the purchase of production materials for subsidiary projects.
5. Providing product maintenance service and technical support.
6. Training subsidiary project personnel and end users of products.
7. Coordinating and consolidating project management. Currently, each foreign-invested enterprise has a separate company structure. An umbrella enterprise can centralize management and streamline the subsidiaries as operating units.
8. Marketing subsidiary products. Usually, each manufacturing FIE in China has to develop its own sales capability. An umbrella enterprise can achieve greater efficiency by establishing one marketing entity.
9. Converting representative offices into umbrella or subsidiary branch offices, thus removing many operating restrictions such as the need to hire personnel through labor service companies.

An umbrella company may provide a range of services to its subsidiaries.

1. Assisting personnel recruitment.
2. Providing technical training, market development, and consulting assistance.
3. Assisting in the acquisition of loans, including providing guaranties.
4. Acting as an agent for subsidiaries in the procurement of machinery and equipment, including office equipment, raw materials, components, and spare parts necessary for production processes.
5. Acting as an agent for SBUs in the sale of products and providing after-sale service.
6. Balancing foreign exchange among SBUs with the approval of the foreign exchange administration authorities.
7. Providing financial support to subsidiaries with the approval of the People's Bank of China.

Without special approval from the Ministry of Foreign Trade and Economic Cooperation, these services can only be provided to SBUs in which the investment company holds at least 25 percent equity.

At present, the allowed scope of operations for umbrella enterprises includes manufacturing, investment in subsidiaries, purchase of inputs and raw materials for SBUs, sales of SBU output, and marketing and operational services. An umbrella enterprise cannot act as a general trading company; that is, it cannot import finished product lines and sell them in China. Its business license must state the industries, projects, or products in which it will invest; it does not have an open license to engage in whatever business it wants. If the umbrella enterprise later wishes to engage in an activity not listed in the license, the change must be approved by MOFTEC and the license amended.

Foreign companies wishing to establish an umbrella enterprise usually must have at least two FIEs in China. Internationally known firms are given preference when applying to establish umbrella enterprises. Like all FIEs, an umbrella enterprise has Chinese legal person status.

According to MOFTEC regulations, Chinese partners in prospective joint investment companies must have a minimum total asset value of 100 million yuan. Foreign applicants for wholly owned or joint investment companies must meet one of two sets of criteria. In one set, the foreign company must have had a minimum total asset value of U.S.$400 million in the year prior to its application, have established one or more FIEs to which it has contributed at least $10 million in registered capital, and have obtained approval for three additional FIE project proposals. Applicants meeting this first set of conditions have the option of establishing an investment company in the name of a wholly owned subsidiary rather than in their own names, which may offer some comfort to foreign investors who want to insulate their corporate headquarters from direct exposure to liabilities in China.

The second set of conditions stipulates that the foreign investor must have established a minimum of 10 FIEs in China and engaged in manufacturing or infrastructure construction to which it has contributed at least $30 million in registered capital. Currently, the investment company itself must have registered capital of at least $30 million.

An umbrella company and its various FIEs are treated by Chinese tax authorities as separate entities; consolidation of revenue and expenditures for tax purposes is not allowed. Subsidiary profits that are remitted to the umbrella enterprise as dividends will not be taxed, however. On the other hand, an umbrella enterprise with no manufacturing of its own will be taxed at 33 percent with no tax holidays. Like all other FIEs, an umbrella enterprise must balance its foreign exchange.

Entry Mode 5: Acquiring Existing Firms

The mergers and acquisitions market in China was virtually nonexistent before 1990. Since then, and particularly since 1994, the number and complexity of deals have grown exponentially and the market has developed in a variety of directions. Acquiring existing firms in China is perhaps the quickest way to expand one's investment in China. This mode is particularly useful for entering sectors formerly restricted to state-owned enterprises. The Chinese government now permits foreign investors to buy all or part of the ownership interests of a wholly Chinese owned or Sino-foreign joint venture. China lacks sufficient capital, technology, and management know-how to meet the needs of industries that are not deemed priorities. Foreign acquisition of Chinese firms gives newly privatized and growing Chinese enterprises easier access to much needed capital for expansion while underutilized assets can be put to profitable use. For these reasons, it is expected that this will remain a long-term government policy (Peng, Luo, and Sun 1998).

Since 1992, China has allowed more than 30 state-owned firms to be listed on international stock exchanges (Rothstein 1996), which denote the shares by different names according to the bourse: N shares are listed on the New York Stock Exchange, while H and S shares are listed on the Hong Kong and Singapore exchanges, respectively. Foreign investors looking to acquire a piece of Chinese industry can now establish a joint venture company limited by shares (a limited company), buy the B shares (in hard currency) of one of the 300 or so state-owned enterprises listed on the Shanghai and Shenzhen stock exchanges, or directly acquire a Chinese firm or other joint venture. These firms may be listed for sale in the property rights markets that have sprung up throughout China. Foreign investors can also buy into a Chinese business by participating in its conversion into a foreign-invested joint stock company.

For a foreign investor, the main advantage of entering the China market through acquisition is that many state-owned firms, though operating in the red, have the potential to operate profitably if they were provided with the right mix of capital, management, and technology (Dong and Hu 1995). Although the Chinese government has declared that ownership of some 1,000 key state firms will remain in government hands, this leaves a huge number of enterprises to be cut loose from state support. Foreign companies will have many opportunities to buy into enterprises in different sectors and regions.

Investing in China through acquisitions offers other advantages as well. The investor may participate in the management and operations of a target firm, as in the case of EJVs and WFOEs, but the investor does not have to do so. As a result, acquisitions not only allow corporate investors to enter China but allow general investors, through holding companies, to gain entry, as in the case of many Hong Kong–based companies. Second, cash flow may be generated in a shorter time than in the case of an EJV or WFOE, since the acquired firm by definition does not have to be built from scratch. Finally, acquisition deals may be more attractive than EJVs or WFOEs because acquisitions offer immediate access to resources such as land use, ready-made distribution channels, and skilled labor, even when targeted firms have been losing money.

Currently, MNCs may also consider acquiring an existing Sino-foreign joint venture via two routes: either the acquisition of the overseas entity holding the foreign interest in the joint venture or direct acquisition at the Chinese local level of the foreign investor's portion of the registered capital. A number of factors will be relevant in deciding which route to take. Acquisition of a foreign holding entity does not change the parties to the joint venture and hence has much lower profile with regard to possible approval requirements. Accordingly, this can be less intrusive and carry less risk of reexamination of the project by the original Chinese approving authority. However, this advantage may be diminished somewhat if the new investor wishes to negotiate amendments to the existing joint venture structure, for example, to amend the constitutional documents (perhaps to strengthen the foreign investor's management control), to alter the percentage of registered capital held by the foreign investor (which may involve separately acquiring an extra tranche from the local party), or to inject additional capital into the joint venture for purposes of expansion (which may effectively change the percentage of registered capital of the parties). In such cases, it would be necessary, in any event, to seek approval from the Chinese approving authority. Another factor in favor of acquiring at the Chinese level is that if the foreign holding entity is not a single-purpose vehicle for the relevant China investment it may not be an appropriate target. Also, two levels of due diligence may be required (and risk involved), one at the foreign and one at the Chinese level. Occasionally, a material change in the holdings of the foreign entity may constitute grounds for dissolving the joint venture under the existing contract. In such cases, acquisition at the Chinese level may be more appropriate. In considering a potential target, various preliminary factors will need to be considered at an early stage of the process. For example, is the business of the joint venture part of a restricted industry, which would make requisite approvals difficult? What does the joint venture's balance sheet look like? Will it need increased investment and can approval for that level of investment be obtained? To what extent will the local partner be able to contribute in terms of business facilitation and finance? This type of question is not, of course, unique to China — the basic disciplines and skills required to carry out a successful acquisition transaction within China do not differ substantially from the international norm.

Foreign investors generally target those enterprises with strong market niches in sectors with some potential for growth. Foreigners are most likely to be interested in, and permitted to exercise management control over, medium-sized firms that are collectively owned enterprises, Sino-foreign joint ventures, or even state-owned, regionally based companies. Many state enterprises have been restructured into limited companies, allowing foreign investors to buy into them by purchasing company shares. But restrictions remain. The restructuring of each state firm and its subsequent listing is subject to government approval. Chinese authorities usually place a ceiling on the amount of foreign ownership interest allowed in state-owned businesses.

A foreign company acquiring a local firm should be familiar with two types of limited companies — those that issue privately held shares and those that issue publicly traded shares. Which form the company takes depends upon the percentage of shares held by the founding parties, who must be legal persons. To set up a private limited company, the firm issues shares that it, or its sponsor, buys back so as to maintain full ownership. By contrast, in publicly traded limited companies, the founding companies may purchase only 30 to 35 percent of the venture's shares and the rest is sold to the public at large. If at least 25 percent of a limited company is foreign owned, it is considered an FIE and accorded preferential treatment. Foreign-funded limited companies require at least 30 million yuan in registered capital. Dividends are distributed in proportion to equity shares. Existing joint ventures may be converted into limited companies pending approval by MOFTEC and the original approval authority.

Investors buying a stake in a Chinese company must first evaluate various risks. Gaining government approval for the transfer of ownership and clearance of property titles is often a difficult hurdle. Foreign investors should be careful to obtain accurate information when buying into a Chinese entity, particularly concerning existing liabilities. Analysis of investment risk should also take into consideration the locality, including the workings of the local bureaucracy, transportation links, and other infrastructure issues, since regional rivalries and aged and inadequate infrastructure often hamper the efficient movement of goods, information, services, and labor throughout many parts of China.

Foreign companies that choose to invest in Chinese companies by buying shares alone should not be under the illusion that they will have a significant voice in running the company. Because foreign investors in a large Chinese enterprise are limited to a minority shareholding position, either in practice or by law in some sectors, they lack the ability to challenge decisions made by the Chinese shareholders on the board of directors. The Company Law in China lacks any provision for minority shareholders to challenge the decisions of the board, as they are able to do in the United States.

While the transformation of China's state businesses can happen on paper overnight, the culture of state domination remains strong, thwarting the implementation of effective business practices. In China, a fundamental ambiguity remains between *shareholding* and *control*. Many Chinese shareholders are typically agents of the state or state-owned enterprises, making it less likely that they will prioritize maximization of profits. The term *red capitalist* refers to the majority of Chinese shareholders who claim to be committed to the bottom line but are reluctant to reduce the numerous welfare benefits of Chinese employees or lay off redundant workers.

Entry Mode 6: Representative Offices

Although technically not considered an FIE, a representative office is a quick and relatively simple way to become acquainted with the Chinese market. No minimum investment is prescribed for establishing a representative office, and this mode is widely used by many foreign companies new to China. This helps foreign companies test the waters before taking the plunge of establishing an FIE within China's complex economy.

Representative offices allow firms to establish contacts with key industrial ministries and begin to build a company's reputation in China. By law, representative offices are prohibited from engaging in direct, profit-making business activities in China. They are allowed to undertake noncommercial activities, including business communications, product promotion, market research, contract administration, and negotiations, on behalf of the head office. Equally important, they can liaise with potential Chinese trading partners, as well as various Chinese commercial and government offices, and can lay the foundations for further investment by promoting the foreign company's name and reputation. Corporate giants like Bechtel and Apple Computer maintained representative offices in China for at least 10 years before organizing legal person status FIEs.

The most apparent advantages the representative office has over other entry modes are its simplicity and flexibility. Unlike an EJV or WFOE, a representative office gives a foreign company a formal presence in China without the complications of an unfamiliar local partner or a substantial financial commitment. A representative office, unlike other investment vehicles, has no minimum registered capital requirements. Many foreign businesses find the establishment of representative offices, though not cheap, an excellent way to become familiar with the Chinese business environment before making a major commitment.

One flexible feature of representative offices is the lack of restrictions on the line of business in which the company can engage. Other entry modes, by contrast, can only participate in sectors and industries designated by governmental authorities. For example, the government discourages foreign participation in media communications except by representative offices. Foreign companies in restricted industries such as insurance, banking, and trading also have found that the establishment of representative offices offers them a platform from which to try to convince government officials to open these sectors to foreign activity.

As the representative office operates independently, it can proceed with liaison, market research, and consulting activities in whatever fashion it sees fit. Closing down a representative office is relatively easy compared to terminating a joint venture. It is also relatively easy for representative offices to hire talented Chinese college graduates or managers who see employment at a representative office as a way to gain exposure to the world of international business or even as a springboard to working at the head office in the future. Such benefits make the representative office an ideal way to explore further investments in China, establish a presence in its various regions, or arrange future investment projects.

This entry mode, however, has several disadvantages. Although establishing a representative office is comparatively easy, a host of regulatory and startup costs makes it quite expensive to maintain. In addition to high labor costs paid to local employees, representative offices must usually pay high rents, as they tend to be located in major cities where office space is in chronic short supply. Of the 24,402 representative offices operating in China as of 1994, 3,802 were located in Beijing, 3,294 in Shanghai, and 6,918 in Guangzhou. Far fewer had been established in interior locations. Moreover, a representative office cannot issue invoices or receive direct payments for its services to Chinese customers. It has also to pay duties on all imported office equipment. At present, the imposed tariffs on computers, photocopiers, fax machines, video and audio equipment, air conditioners, and other office items can be as high as 100 percent. Furthermore, a representative office can officially hire local employees only through one of the four approved management service companies, namely, the Foreign Enterprise Service Co., China International Enterprise Cooperations Corp., China International Intellectech Corp., and China International Talent Development Center. These companies withhold a maximum of 50 percent of the gross pay of local Chinese working in foreign representative offices. Many offices have to pay a substantial bonus directly to the employees to compensate them for the low net pay that results from the management service company's withholding.

Many foreign companies continue to use representative offices as their China headquarters even after they have established other types of ventures in the country. Although the merits of this entry mode make it an invaluable way to sample the fruits of China's current economic dynamism and growth, some foreign investors inadvertently presume that it is a liaison office exempt from taxation. Such misunderstandings have led to substantial penalties imposed by the Tax Bureau. Following one crackdown, official guidelines were issued by the bureau to clarify the types of representative offices that are tax exempt or taxable based on their activities. Nontaxable activities are such that the foreign corporation is not deemed to have a permanent establishment in China. Such a representative office is exempt from taxation, for example, when it only carries out market research, gathers business information, or engages in liaison and other preparatory or ancillary activities related to the manufacture and sales of products by its head office. When tax exempt treatment is desired by an eligible representative office, registration and an application for exemption filed with the Tax Bureau are still required. If the head office is a trading entity (except one that actually purchases and stores goods for further trade) or a consulting firm such as an accounting or legal firm, an advertising agency, a tourist company, or a transport operator, its representative office in the PRC is likely to be taxable for the various service activities rendered to the clients, head office, or other member companies in a group. A representative office that restricts its activities to preparatory or ancillary services in connection with the loan transactions of its banking head office is exempt from taxation. However, if it also provides miscellaneous investment advice or other consulting services, these are taxable.

A representative office that is unsuccessful in applying for an exemption and other taxable representative offices are subject to a business tax of 5 percent on the deemed or attributable income and a foreign enterprise tax of 33 percent on the deemed or attributable net profit. Minimization of tax is possible when appropriate taxation plans are set up in advance. These include choosing one of three (deemed, actual, or cost plus) methods of income and profit determination, entering into approved agreements that distinguish between tax exempt and taxable activities, apportioning taxable activities between the representative office and the head office, tax accounting, and so on. The Tax Bureau must review each representative office to determine whether the chosen method of tax assessment is appropriate or needs to be changed. Existing representative offices should therefore self-evaluate their tax exposure during the previous three years (if any), so that remedial measures can be taken prior to an audit by the Tax Bureau. Strategic handling of the application to establish a new representative office will result in long-term tax savings.

Entry Mode 7: Other Options

Branch

One of the newest options for expanding investment is the establishment of branch offices that undertake business transactions. The 1994 Company Law allows foreign companies to open branches that engage in production and operating activities. An FIE can also open a branch office in another region of the country to expand its operations.

Up until now, only a handful of foreign banks and law firms have been approved to open branch offices. These offices are limited to specified cities, and their scope of business is highly regulated. Branch offices may ultimately offer a relatively simple means of establishing or expanding a corporate presence in China, but the fact that they do not have legal person status means that the foreign parent company is liable if civil charges are brought against the branch. To shield the parent company from unlimited damages, foreign companies interested in establishing branch offices in China should designate an offshore subsidiary as the parent.

Build-Operate-Transfer

Build-operate-transfer is a newly emerging mode of entry into the Chinese market. It is especially useful in the power generation sector and for other large-scale infrastructure projects. For instance, negotiations on one of the first BOT power projects were recently completed. According to officials in southeastern Guangxi, the final contract for the Laibin B power plant will be signed soon with Electricité de France, Britain's National Power International, and Barclays Bank. China's State Planning Committee has ratified 10 more BOT projects calling for foreign operations: the Summer Palace light rail in Beijing, the Zilanda hydropower plant, the Tuoketro B power station in Inner Mongolia, State Highway 104 in Shandong, the Shenyang elevated expressway in Liaoning, the Wuhan light rail line in Hubei, the Yinglongshan power plant in Zhejiang, the Second Nanjing Yangtse River Bridge in Jiangsu, the Shenyang-Beijing Expressway in Liaoning, and the Shenyang second ring road in Liaoning.

A BOT is a guarantee-fee method of cooperation by which an investor identifies a project in a host country, assumes sole responsibility in investing in the construction and operation of the project, and, after recovering its investment and obtaining compensation, returns the project to the local organization in the host country. It is a relatively new means of international capital investment that is applied most often for projects in which the building of infrastructure calls for a huge investment and a long period of construction. It is popular in developing countries short on capital and technology. The first BOT project, implemented in China on a trial basis, was the Beijing-Tongxian Expressway, a collaboration among Beijing civil construction departments and an American company. Construction began in September 1994, with 20 months as the projected time for completion. The approved term of the BOT is 20 years, after which the expressway will be transferred to China.

Due in part to difficulties in working out financing and equity arrangements, the BOT approach is often used together with other entry modes. Foreign businesses may set up BOT project firms by means of either equity or cooperative joint ventures with Chinese partners or wholly foreign owned ventures. Because of their ability to provide foreign investors with returns in excess of their proportional contributions to the venture's total registered capital, CJVs have been the vehicles of choice for BOT infrastructure projects.

Franchising and Licensing

Two forms of contractual arrangements most often used in international expansion are franchising and licensing. Both involve a contract between parties in different countries, but franchise contracts cover more aspects of the operation and are typically of a longer duration than licensing. A licensor in one country makes limited rights and/or resources available to the licensee in a foreign country. The rights and/or resources may include patents, trademarks, technology, managerial skills, and so on. These allow the licensee to produce and market a product similar to the one the licensor has been producing in its home country, without requiring the licensor to create a new operation abroad. For instance, licensees in China and other countries have contracts to produce and sell toys and clothing bearing pictures of Mickey Mouse and other Walt Disney characters.

Licensing is a popular method for profiting from a foreign market without committing sizable amounts of funds. Since the foreign producer is typically 100 percent locally owned, political risk is minimized. Income from licensing, however, is lower than that from other FDI entry modes, although the return on the marginal investment can be higher.

Other potential disadvantages include loss of quality control; establishment of a competitor in a foreign market; improvements of the technology by the local licensee, which then enters the home market; and loss of the opportunity to make a direct investment in the licensee's market.

Most licensing agreements by MNCs have been concluded with their own affiliates or joint venture partners in China. Licensing fees have provided a way to spread corporate research and development costs among all SBUs. They are also a means of repatriating profits in a form typically more acceptable to the Chinese government than dividends.

Compared to licensing, a franchise usually includes a broader package of rights and resources. Production equipment, managerial systems, operating procedures, access to advertising and promotional materials, and loans and financing may all be part of a franchise. McDonald's and Kentucky Fried Chicken (KFC) are examples of foreign companies with franchises in China. This arrangement can lead to the creation of a new business in which the franchise is designed to stand in perpetuity (Chen 1996).

It is important for foreign licensors or franchisors to familiarize themselves with the legal framework for international licensing and franchising in China. Currently, the Regulations on the Administration of Technology Import Contracts (RATIC), promulgated by the State Council in May 1985, are the most comprehensive. In addition, foreign companies should confirm the identity, legal status, and authority of potential Chinese recipients. The simplest verification is a review of their business licenses and, if possible, their articles of association. A foreign supplier should also make sure that the relevant planning authorities in China have authorized the proposed project. Moreover, foreign suppliers must be aware that Chinese law tends to encourage the conversion of a licensing contract into an installment sale plan by forbidding restrictions on the licensee's continued use of the know-how, trademark, or technology received from the foreign firm after expiration of the contract. The RATIC also mandates that license contracts shall generally not exceed 10 years.

Combining Options

Foreign companies can structure their entry into China in many different ways. Some will be more suitable than others depending upon the specific situation and business objectives. A foreign company that is not familiar with the Chinese business environment may want to engage a dependable distributor to sell its goods in China. Firms that want to minimize their investment of capital and resources at the initial stage may find a contract manufacturing arrangement suitable. Some may want to first test the market and establish a relationship with their current and potential customers by setting up a representative office. Those who are knowledgeable about China may consider whether they need a partner at all. Under certain circumstances, they can set up wholly foreign owned enterprises, put in their own management teams, and hire locally to staff their Chinese companies.

Various other forms of doing business in China are also available. Foreign firms should make sure they know all their options before determining the best one. Some options, particularly expanding or buying into an existing FIE or setting up a new one, are attractive because existing legislation and experience make them transparent, feasible, and relatively predictable. Other methods, such as buying into a Chinese enterprise other than an FIE or seeking to establish a branch of the foreign company, may lead investors into uncharted waters. Investors must select among these various options in an environment marked by bureaucratic struggles both within the central government and between the national and local governments.

Inevitably, there are tradeoffs in choosing one entry mode over another. Once a foreign investor decides to pursue an FDI project in China, its choice of entry mode will depend on a wide range of factors. In brief, the selection of entry modes in China depends upon four groups of factors (detailed in chap. 5).

1. Firm-specific factors such as strategic objectives, degree of global integration, firm size and experience, and distinctive competencies such as technological and managerial know-how.
2. Host-country-specific factors, including contextual risk, cultural distance, market potential, market knowledge, infrastructure conditions, intellectual property right systems, and government policies toward and treatment of FDI.
3. Industry-specific factors such as entry barriers, industrial policies of the Chinese government, structural uncertainty, the degree of competition from both local and other foreign firms, and collaboration of suppliers, distributors, and related industries.
4. Project-specific factors such as contractual risk, project size, amount of the investment needed, project orientation (technological, local market, export, or infrastructure oriented), and availability of appropriate local partners.

Figure 5.1 schematically depicts an integrated framework for entry mode selection in China.

It is particularly worthwhile to note that the strategic objective of a project influences entry mode selection. If the project is export oriented, for instance, a WFOE might be a better choice. By manufacturing in the location where factor conditions are optimal and then exporting to the rest of the world, a foreign company may be able to realize substantial location economies and a positive experience curve. This arrangement also gives the company the tight control over marketing that might be required to coordinate a globally dispersed value chain as well as better transfer pricing to avoid various taxes or tariffs. Thus, foreign companies pursuing global strategies may prefer to establish WFOEs.

Special value should also be attached to the nature of an investor's distinctive competency. In particular, it is imperative to distinguish between technological and managerial know-how. If a company's competitive advantage derives from its control of proprietary technological know-how, licensing and joint venture arrangements are not advisable because of the risk of losing control of that technology. A WFOE might be a better choice in this situation. The licensing or joint venture mode can be used for these companies only if the arrangement is structured in such a way as to reduce the risk of a company's technology being expropriated by licensees or joint venture partners (Shan 1991). Companies can arrange to prevent leakage of their most sensitive technologies by only allowing their partners access to production processes that do not expose some kinds of knowledge. Contractual safeguards can also be written into a joint venture contract. Cross-licensing agreements between parties can protect a foreign investor's technological know-how if both parties agree in advance to exchange skills and technologies. Comparatively, the risk of losing control of management skills to franchisees or joint venture partners is not great. This is one reason why many service companies favor a combination of franchising and subsidiaries to control franchisees in China.

Foreign companies in China tend to start with low-risk, low-control options and then advance to higher levels of risk and control as they gain experience and build confidence. The initial market entry is often one of import-export or countertrade. Representative offices, licensing, and franchising may also be considered trial steps. An EJV or CJV may be established as an investment vehicle with intermediate risks. These modes are still dominant in China because they include partnerships with players experienced in the targeted market. They also reduce risk through cost sharing. Thus, they represent an appropriate entry strategy for early market development tactics.

To secure a stronger presence in China, acquisitions, BOTs, WFOEs, or umbrella companies may be required, although many consider these approaches more risky. They are likely to come at later stages in the development of an international diversification strategy in China. These modes, however, enable foreign investors to better control local operations and, more importantly, profit more from the economic boom and market growth. Foreign investors may employ some or all of these alternatives in sequential fashion or use different modes simultaneously with different products or in different regions of China.

Selecting between an EJV and a WFOE is not necessarily an either-or decision. Sometimes a Chinese partner has a strong distribution network or operates in a restricted sector that is attractive to a foreign investor. In such situations, foreign companies can, for instance, surround their WFOE production operation with EJVs that market and sell their products in China. Motorola in Tianjin does exactly that. Since 1993, Motorola has been laying the groundwork for the biggest U.S. manufacturing venture in China. Its $300-million-plus commitment to China focuses on pagers, simple integrated circuits, cellular phones, and (eventually) automotive electronics. The production site in the Tianjin Economic Development Zone is a WFOE; marketing and sales of products will be accomplished through various EJVs with local partners.

Another approach is to consider an EJV and a WFOE in sequence. A foreign investor can make an initial entry as part of an EJV for a fixed period, which is normally stipulated in the duration clause of the joint venture contract. At the end of the stipulated term, it can take over the assets from the Chinese partner and continue to run the operation as a WFOE. This is an attractive alternative if the added value of the Chinese partner is significant but limited to the early stages of the venture. Some EJVs have integrated this option in the termination clause of the joint venture contract.

It is also possible to structure a WFOE under the legal umbrella of an EJV. In other words, the project would be an EJV as a legal entity but would be run and operated as a WFOE. Many foreign partners that have increased their equity stakes in existing ventures are going in that direction. In some cases, they turn their Chinese collaborator into a silent partner with a minority stake.

China has become the largest recipient of FDI among all developing countries. During the past two decades, many operational and managerial problems faced by foreign investors in running FIEs in China have surfaced. Many problems arise because foreign investors have not fully prepared themselves to handle the difficulties associated with the nature of the entry modes they have chosen. As there are many ways to structure an equity or nonequity investment in China, foreign investors should carefully design an investment strategy that best suits their re-source endowments and environmental dynamics. Chapter 5 articulates this issue in detail.

China is by far the largest and most impressive economy in the develop-ing world. When one considers that it also has 1.3 billion people, ap-proximately a quarter of the population of the earth, the potential of its future market is clear. But a number of factors make the selection of entry mode difficult and risky. Economically, there are a myriad of neomercantilist rules and regulations that both restrict and control the flow of FDI within the country. Realistically, putting aside the actual content of Chinese law, it is important to note that there are few legal guarantees for foreign companies, a fact that by itself increases the risks of investing in China. These environmental factors surely have a critical influence on the choice of entry mode for foreign companies.

The Chinese economy will continue to lurch forward as the authori-ties maintain their pragmatic and ad hoc attitude toward market reform and foreign investment. The uncertainties inherent in transforming economies are a source of challenges as well as opportunities. In China, as elsewhere, those investors best prepared to circumvent the former and exploit the latter are apt to survive and prosper. In fact, the growing complexity of the operations of many MNCs in China and the need to better explore market opportunities and more closely coordinate numer-ous strategic business units there have led many firms to set up an inter-SBU network whereby different entry modes are flexibly adopted and strategically integrated.

Mini-case Examples

Mini-case 1: Lion Nathan's Entry Mode Choices

Lion Nathan is a New Zealand–based international company with as-sets of NZ$3.7 billion and a market capitalization of NZ$2 billion. The company has been pursuing an aggressive internationalization path since 1988 and concentrates on its core beverage business with brewer-ies in New Zealand, Australia, and China. Lion Nathan's long-term vision is that of becoming a world-class marketer of beverages within the Asia-Pacific region using the sustainability of its position in Austral-asia to underpin the development of that strategy. In 1997, Lion Na-than's share of the New Zealand and Australian beer markets was 61.1

and 42 percent, respectively. In New Zealand, its leading brands are Lion, Speight's, and Steinlager.

Two investments have been made in China. The first was an 80 percent joint venture investment in a brewery at Wuxi. The second investment was the completion of the first wholly owned foreign brewery in the Suzhou Industrial Park complex in the Yangste Delta.

In April 1988, the company announced that it had sold 45 percent of the company's shares to Kirin, Japan's largest brewery company, for NZ$1.4 billion. The merger of Lion Nathan and Kirin gives them a significant brewing capacity (number four in the world). Kirin is brewed in the northern Shenyang area by China's second-largest brewer, China Resources (Shengyang) Snowflake Brewery. In Zhuhai, in southern Guangdong Province, it has a joint venture with Taiwan's President Group for production for the central and southern regions, but the investment in the Suzhou brewery gives it an opportunity to consolidate its position in China.

Lion Nathan signaled its intention to enter the brewery market in China in 1993 — initially suggesting that it would consider establishing at least one, and possibly two or three, joint venture operations. Within two years, the company hinted that it would have a stake in at least five breweries. Lion Nathan's representatives visited some 45 of the country's 800 breweries and carried out research on a number of firms. The initial investment had required two years and an outlay of NZ$6 million in "doing the homework and getting the learning right." In April 1995, the company acquired a 60 percent interest in a joint venture with the Mashan district government at the Taihushui Brewery (located near the city of Wuxi) for an investment of $32.1 million. The investment included a payment of $7.9 million to the existing owners. That left $24.2 million in the joint venture, $22.3 million of which was to be used to upgrade the brewery. The balance would be used to acquire the land on which the brewery stood. Lion Nathan recognized that there was an opportunity to improve the quality of the beer through application of their own technology. The local manager, who was retained to run the plant, was aware of the Chinese product's shortcomings but had lacked the technology to improve the shelf life of the product, give it better clarity, and make it more drinkable as a warm beer.

The major challenge for Lion Nathan is efficiency in distribution, that is, how efficiently the company can push and pull the product through the system, given China's infrastructure deficiencies. Production efficiencies have also been achieved by improving labor and management practices. When Lion Nathan took over the management at Wuxi, the managers' bonus (about 70 percent of their income) was virtually guaranteed. Lion Nathan decided to guarantee more of the workers' income (60 to 70 percent) and in addition offered a risk bonus of 30 to 40 percent. Lion Nathan also recognized the importance of recognizing cultural differences. Local partners often interpret open debate of brand or marketplace issues by key executives as dissension or indecisiveness since their expectation is that these issues would be resolved before the meeting takes place.

Lion Nathan increased its ownership of the joint venture at Wuxi to 80 percent in January 1996, and brewing capacity was doubled to 120 million liters in June. The company claims that the brewery at Wuxi is one of the few foreign-invested breweries making a profit in China.

In May 1996, Lion Nathan announced that it would commence construction of a new brewery on a green field site within the China-Singapore Suzhou Industrial Park. Initially, the proposal was to build a new facility with a local partner, but the Suzhou site had the advantage of not requiring a local partner. The project was being managed on behalf of the Suzhou provincial government by a group of advisers seconded from the Singapore government, making it relatively easy in the formative stages to get the investment established. With a population of five million, Suzhou is similar in size to Wuxi.

The brewery would have an initial capacity of 200 million liters per annum (equal to the firm's total annual production capacity in New Zealand). Lion Nathan was also able to take advantage of a window, then still available to foreign investors, to import capital equipment free of duty. That scheme ended in June 1997, and a 40 percent duty is now imposed on the imported content of a plant. However, Lion Nathan, through its own *guanxi* networks, was able to establish that the government had to honor approvals of duty-free imports date stamped before January 1, 1997. The brewery was finished ahead of schedule (it was operational in October 1997, effectively 15 months from the time construction began at the plant) and was NZ$20 million under budget (construction had been budgeted at $250 million). Half of those savings would be spent on the launch of Lion Nathan's flagship premium beer, Steinlager. The whole brewery was a turnkey operation in which all equipment was imported from manufacturers in Germany and Holland. The brewery was designed on a modular principle, so that the initial 200 million liter capacity could be doubled at a later date. Currently, it operates one keg and three glass lines that can produce 36,000 bottles per hour. Under the terms of the development contract, other breweries were effectively precluded from establishing plants in the park. Lion Nathan has a strong competitive position in Suzhou relative to other foreign brewers. As the only WFOE brewery, it can reduce production costs through high-volume quality brewing and is not subject to the overmanning levels (and therefore lower productivity) that are experienced by other foreign joint venture brewers.

During 1998, Lion Nathan's revenue, net of excise and sales taxes, rose 3.6 percent to more than NZ$18 billion. The star performer was China, with revenue up 91 percent and 73 percent by volume over 1997. Although the Suzhou brewery has a capacity of 400 million liters it was still operating well under that limit, with total sales in China amounting to 110 million liters in 1998. The investment in China was still operating at a loss (NZ$29.8 million, up from $8.8 million in 1997), but this reflected the planned investment in infrastructure in China resulting from the Suzhou expansion. The chief executive officer of Lion Nathan, Gordon Cairns, claimed that Lion Nathan was one of the best-valued brewing stocks in the world, trading on a multiple of only 9.8 times earnings before interest and taxes, while by comparison the United Kingdom's Whitbread was on a multiple of 11.9, Foster's of Australia was on 13.1, Anheuser Busch of the United States was on 15.7, and Heineken of Holland was on 23.8 (Oram 1998).

In September of 1998, Lion Nathan announced that China would begin producing Steinlager, its premium branded beer in New Zealand, at the Suzhou brewery. In Lion Nathan's game-breaking style, Steinlager will be packaged and distributed in a way that is unique in the Shanghai-Nanjing corridor. Steinlager will be packaged in a 335 ml bottle for the restaurant sector — where consumers are prepared to pay more for beer. Many other premium beers, such as Heineken and Budweiser, are packaged in 335 ml cans for the restaurant sector and 40 ml bottles for the supermarket shelves. Steinlager's distinctive packaging includes a shape similar to that of a Hahn premium bottle, with a waist and a silver fern (a distinctive New Zealand logo) etched into the glass. This fern is not only for branding purposes but to deter black market brewers from producing and selling duplicates. Steinlager also lends itself to a strong brand image since it is a lager, the style of beer that Chinese consumers prefer. As a "stein" type of German beer, it has positive associations, for Chinese consumers associate good beer with German origins.

Mini-case 2: AT&T's Entry Mode Choices

Entry Background
In late 1992, the U.S. telecommunications giant American Telephone and Telegraph Company (AT&T) was trailing far behind a host of

telecommunications equipment suppliers from all over the world that were scrambling for market share in the fast-growing and potentially huge Chinese market. The company had become a late mover because of its hesitancy to enter the newly opened Chinese market and a period of cooling political relations between China and the United States that had commenced June 1989. Thus, AT&T needed to come up with an outstanding entry strategy to make up for lost ground.

The company's involvement with China dates back to a telephone equipment manufacturing facility that had been established in 1918 by its manufacturing arm, International Western Electric. However, like most other foreign firms, AT&T's business relations with China were cut off from 1949 to 1979. When economic reforms began, the Chinese government identified the improvement of the telecommunications infrastructure as a target area for foreign investment. In 1979, China invited AT&T to participate in a joint venture to manufacture switches. The company declined. It was preoccupied with domestic concerns such as the long-running antitrust suit brought against it by the U.S. Department of Justice and the rise of competitors in the long-distance calling market, and it was unfamiliar with Asia in general. In hindsight, AT&T now acknowledges that it made a mistake. In the meantime, many competitors (including Alcatel, NEC, and Siemens) pioneered the establishment of manufacturing joint ventures in China.

With the settlement of the antitrust suit in 1982, AT&T began to turn its attention to international markets. In October 1985, it set up its first China representative office in Beijing. Its first manufacturing facility, an equity joint venture to produce digital transmission equipment, was established in 1989. Two further joint ventures were set up by 1992. However, AT&T still lagged behind its competitors in terms of the size and technology level of its investments in China, and it was unable to set up a switch-manufacturing facility. When the United States imposed trade sanctions in response to the June 1989 Tiananmen uprising, China issued State Council Directive 56, which limited switch arrangements to three existing joint ventures. Thus, AT&T was effectively shut out of the major switch market.

Finally, a window of opportunity opened in October 1992 when the United States and China signed a trade liberalization agreement that included the lifting of Directive 56. The company immediately sent a team of senior executives to China to negotiate a fresh start for AT&T.

The executives searched for a way to differentiate AT&T from its established competitors in China. They were aware that AT&T was not a low-cost producer anywhere and would be much less so in China after its late start. Instead, they identified AT&T's main strength as lying in its combined capabilities in the whole field of telecommunications equipment and services, the result of its long history of providing telecommunications services in the United States. The company had expertise in the software that ran the telecommunications equipment and in network management. In contrast, most of its competitors supplied equipment exclusively.

The company set out to impress Chinese officials with its comprehensive capabilities and size. An eight-member team from the State Planning Commission was invited to the United States to tour AT&T's business units, manufacturing facilities, and the world famous Bell Laboratories research and development facility. Negotiations proceeded quickly and culminated in a memorandum of understanding (MOU) signed by AT&T and the State Planning Commission in February 1993.

The MOU did not bind AT&T to investing particular amounts in specified joint ventures. Rather, it established a "long-term comprehensive partnership" between AT&T and China and identified 10 areas in which the parties might jointly pursue business opportunities. China committed to organizing the relevant ministries and agencies, which would help identify possible local partners. The company took on obligations regarding technology transfer, joint research and development (R&D), and training for Chinese nationals. The first phase of cooperation would focus on switching, microelectronics, and network management joint ventures and on the establishment of a Bell Labs facility in China. At the end of the first phase, the parties would jointly study further areas of cooperation.

In May 1994, AT&T signed an agreement to invest $150 million in China over the next two years. Pursuant to the MOU and the 1994 agreement, AT&T established three more joint ventures between 1993 and 1996, including switch-manufacturing facilities in Qingdao and Chengdu. The former is its largest outside the United States.

In order to implement the MOU and compete effectively in the Chinese market, AT&T restructured its business organization. Since 1989, all of AT&T had been organized into 21 business units following product lines in order to decentralize decision making and improve market responsiveness in the previously monolithic organization. In China, the business units had operated independently, sometimes at the expense of losing synergistic opportunities. This structure conflicted with AT&T's strategy under the MOU of showing a united front to the Chinese government and drawing on all of its capabilities to deliver complete, integrated solutions to its Chinese customers.

As a result of the campaigning of AT&T's China head, Bill Warwick, a China business unit called AT&T China was created in July 1993.

It was given independent responsibility; primary responsibility in marketing and manufacturing strategies, product offerings, and pricing; and the power to redistribute revenue among its business units in China. The business units would report to Warwick as well as their business unit heads in the United States. In addition, AT&T China would report directly to the AT&T CEO, Robert Allen. It was the first case of AT&T employing a "global and local" matrix strategy.

Analysis

When AT&T rebuffed China's request for a switch joint venture in 1979, it made an error in judgment that had severe and long-lasting repercussions for its prospects in the Chinese market. After AT&T awoke to the promise of the China market in the late 1980s, it had to play catchup with the many accomplished competitors that had already established themselves in China. If AT&T had merely continued to add joint ventures one by one, without doing something remarkable, it would always have lagged behind its competitors and its joint ventures would have received relatively little attention and special treatment from the Chinese government.

In light of this, the signing of the MOU was a bold strategic move that created a fresh image for AT&T in China and accelerated the establishment of new joint ventures. The company needed to distinguish itself clearly from its rivals. By means of the MOU and the U.S. tour preceding it, AT&T brought home to the Chinese government its sheer size and broad capabilities. There is a saying that when doing business in China it is good to ride a large horse, and AT&T showed that it had the largest horse of all.

The MOU was a large and very public statement of AT&T's commitment to China—a quality strongly desired by the Chinese. It especially needed to make such a statement because of its previous hesitancy in entering the market. The MOU helped to repair the poor relations between AT&T and the Chinese government and created *guanxi* between company executives and key officials in the industry. It committed the Chinese government to smoothing the way for AT&T to set up new joint ventures. The MOU changed the nature of and imparted a new significance to all of AT&T's subsequent activities. Each new joint venture would now be given particular notice and be regarded as part of a pattern established by the MOU, reinforcing AT&T's commitment.

Having said that, the MOU's function was limited. It did not in itself build joint ventures or gain market share for AT&T. It was an excellent public relations tool, but it had to be followed up with good entry and operational strategies in order for AT&T to win a share of a competitive market. It seemed to be making good headway — by 1995 it had 5 percent of the switch market and even more in the transmission equipment and optical fiber markets.

The reorganization of China operations to better fit local conditions was an essential move. Without it, AT&T could not have delivered on its promises in the MOU nor implemented its strategy of providing one-stop solutions. Perhaps more so than in any other market, foreign firms need to adopt special business strategies and tactics in China. A firm that primarily follows a global approach is unlikely to succeed.

All six manufacturing facilities established by AT&T prior to 1996 took the form of joint ventures rather than wholly foreign owned enterprises. This was almost inevitable. The Chinese government was keen to encourage the transfer of technology and knowledge from foreign telecommunications firms to the local industry, and so it more or less required the joint venture structure (the exceptional case of Motorola is discussed later). Moreover, AT&T as a late entrant did not have the bargaining power to convince the Chinese government to let it do otherwise. A late entrant probably has to promise more than a first mover in the way of technology transfer. In fact, a key sweetener in the MOU signed by AT&T was a commitment to engage in technology transfer, R&D, and training.

The company may not have chosen a WFOE structure if given a free choice in the matter. It was a relative newcomer to the Chinese market and may have welcomed the market knowledge and operational expertise of a local partner. This inexperience was compounded by the fact that AT&T was not active in the international arena generally, as its past efforts had been focused almost exclusively on the U.S. markets. Its purpose in entering China was to sell equipment in the local rather than the export market, which again points to the superiority of a joint venture structure. Furthermore, its key customers were the Ministry of Posts and Telecommunications and regional Post and Telecommunications Administrations rather than individual consumers. Its local partners were likely to have strong existing contacts with these government authorities.

Motorola is the exception that proves the rule in the telecommunications industry. It was an early mover and major investor in China and enjoyed good relations with the government. Even so, when Motorola requested permission to set up a WFOE in early 1989, the Chinese government balked at the request and pressed for a joint venture. The key factor that changed the government's mind was Motorola's continued presence in China and its support of the government during and after the events of June 1989.

Postscript

In September 1995, AT&T declared that it would split into three separate companies — a telecommunication carrier and service provider (the "new" AT&T), a computer manufacturer (NCR), and a telecommunications equipment manufacturer (Lucent Technologies). Lucent began operations in February 1996. It took over most of the old AT&T's operations in China. Since foreign firms are prohibited from involvement in telecommunications service provision, the name AT&T will seldom be heard in China in the near future.

The loss of the well-known AT&T name and its service provision expertise will require a revision of the strategy described in the preceding sections. Clearly, Lucent is more poorly equipped to offer the one-stop shopping experience of the old AT&T. It is difficult to obtain a clear picture of Lucent's performance in China since 1996. Two further manufacturing facilities have been or are being set up — the Lucent Technologies Qingdao Power System in 1996 (interestingly, its first WFOE) and Guoxin Lucent Technologies Network Technologies, a Shanghai joint venture announced in 1999. Alcatel's Shanghai Bell still dominated the switching market in 1998, with one-third of the market, while Lucent had less than 10 percent. But Lucent is said to be a leader in transmission technology and data communications, and it is poised to take the lead in providing Code Division Multiple Access (CDMA) wireless phone technology if the Chinese government adopts the CDMA standard.

Mini-case 3: Honda's Entry Mode Choices

Honda is the fourth-largest Japanese manufacturer of automobiles and the world's largest producer of motorcycles. It operates its own plants or joint ventures in Taiwan, Thailand, Vietnam, China, India, and Indonesia. The method of entry for Honda has varied from country to country as the company has adapted to the local environment at the time of entry. The method of entry ranges from simple export to joint ventures and wholly owned subsidiaries.

Honda's first plant outside of Japan was established in Taiwan in 1961. Initially, this plant was just a base for "knockdown" exports of motorcycles. In 1969, it followed with the production of automobiles. This was the first example of foreign direct investment for Honda in another Asian country. Now Taiwan is a major producer of motorcycles for Honda. The Taiwanese plant exports to Europe, the Middle East, China, and Africa. Honda's entry strategy was one of exportation, and as the country grew economically so did the company's target market and the level of FDI by Honda.

TABLE 4.1. AT&T's Joint Ventures in China, 1989–95

Joint Venture	Date	Partners	Products
AT&T Shanghai	1989	AT&T: 50% Shanghai Optical Fiber Communications Corp.: 28% Shanghai Telecommunications Equipment Factory: 22%	Digital transmission equipment
AT&T China (communications equipment)	1991	AT&T: 50% Shanghai Telecommunications Equipment Factory: 50%	Network products, including loop system components and digital data network systems
AT&T Beijing (fiber-optic cable)	1992	AT&T: 60% Beijing Optical Communications Co.: 20% China Beijing General Electric Wire and Cable Co.: 15% China National Posts and Telecommunications Industry Corp.: 5%	Fiber-optic cable
AT&T Qingdao (telecommunications systems)	1993	AT&T: 51% Qingdao Instrument and Meter Bureau: 34% Shandong PTA: 15%	5-ESS switches
AT&T Chengdu (telecommunications equipment)		AT&T: 76% Sichuan Posts and Telecommunications Switching Equipment Plant: 24%	Switching systems
AT&T Tianjin (cable)		AT&T: 60% Tianjin Electric Wire and Cable Co.: 40%	Cable products for telephone switches

In Thailand, Honda started with the creation of the Asian Honda Motor Co., Ltd., in 1964. Now, all automobiles designed for use in the Asian region are produced at the Ayutthaya plant of Honda Cars Manufacturing. This plant has more production capacity than any other in the region. Vietnam, Cambodia, the Philippines, Japan, Laos, Indonesia, China, and even Japan are some of the countries to which this plant exports. The main product of Honda in this region is its motorcycle. In Thailand, Honda enjoys a market share greater than 60 percent thanks to a high degree of local content and brand name recognition. The motorcycles produced in Thailand have an 85 percent local content ratio. In the near future, Honda wants to raise the ratio to 95 percent. This move will allow Honda to insulate itself from the foreign exchange fluctuations of the Thai baht.

In Vietnam, production of motorcycles began in December 1997. However, Honda has been a market leader and the vehicle of choice for affluent Vietnamese for over 30 years. How was this possible with the import ban that was imposed from 1972 to 1994? Relatives of Vietnamese living in the United States and other countries shipped vehicles back as gifts, and 800,000 Honda Cubs had been imported during the Vietnam War. As a result, Honda was the dominant name in the marketplace despite not generating a single sale from the country in over 20 years. Currently, Honda enjoys a 70 percent market share of new motorcycle sales and a 90 percent share of both new and used motorcycle sales. However, the motorcycles that Honda produces in Vietnam are still expensive on a relative basis. According to one Honda executive, the 27 million dong (U.S.$2,100) required for a 100 cc Super Dream would take an average Vietnamese worker three years to save. Honda chose to pursue a joint venture in Vietnam because of a high tariff of 60 percent, but the joint venture became a necessity when the Vietnamese government decided to reimpose a ban on motorcycle imports as part of its efforts to reduce its trade deficit and encourage local industry. In this case, Honda began its entry with exports and was barred from furthering its investments by the political-legal environment. When that environment became more receptive to business, Honda was able to pursue a joint venture and begin local production.

The mode of entry for Honda in China was somewhat different. Honda entered China's automobile market to produce Accords and engines when the joint venture of French car manufacturer Peugeot Citroen failed. Honda took over that company's plant and formed joint ventures with Guangzhou Auto Group Corp. and Dongfeng Motor Corp. The Guangzhou Honda Automobile Co., Ltd., has a capitalization of $140 million, and the Dongfeng Honda Engine Co., Ltd., has a capitalization of $60 million. In each of these joint ventures, Honda has a 50 percent stake. These two ventures will start pilot production in early 1999, with full production beginning in the fall of that year. When production begins, Honda will be the first Japanese car maker to produce its automobiles on Chinese soil. Toyota sells its Daihatsu cars in China but under a licensing agreement. At the outset, 40 percent of the parts will be purchased locally, with that percentage expected to rise every year. In the case of China, the method of entry could be viewed as an equity joint venture.

Honda Motor Corp. generally pursues a low-risk strategy of entry by export. Honda's competitive strategy is based on differentiation in the form of brand recognition and quality. This strategy works especially well in brand-conscious cultures such as Vietnam's, where Honda has a 70 percent market share despite availability of the lower-priced models of Yamaha and Suzuki. The company makes its presence known through community activities and by sponsoring events. In Thailand, Honda maintains a traffic safety center outside of Taipei. Honda also sponsors golf tournaments in the region. After the local market is receptive to the brand name, Honda either establishes a plant or enters into a joint venture in the host country. After the plant is established, Honda will encourage parts makers to build factories in the region so that it can procure parts locally, increasing the self-sufficiency of the plant. This move reduces the company's foreign exchange risk and lessens the necessity for the parent company to use its resources on an economic forecasting and hedging department. Honda generally enters a market with motorcycles, as its research shows that consumers in developing countries will buy motorcycles when household income reaches approximately U.S.$1,000. After the income level rises to greater levels, Honda begins to produce and market automobiles in the local market. No Asian country has reached the level of development of Japan yet, but one would assume that Honda will further develop its strategy of differentiation as other countries progress economically. Honda probably will make its automobiles more environmentally friendly and customizable as well, as they will be in the next few years in Japan.

Despite its general strategy for entry into another country, Honda will make exceptions if the opportunity presents itself. For example, it would not have been able to expand its automobile business to China if it had not pursued a joint venture. If it had not pursued this opportunity, Honda would have missed expanding into the automobile industry's "promised land," where there are 6.6 automobiles per 1,000 people (as opposed to 600 per 1,000 in Japan and 720 per 1,000 in the United States). If other such profitable opportunities arise, Honda will likely pursue them in the same fashion.

Honda has a well-planned and time-proven method of entry into other Asian countries. The method of entry and the progression that follows is a good fit with the company's competitive strategy of differentiation. The encouragement of the use of a high level of local content helps Honda produce its products with firmer assumptions of costs and thereby revenues. If Honda maintains this strategy and keeps expanding its plants, it will remain a major player in the Asian motorcycle market and will be well positioned for the expected growth of the automobile market.

CHAPTER 5

Entry Mode Selection: Factors and Decisions

MNCs can structure their entry into the Chinese market in many different ways. Some are more suitable than others, depending upon a variety of situational contingencies. Inevitably, there are tradeoffs in choosing one entry mode over another. Once a foreign investor decides to pursue a FDI project, its choice of entry mode will depend on a wide range of factors. Broadly, these contingencies can be classified into country, industry, firm, and project categories. Foreign firms should make sure they know all possible options for entry into a target country before determining the best one. This chapter delineates all major factors that are associated with the entry mode selection and articulates the impact of each of these factors on entry mode decision.

Literature Background

Entry mode selection is an important decision in international expansion since it is tied to an MNC's core competency contributions, control over subsidiaries, parent-subsidiary relations, and vulnerability to external changes in a host country (Gomes-Casseres 1990; Hill, Hwang, and Kim 1990). By choosing an entry mode that fits internal capabilities, strategic goals, and environmental contingencies, an MNC can also prevent the exposure of distinctive technologies, mitigate transactional hazards that may be precipitated during resource dispersal or interactions with contextual forces, and boost the economic rents derived from tacit knowledge (Gatignon and Anderson 1988). In recent years, Dunning's Ownership-Location-Internalization (OLI) paradigm, transaction cost theory, bargaining power theory, and the organizational capability paradigm have emerged as the leading theories for explaining choices of entry mode during international expansion.

Dunning's (1980, 1988) eclectic, or OLI, paradigm stipulates that the choice of entry mode during international expansion is influenced by three types of determinants (OLI advantages): ownership advantages of a firm, location advantages of a market, and internalization advantages of integrating transactions within the firm. First, MNCs must possess superior assets and skills that can earn economic rents high enough to counter the higher cost of servicing international markets. Once an MNC's technological, operational, organizational, and financial competencies are strong enough, it may opt for a high-risk mode of entry that has greater potential for high returns. Second, MNCs interested in serving foreign markets are expected to be selective and favor entry into more attractive markets. In countries offering high market potential, investment modes are expected to provide greater long-term profitability to firms compared to noninvestment modes such as export. Once a mode is chosen, the interactions between these factors and the mode will be largely exogenous, meaning that it will not be economically feasible to switch entry modes once an MNC has entered the target market. Finally, entry mode selection must be determined by the requirements of global integration and internalization. When high integration is required, high-control entry modes are preferred. By contrast, low-control modes may be more appropriate for MNCs that do not desire integration with the target host country.

Transaction cost theory suggests that the governance structure an MNC chooses for a venture is driven by a desire to minimize transaction costs (Anderson and Gatignon 1986; Hennart 1989; Williamson 1985). If transaction costs are low, a rational firm will prefer that its transactions be governed by the market. However, if the costs of adaption, performance monitoring, and safeguarding against the opportunistic behavior of other parties are too high, the firm will prefer an internal governance structure (e.g., a wholly owned subsidiary). Specifically, a high-control entry mode may be chosen if (1) the uncertainty of demand for an MNC's products or services in a foreign market is high; (2) foreign market attractiveness is high; (3) the cultural distance between an MNC's home country and host country is high; (4) the specificity of the assets that an MNC contributes to the foreign venture is high; or (5) the need for local contributions such as indigenous capital, technology, and skilled manpower is low.

Bargaining power theory argues that the specific mode chosen by an MNC depends on the relative bargaining power of the firm and that of the foreign government (Boddewyn and Brewer 1994). Bargaining power refers to the bargainer's ability to set discussion parameters, win compromises from the other party, and skew the outcome of the negotiation toward its desired ownership alternative. Access to foreign markets is controlled by political actors at home and abroad, so the initial market entry decision must take into account political imperatives (Gomes-

Casseres 1990). A major source of a host government's power is its ability to control market access and supply or withdraw investment incentives. An MNC's bargaining power stems from its ownership advantages. Therefore, bargaining power theory assumes that MNCs typically negotiate with foreign governments for a high-control mode of entry, since these are the most desirable arrangements in terms of the sustained ability to dominate the market and protect proprietary technology. By contrast, host governments often prefer investing firms to use a low-control mode when entering their countries because such modes help transfer technology and know-how to local firms and allow them to share in the profits derived from the success of FDI projects.

Another line of argument addressing the entry mode decision focuses more closely on a firm's capabilities (Agarwal and Ramaswami 1992; Teece, Pisano, and Shuen 1990). In general, high-control and internalized entry modes provide competitive advantages. They would be preferable in domains where the firm has a strong knowledge base and possesses the necessary routines, since incremental costs are marginal (Teece 1983). This increases the efficiency of resource utilization and the effectiveness of its transfer in-house. When the firm lacks the requisite capabilities, it may be too daunting to operate in a new context within an acceptable time frame or cost limit. A more effective, less costly alternative might be to supplement the firm's resources by grafting on new knowledge gained from the experience of other firms (Hamel 1991). When knowledge resources are the primary concern, interfirm collaborations will involve restructuring the information boundaries of each firm and managing knowledge flow. Foreign direct investment made through a wholly owned subsidiary results in the perpetuation of a firm's routines. Most MNCs find that joint ventures enhance the capabilities of their core businesses. The development of all necessary know-how in-house is viewed as too slow a process; joint ventures provide the structural mechanisms that allow more extensive exchanges of knowledge.

An MNC is expected to choose the entry mode that offers the highest risk-adjusted return on investment. A firm's choices are also determined by behavioral factors such as resource availability, bargaining position, and the need for control. Therefore, the four theories just described contribute different, complementary perspectives to our understanding of entry mode choice. While transaction cost theory serves to explain the risks of various entry modes, bargaining power theory describes the control effects of each mode. While the OLI paradigm offers more insight into the rationale behind various entry modes, the organizational capability paradigm sheds more light on the need to commit or acquire resources in different entry modes. Collectively, all four theories have greater explanatory power than any single theory in describing the underlying contingencies of entry mode selection. They hence serve as a theoretical foundation for the following hypotheses.

This chapter suggests that the selection of entry modes in China depends upon the following four groups of factors. First, selection is influenced by Chinese macroenvironmental factors such as government intervention, property rights protection, and environmental uncertainty. Like other emerging economies, the Chinese market is characterized by frequent changes in the regulatory framework, limited protection of industrial or intellectual property rights systems, and a volatile national environment (economic, sociocultural, political). Second, industry-specific factors such as sales growth, asset intensity, and growth in the number of firms have an influence on the choice of entry mode. Despite improvements in recent years, the industrial structure in China remains one of the bottlenecks hampering economic development. Third, the entry mode choice is associated with firm-specific factors such as knowledge protection, global integration, and host country experience. Limited protection of intellectual property rights in China necessitates knowledge protection and global integration by firms. Finally, in selecting an entry mode, project-specific factors such as project orientation, size, and location must be considered. Many governments treat FDI projects differently according to these dimensions. Projects with different traits often imply different potentials for economic returns and risks. The following section discusses each of these factors at multiple levels in detail. Figure 5.1 schematically shows an integrated framework for entry mode selection.

National-Level Factors

A number of exogenous macroenvironmental factors have an impact on the choice of entry mode. First, *Chinese government FDI policies* may directly or indirectly influence entry mode selection. The laws on FDI in certain regulated industries (e.g., automobiles, telecommunications, and insurance) may mandate that foreign firms must choose joint ventures, as opposed to wholly owned subsidiaries, as an entry mode. This policy holds particularly true in pillar industries or those vital to the economic development of the host country. Multinational companies with different entry modes are treated differently in terms of taxation, infrastructure access, local financing, and resource or material procurement by the central or local government. For instance, joint ventures in technology-intensive sectors often enjoy preferential corporate income

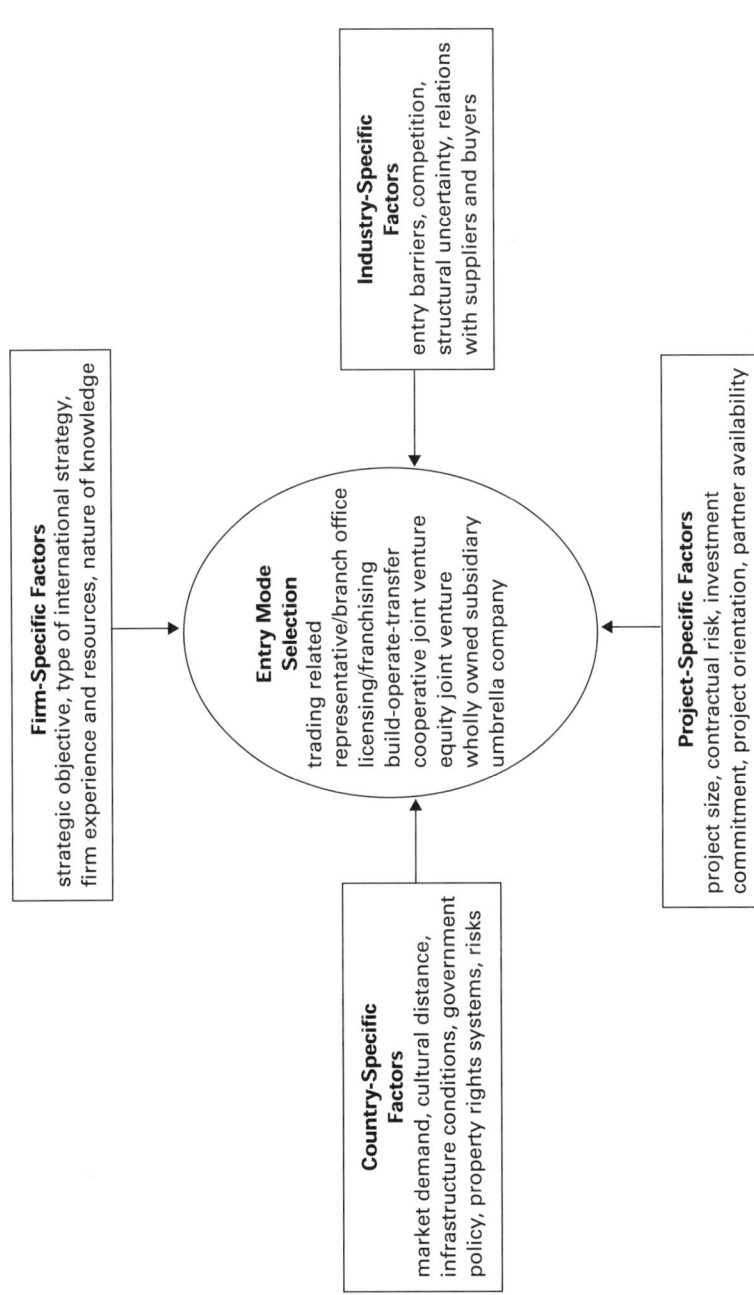

Firm-Specific Factors

strategic objective, type of international strategy, firm experience and resources, nature of knowledge

Industry-Specific Factors

entry barriers, competition, structural uncertainty, relations with suppliers and buyers

Entry Mode Selection

trading related
representative/branch office
licensing/franchising
build-operate-transfer
cooperative joint venture
equity joint venture
wholly owned subsidiary
umbrella company

Country-Specific Factors

market demand, cultural distance, infrastructure conditions, government policy, property rights systems, risks

Project-Specific Factors

project size, contractual risk, investment commitment, project orientation, partner availability

Fig. 5.1. Entry mode selection in international expansion: an integrated model

tax rates. This idiosyncrasy influences entry mode selection because it has implications for expected risk-adjusted profitability.

Second, the *conditions of the infrastructure and support industries* will affect the extent to which an MNC plans to commit distinctive resources to Chinese operations and the degree to which it perceives operational uncertainty and contextual unpredictability. These in turn influence the entry mode option. In practice, MNCs often have to make a tradeoff between two different control mechanisms. On the one hand, the wholly owned subsidiary option can enable the MNC to maintain better control over its internal operations than the joint venture mode does, thus reducing its vulnerability to contextual volatility. On the other hand, a wholly owned subsidiary is at a disadvantage relative to a joint venture in counteracting environmental risks in a complex, hostile, or uncertain setting. This is due in large part to the lack of a Chinese partner who would otherwise help mitigate these contextual differences. To appropriately select an entry mode, an MNC needs to gauge whether internally induced uncertainties outweigh externally induced variabilities or vice versa.

Third, *property rights systems* and other legal frameworks in China appear to be increasingly important to entry mode selection. This is because technological competencies and tacit knowledge are emerging as prominent determinants of an MNC's sustained competitive edge in the Chinese market. Without sufficient legal protection, an MNC's property rights and tacit knowledge, such as trademarks, brand names, know-how, patents, copyrights, and the like, will expose it to possible infringement and piracy by local firms. Under such circumstances, the MNC may have to use a high-control entry mode such as a wholly owned subsidiary or a dominant equity joint venture.

Fourth, *host country risk* in China as perceived by an MNC may affect its resource commitment, strategic flexibility, and expected return-risk tradeoff, which in turn impacts the selection of entry mode. The managers of MNCs have to deal with a variety of host country risks including general political risks (e.g., instability of the political system), ownership/control risks (e.g., price controls or local content requirements), and transfer risks (e.g., currency inconvertibility or remittance control). When these risks are high, the MNC is advised to limit its exposure by reducing its resource commitment and increasing its ability to exit from the market quickly without incurring a substantial loss should the environment worsen. This suggests that, other things being equal, licensing and joint ventures will be favored over wholly owned subsidiaries when country risk is high. Joint ventures with Chinese partners experience a relatively low rate of expropriation compared to wholly owned subsidiaries. This is because joint ventures have Chinese equity partners who may have some influence on government policy and a vested interest in speaking out against expropriation.

Fifth, *cultural distance* between the home country and China influences foreign entry decisions and processes. Over time, MNCs learn how to overcome cultural barriers and move from low-risk (e.g., representative or branch offices, licensing, and franchising) to high-risk entry modes (e.g., dominant equity joint ventures, wholly owned subsidiaries, and umbrella companies) and move from culturally proximate countries to more distant ones. The perceived distance from the home country and China in terms of culture, economic systems, and business practices also determines location familiarity; the shorter the perceived distance, the greater the familiarity. Perceived distance is a function of both basic psychic distance and the firm's prior experience in that culture. The greater the perceived distance between home and host countries, the more likely it is that MNCs will favor licensing or a joint venture over a wholly owned subsidiary. Not being comfortable with the culture, economic system, and business practices in China causes executives to shy away from direct investment. Faced with the uncertainty of the unknown, an MNC may be unwilling to commit substantial resources to Chinese operations since such a commitment would substantially reduce the MNC's ability to exit without cost if the host market should prove unattractive.

Sixth, *demand conditions* affect expected net return and firm growth during international expansion. One of the prominent features of the Chinese market is the diversity and variability of market demand conditions across different industries, regions, and periods of time. These environmental dynamics affect resource commitment, strategic orientation, and entry mode decision. When future demand in a target sector or region is unknown, an MNC may be unwilling to invest substantial resources. Extensive resource commitments may limit the firm's ability to reduce excess capacity or exit from the Chinese market without incurring substantial sunk costs if demand should fail to reach a significant level. As has been argued elsewhere, uncertainty as to future demand conditions is likely to be greatest in either embryonic or declining industries. Thus, MNCs may favor low-resource-commitment modes of entry when the Chinese market is in its embryonic or declining stage (e.g., licensing). When demand conditions become more stable and predictable, as tends to happen in mature markets, the MNC is better able to identify the optimal capacity needed to serve Chinese consumers. However, this does not imply that the MNC will have a preference for a particular entry mode. Indeed, the MNC is likely to be indifferent.

Factors other than demand conditions will determine its choice of entry mode when the target sector is mature.

Finally, *environmental uncertainty* is an important contingency for the entry mode decision. The impact of environmental volatility on firm operations is normally enduring and fundamental. As entry mode choice is associated with the level of risk exposure as it is perceived by managers, it is necessary for MNCs to make sure that the chosen entry mode will minimize such an impact on firm operations and/or that the firm has a sufficient ability to mitigate against uncertainties if it is opting for a high-risk mode. When uncertainty is high, a greater degree of ownership potentially entails more switching costs should undesirable events occur. Ownership of strategic assets may deprive the owner of the flexibility of making a low-cost exit from a market. Therefore, firms tend to shun ownership under such conditions. Unlike contractual risks resulting from the exposure of transaction-specific assets, which can be neutralized or mitigated through internalization of intermediate markets, uncertainty and risks embodied in the contextual environment are usually beyond the control of the firm. This also causes the firm to shy away from ownership. Thus, MNCs should consider lower levels of equity ownership as environmental risks increase. Although large MNCs are usually able to bear some risks, empirical evidence indicates that the willingness of MNCs to commit equity in a foreign market (such as China) is inversely related to perceptions of the uncertainty of doing business in a host country (Gatignon and Anderson 1988).

Industrial-Level Factors

Various industry-specific factors such as entry barriers, industrial policies set by the host government, structural uncertainty, the degree of competition from both local and other foreign firms, and relationships with suppliers and distributors are important considerations underlying entry mode selection. First, the *nature and degree of competition* from either local or other foreign businesses in China may have a direct impact on whether an MNC chooses an arm's length approach to its contract or sets up an internal organization to undertake business transactions. Licensing can be viewed as an arm's length contractual relationship; setting up a wholly owned subsidiary, by contrast, involves an extension of the MNC's organizational boundaries and a commensurate reduction in the firm's strategic flexibility. When competition is volatile, any reduction in strategic flexibility is not economically advisable. A volatile market is one in which rapidly changing technological, macroeconomic, social, demographic, and regulatory factors produce a situation of intense competition, be that on the basis of price, marketing expenditures, or investments. Such conditions require quick responses from the MNC. Insofar as resource commitments limit an MNC's ability to adapt to changing market circumstances without incurring substantial sunk costs, an MNC theoretically favors entry modes involving low resource commitments when competitive pressures in the Chinese market are intense.

Second, *entry barriers* into a target Chinese industry constitute a significant impediment to entry mode selection. When such barriers are high, MNCs have very little freedom to choose among entry modes. MNCs often have no choice but to accept host-government-instituted modes of entry into certain industries. Broadly, these barriers result from either industry- or government-induced factors. Of the former set, possible factors include a large minimum scale, high capital requirements, high exit costs, superfluous production capacity, predatory selling prices, supply and distribution monopolies, and superlative customer loyalty. Among the latter set, possible factors include policies such as control over entry, local partner, location, timing, and equity along with financing policies, tax law, scarce resource procurement, infrastructure access priorities, and so on.

Third, *structural uncertainty, complexity, and hostility* may lead MNCs to use high-control or low-commitment entry modes such as representative offices, licensing, franchising, loosely structured cooperative joint ventures with little resource commitment, or minority equity joint ventures. The impact of an industry's structural dynamics on MNC operations is normally enduring and fundamental. It is necessary for MNCs to ensure that the chosen entry mode will minimize such an impact on firm operations and/or that the firm has a sufficient ability to mitigate against such dynamics if it is opting for a high-risk entry mode. This suggests that MNCs should consider various factors at different levels simultaneously in the process of making an entry mode decision.

Fourth, *availability and favorability of supply and distribution* in the target Chinese industry will determine the rationalization of value chain linkages needed for an MNC's local operations and the vertical integration of other units within the MNC network. Although this impact is firm specific, depending upon the firm's objectives, competencies, and strategies, relationships with Chinese suppliers and local distributors can influence the firm's product quality, on-time delivery, customer responsiveness, and competitive power, which in turn affect profitability, sales growth, liquidity, and asset efficiency. When an MNC relies more on local resource procurement and/or emphasizes the Chinese market, it is more vulnerable to industrial linkages with suppliers and distributors.

Entry modes involving partners turn out to be the superior choice when the MNC needs but lacks industrial linkages in China.

Finally, *its relationship with Chinese buyers* may affect an MNC's growth potential, resource commitment, and strategic orientation. These in turn affect the entry mode selection. When an MNC has strong, diverse linkages with various buyers, customers, and end users established through previous export or import (direct or indirect) businesses, it is advisable for the firm to employ a high-resource-committed mode such as a dominant joint venture, wholly owned subsidiary, or umbrella company. By contrast, a firm may use a low-resource-commitment mode such as a representative office, licensing, franchising, or a minority or split joint venture to enter the Chinese market. As it takes time to build and develop relationships with various buyers, entry mode selection is an evolutionary process that relies heavily on linkages with Chinese customers.

Organizational-Level Factors

Entry mode selection is contingent on several firm-specific traits as well. First, a firm's *resource munificence* in internationalization will influence its ability to explore market potential and achieve a competitive edge in the Chinese market. It affects the entry mode decision because it impacts resource commitment, control mechanisms, partner selection, and knowledge transfer. A foreign investor that lacks these resources but wishes to share in the risks associated with having them is often compelled to enter the market through a joint venture in which its resource commitment will be minimized. Firms having less knowledge about the Chinese market tend to reduce their strategic risk through licensing agreements or joint ventures rather than the wholly owned modes. Some firms use acquisition to procure a new set of resources, while firms using the new venture mode (i.e., greenfields) rely on their previously developed resources. A firm will use the joint venture mode to rectify a resource deficiency only if it is willing to risk providing access to such resources and can find suitable Chinese partners with appropriate resources to share. The critical factor is finding partners predisposed to provide such access to resources. This predisposition must be based on interfirm trust and a perception that sharing resources will not negatively impact either firm. An MNC will tend to favor an acquisition mode if it cannot find a suitable partner to provide access to required resources or if it is not itself willing to provide access to internal resources because it fears the risk of their exposure.

Second, *the nature of strategic assets or knowledge* may affect an MNC's competitive and control capabilities. If it has tacit strategic assets or distinctive knowledge, a wholly owned subsidiary mode increases the firm's ability to use that knowledge. Thus, tacitness is positively related to degree of control. In general, the risk of knowledge exposure is perceived by management to be lower when the exposed resources are peripheral or if the core competencies are difficult to imitate or transfer. A firm unnecessarily exposing its critical resources may accidentally provide its Chinese partner with a competitive advantage in the future. Therefore, the perceived nature and type of resources being exposed are important to the entry mode selection process.

It is imperative to distinguish between technological and managerial know-how. If a company's competitive advantage derives from its control over proprietary technological know-how, licensing and joint venture arrangements are not advisable because of the risk of losing control of that technology. A wholly owned subsidiary might be a better choice. Licensing or joint ventures can be used only if the arrangements are structured so as to reduce the risk of the technology being expropriated by licenses or joint venture partners. Companies can arrange to prevent leakage of their most sensitive technologies by only allowing their partners access to limited production processes. Contractual safeguards can also be written into a joint venture contract. Cross-licensing agreements between parties can also protect a foreign investor's technological know-how if both parties agree in advance to exchange skills and technology. Comparatively, the risk of losing control over management skills is not that great. This is one of the reasons why many service MNCs favor a combination of franchising and subsidiaries that control its franchises.

Third, an MNC's global integration requirement may influence the entry mode choice. This choice can help balance the parent firm's global integration requirement with its Chinese subsidiary's local responsiveness requirement. Entry mode selection is one of the major tools for implementing an MNC's transnational strategies, wherein both global integration of worldwide businesses and local responsiveness to Chinese operations are needed for a diversified business. A full ownership entry mode is the most important mechanism for internalizing global businesses. The wholly owned mode enables the investor to better control venture activities, hence facilitating an internalization of geographically dispersed businesses within an integrated network. It can also stimulate operational synergies derived from vertical integration, production movement, information transfer, and political power and financial synergies resulting from transfer pricing, tax avoidance, risk diversification, profit margin increase, and capital structure improvement. If required integration is low, ownership control will become less imperative and the joint venture mode will be selected in the search for economic benefits that cannot accrue in wholly owned subsidiaries.

Fourth, a firm's *strategic goals* in entering China are one of the foremost determinants underlying entry mode selection. It is widely realized that foreign venture success is a function of how the firm enters the target market. When an MNC attempts to pursue market share in China, high-commitment choices such as cooperative or equity joint ventures, wholly owned subsidiaries, and umbrella companies are better because they enable the firm to have a deeper, more diverse involvement with the indigenous market, which provides more opportunities to accumulate culture-specific experience. If an MNC aims only to exploit factor endowment advantages such as cheap Chinese labor, low-commitment entry modes such as subcontracting, compensation trade, coproduction, cooperative arrangements, and minority equity joint ventures may be superior to other options because the risks and costs are low. If an MNC aims at overall corporate efficiency maximization, tight coordination is necessary for the effective execution of its strategies. This tight coordination may be difficult to accomplish in coalitions or through licensing. Such agreements link a foreign entrant to independent firms with different strategic motivations and a potential for conflict. Therefore, high-control entry modes are a better choice when tight coordination within an MNC network is necessary. Specifically, by manufacturing in a location where factor conditions are optimal, then exporting products to the rest of the world, a foreign company may realize substantial location economies along with a positive experience curve. This arrangement also gives the company the tight control over marketing that is required for coordinating a globally dispersed value chain. It can also engage in transfer pricing to avoid various taxes or tariffs. Thus, foreign companies pursuing global strategies may prefer to establish wholly owned subsidiaries.

Finally, *experience with the Chinese market* reduces the uncertainty associated with assessing the true economic worth of entry into China. It follows, therefore, that MNCs with little or no experience with operations in China will try to limit their risk exposure. Such firms prefer low-control, low-resource commitment entry modes such as exports, subcontracting, international leasing or franchising, and countertrading. In contrast, MNCs with significant China-specific experience prefer high-control, high-resource commitment entry modes such as cooperative or equity joint ventures, wholly owned subsidiaries, and umbrella investment companies. In addition, firms can be expected to pursue a wholly owned entry mode relative to a joint venture as they gain experience in the local environment. A foreign company that is unfamiliar with the

Chinese environment may want to engage a dependable distributor to sell its goods. Firms that want to minimize capital and resource investments at the initial stage may find contract manufacturing suitable. Some may want to first test the market and establish a relationship with their current and potential customers by setting up a representative office.

Project-Level Factors

In the course of entry mode selection, MNCs also need to consider some attributes of the FDI project itself. These attributes are associated with resource commitment, strategic orientation, and transaction costs, which impact the choice of entry modes associated with the Chinese market. First, *project size* influences the extent of control sought by an MNC. Firms may shy away from wholly owned entry mode in favor of a joint venture when the project is large. Investors deal more cautiously with transactions that involve greater investment commitment. A large investment implies higher startup, switching, and exit costs and thus involves higher financial and operational risks. In order to reduce such transaction costs, firms become more circumspect when considering an entry mode. Moreover, a firm's commitment is positively related to its expected stake, that is, the perceived importance of possible gains or losses associated with the investment commitment. When the stakes are high, firms are likely to enter China more cautiously. Therefore, risk and cost-sharing entry modes are favored.

Second, *project orientation* (i.e., export oriented, technologically advanced, local market oriented, import substitution, or infrastructure oriented) influences an MNC's resource dispersal and strategic orientation and therefore influences firm behavior in terms of governance structure and entry mode. For example, other things being equal, MNCs investing in import-substitution projects in China may be inclined to establish partnerships with local government agencies or state-owned enterprises holding monopoly positions since this type of FDI project is markedly vulnerable to host government control and hindrance. If a project is local market oriented, the MNC may choose the cooperative or equity joint venture mode as the Chinese partner can provide distinctive supply and distribution channels, governmental networks, and culture-specific business knowledge and experience. If a project is technologically advanced, the firm may opt for the wholly owned subsidiary mode to protect its know-how or the joint venture mode if it needs complementary technologies or knowledge from a partner firm. Finally, when a project is infrastructure oriented, the

MNC may apply the build-operate-transfer mode if it plans on having only a short-term run or the majority joint venture mode if it has a long-term strategic plan and is willing to take risks.

Third, *contractual risks and costs* associated with a particular FDI project may affect an MNC's commitment, contribution, and control. Licensing may avoid the resource commitment associated with opening up a foreign market. However, if an MNC grants a license to a Chinese business to use firm-specific know-how to manufacture or market a product, it runs the risk of the licensee, or an employee of the licensee, disseminating that know-how or using it for purposes other than those originally intended. Similar arguments can be made with respect to joint venture partners. In a complex and uncertain world populated with economic actors of bounded rationality and opportunistic tendencies, the costs of negotiating, monitoring, and enforcing contracts are not trivial. There is always the possibility of unanticipated contingencies giving rise to opportunistic actions against which the MNC has no defense. By establishing a wholly owned subsidiary in China, an MNC can reduce dissemination risk and therefore economize on the transaction costs of licenses or ventures. If the reduction in transaction costs exceeds the bureaucratic costs of establishing and running an internal market to transfer know-how, establishing a wholly owned subsidiary makes the most sense.

Finally, *the availability of proper Chinese partners* for a particular project may affect an MNC's entry ability and choice. An MNC's ability to establish a joint venture or utilize any other form of unintegrated entry depends on the availability of capable, trustworthy partners. In the absence of acceptable local partners, the MNC may be forced to establish a wholly owned subsidiary. When an MNC has a variety of choices in partner selection, it will have much greater freedom in choosing among entry modes ranging from trade-related and build-operate-transfer modes to cooperative and equity joint ventures. The availability of acceptable local partners boosts the effectiveness of entry mode selection.

In sum, the entry mode choice associated with the Chinese market depends upon four groups of factors: (1) country-specific factors, including government FDI policies, conditions of infrastructure and support industries, property rights systems and other legal frameworks, macro-environmental, cultural distance, demand conditions, and contextual uncertainty; (2) industry-specific factors such as the nature and degree of competition, entry barriers, structural uncertainty, complexity, and hostility; (3) firm-specific factors such as resource munificence, the nature of strategic assets or knowledge, global integration requirements, strategic goals, and China-specific experience; and (4) project-specific

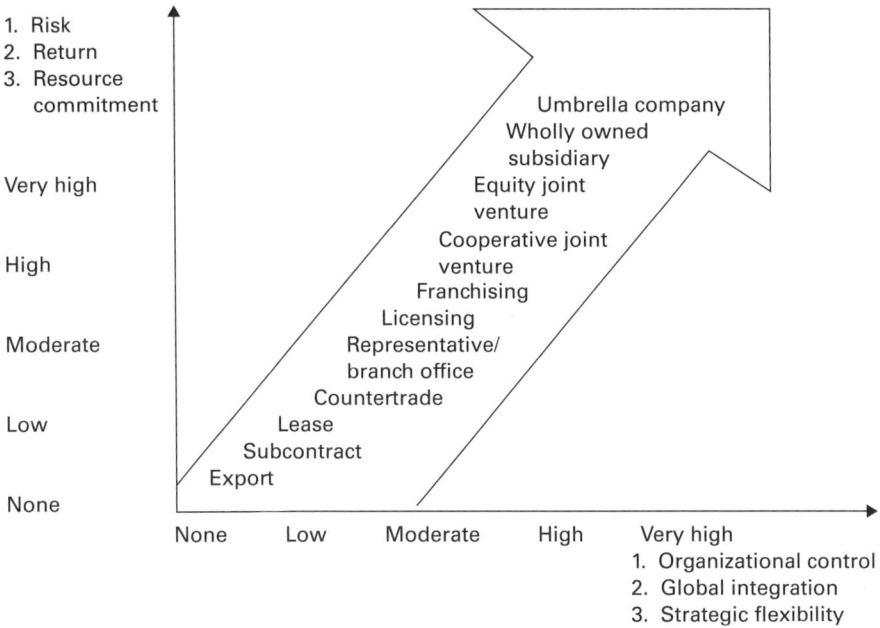

1. Risk
2. Return
3. Resource
   commitment

Very high

High

Moderate

Low

None

Umbrella company
Wholly owned
subsidiary
Equity joint
venture
Cooperative joint
venture
Franchising
Licensing
Representative/
branch office
Countertrade
Lease
Subcontract
Export

None   Low   Moderate   High   Very high

1. Organizational control
2. Global integration
3. Strategic flexibility

Fig. 5.2. Critical implications of various entry modes

factors, including project size, project orientation, contractual risks and costs, and the availability of proper Chinese partners.

This discussion may serve as a useful tool for selecting an appropriate entry mode that fits both external forces (at the country and industrial levels) and internal competencies (at the firm and project levels). Among a wide range of entry mode choices, it is up to international managers of each firm to opt for the one most appropriate to the firm's capabilities, goals, and risk propensity. It is important that each entry mode decision be considered in light of contextual factors such as market demand, government policy, country risk, entry barriers, and industrial competition. This may allow the MNC to effect a strategy that derives the maximum possible benefit from Chinese markets.

Figure 5.2 summarizes the implications of various entry modes in terms of risk, return, control, integration, commitment, and flexibility. Individual firms should combine this general framework with specific firm characteristics and situational contingencies. These dimensions can serve as base points for MNC managers considering various entry modes. Overall, risk, return, control, integration, commitment, and flexibility all increase step by step through the sequence of trade-related modes; representative or branch offices; licensing, franchising, or BOT; cooperative joint ventures; equity joint ventures; wholly owned subsidiaries; and umbrella investment companies.

Survey Results

I conducted a mail survey of senior managers in foreign ventures (EJVs and WFOEs) in China during 1996–97 with a focus on the coastal areas (the Yangtze and Pearl River deltas). After two rounds of reminders, there were 174 complete responses, including those from 102 equity joint ventures and 72 wholly owned foreign subsidiaries (detailed information about the survey and variable measurement is available from the author). The following results were observed.

First, when perceived governmental intervention or environmental uncertainty in China is high, MNCs tend to choose the joint venture mode. When perceived property rights protection is low, MNCs are more likely to employ the wholly owned subsidiary entry mode.

Second, when asset intensity of a target Chinese industry is high, MNCs seeking long-term profitability tend to choose the wholly owned mode while those MNCs seeking risk diversification are more likely to opt for the joint venture choice. Although industry sales growth is not related to entry mode decision, the growth of the number of firms in an industry is associated with a preference for the wholly owned entry mode.

Third, when the necessity for knowledge protection or global integration is high, MNCs tend to choose the wholly owned mode. The likelihood of choosing the wholly owned mode is also an increasing function of an MNC's China-specific experience.

Finally, when an FDI project is located in an open economic region, an MNC is more likely to use the wholly owned entry mode. If a project site is in a less-developed, less-open region, firms appear to prefer the joint venture choice. Project orientation and size are not systematically associated with the entry mode decision.

Foreign investors may be able to draw some lessons from these findings. Selecting an appropriate entry mode should fit both external forces (at the country and industrial levels) and internal contingencies (at the firm and project levels). Among a wide range of entry mode choices, it is up to the international managers of each firm to opt for the one most appropriate to the firm's capabilities, goals, and risk propensity. Government controls over market supply are being lifted, promising enormous opportunities for MNCs. It is important that each entry mode decision be considered in light of contextual factors such as government policies, intellectual property rights systems, environmental uncertainty, and industrial structural attributes as well as organizational and project traits such as knowledge protection, global integration, local experience, and project location. This may allow the MNC to effect a strategy that derives the maximum possible benefit from a Chinese market in which it invests and operates.

Financial Comparison between EJVs and WFOEs

Using archival data obtained from the Jiangsu Provincial Commission of Foreign Economic Relations and Trade, I compared 48 randomly selected sample EJVs with 48 sample WFOEs with regard to several key financial variables. The two groups were matched in their industrial distribution.

As table 5.1 shows, although there is no significant difference in the level of return on assets (ROA) for EJVs and WFOEs, the profit margins show significant disparities. The gross profit margin (sales minus variable costs divided by sales) is lower for WFOEs than for EJVs.

TABLE 5.1. Mean Difference Comparisons between EJVs and WFOEs

Variable	EJV	WFOE	t-Value
Profitability			
Return on asset before tax	.21	.18	−1.33
Return on asset after tax	.15	.14	−0.46
Gross profit margin	.71	.69	−0.95
Operations profit margin	.23	.26	2.48**
Efficiency			
Receivable turnover	9.86	10.33	.42
Inventory turnover	9.23	9.45	.12
Total asset turnover	1.39	1.21	−1.83*
Liquidity and financial risk			
Current ratio	1.90	2.35	2.67**
Cash liquidity	.10	.09	−0.75
Debt ratio	.37	.29	−2.68**
Interest coverage	13.24	17.55	1.04
Growth opportunity			
Local sales growth	.18	.17	−0.78
Export growth	.08	.15	2.91**
Lerner index	.05	.06	0.25
Net profit growth	.14	.12	−0.56

Note: $*p < .01$ $**p < .001$

However, when all other expenses beyond direct costs are taken into account, WFOEs are more profitable than EJVs, as is shown by their higher operating profit margin (sales minus variable and fixed costs divided by sales). This suggests that WFOEs on average have higher variable costs in relation to total revenue than EJVs do and that they may have lower fixed costs than EJVs due to their lower overhead expenses — caused by, for example, lower interest and depreciation — or less allocation of certain social or transportation expenses not incurred by the WFOEs but by the local social or transportation authorities because there is no Chinese partner involved.

Compared to WFOEs, EJVs have similar levels of accounts receivable and inventory turnover but a moderately higher level of total assets turnover, suggesting that certain current assets (except accounts receivable and inventory) and fixed assets might dedicate a greater role to an EJV's total assets efficiency than to a WFOE's.

As a measure of liquidity, the current ratio is significantly lower for EJVs than for WFOEs. One possible reason for this is that EJVs, which are usually in partnership with Chinese state enterprises, may have better banking relationships, which warrants maintaining this low current ratio without impairing their routine business activities. In the meantime, the debt ratio is significantly higher for EJVs than for WFOEs, which may also explain their lower interest coverage ratios. The higher debt ratio for EJVs can be explained by the fact that many foreign investors in joint ventures, particularly those funded in Hong Kong and Taiwan, often contribute a portion of the investment capital they committed to in official agreements.

None of the domestic market growth measures reveals significant differences between EJVs and WFOEs, indicating that both groups of firms have similar growth opportunities. However, the export growth rate is significantly higher for WFOEs than for EJVs, suggesting that foreign investors aiming to pursue Chinese market entry are more likely to choose the joint venture mode since utilization of the existing market power and distribution networks possessed by the Chinese counterparts is commonly viewed as the best short way to enter this unfamiliar territory. On the other hand, foreign investors attempting to minimize production costs by manufacturing in China and then exporting to international markets are more likely to employ the wholly owned subsidiary mode.

This comparison provides some lessons for international managers. First, WFOEs have demonstrated superior financial efficacy over EJVs in terms of asset efficiency and financial risk reduction. If the strategic goal of an investor entering the Chinese market is to pursue optimal asset synergies and/or risk reduction through globalization of its operations and management, the WFOE is a superior entry mode to the EJV. Second, if the strategic objective of the investor is to pursue local market share, the EJV is a better option than the WFOE, all other factors being equal. Alternatively, if the strategic mission of the investor is to pursue the benefits of cost minimization through exports, the WFOE turns out to be a superior choice over the EJV. Finally, if the investor contributes distinctive resources to the venture and does not want these resources to be exposed to the local partners, the WFOE can enable the investor to retain greater control over venture businesses. Thus, it constitutes a superior mode over the EJV.

Mini-cases

Mini-case 1: ARCO's Experience in China

The Atlantic Richfield Company (ARCO) began operating in the United States as an oil refining and marketing company. Its primary businesses are oil and natural gas. At one time, it diversified into chemicals and coal, but more recently it has begun to spin off or sell these product divisions. Although Atlantic Richfield is not one of the top oil companies in terms of size or sales, it is a leader in the industry in its use of cutting-edge technology, which has enabled it to obtain greater efficiency in draining oil and gas fields. Besides its domestic operations, it now operates in many countries worldwide. Its four main international operations are in Algeria, China, Indonesia, and the United Kingdom. It has made significant inroads into the Chinese market by controlling the Yacheng natural gas field off the coast of Hainan Island. It is mainly involved in strategic alliances, acquisitions, and new wholly owned subsidiaries.

Atlantic Richfield established commercial relations with China in 1978 and was the first foreign company to sign an offshore oil contract with China in 1981. In 1983, it discovered a gas field in the South China Sea, near Hainan Island, known as Yacheng 13. It set up China's first natural gas production facility there. The gas field required two subsea pipelines, one to Hong Kong and one to Hainan Island. The pipeline to Hong Kong is the second largest in the world, stretching nearly 500 miles. The gas is piped to the Castle Peak Power Co. in Hong Kong for refining and processing in order to meet the growing demand for energy in the Asia-Pacific region. The gas piped to Hainan Island is used for power generation and a fertilizer plant. The company began selling gas from Yacheng 13 in 1996.

Another partnership was formed in 1997 between ARCO and the

China National Offshore Oil Corp. for the development of the Ledong natural gas fields. The two companies had cooperated previously in developing Yacheng 13. For the Ledong project, they combined complementary resources to determine the economic viability and possible development of the gas fields.

Besides the Yacheng 13 and Ledong gas fields, ARCO has several other stakes in China. It has concessions in the San Jiao and South Hedong coal bed methane blocks in northeastern China. It also has ties with the Zhenhai Refining and Chemical Co., in which it purchased a 10 percent interest in 1994. In 1996, it purchased convertible bonds that gave it a 20 percent interest. It is also considering several joint projects with Zhenhai.

The ARCO Coal Company and China's Shenhua Group, Inc., formed a partnership in 1996 that illustrates the importance of compatible goals and complementary skills between partners. The partnership had the main objective of evaluating the economic viability of various coal mine and power plant projects in north-central China. It was understood that in the future there would be a possibility of cooperation in the development of such projects. Each company complemented the other. As one of the largest coal companies in the United States, the ARCO Coal Co. provides expertise and resources. It operates surface and underground coal mines in both the United States and Australia. The Shenhua Group is in charge of the development and operation of the Shenfu/Dongsheng coal field in Shaanxi and Inner Mongolia Provinces. It is also involved with related railways, power plants, the Huanhua seaport, and auxiliary businesses and projects.

In 1998, ARCO and the China United Coal Bed Methane Corp. signed a production-sharing contract. They will evaluate the commercial potential of three coal bed methane projects in Shanxi Province. The three projects are known as Sanjiao, Sanjiao Bei, and Shilou. All three cover about 1,930 miles and are located in the Hedong Coal Basin. ARCO has been in the coal bed methane business for more than 10 years and has the most efficient project in the San Juan Basin/Four Corners area of the United States. The China United Coal Bed Methane Corp. was established by the Ministry of Coal Industry, the Ministry of Geology and Mineral Resources, and the China National Petroleum Corp. The company's primary objective is to supervise and administer the development of the coal bed methane industry in China.

Macroenvironmental factors that affected ARCO's entry mode selection included the potential demand for its products and services and China's strict government policies. ARCO International Oil and Gas is the division of ARCO in charge of exploring, developing, and producing oil and gas outside the United States. In 1978, high-ranking officials of the Chinese government met with ARCO senior managers to discuss China's interest in developing its oil, natural gas, and coal resources effectively and quickly. China needed a joint venture with a firm outside the country that could supply the know-how and services it needed. This obvious demand provided a great opportunity for ARCO. In part because of the government's interest in developing its natural resources, the firm did not have to deal with as many tough government policies and corruption as did other foreign companies attempting to enter China. For this reason, the Chinese dubbed ARCO the "lucky company." In 1982, the ARCO China subsidiary became the first foreign company to be awarded offshore oil exploration rights.

One industry-specific factor that concerned ARCO was competition. After lengthy discussions with officials from China's Ministry of Foreign Affairs and other participating departments, ARCO agreed to a contract in which it would finance resource exploration, jointly develop and produce the fields, and then transfer operations to the Chinese in exchange for a share of the profits. It was also required to train a number of Chinese managers who would be able to handle operations after ARCO's withdrawal. The company agreed to such broad terms because this gave it first-mover advantages, including a considerable edge over future competitors.

The company had some difficulty with China's tax laws and industrial regulations, which had not been set up to handle foreign firms. Laws had to be developed for specific situations, which made the negotiation process very time consuming. One difficult rule was that major joint ventures were expected to generate enough hard currency to be self-sustaining. Despite these problems, the first contract between ARCO and China, signed on September 19, 1982, gave ARCO a 70 percent interest in the 2.2 million acre Yingge Hai block. Santa Fe Minerals was the junior partner, with a 30 percent interest.

Before any type of planning could commence, ARCO had to determine its firm-specific objectives. Its interest in China primarily focuses on growth opportunities to increase the size of its potential market and achieve higher rates of return. Another objective is gaining access to China's resources. Although ARCO went to China to find oil, it initially discovered other forms of natural resources like gas and coal. The Yacheng 13 project has approximately three trillion cubic feet of recoverable reserves and a projected field life of 20 years. There are also ongoing projects in northeastern China in San Jiao and the South Hedong coal bed methane blocks and in the Ledong natural gas fields in the South China Sea. Thus, China clearly met one of ARCO's objectives.

Other factors ARCO had to consider were firm experience and knowledge. It had no problems in this respect since it has been in operation since 1966 and has an excellent history of finding and developing natural energy resources. Its experience and technical knowledge have increased its chances of successful expansion overseas.

Project-specific factors include project size and partner availability. The most significant project in China is the Yacheng 13 gas field, discovered in 1983. It was China's first productive offshore gas field. It cost about $1.1 billion to develop and required the construction of two offshore production platforms as well as onshore receiving facilities. A 480-mile subsea pipeline was also built to transport gas from the site to Hong Kong. It is the world's second-longest offshore gas pipeline, and the project altogether is the largest energy investment in China. Three firms, the China National Offshore Oil Corp., ARCO China, Inc., and the Kuwait Foreign Petroleum Exploration Co., jointly developed the Yacheng 13 project. Partner availability was not, therefore, a major problem for ARCO.

The company first entered China in cooperation with the Chinese government through the Chinese National Offshore Oil Corp. by forming a strategic alliance with Santa Fe Minerals. Later ARCO made acquisitions and then created a new wholly owned subsidiary, ARCO China, Inc., which now has its headquarters in Hong Kong. This subsidiary, in turn, has partnered with other companies in some of the largest natural resource development projects in the world.

Mini-case 2: 3M's Experience in China

Minnesota Mining and Manufacturing (3M) has been a multinational corporation since 1951, when it made its first direct investment abroad. By 1985, 3M was operating in 52 principal locations outside the United States and its products were being marketed and sold in a total of 135 countries. According to *Fortune* magazine, in 1984 3M had sales worth $7.7 billion, of which 34 percent were from its international operations. It had approximately 86,707 employees. Its subsidiaries employed roughly 36,450 people, of which fewer than 100 were United States citizens.

Since late 1978, the Chinese government has focused on modernizing and industrializing China. Many of its plants and equipment were old and outdated. It lacked the technology and technical skills it would need to compete with other industrialized economies. Another problem was low worker productivity. Chinese companies lacked the management skills required to increase worker productivity and output. A third major problem with the Chinese economy was that central planners determined prices. This meant that prices did not reflect the costs of production or market supply and demand.

During this time, foreign companies wanting to do business in China did so through joint ventures or by sending in sales representatives. All joint ventures had to be authorized by the Foreign Investment Control Commission. Foreign partners were required to hold at least 25 percent of the company but could own more with approval. Laws concerning joint ventures required foreign companies to provide equipment and technology. Consignment arrangements, in which the foreign firms supplied capital, raw materials, and equipment and were paid with manufactured goods, were common.

At that time 3M had an office in Hong Kong called 3M Far East Ltd. In the early 1970s, a position was established to provide service to Hong Kong customers who were reselling 3M products to China. Soon this position grew into a department called the China Trade Division. In the early 1980s, 3M decided it was an opportune time to enter China. 3M's representatives in China were given the assignment. The catch was that 3M did not want to enter through a joint venture but with a wholly owned subsidiary. At that time, the PRC had no operations of that kind. A long battle ensued before 3M could successfully pursue this entry method.

The company viewed this unique entry method as a great opportunity for both 3M and China. It felt it had the experience and technical know-how to help shape China's future. It would be the first entrant into China as a wholly owned subsidiary; together with the Chinese government it would help develop policies and regulations for future corporations and would gain status as a founder. There were still many uncertainties, such as China's political climate and slow-moving, multilayered bureaucratic system, but 3M felt that being first in China's virtually untapped market would be worth the risk.

The company began investigating entry into China on an informal basis. It first determined its criteria: it would only enter China as a wholly owned subsidiary, it would produce for the Chinese market, it had no plans to export from China, and it would enter only if the initial investment was small. It next decided that it would produce whatever China needed; electrical and telecommunications products seemed to be the best choice.

There were several reasons for this product choice. China already had manufacturing facilities that could produce these types of products, but the demand for them was still great. These product lines could be established with a relatively low front-end investment and would present good opportunities to expand the line. The company's first location

choice for operations was Shanghai because it was the most industrialized city and its officials were used to dealing with Western corporations.

It was important to 3M that it be perceived as a company genuinely
interested in serving the Chinese market. It knew that concepts such as
guanxi and "face" were important to the Chinese. Because of this, 3M
decided that the Chinese would rather deal with the head office than
sales representatives. The importance of status was never forgotten. In
1980, a 3M representative by the name of Marshall went to China with a
proposal and began negotiations with the Ministry of Foreign Trade and
Economic Cooperation in Beijing. Much to 3M's surprise, the ministry
seemed open to the idea of a wholly owned subsidiary, but it lacked the
regulations and experience needed to deal with this type of setup. Marshall quickly learned to be diplomatic and polite while pressing the
issues that 3M considered important. After several meetings over the
course of many months, negotiations reached the State Council level.

Negotiations with the State Council began with a discussion of hypo-
thetical situations. Marshall would explain what 3M would like to do if
given a particular opportunity. He concentrated on what the company
could do for China, emphasizing that China would bear no risks with a
wholly owned subsidiary. The success or failure of the operation would
lie solely with 3M. This would give China the opportunity to gain experience and formulate regulations for subsequent firms wishing to enter the
country. One of the most important arguments was that 3M was a good
corporate citizen with experience in several other countries and, most
importantly, willing to develop and train local Chinese managers. Its
policy of staffing subsidiaries with local citizens was of the utmost importance to the Chinese.

The company was given official approval and told to meet directly
with Shanghai Electrical Machinery Co. to make a deal. At Shanghai
Electric, 3M found politeness and acceptance but not encouragement.
Its presence would mean much work and very little payoff to Shanghai
Electric, which had to run its own businesses and operations.

By the spring of 1981, Marshall was fighting on two fronts. He was
arguing 3M's benefits at the national policy level in Beijing and at the
operational level in Shanghai. The biggest impediment seemed to be
China's desire to have 3M export from China, a commitment the firm
did not want to make. Marshall meanwhile encouraged officials to tour
subsidiaries in other countries and witness the benefits that 3M could
bring to China. Four officials from the Ministry of Foreign Affairs in
Beijing and two from the Shanghai Investment and Trust Co. embarked
on a tour of subsidiaries. This tactic worked well for 3M. At the end of
the trip, the Chinese officials gave immediate verbal approval. After

some delay, in October 1983 3M received an official written license to operate in China.

Further problems included determining what name 3M would use. It wanted to use *China* in the title of its subsidiary, but government officials did not approve. It felt that the name would be helpful when it was time for 3M to expand into other areas of China. It did not want to be limited to operations in Shanghai. The Chinese government eventually allowed the country name to be included in the title. On November 10, 1984, 3M signed a 15 year contract; on March 15, 1985, the Shanghai plant officially opened.

Most corporations that enter China do so through joint ventures. The Chinese government encouraged joint ventures because they allow the country to absorb technology and gain more earnings through export. For several reasons, 3M was not interested in a joint venture. Because of its array of products, it did not believe that any Chinese firm would make an appropriate partner. In its opinion, no Chinese company had compatible resources or even the ability to understand the scope of 3M's operations. Other joint ventures were encountering problems with Chinese employees who were unwilling to change their work habits. One major benefit of a joint venture is the ability of the foreign firm to gain access to the host country's existing customer base and marketing methods. Since capitalism was relatively new to China, however, these benefits were mostly lacking during the 1980s. A wholly owned subsidiary, on the other hand, promised several advantages to China. One was that the country would bear no real financial risk. China would gain important management skills in improving productivity, organizing inventory systems, and running efficient operations. In addition, 3M would employ Chinese citizens who would learn valuable skills. Most importantly, China would gain new technology and effective managers.

There were both advantages and disadvantages for 3M in having a wholly owned subsidiary in China. The disadvantages were the high costs and risk associated with all wholly owned subsidiaries. It knew from the beginning that getting the Chinese government to approve a wholly owned subsidiary would be time consuming and expensive. The fact that 3M would be the first organization of this type to enter China increased the risk. The fact that China did not have any regulations or experience in dealing with wholly owned subsidiaries would have been reason enough for many companies to avoid this entry mode.

The company looked forward to being a pioneer in the new territory. It viewed being the first wholly owned subsidiary in China as a learning experience. It wanted to help shape policy. From the beginning, it held its ground and proved to the government that it was serious about making a long-term commitment to China and its people. It wanted to manufacture in China for the Chinese market and planned to reinvest its earnings within the country. For the most part, China and its people could only benefit from 3M's presence. The long delays and frequent hassles were well worth the trouble to 3M because it gained what no other American corporation then had: access to the newly emerging and virtually untapped Chinese market.

Mini-case 3: Occidental's Experience in China

International joint ventures are increasing in importance globally. Motivated by opportunities such as market access, technological access, and cost and risk reduction, more corporations are using alliances to compete within their industries worldwide. However, history shows that such alliances are not always successful. The case of Occidental Petroleum (OPC) displays the intricacies of establishing a joint venture in China. This joint venture between OPC and a host of partners from the Peoples' Republic of China has been characterized by constant economic, technical, and bureaucratic problems.

Occidental Petroleum Corporation consists of a petroleum operation, a coal exploration business, a chemical business, and a nationwide retail operation in the United States. Primarily an oil company, OPC employs more than 78,000 people in over 100 countries worldwide. With annual sales around $10 billion in the 1980s and the early 1990s, OPC was among the top 10 major energy firms in the United States. Its strategy emphasized foreign production, and it maintained facilities in Argentina, Bolivia, Canada, Ecuador, Malaysia, Pakistan, and the Philippines.

In 1979, the Peoples' Republic of China instituted an "open door" policy to help speed industrial development. One of the primary goals of the government was to develop its energy sector, which in turn would support the industrial development of the rest of the nation. Among its various resources, coal was most important. China's proven coal reserves exceed 900 billion tons, behind only the Soviet Union and the United States. Total estimated reserves are in the neighborhood of 2 trillion tons; at current production levels it would take 2,000 years to exhaust the supply. But, despite this abundant coal supply, China lacked the capital and technology to exploit its coal in sufficient qualities to meet the country's energy needs. China's goal of modernization was in jeopardy; therefore, the search for a foreign partner to help develop the country's energy resources was a top priority of the open door policy.

In 1980, China opened its premier coal mine, the Antaibao, in the province of Shanxi, to international bidding. Eight Western firms participated in the bidding, including three from the United States, two from Germany, one from France, and one from Japan. In the end, the Occidental Petroleum Corporation beat out all of its competitors.

Occidental's CEO and chairman, Armand Hammer, was the driving force behind the joint venture. Hammer was a well-respected, dynamic, and charismatic leader noted for his legendary achievements in the international arena. He struck one of the first deals between a Western businessman and the Soviets in the 1930s, supplied them during the Second World War, and has traded with Eastern Europe since the 1970s. When China initiated its open door policy in 1979, Hammer was naturally a top prospect. China desperately needed to prove that its policy was credible and that direct investment from abroad was genuinely welcome. Its political leaders selected Hammer as an emissary who could bridge the gap between China and the Western world.

In return, Hammer responded to Chinese inquiries with enthusiasm. He saw the situation as an opportunity for OPC to expand its global operations and capitalize on some first-mover advantages. True to his nature, Hammer took a high-profile approach and befriended China's supreme leader, Deng Xiaoping. This would be the start of the Antaibao coal mining venture between OPC and a coalition of Chinese firms led by the Chinese National Coal Development Corp. (CNCDC).

From the late 1970s to the early 1980s, OPC saw its profits decline. It hoped to reverse this trend with an equity joint venture in China that would develop a mining operation in the Chinese province of Shanxi. The agreement, initiated in 1982, created a fifty-fifty joint venture between OPC and a Chinese consortium consisting of the China Coal Import/Export Corp., the China International Trust and Investment Corp., the province of Shanxi, and CNCDC.

The fifty-fifty equity joint venture, dubbed the Antaibao Project, called for $700 million in capital endowments, with each side of the partnership contributing an initial $200 million. The remaining $300 million was to be syndicated by 39 international banks. Each side would guarantee 50 percent of the loan. The project would employ 3,000 workers of which 20 to 30 would be Occidental expatriates. Furthermore, OPC agreed to export 75 percent of the total output and assume complete responsibility for marketing the coal in the export market.

A joint venture may have been the wrong mode in this situation. However, it may have been the only option given China's development policies. Joint ventures tend to succeed only if the partners have complementary skills, resources, financial assets, and a congruence of needs, strategies, and operating methods.

The most important factors that lead to the selection of an equity joint venture as a mode of entry are firm specific. The decision that led to OPC's selection of a joint venture was based on the firm's technological skills and international experience and the expanding market opportunities available in China. Although firm experience was satisfactory, the joint venture was doomed to failure because each partner had different strategic goals. From the beginning, the goals of the Chinese partners were linked to the goal of their government. China's strategic goals were to validate and promote its open door policy and curb the suspicions of the West. China saw its new policy as a vehicle for modernization. Despite its abundant coal supplies, China lacked the capital and technology needed to exploit it. It sensed that the United States possessed the necessary advanced technology and abundant capital. Courting American investment was of strategic importance. On the other hand, OPC was experiencing a slowdown in earnings and viewed the joint venture as a new avenue for foreign exploration and production that ultimately would lead to growth in sales and earnings. This fundamental difference eventually led OPC to make promises that were undeliverable. Driven by grand illusions of future profits, OPC began making extravagant promises before a feasibility study had even been launched. When these promises proved to be undeliverable, the degree of trust and cooperation on the part of the Chinese diminished. As disputes arose and the venture began showing signs of inevitable failure, the government intervened to enforce a solution. The political leadership of China could not afford to lose face by letting its open door flagship venture fail.

Other clashes arose on the operations and production side of the venture. The Americans wanted to reduce the production of high-sulfur coal, which could only be sold on China's domestic market and for local currency. They wanted to increase the production of low-sulfur coal for the export market. However, at that time world coal prices were falling and the Chinese insisted on decreasing production of low-sulfur coal due to the shrinking export market. They claimed that the continued production of export coal would only result in large inventories and increased costs. Disagreements like these fueled the fire that would eventually incinerate the venture.

The country-specific factors that helped initiate the joint venture entry mode were market demand and government policy. Occidental saw the Antaibao joint venture as a great opportunity for entering a new market and expanding its revenues. The demand for coal in China was extremely high. Of the various energy resources, coal was the most important. Three-quarters of the country's energy demand was met by coal. Furthermore, Occidental's CEO had a good relationship with China's political leadership. The strong central government led Hammer to believe that he could count on essential support in terms of infrastructure. This connection with the central government, in theory, should have helped alleviate some of the international obstacles that arose. In the end, however, central planning had devolved to the extent that the Antaibao project faced bureaucratic anarchy, and the help Hammer had hoped for proved less effective.

Industry-specific factors were also significant in influencing the selection of the joint venture mode. In the coal industry, entry barriers such as high capital costs probably helped encourage the partnership. The risk of uncertainty is also reduced when partners are added. The joint venture helped China obtain the capital resources and technology it needed to conduct more efficient mining operations. The benefit to Occidental was that the uncertainty of operating in China could be transferred to its partners.

Initially, there seemed to be many advantages to the joint venture mode. Occidental would benefit from the knowledge of its local partners and the support of the government. It could expand its presence into China and increase its profits. It could obtain a first-mover advantage in a country that was traditionally isolationist. The Chinese coalition in return would receive U.S. mining technology and capital resources to help modernize their country. Finally, the joint venture would validate China's open door policy.

Unforeseen were the intricate problems associated with joint ventures and doing business in China. The partners were unable to build lasting trust. Occidental never really understood the concept of *guanxi,* which was prevalent in China. Although Hammer had established strong *guanxi* with the central government, he failed to develop close *guanxi* relations with his local partners. The provincial authorities also set up obstacles. Instead of working together, all sides blamed the others for the problems that arose. In fact, many OPC officials believed that the Chinese partners had deliberately exacerbated the problems.

The Antaibao joint venture was obviously not successful. Although the agreement seemed likely to benefit all parties, it failed because it lacked a fundamental structure for success. The strategic goals of the partners were not aligned. Each partner, blinded by personal goals, refused to make concessions for the betterment of the venture. A joint venture's success is highly dependent on common or complementary goals. If there are large variances in the strategic goals of the partners, there will be more potential for problems.

Mini-case 4: Otis's Experience in China

Otis Elevator, a wholly owned subsidiary of United Technologies Corp., is the world's largest manufacturer and servicer of elevators, escalators, moving walkways, and shuttle systems. These products are quite profitable in China, which has the world's largest elevator market. Otis Elevator has captured a notable 25 percent of this market and expects growth to continue.

The Chinese market for elevators, escalators, and other equipment (moving a potential 1.2 billion people a day) is enormous. Just a few years ago, experts claimed that China's elevator market could easily increase by more than 10 percent per year until the turn of the century. The Chinese market is therefore large enough to accommodate all of the world's elevator manufacturers. Considering the vastness of the market, the 25 percent market share that Otis possesses is overwhelming. Its presence in the market is so predominant that its two most threatening competitors, Schindler and Mitsubishi, share only another 25 percent, making the market oligopolistic. Aside from these two, Otis leads 123 registered elevator manufacturers in China, the majority of them holding only single-digit percentages of the market. Although Otis dominates the industry, it has not become complacent or allowed production and morale to diminish. It remains focused on product innovation.

In 1982, Otis was granted approval by the Chinese government to begin operations in China. The Chinese government was pleased by Otis Elevator's presence because it believed that additional competitors to China-Schindler Elevators would promote competition in the elevator business, which would ultimately increase quality and efficiency. In 1984, Otis entered into a partnership with the Tianjin Lift Co. and China International Trust and Investment Corporation (CITIC) and set up its first operation in Tianjin. This partnership not only manufactures a full range of products but uses its extensive distribution network to install and service these products throughout the country.

Otis's second joint venture in China, the Beijing Otis Elevator Co., Ltd. (BOEC), was formed in 1992. This partnership between Otis and the Beijing Equipment Installation Engineering Co. installs, services, and modernizes elevators and escalators in the Beijing area. Also in 1992 the Guangzhou Otis Elevator Co., Ltd. (GOEC), was formed to capture the increasingly important southern market. In 1993, Otis established the Shanghai Otis Elevator Co., Ltd. (SOEC), the first foreign joint venture elevator company in Pudong. It is a partnership between Otis, CTOEC, and the Shanghai SITICO Enterprises Co., Ltd. Prior to making any foreign direct investments in China, Otis set up branch offices to study the factors involved. Establishing local branch offices allowed it to establish a presence in the local market without having to commit to it. As of now, there are 35 branch offices throughout China.

In the early 1980s, China's population was rapidly growing and the cities were severely overcrowded. The Chinese government and Otis Elevator realized that skyscrapers would be needed in the near future. Therefore, there were plenty of opportunities for companies like Otis to make a higher return on investment. The government, seeing the advantages of an open market, encouraged competition within the industry.

The cultural differences between the United States and China are vast. Chinese managers have been trained to produce and manufacture products efficiently but not to maximize profits. Government policies protect the interests of Chinese firms, and privatization and foreign ownership are controlled. Overall, the risk of doing business in China was high at the time Otis entered the market because the Chinese political system had just recently permitted foreign direct investment. There were many uncertainties about the role the government would play.

Firm-specific factors included Otis Elevator's prior business experience in China. It did not, however, have any joint venture experience. Project-specific factors depend on the location of the investment and the needs of the market, which determine such things as project size. The Tianjin joint venture had an initial investment of $5 million dollars. Industry-specific factors included entry barriers, competition, structural uncertainty, and relations with suppliers and buyers. At the time Otis entered the market, the Schindler Elevator Co. of Switzerland was the only major competitor. There was no fierce competition for small projects, however, because demand was much greater than supply. Since the government wanted new competitors in the elevator business, there were little or no entry barriers. After Otis entered the market, buyers benefited from having more choices. The relationship with suppliers depends on the bargaining power of local partners. Otis's partner, the Tianjin Lift Co., is a major firm that has established a rapport with local suppliers. Therefore, Otis did not need to worry about supplier reliability. As a result of analyzing these factors and previous success stories, Otis chose to form equity joint ventures with local companies. This strategy allows Otis Elevator to assemble, manufacture, and service elevators in the local market. The Tianjin Otis Co. has two local partners, the Tianjin Lift Co. and CITIC. Otis Elevator sought a partner that had the capability to manufacture high-quality elevators and escalators. The Tianjin Lift Co. was willing and able to provide labor, equipment, infrastructure, and capital. It also shared a common interest with

Otis in wanting to dominate the elevator business. Its management was willing to adopt Otis Elevator's management style while Otis agreed to provide training for Tianjin workers to raise their technological skills. Similarly, Otis invested $2 million in building a training facility in Guangzhou. The partners in the Guangzhou Otis Elevator Co. are Otis Elevator and the Guangzhou Nanfang Elevator Factory, which is a lift manufacturer operating under the Guangzhou Bureau of Mechanical and Electrical Industry.

CHAPTER 6

Equity Ownership: Factors and Decisions

Equity ownership, a sharing arrangement, is an inseparable decision from entry mode selection and a subchoice of every cooperation-based entry mode option. This decision has critical implications in risk sharing, resource allocation, knowledge commitment, environment vulnerability, strategic flexibility, and organizational control. This chapter addresses the importance of equity ownership and various factors, both internal and external, that affect the equity ownership decision. The relationship between equity ownership and joint venture control is also illuminated. The final two sections present the results of a survey recently conducted in China and several mini-case examples.

The Importance of Equity Ownership

An equity ownership arrangement concerns the equity distribution and ownership structure established by partners in a joint venture (JV). It specifies the proportion of each partner's investment and in most instances the profit remittance from the venture. Equity sharing is an important aspect of investment since it is closely tied to the firm's core competency contributions, control over subsidiaries, bargaining power with local partners, globally integrated synergy, and parent-subsidiary relations.

Value-generating assets increasingly include created (e.g., human capital) rather than natural assets. Most of these created assets are intangible and ownership specific, and they often constitute the major contribution brought by one party to a joint venture. Under these conditions, the equity distribution within a JV is critical, particularly when the partner firms are pooling core competencies in the venture. Equity distribution can also affect the ability and propensity of a JV to influence environmental factors.

A JV's relative strength within an interdependent, multinational network can reduce its vulnerability to host government intervention.

135

The reverse is also true. That is, the higher the degree of dependence of the venture on local relationships the more the venture will be prone to political or other contextual risks. In general, if a JV's interaction with the local environment is high, the parent should decentralize power and disperse more resources to the venture. Conversely, since the foreign partner's control over local operations is positively related to its equity status, higher ownership will lead to a lower degree of dependence on local relationships. As a result, it is likely that the greater the portion of equity owned by foreign investors the lower the risks and uncertainty assumed by their JVs will be.

Although large MNCs are likely to be able to bear more risk, empirical evidence indicates that the willingness of American firms to commit equity in a foreign market is inversely related to the perception of uncertainty of doing business in the host country (Stopford and Wells 1972; Gatignon and Anderson 1988). However, allowing an indigenous partner to assume a larger share of a JV not only implies potentially lower switching costs but ties the interest of the partner to that of the foreign venture. To the extent that transactional relationships cannot be separated from contextual ones, the structure of a sharing arrangement that shifts the economic interests of the party to the venture lowers contextual as well as transactional uncertainty and risk.

The equity ownership arrangement can be structured in such a way as to shift more of the contextual risk of the venture to the local partner, thereby reducing its propensity to influence changes that might benefit itself to the detriment of the joint venture or the parent itself. Although having a larger share may also allow one partner to extract benefits from the venture, a minority partner can keep and exercise control by carefully structuring the joint venture operations.

When entering China, foreign investors are sometimes able to exercise even greater control than their equity levels would suggest. This is due to the nature of their contributions (e.g., advanced technology) and more sophisticated knowledge of control mechanisms. Control that results from competency and managerial efficiency may lead to greater effectiveness than would be the case elsewhere.

The possession of key resources by one partner in a JV can make the other parties involved dependent on that partner. An entity that has the option to either contribute or withhold a key resource or input has greater bargaining leverage. This is especially important if the resource is irreplaceable or nonsubstitutable in nature. The partner controlling the resource will have more potential partners to choose from than the partner without that resource. The partner that lacks resources will be in a subordinate position during JV negotiations. Equity ownership is therefore unlikely to be symmetrical in the event of a dominant partner.

Bargaining power can also be derived from pressures to cooperate, available resources, commitment, and the strengths and weaknesses of each partner. In JV negotiations, the partner with the greatest bargaining power will generally achieve the highest level of control, which will later allow that partner to dictate the activities of the JV and hence achieve its own objectives. Goal attainment during the JV negotiation process can therefore be gauged in terms of achievement of control. These kinds of JV ownership can be identified for an individual firm using equity share as a proxy for control: majority ownership, minority ownership, and split-over ownership (50 percent each in the case of two partners).

Equity distribution determines ownership structure and the relationship among venture partners. A majority equity holding means that that partner has more at stake in the venture than the others. Normally, the equity position will be associated with an equivalent level of management control in the venture. In other words, control based upon equity ownership is often direct and effective. The correspondence between holding equity and managerial control is not always exact. It is possible for a partner to have a small equity holding but exercise decisive control. Usually, however, management control reflects ownership, especially in the international context.

When both partners want to be majority equity holders, sharing arrangements often end up equally split. A fifty-fifty ownership split ensures that neither partner's interests will be quashed. It best captures the spirit of partnership and is particularly desirable in high-technology joint ventures as insurance that both partners will remain involved with the venture's technological development. Equally distributed ownership is the only way to ensure that top managers from each parent firm will stay interested enough to avert problems in the venture.

Because a fifty-fifty equity-sharing arrangement ensures equal commitment from each partner, decision making must be based on consensus. This often results in a prolonged decision-making process that can lead to deadlock. The success of fifty-fifty equity ventures relies strongly on the synergy between partners over issues ranging from strategic analyses to daily management of the venture. It is important that partners speak a common language, have similar background knowledge, and share a set of short- and long-term objectives. By contrast, partners coming from diverse market environments with different business backgrounds and conflicting goals often have a hard time making a fifty-fifty venture a success. A fifty-fifty equity share is more likely to lead to problems in the internal management of the venture when it is necessary to carry out tasks about which the partners do not fully agree. Leadership and coordination systems in general become difficult.

The issue of which pattern of ownership best ensures joint venture success has been a puzzle to academics and practitioners alike. Instead of arguing for one type of ownership, it seems to me that the success of equity ownership and JV relationships is not a simple, linear linkage. Rather, it is a complex, nonlinear association in which many factors may affect either JV ownership and success or moderate their linkage. By the same token, it is difficult to judge whether or not majority ownership outperforms the other options. Sometimes the question itself does not even make sense. Different MNCs attach varying importance to the equity ownership level in JVs depending upon their strategic goals, integration requirements, resource dependence, firm experience, and alternatives for bargaining power, to name just a few factors. A firm that does not care about equity level because it has many other alternatives for gaining bargaining power and JV control cannot be analyzed in terms of equity-performance relations.

Recognizing this complexity, I suggest a few approaches to understanding the equity-performance relationship. First, it should be understood that negotiating an appropriate sharing arrangement is an important investment strategy in international expansion. No matter how different this factor is to individual MNCs, it is certainly one of the primary sources of bargaining power, a prominent control mechanism, and a predominant force protecting the firm's proprietary knowledge and strategic resources. As such, the critical nature of sharing arrangements should not be underestimated. At the same time, sharing arrangements are not universally important. Both their antecedents and their implications are heterogeneous among different international firms. This heterogeneity stems from internal goals, capabilities, and strategies as well as external contingencies such as different environments, industries, and partners. Finally, the sharing arrangement is not the only contributing factor in bargaining power and managerial control. Of all the control choices available to a firm, it is important to opt for those that will provide most benefits and, even more importantly, combine them effectively in order to earn the maximum rents at the lowest cost. In addition, each firm should properly assess the importance of the sharing arrangement to the firm. For this purpose, it must analyze the relevant antecedents and expected effects of such arrangements.

Strategic Factors Affecting Equity Ownership

Broadly, factors influencing an MNC's choice of equity ownership in JVs in China include strategic (internal) antecedents and environmental (external) contingencies. In today's world economy, organizationally embedded strategic assets have become increasingly critical to the accomplishment of sustained competitive advantages as they affect both rent generation and new resource creation. Strategic assets are imperative to success in the Chinese market, largely determining the ability to achieve a competitive position and true market power there. An MNC's possession of strategic assets can also make a Chinese partner more dependent on it. An entity that has the option to either contribute or withhold a key asset has greater bargaining leverage. Equity sharing is of the utmost importance in protecting those strategic assets that are contributed to a Chinese venture.

When a sharing arrangement is structured to reduce transaction costs and accrue economic benefits by protecting or utilizing a firm's strategic assets, strategic antecedents become its exogenous determinants. Strategic antecedents generally refer to firm-level factors that significantly influence the attainment of strategic goals in the course of allocating and utilizing geographically dispersed yet globally integrated strategic assets. Among these factors, proprietary knowledge protection, strategic and market orientations, product or market breadth, global integration, and the strategic objective itself can affect the extent to which an MNC depends upon or interacts with the host environment of its JV. A firm's vulnerability and exposure to the Chinese market environment are usually increasingly important functions of this dependence. As an important vehicle for manipulating risk propensity and controlling contextual and contractual variations, equity sharing becomes the governance mechanism linking strategic antecedents and risk control. These antecedents affect the optimal level of equity share, which in turn controls the transaction hazards that result from interpartner conflicts or external contingencies.

The governance structure, including equity share, is significantly influenced by the desired use of strategic assets. Strategic assets essential to the rent-earning potential of resources in the compound asset bundle have a major impact on sharing arrangements and other entry strategies. More embedded, diffuse resources result in greater use of internal control over transactions and dominant control over equity distribution. Protecting such resources and implementing operational strategies are moderated by an MNC's bargaining power vis-à-vis its Chinese partner. A partner with greater bargaining power will generally achieve a higher level of JV control, which will eventually allow that partner to dictate JV activities and achieve its own objectives. As equity sharing is a source of this power, it can serve to enable an MNC to smoothly implement policies relating to strategic factors.

Strategic Orientation

In order to monitor JV operations in China, MNCs are becoming increasingly reliant on strategic orientations, which serve to balance global integration and local responsiveness. By controlling the *proactiveness* of JV, an MNC can manipulate a venture's economic exposure and operational vulnerabilities to the environmental dynamics in China, adjust its market effectiveness or cost efficiency, and manage its innovativeness and adaptability to the host environment. As investment commitment and resource inputs are increasing functions of proactiveness, a more proactive JV implies a greater necessity for a high equity share. This arrangement helps the MNC protect the distinctive competencies it contributes to the venture and ensures that they will be used effectively to pursue maximum compensation. A highly proactive orientation necessitates a competitive strategy that includes superior process innovation, product differentiation, and market adaptability. A high equity share boosts the effectiveness and efficiency of such competitive strategies. By contrast, an MNC with a low proactive orientation may not need a dominant equity share because its rigid, noninnovative, and nonadaptive posture does not require dominant decision-making power and organizational control.

Futurity is another important dimension of strategic orientation that affects a firm's ongoing commitment to long-term cooperation and its propensity to take risks. When an MNC seeks longer futurity for its Chinese JV, the venture will be seen as more strategically important. Its stakes and payoffs become more dependent upon the JV's profitability and stability. This in turn requires a greater equity share to ensure that the MNC can control operations and management. Thus, the desired focus on the future may be linked to equity sharing in the same direction. Moreover, as high futurity implies an expected long haul, often targeting competitive position and market power in the Chinese market, MNCs seeking high futurity must constantly commit distinctive resources to the venture. This requires high profit sharing, and hence high equity ownership, to compensate for the MNC's continuous investment and longitudinal contributions.

Market Orientation

JVs can pursue economic benefits from either the host or export markets. Unlike the export market, with which an MNC is often globally integrated, a host Chinese market is often more volatile, complex, and unpredictable. Because MNCs focused on the Chinese market rigorously interact with and rely upon external forces in the industrial, macroeconomic, and sociopolitical environments, they are more vulnerable to environmental contingencies than are MNCs operating an in export market. When an MNC targets globally coordinated export channels, it is not imperative to have a dominant equity share in its JV since global coordination systems safeguard transactions from internal or external uncertainties. When an MNC aims at a host Chinese market, however, a high level of equity share is necessary so as to engender organizational control over venture activities, which in turn helps mitigate contractual hazards derived from interpartner conflict or contextual dynamics. In addition, MNC managers are generally less knowledgeable about indigenous economies than export markets, thus intensifying their reliance on equity sharing and accordingly demanding greater equity control. Finally, firms with different market orientations have different perceptions of the importance of JV operations, leading to varying needs for equity control. Financial returns are generally more important to MNCs focused on the host market than to export-focused investors since the latter can generate additional economic benefits that the former cannot secure (e.g., financial and operational synergies from vertical integration or transfer pricing). Thus, equity share will be positively related to a host market orientation but inversely associated with an export orientation.

Knowledge Protection

Protecting a firm's proprietary competencies (technology, know-how, brand names, trademarks, copyrights, patents, etc.) without leakage to the partner or other local businesses constitutes one of the predominant managerial requirements for venture success. Sharing arrangements are major control mechanisms safeguarding a firm's proprietary assets and knowledge. A high equity share increases an MNC's ownership control, which is manifested in either overall or specific controls over JV operations and management. Everything else being constant, a higher equity control will better protect a firm's tacit knowledge and strategic resources. Equity control also fosters the attainment of economic benefits earned by gaining proprietary knowledge through a strong competitive position, great bargaining power, or high profit sharing. A high equity share helps ensure the best deployment of an MNC's strategic assets without giving rise to uncompensated leakage to others. The greater the tacitness of proprietary knowledge or the perceived economic rents from such knowledge the greater the need will be to maintain a high equity share. Level of equity is therefore an increasing function of the need to protect resources and knowledge.

Resource Dependence

Interpartner complementarity may arise in a specific area such as product development and process innovation or in a combination of different functions or phases in the value chain (e.g., technological skills versus marketing expertise for the same product). When an MNC greatly needs a Chinese partner's complementary resources, a dependent relationship arises. In this situation, the MNC will have less bargaining power when asking for ownership control. This suggests that a foreign firm can acquire a Chinese partner's complementary skills only at the expense of ownership control. When the importance of acquiring a local firm's tacit, complementary knowledge outweighs that of maintaining high equity control, dominant sharing arrangements are subordinated to interpartner learning. Under this circumstance, the foreign firm may accept a low equity share if the Chinese firm asks for a greater percentage of ownership. In general, an MNC seeking to tap a partner's knowledge by forming a JV does not need to maintain JV longevity and stability and finds it unnecessary to make a strong commitment, take financial risks, or maintain managerial control.

Global Integration

Equity ownership arrangements can help balance global integration with local responsiveness in China. All international expansion decisions are integral parts of an MNC's global network. Equity sharing is one of the major tools for implementing an MNC's transnational strategies, wherein both global integration and local responsiveness are needed for a diversified business. When a higher degree of global integration is demanded, greater equity ownership in a JV becomes necessary. This enables the investor to better control venture activities, hence facilitating an internalization of geographically dispersed businesses within an integrated network. If the required level of integration is low, equity share will be less significant and imperative. Low equity status may be acceptable to a firm in this situation.

Strategic Integration

Decisions about entering China must align with a firm's strategic motivations. As equity sharing is associated with risk-taking propensity and resource commitment, an MNC should structure it in such a way as to help accomplish its strategic goals without taking excessive risks. If a JV is designed to share financial risks and operational uncertainties with local firms, a low level of equity may be advisable. The MNC would not only lower its commitment and contributions, thus diversifying risks, but also create better ties with a partner seeking managerial control, thus stimulating interfirm collaboration. Therefore, an MNC pursuing risk diversification is likely to maintain a lower equity share, all other things being constant.

When an MNC intends to use a JV to bypass entry barriers to the Chinese market or gain access to scarce resources there, it may consider accepting a lower equity share. This arrangement alleviates the firm's commitment, risk taking, and contributions without hindering the market entry or resource access. When an MNC allows a local partner to dominate equity control, JV formation is often more easily ratified by the Chinese government and the venture more readily receives access to resources from the local government.

By contrast, if an MNC pursues sustained economic benefits such as long-term profitability, an enduring competitive position, and market power, it is necessary to invest tacit knowledge and distinctive resources in its local operations. In this situation, ownership control is critical. It increases profit sharing earned with the firm's contributions but also ensures an advantageous position that can protect proprietary knowledge. Because operational and managerial stabilities are fundamental to an MNC's long-term investment, a high equity share and the managerial control derived thereby can serve as stabilizing devices that will help a venture flourish over the long term according to the MNC's desired goals, plans, and strategies.

Firm Experience

When an MNC enters uncharted waters such as the Chinese market, it will be less proactive and risk taking in its commitments to local operations. This will be further reflected in its sharing arrangements. Specifically, firms will be more prudent and tactful in undertaking investment and resource dispersal to local ventures when they are unfamiliar with the dynamics of the local environment or have not yet accumulated enough culture-specific experience in the host country. When they still face the liabilities of foreignness, circumspect and evolutionary behavior is an appropriate alignment with external contingencies. As equity ownership level is positively associated with investment commitment, discreet behavior will be mirrored in a low equity percentage. Thus, it can also be expected that firm experience and environmental familiarity will be positively linked to equity level. This implies that as an MNC accumulates more China-specific experience it will increase its equity commitment to the local venture, everything else remaining constant.

Expected Investment Commitment

Expected investment commitment is often manifested in investment size, venture turnover or duration, and capital requirements. When the required commitment is high, the firm is inevitably subject to greater financial risk and economic exposure. Under these circumstances, the foreign company may be more circumspect with respect to equity contribution. Unless the company aims to launch the project at whatever cost (e.g., as in pioneering in the market as the first mover), the firm will usually opt for a low percentage of equity status when the joint venture project is extremely large, has a high capital requirement, or has a long investment turnover. This arrangement decreases the firm's resource commitment, thus reducing its financial risks and operational variabilities. Further, it may make the partner more cooperative and dedicated to the venture, as the partner has a bigger stake in the joint project.

Environmental Factors Affecting Equity Ownership

Equity ownership level is associated with the level of risk exposure as it is perceived by international managers. Equity sharing may be structured to control exposure to uncertainty and mitigate risk taking. The transaction cost implications of the degree of integration or the extent of ownership of strategic assets become increasingly complicated under uncertain conditions. When uncertainty is high, a greater degree of ownership potentially entails more switching costs should undesirable events occur. Ownership of strategic assets may deprive the owner of the flexibility needed to make a low-cost exit from a market. Therefore, firms tend to shun ownership under such conditions. Unlike the contractual risks resulting from the exposure of transaction-specific assets, which can be neutralized or mitigated through internalization of intermediate markets, uncertainty and risks embodied in the contextual environment are usually beyond the control of the firm. This also causes the firm to shy away from ownership. When operating in a foreign location, investment in assets that cannot be deployed is inevitable. When a host environment becomes risky, foreign investors are less likely to invest in such assets. This implies that MNCs favor lower levels of equity ownership as environmental risks increase.

A societal profile of a host country includes the industrial (or task) and national (or institutional) environments. Both the industrial and national environments affect the level of perceptual risks and uncertainties, thus influencing equity sharing. Industrial environment components, including customers, suppliers, and competitors, all shape the nature and intensity of competitive pressure and contextual threats, influence the input-output dynamics in local industries, and affect the resource munificence needed for venture operations. National environment components, such as regulatory, sociocultural, economic, and technological aspects, determine the variability and unpredictability of the institutional context and represent a major source of contextual risks that are difficult for JVs to control. In a dynamic Chinese environment, these environmental components become more apparent as contextual risks because of incomplete transformation about the market, ambiguous property rights systems, and uncertain and inconsistent government policies.

Local environments are characterized by both the source (components) and the nature (dimensions) of their impact on firm behavior. A few dimensions for each environmental component, such as *dynamism, complexity,* and *hostility,* can independently or interactively affect the perceptions of MNC ventures concerning uncertainty in the host Chinese market. Perceived uncertainty depends on these environmental dimensions, which then determines the nature of strategic choices such as levels of equity share. Environmental dimensions also affect a firm's ability to obtain non-equity-based managerial control over a JV, process information, and scan the environment of a local market.

Environmental Dynamism

Dynamism concerns the variability and unpredictability of environmental components. A variable environment elevates the transaction costs of doing business, the switching and exit costs of investing, and the difficulties of establishing organizational control, managerial planning, and global integration. Investors, whether foreign or local, tend to be less proactive within a variable environment. Therefore, an MNC's equity level in a Chinese JV may be inversely related to expected environmental variability. On the other hand, an unpredictable environment increases the costs of searching, scanning, interpreting, and examining information, hampers cash flow and liquidity management, and reduces the economic benefits earned from contributed resources. As a result, MNC managers perceive an unpredictable environment as having a high risk premium and great investment uncertainty. This attenuates their strategic commitments, thus mitigating the rationale of maintaining a high equity share, all other things being equal.

Environmental Complexity

Complexity refers to the diversity and heterogeneity of environmental components. A diverse, heterogeneous environment increases the liability of foreignness and poses more difficulties for firms adapting to environmental contingencies. This in turn propels the costs of doing business abroad, adaptation, and innovation. A diverse, heterogeneous environment at the industrial level may reduce economies of scale, increase the costs of sourcing, and inflate expenditures on product differentiation. At the national level, it may narrow a firm's economy of scope, rule out certain business potentials, and increase information costs. Asset specificity also increases, leading to greater transaction costs and contractual uncertainty. When a firm confronts a complex environment, it also faces more difficulties in making strategic decisions and deploying productive resources internationally. Correspondingly, the degree of social integration is generally low when an indigenous context is diverse and heterogeneous. High costs and risks and low integration attenuate the rationale for holding a high equity share, suggesting that an MNC's equity share will be an inverse function of environmental heterogeneity.

Environmental Hostility

Hostility involves the criticality and deterrence of environmental components. A more hostile environment increases the likelihood that foreign investors will shy away from that location or commit less to local projects because this will involve more risk and volatility. A hostile environment often creates not only contextual uncertainties but contractual risks. Such risks are mirrored in uncertainties occurring in resource procurement, supplier relationships, distribution arrangements, infrastructure access, government support, and interpartner cooperation. In the language of game theory, two firms in a hostile environment are likely to be more opportunistic because each player suffers from the inability to achieve the Nash equilibrium that contributes its best payoff. In response, an MNC may minimize its transaction exposure to a joint project and reduce its investment commitment to the JV, thus alleviating the need for a high equity share. When an environment is hostile, an MNC needs to commit more to the environment if it aims to reduce its vulnerability to the local context. On the other hand, more commitment implies more risk taking in such an environment, as contextual hostility often outweighs the managerial ability to control it. Risks in this situation are very difficult to diversify. This reinforces an MNC's rationale for investing with a low equity share.

Government Regulations

Finally, regulations and rules on equity ownership arrangements enacted by the Chinese government have a direct impact on a firm's choice of ownership level. These regulations and rules are normally manifested in joint venture laws, FDI policies, or industrial policies. Today more and more Chinese industries, including some previously prohibited or restricted ones (e.g., airlines, mining, insurance, and health care), have been opened up to foreign investors. However, MNCs entering these newly opened industries generally have to accept the joint venture mode and, more importantly, maintain a minority status. On the positive side, minority equity may help the MNC mitigate its vulnerability to environmental uncertainty in these industries, thus reducing its economic exposure to external contingencies. On the negative side, minority equity impedes the MNC's growth potential in these regulated industries.

Equity Ownership and Control

In general, equity ownership has a positive effect on managerial control over the Chinese JV via both direct as well as indirect paths. A direct effect occurs when equity control contributes to higher overall or specific control over the venture operations and management. This may be manifested in areas that are positively associated with equity level such as percentage of board membership, nomination of general and deputy general managers, and structural controls. An indirect effect occurs when equity ownership first leads to greater bargaining power, which in turn heightens the firm's managerial control over JV activities in China. In practice, these two effects often take place simultaneously.

Bargaining power refers to the relative influence each partner exerts over the outcome of negotiations. The main factors that influence the relative bargaining power of a JV partner include (1) the partner's control over important resources needed by the venture, (2) the relative strategic importance of the venture to the partner, (3) the availability of alternative arrangements, and (4) host government intervention.

In the business world, relative bargaining power can be measured by the key resources or core competencies contributed by partners to the joint venture. These core resources include:

1. Production machinery or equipment that is unavailable in host economies.
2. Technology or know-how that is useful for production but unobtainable in the indigenous market.
3. Prestigious technical personnel.
4. Management skills and accounting and financial management personnel.
5. Established brands, particularly those popular in international markets. These brands can also be valued as intangible assets and foreign capital contributed by foreign investors.
6. Patents, franchises, and licenses.
7. Government relations, which are particularly important to a large investment project subject to ratification by the local government.
8. Distribution channels. Foreign partners who possess international distribution channels are not only preferred by the local partner but also favored by the host government.
9. Research and development. Upgrading the products and introducing new styles, attractive packaging, fresh colors, and beautiful images are demanded due to changing purchasing habits and utility priorities.
10. Experience in international operations. Both the government and the Chinese partners often view JVs as windows to the outside world. The Chinese company may have more confidence in future cooperation when it perceives that the foreign partner has great competence in global business.

Relative bargaining power is the underlying determinant of the extent of the impact a partner is able to exert over decision making in the joint venture. The higher the relative bargaining power the greater the extent and scope of managerial control it will achieve over joint venture activities. Effective managerial control is accordingly perceived as a consequence of the bargaining process. The linkage between bargaining power and the level of cooperation or conflict between joint venture partners can be explored both directly and indirectly. The direct effect of relative bargaining power on cooperation is examined by explicitly testing the relationship between bargaining power and conflict between joint venture partners. Where relative bargaining power is equally matched, cooperation tends to be low because of deadlocks in the decision-making process. Unequal power distribution enables one party to "force" the other to cooperate. The higher the bargaining power of one partner relative to that of the other the lower the level of conflict between partners will be.

Questions of ownership and control are often complex when Chinese partners encounter significant external interventions in both ownership and control. Historical concepts of equity ownership in China do not accord with the Western model of legally protected property rights. The interests of JV owners are usually both complementary and conflictual, so they are always potentially competitive. In the case of an oligarchic ownership configuration, the actions of the large players are highly interdependent but theoretically unpredictable, just as with the behavior of a few large competitors in an oligopolistic industrial structure. This adds considerable complexity to the relationship between equity sharing and control. Further, in establishing JVs to exploit complementarity between partners the dominant firms create foundations for control that derive not from formal ownership but from the specific resources, knowledge, and skills they provide. Since these assets are within the possession of the partner firms and have intrinsic value, they amount to ownership factors. These property rights convey powers of control that may be recognized in formal contracts or exercised on an informal, noncontractual basis. The linkage between the sharing arrangement and control in Chinese JVs is thus considerably more complex than in either single monolithic firms or wholly owned subsidiaries.

Control involves the processes by which a firm influences the activities and outcomes of its members and subunits through the use of power, authority, and a wide range of mechanisms. Managerial control of JVs focuses on the degree of power a parent company has vis-à-vis key functions and decisions that are potentially important to the performance of the JV during its operations in China. It helps the parent firm ensure the most effective and efficient use of its distinctive resources or knowledge, thus optimizing the benefits of these resources. Ineffective or insufficient control over a JV limits the parent firm's ability to coordinate abilities, exploit resources, and implement strategies. Exercising control over some or all JV activities in China helps protect the firm from premature exposure of its strategies, technological core, or other proprietary components.

Control is imperative given the potential for interpartner conflict during the formation or operational stages. During the formation stage, goal heterogeneity, low trust, resource homogeneity, and ambiguous contracts are endogenous factors that intensify subsequent interfirm conflict. During the operational stage, opportunistic behavior, differences in operational policies, the emergence of local contingencies, and changes in strategic goals and plans can result in conflict that may impair the creation of expected synergies. Increasing formalization and monitoring of interpartner relations can also lead to dissent between parties struggling to maintain organizational autonomy in the face of growing interdependence. Moreover, the increase in resource transactions between foreign and Chinese partners over time implies that their domains will shift from being complementary to more similar. This increases the likelihood of territorial disputes and competition. Cooperation and stability within a JV require some form of institutionalized mechanism to control opportunism and guarantee the fair sharing of rewards.

As organizations expand overseas, increasing in both complexity and diversity, the demand for monitoring, coordinating, and integrating their activities and resources increases. When operating in a highly complex, dynamic environment such as that of China, an interfirm network tends to be more vulnerable to environmental changes and conflict between parties. Environmental change and uncertainty become a serious external threat to the venture. Such vulnerability requires special bonds between the parties if stable and honest transactions are to be sustained. Joint venture management needs to develop institutional control mechanisms because the norms of reciprocity and trust are likely to be insufficient.

Managerial control, the process and techniques by which parent firms influence JV operations and work to attain their objectives, enables a firm to reduce transaction costs that would limit a strategy's benefits. Controlling resource applications may determine actual rent extractions, and controlling leakages of proprietary knowledge prevents the uncompensated transfer of capabilities. Insufficient or ineffective control can limit the parent firm's ability to effectively coordinate activities, utilize resources, and implement strategies. JV success is a function of the fit between the parent's criteria for success and how well the parent controls activities related to these criteria.

In formal terms, ownership is the legal possession of assets. It is normally defined in terms of three fundamental rights: (1) the right to possess an asset and/or its financial value, (2) the right to exercise control over the asset, and (3) the right to information about the status of what is owned. Owners also have the right to transfer assets and receive an income or return from them. Equity has constituted the conventional concept of ownership. A full conception of ownership, applicable to JVs, incorporates equity, contractual, and noncontractual components. Equity is the most readily valued ownership component, and noncontractual inputs are the least readily valued. Equity and contractual inputs approximate task- or operational-related complementarities, while noncontractual inputs approximate partner- or cooperation-related complementarities and competencies. The equity-sharing arrangement serves as the core of this threefold distinction scheme (see table 6.1).

The control potential offered by equity share operates through the right to manage that it conveys. This right is most tangibly manifested in the appointment of members to the JV board. While the board rarely intervenes in the ongoing management of a JV, it does typically enjoy the power of final approval for major strategic and financial decisions. In reality, boards of directors find it extremely difficult to master the complexities that such decisions present. It is in any case normal to close off most, if not all, alternative options through decisions made by management well before the matter is presented to the board. Nevertheless, certain members of the board are often seen to carry particular weight, and serious attempts will be made to lobby them before a final decision is reached. The authority of these board members does not necessarily rest upon equity ownership; it may also derive from their representation of nonequity components.

Contractual ownership inputs often specify control rights in JV contracts. These rights contrast with those stemming from equity ownership in that they are specific to certain areas or items rather than of a general nature. Thus, the provision by a partner of its internationally established brand name may be accompanied by a formal agreement restricting the use of that name. Similarly, partners will often endeavor to secure contracts preventing leakage of its proprietary technology through its JV partner(s) to other firms. Contractual rights in this area can extend to specifications of who shall use and manage the technology and a schedule of royalty payments.

The exploitation of technological advantages and their combination with access either to low-cost labor or attractive new markets provide the rationale for many JVs in China. Technology is today typically the

TABLE 6.1. Ownership Components and Control

Ownership Inputs	Examples of Inputs	Control Potential
1. Equity Sharing	Equity finance, land and equipment valued as equity	Right to representation on the board Occupancy of key managerial positions
2. Contractual	Contracted inputs such as technology transfer and transfer of rights to use brand names	Control over designated areas of technology, input resources, and access to brand names, marketing channels, etc.
3. Noncontractual	Managerial competencies, training	A partner's possession of advanced management systems, training and human resources management expertise, strong organizational culture

most distinctive resource provided by a partner company to a Chinese JV and therefore carries with it the potential for exercising control. In sectors where technology is a key resource, asymmetric technological information allows technology to dominate marketing skills and financial capital. The technological superiority of Western firms in ownership is likely to provide these firms with the ability to compete successfully in the Chinese market. Proprietary technology from a parent company is one of the few factors that strongly influence the competitive position and performance of a Chinese JV.

Sharing and contractual inputs (numbers 1 and 2 of table 6.1) normally represent a need for tight control over JVs by their parents, for in these categories they risk losing equity and proprietary knowledge. Controls tighten as the value and scope of these resources increase and the intensity of resource transfer between parents and JVs rises. The strength of the controls that must be exerted depends on how much interaction is needed between the venture and the firm's other business units in order to achieve the objectives of that venture.

Number 3 in table 6.1 concerns ownership inputs provided on a *noncontractual* basis. These normally present less need for tight controls than is the case with financial, technological, or marketing inputs. By and large, these inputs are expected to be items that increase the ability of the partners and their staffs to work together effectively or develop the managerial and technical skills of the JV directly. In addition to expert authority, which derives from possessing valued technical competencies, the skills of organizing complex operations, promoting multicultural integration, nurturing trust between staff members, and promoting the indigenous learning process within the JV (as opposed to the transfer of knowledge to it) are likely, through their very results, to generate a willingness to accept the authority of the owning partner that provides them. Since such skills are directed toward the development of the JV itself, they also create a basis through which the venture may eventually secure freedom from parental control. An increase in trust, knowledge sharing, interpersonal networks, and learning capacity enables the Chinese JV to act more autonomously, especially when there are significant uncertainties and peculiarities in the Chinese competitive environment. A heavy investment in noncontractual ownership inputs is likely to be accompanied by the attempt to build a basis for cultural control through the socialization and identification process.

This discussion has shown how different categories of ownership input provide different potential control options for Chinese JV activities. This suggests that the owning partners of a JV may possess a capacity to exercise control in selected areas of its operations. The fact that technology is a dominant input in technologically intensive sectors also implies that control over that area may provide the key to overall control of the JV. Likewise, in a sector such as fast-moving consumer goods, marketing skills and brand strength are likely to be dominant inputs and hence will furnish the basis for overall control. Whether or not the potential for selective control is actually realized depends upon its recognition by the managers concerned. The continued equation of control rights with a majority equity stake inhibits this recognition. On the other hand, while control over a key nonequity input provides the potential for dominance within a Chinese JV, possession of the legal rights that stem from a majority equity holding position can obviously add to the legitimacy of that control.

Survey Results

A nationwide mail survey of general or deputy general managers representing the foreign parties in Sino-foreign equity joint ventures was undertaken by the author in China in 1997. Based on the *Directory of Foreign-Invested Industrial Enterprises* compiled by MOFTEC, and published by Economic Daily Press, Beijing, in 1996, and the *Top 22,000 Businesses in P.R.C.*, published by China International Business Investigation Co., Ltd., in 1996, I sent both English and Chinese versions of the questionnaire to 450 JVs throughout the country through an independent contractor working in China. After two rounds of reminders, there were 129 completed responses. Analysis of these sample firms suggested the following results.

First, both the proactiveness and futurity a foreign party seeks are positively associated with equity share. Strategic orientation is linked to equity share in that a more ambitious or longer term posture aligns with a higher equity share. As an increasing function of intended proactiveness and futurity, equity sharing serves as an organizational mechanism ensuring implementation of innovative, adaptive, and proactive strategies and attainment of a maximum payoff from long-term commitments.

Second, market orientation (host market versus export market) was not found to be related to equity share. In China, market orientation may be not significantly important in relation to sharing arrangements. For firms facing intervention by the local government or operating in a more hostile industry, high equity control may be necessary regardless of market orientation. Equity control remains crucial to export-oriented JVs, as they still have to rely on or interact with local suppliers, relating industries, infrastructures, and governmental authorities.

Third, an MNC's equity share is positively related to the extent to which it needs to protect its proprietary knowledge. The need for knowledge protection drives up the level of equity share, which helps safeguard them from the threat of leakage to partners and local businesses. Thus, MNCs in China are encountering a dilemma. They must balance the need to contribute proprietary knowledge as a result of increasing competition and preemptive goals and the need to protect such knowledge in an environment where the industrial and intellectual proprietary rights system is underdeveloped and poorly enforced. A sharing arrangement may act as an important managerial mechanism to alleviate this dilemma.

Fourth, an MNC's dependence on a local partner's resources, skills, and knowledge is significantly and negatively associated with equity sharing. The greater the dependence the lower the equity MNCs tend to maintain. Equity levels seem to yield to the acquisition or accumulation of a local partner's country- and firm-specific knowledge. In this regard, equity sharing is a means of implementing an MNC's primary goal in JV formation, that is, to acquire a partner firm's learning, experience, and knowledge. Although Chinese firms are generally less technologically competent than Western MNCs, they do possess distinctive resources and knowledge (e.g., possession of distribution channels or marketing expertise and knowledge about the market and policies) upon which MNCs must rely.

Fifth, global integration is an important strategic antecedent underlying equity sharing. It is positively associated with equity share at a significant level. The greater the need for global integration the higher the MNC's equity share in a JV will be. A high equity share helps an MNC ensure the internalization and integration of its JVs, as strategic goals, managerial philosophies, and corporate cultures often vary between parties.

Sixth, among three constructs of strategic intention, market entry and long-term economic benefits are significantly associated with high equity share whereas risk diversification is not. As table 6.1 shows, while the desire to obtain long-term benefits is positively related to equity share the market entry intention is negatively linked. Unlike MNCs pursuing market entry, access to local resources, or the bypassing of entry barriers, firms seeking a long-term presence in the host market attach greater importance to organizational control over JV activities and economic exposure and thus require a high equity share. Companies attempting to transcend entry barriers often have little bargaining power over local partners or indigenous governments. Thus, equity level may be subordinated to the achievement of market entry and presence. The reason why the risk-sharing objective is not related to equity sharing may lie in the possibility that risk sharing is not usually an MNC's utmost strategic concern when entering the Chinese market. When risk sharing is not the primary concern, equity sharing will be used to help fulfill other strategic goals and benefits.

Seventh, environmental complexity and hostility as these are perceived by MNC managers are found to be significantly and negatively associated with equity sharing whereas environmental dynamism has no systematic influence on the sharing arrangement. The explanation for this may reside in the fact that MNCs pursuing long-term economic benefits in China are largely unaffected by its environmental dynamism. Although an emerging market such as China's is characterized by a variable industrial and national environment, MNC missions, aims, and interests seem to be unabated when they are investing and operating there. Dynamism implies that there are market opportunities MNCs can preempt. A positive linkage between dynamism and a long-haul intention, a positive antecedent of sharing, may somewhat offset the inverse relation between dynamism and equity.

Eighth, a significant yet negative relationship between equity share and environmental complexity suggests that an MNC's sharing-arrangement behavior is influenced by the perceptual complexity of the external context. A complex industrial environment may increase contractual hazards and transaction costs, while a complex national environment may elevate information costs. Under these circumstances, MNCs tend to avoid maintaining high equity and risk. Similarly, when MNC managers perceive the environment as hostile, they may reduce transaction exposure and investment commitment by holding a low equity share.

Finally, JV size in terms of number of employees is negatively associated with equity share, whereas the capital required for a startup investment is not associated with sharing arrangements. Greater organizational size implies more risk taking and commitment, and thus it is inversely related to equity level. However, the amount of startup investment may be determined by project characteristics or government regulations; it is not necessarily related to sharing decisions.

The managerial implications of these findings can be further highlighted as follows. First, sharing arrangements are an important investment strategy in international expansion. No matter how different it is to individual MNCs, it is certainly one of the primary sources of bargaining power, a prominent control mechanism, and a predominant force protecting the firm's proprietary knowledge and strategic resources. Second, equity sharing is such a complex decision that it has to be combined with an MNC's strategic needs, resource commitment, knowledge protection, global integration, and strategic orientation. Equity sharing can be utilized to help fulfill such strategic issues. Moreover, as an important element of entry and cooperative strategies, sharing arrangements must align properly with a host environment at both industrial and national levels. Third, the criticality of equity sharing as a vehicle to control risktaking and enhance rentgeneration should not be underestimated. Equity sharing serves as a bridge connecting resource and performance, a lever adjusting economic exposure and risk propensity, a device escalating bargaining power and organizational control, and a system bolstering implementation of strategies and policies in JVs.

Mini-case Examples

Mini-case One: The Esquel Group's Experience in China

Founded in 1978, the Esquel Group is one of the world's largest cotton apparel manufacturers. The company, headquartered in Hong Kong and with more than 20 factories in Malaysia, Singapore, China, Jamaica, and Mauritius, has more than 30,000 employees. It annually produces more than 48 million garments and 24 million yards of woven and knit fabric. The company's product range features a wide variety of men's and ladies' pure cotton and chief-value cotton apparel. Strategic integration in the areas of cotton farming, spinning, weaving, knitting, dyeing, finishing, and accessory manufacturing has enabled the company to employ strict quality controls at every stage of production and respond quickly to changes in the market. The company's customers include famous fashion brands like Polo Ralph Lauren, Tommy Hilfiger, Nordstrom, Marks & Spencer, and Fila, which supply the U.S., Japanese, and European markets.

The Esquel group began investing in China in 1978. It gradually increased its holdings in the cotton textiles and manufacturing sector to its current portfolio of 12 factories, which are located primarily in the Guangdong, Jiangsu, Zhejiang, and Xinjiang Provinces. Annual output exceeds 12 million garments and 24 million yards of quality cotton fabric.

Of its six main manufacturing factories in China, the Esquel Group wholly owns three and has controlling stakes in three joint ventures. Of the three wholly owned factories, one supplies the whole group with high-quality yarn made from the world famous raw cotton of Xinjiang. The other two produce all the woven and knitted fabric needed by the garment factories. One factory, Golden Field United Textiles, Ltd., also produces garments that are mainly exported to the Japanese market, where there is no quota on textile products from China. Golden Field, the firm's first factory, was initially a joint venture between Esquel, a small cotton mill in Guangdong Province, and a Japanese textile company. This format lowered the company's risk in investment in mainland China when the Chinese government's policy was not yet stable. As it gained confidence in long-term investment in China, the company bought out the other two partners' interests one and five years later, respectively, in order to obtain full control over production. Except for the three garment factories in Jiangsu and Zhejiang Provinces, for which the company used the joint venture format in order to get a high export quota, the company wholly owns all its manufacturing facilities. This ensures high-quality products that can serve the high-priced segment of Western apparel retailers.

The company began cooperating with China immediately after it was founded in 1978 and just as China was implementing its open door policy to encourage foreign investment. At that time, the company's factories in Malaysia and Singapore were suffering from increasing labor costs. In order to avoid the risks associated with being a first mover, Esquel began with a cooperative arrangement with the Changzhou No. 1 Garment Manufacturing Co. Esquel transported fabric and accessories to the factory and got back finished garments. Having gained more confidence in the Chinese government's policy, the company made a joint venture investment in the factory in 1995 to ensure the high quality of its products. It later injected more money and gained full control over production.

Before the joint venture, the Changzhou No. 1 Garment Manufacturing Co. already had a good manufacturing facility located in Changzhou city, 165 km from Shanghai and 60 km from Zhangjiagang, another important harbor in China. Changzhou is an important industrial base in Jiangsu Province, with comparatively good infrastructure and more than 30 percent average growth in its GDP. Jiangsu Province is one of the more economically developed provinces in China, and it is particularly famous for its advanced textile industry. This has provided the joint venture company with easy access to the high-quality fabric and accessories of the area.

The other two partners in joint venture projects are the Jiangsu Garment Import and Export Co. and the Jiangsu Knitting Textiles Import and Export Co. With these two partners, the joint venture company can get much higher quotas for export to the U.S. market. Since the Esquel group holds 51 percent ownership in each of the two projects, and later increased its percentage by injecting further investment, it was assured of control over production and lowered its costs at the same time.

For a long time after Esquel's initial investment in China, all its manufactured products were exported to Western countries. China was only a manufacturing base. In 1995, Esquel decided to establish a fashion brand aimed at the huge market of 1.2 billion Chinese consumers. Initially called Shirt Stop and later PYE, the new brand took advantage of the production facilities and experience in design gained by serving the big U.S. and European fashion companies. The company used the franchise format to set up stores selling pure cotton apparel under the new brand name. Within two years, there were more than 100 PYE stores in Beijing, Shanghai, Guangzhou, Dalian, and other cities in China. However, rapid expansion exacerbated problems such as the firm's lack of retail experience, especially in marketing and inventory management. By 1998, it had lost more than a million dollars in its new retail business.

In analyzing the company's strategy, it was found that the fashion market project does have its attractions. Compared to Esquel's cotton apparel, most Chinese products are of much lower quality and unattractive design. With the emergence of more affluent consumers in China, more people are able to afford the company's higher priced products, which are still cheaper than foreign name brands. With production facilities and offices in mainland China, the company can react quickly to changes in the market and has lower transportation and management costs than outside manufacturers do. In spite of its loss, the company is still confident that it will realize long-term profitability in retailing apparel in China. It plans to open more stores in the near future.

The chairman of the Esquel Group, Margie Yang, clearly knows the importance of the *guanxi* network in conducting business in mainland China. Esquel participates actively in events supporting China's economic development and educational projects. The company donated Rmb 1 million to the Chinese government for irrigation projects in Xinjiang. It donated another million to found a high school in Guangdong Province. In August 1996, it donated another 300,000 to the provincial government of Xinjiang to support local education and 500,000 to help provide electricity to a country where the company is going to establish another cotton spinning project. In addition to donations and active cooperation with local governments, the company invites government officials and guests to visit its factories and sample its products. This effort has resulted in a very good relationship with the government, which greatly facilitates the company's business in China.

Mini-case 2: Kodak's Experience in China

Kodak is primarily engaged in developing, manufacturing, and marketing consumer and commercial imaging products, with sales in excess of $14 billion in 1997. It first entered China's market by exporting domestically produced components and importing products for domestic sales. China's photographic film market is the third largest in the world, subordinate only to those of the United States and Japan. Consumers bought over 170 million rolls of film at retail stores in 1997, representing 6 to 7 percent of worldwide film consumption. Kodak's research indicates that there is great pent-up demand for conventional photography in the $800 million Chinese photographic and paper markets. Its revenue in China approached $250 million in 1997.

Although the Chinese government put some constraints on wholly foreign owned enterprises in the early 1980s, Kodak managed to invest in two of them, the Kodak Electronic Products (Shanghai) Co. and the Kodak Photographic Equipment (Shanghai) Co. Both produce camera components for export and a small amount of photographic equipment for domestic sales. Kodak has also invested about $12 million in Xinhui KH Optical Co., a contractual joint venture between Xinhui and Guangdong that produces optical lenses. Kodak's aggressive marketing campaigns and nearly a dozen representative offices around the country have cornered around 3,700 exclusive outlets throughout China. However, as most foreign companies find, exporting and importing can be costly. Even going through the gray channels costs money. Kodak realized that it needed to lower its costs and gain better control of distribution and sales. Its next step was to establish domestic production and distribution facilities in China.

In early 1998, following more than two years of negotiations involving the ministries of Foreign Trade and Economic Cooperation, Chemicals Industry, Light Industry, Machines Industry, and the State Economic and Trade Commission, Kodak announced that it would invest more than $1 billion in China over the next several years, one of the largest investments ever made by a U.S. company. The investment will mainly be used to upgrade technology, improve manufacturing, and expand the distribution and marketing capabilities needed to build a strong domestic Chinese photo industry. Kodak strongly believes that China will one day be the world's largest photographic market. It has therefore chosen to set up both a joint share company and an umbrella company as vehicles for its investments.

Kodak has formed a company-controlled umbrella, or holding, company, the Kodak (China) Co., Ltd., and a company-controlled joint share, or limited liability, company, the Kodak (Wuxi) Co., Ltd., to produce and market color film, medical and industrial X-ray film, and other products in China and elsewhere in Asia. Based in the city of Shanghai, the Kodak (China) Co. purchased the assets of two Chinese photographic enterprises, the Shantou Era Photo Materials Industry Corp. and the Xiamen Fuda Photographic Materials Co., Ltd., both of which produce color film and paper. A third Chinese enterprise, the Wuxi Aermei Film and Chemical Corp., which is based in Wuxi city and makes medical and industrial X-ray film, transferred its primary assets to the Kodak (Wuxi) Co.

The Kodak (China) Co. will require about $385 million in capital and a $1.1 billion investment, which will be used for technical upgrading of existing equipment in Xiamen Fuda and Shantou Era. The Kodak (Wuxi) Co. will require about $45 million in capital and a total investment of $80 million, which will be used in the improvement of existing Wuxi product lines and a new project producing chemicals for film development. In addition to joint share products, Kodak is also financing the construction of a $650 million, 430,000 square meter production plant in Xiamen. This will be one of Kodak's largest production plants worldwide. It will complement the Xiamen Fuda and Shantou Era operations by producing emulsion, color film, and paper for consumer and professional use. Kodak will also invest more than $400 million to build an industrial park in East China's Fujian Province. The park, located in the Haicang Development Zone of Xiamen City, will become a major production base for Kodak film. To ensure steady growth rates in China, Kodak will also create new distribution networks and enhance its marketing activities.

Several factors can explain Kodak's entry mode selection. The new companies not only give Kodak access to a huge market, but they also demonstrate the firm's commitment to China and its willingness to share technology and managerial expertise. The companies will also provide Kodak with more flexibility. Their structure will enable foreign and Chinese investors to participate in each enterprise while at the same time providing greater operational scope and management flexibility than would be permitted by either a joint venture or a wholly foreign owned enterprise. They will also enable Kodak to operate an integrated company across tax jurisdictions, with production facilities in two provinces and its headquarters in a third. Kodak feels that the umbrella company will be free to expand its operations anywhere in China by buying up the productive assets of other state owned enterprises or establishing branch offices.

This arrangement will eliminate most of Kodak's potential competitors in China. With Xiamen Fuda, Shantou Era, and Wuxi as partners, the China Lucky Film Corp. (which now has about 7 percent of China's roll-film market) will represent Kodak's only domestic competition. Kodak also hopes that the move will give it an edge over global Japanese competitor Fuji Photo Film, which has been distributing its photographic film and paper products in China since 1980 and now has about 48 percent of the market.

During the joint share negotiations, Kodak stressed the importance of having the right company structure. It quickly identified the equity distribution, degree of management control, and corporate flexibility it would require to make its billion dollar commitment work. It now owns 80 percent of the shares in Kodak (China), with Xiamen Fuda Photographic Materials and Shantou Era Photo Materials owning 10 percent each. Kodak owns 70 percent of the shares in Kodak (Wuxi).

Kodak's strategic objectives greatly influenced its desire for control. It will be able to lead the management and operation of the companies as they manufacture, market, distribute, sell, and support Kodak brand products throughout China. Kodak's expected investment commitment also influenced its demand for a majority position. It felt that it should hold a majority of the equity since it had offered to buy three failing state-owned enterprises, build them up with cash and the latest technology, and provide employment for more than 2,000 workers.

Kodak appointed David Swift, chairman and president of Kodak's Greater China Region, to serve as chairman of both new joint share companies. Swift had previously served as vice president and chief operating officer of the Digital Product Center and has been with Kodak for many years. Having Swift chair both companies was also crucial in ensuring company control.

The board of directors for both joint share companies will be stacked with Kodak members. Kodak (China), for example, will have a board of directors consisting of 10 members, eight of whom will be appointed by Kodak. With such a large majority, Kodak will have the flexibility and control it needs to make the project a success.

Mini-case 3: Boeing's Experience in China

Over the past 80 years, Boeing has emerged as the world's largest producer of aeronautical products, including commercial aircraft, military aircraft, helicopters, missiles, rockets, the space shuttle, the space station, and satellites. Boeing has enjoyed first-mover advantages in the Chinese aircraft market. Of the 400 jetliners operating in China by 1999, 288 were built by Boeing.

China's economy is unique in that it offers varying entry modes to foreign firms. Boeing's entry into the Chinese aerospace industry has been characterized by an extensive network of working relationships and has gradually evolved from exporting to EJVs. For most firms just entering the global market, exporting is favored because it allows them to avoid the costs of establishing manufacturing operations in the host country while achieving experience curve effects and location economies. Boeing first began exporting to China in 1972 when China's flagship carrier, the Civil Aviation Administration of China (CAAC), ordered 10 707s. Boeing continues to export its aircraft to China's airlines and currently owns a 72 percent share of them.

During the late 1970s, Boeing increased its involvement with China through what is characterized as industrial cooperation. It established two BOT operations for the production of major parts and assemblies. The Xian Aircraft Co. is responsible for the coproduction of 737 vertical fins, horizontal stabilizers, forward access doors, and 747 trailing edge ribs while the Shenyang Aircraft Company oversees the production of 757 cargo doors and 737 tail sections. Overall, more than 2,900 planes currently flying worldwide include major parts and assemblies built in China.

During the 1990s, Boeing participated in several joint ventures. It invested $11 million in the Taikoo Aircraft Engineering Co. (TAECO), a joint venture with Cathay Pacific, Singapore Airlines, Japan Airlines, the Xiamen Aviation Industry Co., and the Beijing Kai Lan Technology Development Service Co. (a wholly owned subsidiary of Aviation Industries of China [AVIC]). More recently, Boeing has entered into an equity joint venture with the government-controlled AVIC and the Hexcel Corp. for the production of composite parts for commercial planes.

Finally, Boeing entered China's market through development programs. At the request of China, Boeing has provided assistance in developing China's air transportation infrastructure. With an emphasis on management skills training, improving safety, and increasing capacity, Boeing has built a spare parts center in Beijing; hosted Chinese manufacturing specialists to further industrial cooperation; provided customized training for accident investigation, piloting, and maintenance; assisted in air traffic control management training programs; helped airlines establish safety departments and programs; provided Boeing-owned simulators to China's CAAC Flying College free of charge; trained more than 2,000 pilots and mechanics; and established its Boeing Asia headquarters in China.

As Boeing's relationship with China continues to progress, the company hopes to eventually establish a wholly owned subsidiary to manufacture aircraft there. Currently, the Chinese government is opposed to such a move because it would rather gain access to Boeing's technologies and manufacturing methods.

A joint venture valued at $63 million, TAECO is managed by its majority shareholder, the Hong Kong Aircraft Engineering Co., Ltd., and specializes in Boeing 747, 737, and 757 maintenance, repair, and overhaul services. The venture had been operational for a year and a half before Boeing joined Singapore Airlines, Cathay Pacific, and Japan Airlines as an equity shareholder. Boeing's entry represented a first for the company in China. It was an effort to broaden its business into other aspects of commercial aviation such as maintenance and pilot training. TAECO was selected because of its specialization in Boeing aircraft. With Boeing's involvement, the venture will now be able to expand its range of services. In addition, all of the shareholders have ordered a total of 537 Boeing jets. Boeing's involvement thus expands its presence and network in the Chinese marketplace, giving it the advantage of exporting its planes to airlines there while providing skilled maintenance and modifications.

Boeing's entrance into the TAECO joint venture was achieved at the price of $11 million, which gave it a 9.09 percent share. The investment was a combination of new and vendor shares from existing shareholders. The majority shareholder, TAECO, now owns 41.82 percent. Cathay Pacific, Singapore Airlines, and Japan Airlines each hold a 9.09 percent share, similar to that of Boeing. Xiamen Aviation owns 13.64 percent, while the Beijing Kai Lan Technology Development Service, a wholly owned subsidiary of the aviation regulatory body CAAC, holds an 8.18 percent share.

Boeing's second joint venture, the BHA Aero Composite Parts Co., was established in 1998 after two years of negotiations. The partners in this operation are Boeing, Hexcel, and the local AVIC. All three partners have an equal equity share. Boeing has agreed to purchase the joint venture's production output (composite parts for secondary structures and interior applications for commercial aircraft) for a minimum of 20 years. Its goal is to produce composite parts for secondary structures and interior applications for commercial aircraft. A subsidiary, Boeing Commercial, is directly involved in the manufacturing of aircraft, missiles and parts, helicopters, and electronic components, including computer and software products. Its capabilities are highly compatible with those of Hexcel, a company of about 4,600 employees that acts as an international manufacturer and marketer of light, high-performance, composite materials, parts, and structures for the aerospace, defense, recreational, and general industrial markets.

Mini-case 4: Daewoo's Experience in China

Daewoo Motors has overseas production plants located in China, Vietnam, Uzbekistan, the Czech Republic, India, Iran, Poland, Egypt, and the Ukraine. Daewoo's entry into China began during the mid-1990s. It would be considered a middle or late mover due to the fact that it was not the first automotive company to enter into China. It entered China around 1997 with the previously mentioned joint ventures. It began its investments in China with some auto parts plants in and around Shandong Province, specifically in the cities of Yantai, Qingdao, and Weihai. Auto parts have become a major industry in the Yantai Development Zone.

Yantai is located at the eastern tip of Shandong Province. It borders the Yellow Sea on the south and the Bohai Sea on the north. It is an area known for its pleasant climate, with mild winters and moderate summers. This area is under the jurisdiction of a municipal government and consists of four urban districts (Zhifu, Fushan, Laishan, and Muping), five cities (Longkou, Laiyang, Laizhou, Penglai, and Zhaoyuan), and three prefectures (Qixia, Haiyang, and Changdo). The total area, about 13,506 square kilometers, is inhabited by 6.35 million people. The economy of Yantai has done well due to its position in the national market. Rather than facing stronger rivals by competing in the same industry, this area produces niche items that enjoy limited competition and strong demand.

This area boosts 30 kinds of minerals, including gold, silver, copper, iron, and marble. Yantai also produces a vast amount of agriculture products, which include wheat, corn, sweet potatoes, pears, grapes, apples, and chestnuts. Seafood is another plentiful resource of this region, which boasts prawn, fish, scallops, and abalone. Yantai has established a stable industrial base in light industries, foodstuffs, textiles, electronics, machinery, chemicals, building materials, silk, instruments, chemicals, metals, and coal. There are four main traditional industries within this region: wine, canned food, wooden-frame clocks, and padlocks. Several emerging industries include automobiles, power machinery, freezers, computers, spandex, and leather products. Air transport is available to major areas and cities throughout China, including Beijing, Shanghai, Guangzhou, Harbin, Shenzhen, Wuhan, and Shantou. Two of Yantai's eight ports, Yantai and Longkou, are open to international shipping and have a capacity of over 12 million tons. The Yantai port has nine berths that can handle cargoes of over 10,000 tons. There are also passenger liners to Tianjin and Dalian and cargo freight service to international ports in Japan, the United States, Canada, Korea, Hong Kong, Singapore, and elsewhere.

Qingdao is located on the western tip of the Shandong Peninsula. It has a maritime climate that is warm in winter and cool in summer. Qingdao is one of the most important "coastal open economy" cities in Shandong. Within this city, there is economic administrative power similar to that of a provincial government. This area is also under the jurisdiction of the municipal government, which includes seven urban districts (Shinan, Shibei, Sifang, Licang, Huangdao, Laoshan, and Chengyang) and five county-level cities (Jiaozhou, Jimo, Pingdu, Jiaonan, and Laixi). The total area comprises about 10,654 square kilometers and has a population of 6.79 million.

Qingdao was once known as the gingham city and a producer of quality beer. Today it contains large factories that produce many consumer items and garments as well as tractors, diesel locomotives, television sets, rubber tires, bicycles, and refrigerators. The leading industries in this area are textiles and garments, light industry, chemicals, machinery, and electronics. Qingdao's port has an ice-free harbor that ships large consignments of garments, yarn, cotton, and polyester fabric, leather footwear, electrical appliances, and other products to ports in over 100 countries and regions throughout the world. Its largest trade partners are Japan, South Korea, the United States, Hong Kong, Germany, and Canada.

Daewoo Motors has entered the Chinese automotive industry through joint venture distributorships. The two joint ventures are First Automotive Works–Daewoo Automotive Engines and Shandong-Daewoo Automotive Components.

The first project was FAW-Daewoo Automotive Engines in East China's Shandong Province. The first enterprise in China to produce automobiles, FAW was founded on July 15, 1953. It became one of the first "grade one" companies in the automotive industry. It achieved the top spot in the industry in volume of production, sales, and exports in 1996. Today FAW-Daewoo is China's largest sedan engine manufacturer. It went into production in October 1999 with three plants in Yantai, Weihai, and Qingdao. There was an initial investment of Rmb 5.7 billion or about $688 million. Within the three plants, there are 60 advanced production lines that manufacture more than 20 types of sedan engines. It is expected that these plants will eventually achieve a combined annual output of 300,000 engines.

The second project, the Shandong-Daewoo Auto Parts and Components Co., Ltd., is a joint venture with the Shandong Automotive

Industry Corp. It also commenced operations in October 1999 with an investment of Rmb 2.1 billion, or $254 million. The company mainly produces brake, steering, air-conditioning, and suspension systems for sedans. The annual output capacity is expected to reach 300,000 units.

Daewoo hopes that this network of Chinese and Korean companies will provide a component supply base when it opens an automobile plant in the future. There have been plans since 1998 between Daewoo and FAW to set up a joint venture car assembly plant that will be operational by the year 2000. This plant will produce Lanos models and have an annual capacity of 150,000 units. The engines and other key components are to be produced in China.

There have been plans for a car assembly plant to be running by the year 2000 with a fifty-fifty investment by FAW and Daewoo. The joint ventures of FAW and the Shandong Automotive Industry Corp. can be deduced to have either a fifty-fifty basis or a majority investment by the local company.

Mini-case 5: Peugeot's Divorce

China's automotive bureaucrats liken PSA Peugeot Citroen's troubled automobile joint venture in Guangzhou to a failed marriage: if two partners do not get along, they should separate. Although optimism pervaded the union at the outset in 1985, troubles at the Guangzhou Peugeot Automobile Corp. (GPAC) surfaced quickly and by early 1997 the French investors had decided to withdraw from the joint venture. Despite the French pullout, Guangzhou officials insist that the Chinese side will soon find a new "spouse." French enterprises interested in taking Peugeot's place in the partnership, however, would do well to heed the lessons of this failed Sino-foreign enterprise. They might also consider Guangdong's tarnished history of auto-related joint ventures, as Peugeot's decision to pull out of GPAC was as much the result of Guangdong's uneven investment environment as the company's own errors.

Start-up Missteps
Peugeot was one of the first foreign automakers to approach Guangzhou officials in the early 1980s about creating an industrial alliance. Four years of negotiations culminated in the $52 million GPAC joint venture in 1985. Peugeot held 22 percent of the company, the National Bank of Paris took 4 percent, and the International Finance Corp. held 8 percent. The PRC investors were Guangzhou Automotive Manufacturing (GAM), with 42 percent; the Guangzhou branch of the Industrial and

Commercial Bank of China, with 4 percent; and the China International Trust and Investment Corp., which held the remaining 20 percent. The 50,000-vehicle production target was to include light trucks, sedans, and station wagons.

Guangdong initially appeared to be a logical site for the new factory. The province had one of the highest standards of living in the country and extensive experience with joint venture projects. Moreover, with Guangdong far from Beijing's watchful eye, Peugeot officials anticipated a greater degree of managerial autonomy than a plant in northern China might enjoy. Local government support for the joint venture also seemed strong.

Yet these apparent advantages could not shield the Sino-French joint venture from its share of difficulties. During the setup phase, for example, Peugeot discovered that GPAC workers—formerly employed at the GAM bus and truck factory—had inadequate skills. Consequently, Peugeot had to spend more than was anticipated on both training PRC workers in Europe and sending French managers to China.

Commitments to localize parts production posed additional stumbling blocks for GPAC. Although the joint venture contract called for GPAC vehicles to reach a 90 percent Chinese content level within five years of start-up, the French partner found few suppliers of quality parts in Guangdong and was prohibited by Guangzhou officials from sourcing from other regions. Peugeot, for its part, was slow to establish joint ventures in parts manufacturing—a key to Volkswagen AG's success in Shanghai. The company thus had to assemble automobiles largely from imported parts, which proved costly when the French franc appreciated some 110 percent against the renminbi in the late 1980s. The resulting rise in the price of imported parts, together with PRC localization and consumption taxes totaling more than Rmb 45,000 ($12,000, based on the 1989 exchange rate) per vehicle, substantially raised the retail price of finished vehicles. In early 1990, for example, the company's model 505 station wagon sold for Rmb 200,000 ($54,000), while Shanghai-Volkswagen's Santana, which was subject to similar taxes, sold for Rmb 180,000 ($49,000). As a result, GPAC's growth slowed.

Stiff Competition
GPAC's troubles were aggravated by stiff competition from Shanghai Volkswagen. The Santana had achieved 75 percent local content by 1992 and thus was able to keep production costs and sales prices relatively low. Although GPAC had reached similar levels of domestic content by 1994, its least expensive station wagon cost Rmb 170,000 ($21,000), compared to Rmb 135,000 ($16,000) for the least expensive Santana model, in 1994.

Moreover, the quality of both GPAC parts and finished vehicles remained poor. Because the local government objected to sourcing from plants outside Guangzhou, GPAC was forced to use local parts that often failed to meet international standards.

Some of Peugeot's management decisions also contributed to GPAC's competitive weaknesses. The company reportedly repatriated most of its profits and made relatively few changes to its 1980 Sera products, whereas Volkswagen reinvested profits and refined its production, introducing a new Santana 2000 model in the mid-1990s. The GPAC sedan also had problems finding a market niche, as its large engine's high fuel consumption precluded the car's use as a taxi and its outdated design failed to attract Chinese buyers. Compared to the Audi 100 — made in Changchun by a joint venture between Audi AG, a subsidiary of Volkswagen, and China's First Automobile Works (Group) Corp. — the GPAC sedan lacked the prestige that status-conscious private and government consumers sought in a vehicle.

In addition, GPAC was not as high a political priority for Guangzhou officials as was the Volkswagen plant for the Shanghai government. While the Shanghai municipality invested Rmb 5 to 6 billion ($600 to $700 million) to aid Volkswagen's endeavor, Guangzhou officials only contributed about Rmb 1 billion ($120 million) to help GPAC. Further, because of Guangzhou's laissez-faire approach to production and consumption, city leaders were reluctant to urge government officials or enterprises to purchase GPAC's vehicles. In Shanghai, by contrast, the city's taxi company was one of the largest purchasers of Volkswagen Santanas. Further, in 1996 the Shanghai municipal rules on engine size for taxis effectively eliminated Volkswagen's competitor in the city, the Tianjin Charade, from the taxi business. Ironically, while GPAC's remoteness from Beijing protected it from central government interference, the southern China venture did not rank high on Beijing's planning agenda. The lack of a central government partner meant that PRC leaders would do little to forestall the joint venture's decline.

Pulling Out

In 1989, one Peugeot official noted, with what now seems painful intuition, "If we had to make the decision to come to China over again, knowing what we know, we wouldn't come." Even a rise in the production of cars and light trucks from about 2,700 in 1987 to a peak of 22,500 in 1992 did not renew French officials' hopes for success. By 1994, production had begun to falter and the venture fell into the red. That year, GPAC produced only 4,485 sedans and station wagons and 1,241 trucks, and the company recorded losses of Rmb 100 to 200

million ($12 to $24 million). Although production during 1995 re-
bounded to roughly 8,000 cars and trucks, GPAC's losses rose to Rmb
320 million ($39 million). Shanghai-Volkswagen's 1995 profits, on the
other hand, reached Rmb 2 billion ($240 million). In 1996, GPAC
manufactured only 2,400 vehicles, and Guangdong officials estimate
that production will not reach 1,000 units in 1997.

Although Peugeot decided in February 1998 to withdraw from
GPAC, the joint venture has not proven a complete failure for the two
sides. Peugeot exported thousands of car kits and parts to Guangzhou
from France, amassing profits for the home company. The venture imparted valuable lessons that Peugeot can incorporate into the operating
plan for its venture in Hubei Province, which continues to produce
Citroen vehicles. And the Guangdong and Guangzhou authorities are
sure to consider the lessons of GPAC as they press ahead with efforts to
strengthen the automobile sector in the province.

Indeed, neither Peugeot's withdrawal from GPAC nor Guangdong's uneven history in auto production has diminished foreign investors' appetite for building cars in the province. Peugeot's pullout created
a vacuum for foreign manufacturers seeking a share of China's automobile market. These included Daimler-Benz, General Motors, Opel,
Honda, and Hyundai. Although Beijing is promoting Changchun in Jilin
Province, Shanghai, and the Wuhan-Shiyan region in Hubei Province as
future automobile production centers and the Ninth Five Year Plan
(1996–2000) does not identify new sites in China for such production,
Guangzhou remains on foreign investors' lists as a potential investment
location. In addition, PRC import tariffs on finished sedans of 80 to 100
percent of the import price will continue to act as an incentive for
foreign companies to establish China-based production facilities rather
than merely export to the PRC. And Hong Kong's closer integration
with the Guangdong economy could spur further growth in the region,
prompting an increase in automobile sales.

In May 1997, Guangzhou officials seriously considered Opel's proposal to fill the vacancy left by Peugeot but cautioned that the city and
Opel were only "dating" and that observers should "wait for them to
announce their marriage." With backing from General Motors, Opel
possesses the financial might to sustain a program of factory modernization and the production of a late-model vehicle. Opel also could draw on
its prior experience marketing Corsa and Astra models in Latin America
and Eastern Europe. Should Guangzhou permit parts to be imported
from outside the region, Opel would be able to tap the 14 Delphi Automotive Systems parts makers scattered throughout China's coastal region to
meet local parts requirements. General Motors' plan to manufacture

Buicks in Shanghai could also provide an opportunity for Opel to further expand its parts-sourcing base.

An Uneven Track Record

Peugeot's automotive venture was not the first to go sour in Guangdong. In 1989, Huizhou officials welcomed the Korean-American representatives of Panda Motors, which promised to inject $1 billion into a plant in the coastal city to build cars for export. But Panda lacked any experience in making cars and appeared to be a front for the Unification Church, which evidently was using the venture to gain a foothold in China. In 1996, having failed to produce a single car, the venture held an official closing ceremony.

In 1995, Germany's Mercedes-Benz AG, a division of Daimler-Benz, signed an agreement to produce minivans in the western Guangdong city of Zhanjiang and engines in the island province of Hainan. The projected combined investment for the venture totaled nearly 5.6 billion yuan. Daimler-Benz held a 45 percent stake, and production capacity was scheduled to reach 60,000 vehicles and 100,000 engines by 1998. The project's viability is presently in question, however. Reportedly, Chinese officials have insisted that the German company guarantee a return on the investment and lower production costs. The German company is seeking solutions to keep the venture on track.

Unapproved though locally supported production facilities have further plagued the development of the automobile market in Guangdong. These small plants assemble cars from kits that are imported, sometimes illegally, from a variety of Western manufacturers and realize quick profits. By the mid-1990s, 70 or 80 such facilities existed in Guangdong, with most making fewer than 100 vehicles per year. Although the provincial government opposes such activities and claims that many plants have been closed, several factories continue to assemble and sell late-model Western cars, trucks, and related parts in Guangdong, which constitutes about 10 percent of China's total automobile market.

Discerning which way the political winds are blowing for the auto sector in Guangdong is proving difficult. In March 1997, Guangdong governor Lu Ruihua declared that automobiles would no longer be considered a "pillar" of the provincial economy. Lu also noted that Guangdong is better known for its light industries and should base its continued growth on consumer electronics, housing, textiles, and similar sectors. Guangdong auto officials, however, cautioned that Lu's declaration regarding pillar status for automobiles was targeted at the uncontrolled independent assemblers and was not to be misinterpreted as the province's withdrawal of support for large, officially sanctioned projects in the sector. Officials in Beijing's Ministry of Machine-Building Industry also pointed out that there has been little change of late in Guangdong's automobile investment patterns.

The troubled past for the automobile industry in Guangdong raises doubts about whether any of the potential suitors for its factory are likely to find happiness in a joint venture marriage. Parts procurement would have to expand beyond Guangzhou's boundaries for any other manufacturer to succeed. More problematic, however, is the current dominance of the Santana. Nevertheless, possessing significant financial reserves, a commitment to quality, and instant access to domestic parts to build a late-model vehicle might be the keys to success in China's large, protected market. And, of course, potential entrants now have the benefit of GPAC's experience from which to learn.

(Adapted from Eric Harwit, "Guangzhou Peugeot: Portrait of a Commercial Divorce," *China Business Review* [November–December 1997]: 10–11.)

PART 3
Entering and Operating in China
Case Studies

Nokia

Nokia is the world's largest mobile phone manufacturer and the leading supplier of digital mobile and fixed networks. It also supplies multimedia equipment, satellite and cable receivers, computer monitors, and other telecommunications products. Based in Finland and headed by President and CEO Jorma Ollila, the Nokia Group is composed of five main divisions: Nokia Telecommunications, Nokia Mobile Phones, Nokia Multimedia Network Terminals, Nokia Industrial Electronics, and the Nokia Research Center. It also has an additional division, the Nokia Ventures Organization.

Nokia's stock price as of November 30, 1998, was U.S. $95.00, as listed on five European stock exchanges and the New York Stock Exchange. In 1998, Nokia's net sales from 130 countries grew by 34 percent to a total of $9.8 billion. It sold more than 21.3 million mobile phones, capturing a global market share in excess of 21 percent. In its third quarterly report of 1999, its net sales totaled 20 million Finnish marks ($12.4 million), an increase of 62 percent.

In 1865, a Finnish man named Fredrik Idestam founded the Nokia Corp. as a forestry enterprise that grew to become one of Europe's largest tissue manufacturers. Nokia's neighbor, the Finnish Rubber Works, produced rubber bands, industrial parts, raincoats, rugs, balls, tires, and galoshes. In 1922, the Finnish Rubber Works bought a cable company, the Finnish Cable Works. In 1967, these three companies were merged to form the Nokia Group, with Bjorn Westerlund supervising 460 employees. Shortly thereafter, Nokia began developing commercial products such as telephones along with infrastructure products. By the 1980s, Nokia had become Europe's third-largest television manufacturer and the largest information technology company in the Nordic region.

During the early 1990s, Nokia decided to focus on telecommunications. When the cellular boom hit the market, it was the first company to deliver the total Global System for Mobile Communication (GSM) system, including both telephones and telecommunications infrastructure. Today, Nokia's core business has evolved into development, manufacturing, and delivery of operator-driven infrastructure solutions and end-user mobile phones and other terminals. It has facilities in more than 45 countries and research and development centers on four continents. It now has more than 42,000 employees worldwide.

The Asia-Pacific region accounts for 23 percent of Nokia's market, with China the third-largest market after the United States and the United Kingdom. Thanks to successful investments in the GSM network system, Nokia was able to sign on with the Shanghai Post and Telecommunications Authority in China. This was its biggest expansion agreement in 1997. Nokia entered China in the early 1980s. In October 1994, the first official GSM call in China was made by Post and Telecommunications minister Wu Jichuan, using a phone and a network both delivered by Nokia. As the popularity of GSM networks continues to increase in China, the delivered subscriber line capacity on Nokia's GSM 900 and GSM 1800 networks there has broken the 10 million barrier. Nokia is also the first and only telecommunications company in China to have large-scale manufacturing facilities for complete GSM infrastructure, Nokia DX200 mobile switching centers, base stations, base station controllers, operation and maintenance centers, voice mail systems, and cellular transmission equipment. Nokia also provides implementation services and training to local units such as the Yunnan Post and Telecommunications Administration. It has established a research facility in Beijing that focuses on applying the latest technology to products and solutions for the Chinese market. The unit also cooperates with the Chinese research and development community in order to provide input on China's requirements for global projects. Nokia's 1997 interim report continued to highlight the importance of the Asia-Pacific market and consumer demand for mobile phones.

External Environment

Nokia has little to fear from new competitors because of high entry barriers and start-up costs for new companies. Its major existing competitors in China are Motorola and Ericcson. Despite much rivalry among existing telecommunications firms, Nokia holds a very strong position because it is the only company to have a large GSM manufacturing facility in China. Most of China runs on the GSM network, so Nokia is dominant in this area. In order for companies like Qualcomm, a U.S. based telecommunications company, to enter China, they would have to convince Chinese regulators to switch to systems such as the Code Division Multiple Access network. Qualcomm has accused both Nokia and Ericcson of scaring Beijing into sticking with GSM by claiming that the

CDMA network would complicate the industry. Currently, 20 million mobile phone users in China use the GSM network. If users were to switch to phones that use the CDMA network, they would only be able to use their phones in limited areas. For this reason, customer loyalty is very high. It also means that buyer bargaining power is low.

The telecommunications industry in China is tightly controlled. Foreign companies are barred from owning or operating telecommunications networks there. To break into the industry and expand its GSM network, Nokia had to sign agreements with various Chinese companies. It now supplies them with the GSM network. Therefore, telecommunications companies such as Qualcomm would also have to persuade Chinese telecommunications companies to switch to the CDMA network.

The bargaining power of suppliers is high, as a few large companies dominate the telecommunications market in China. Satisfactory substitutes are not available, although if Beijing ever decides to switch to a CDMA network the risk of substitutes would increase.

China is currently in a period of deflation. Corporations are cutting costs to keep up with falling prices. China's policy concerning deflation is to maintain its current exchange rate. Officials feel that this move will reinflate the economy. In order to accomplish this, China needs to maintain a growth rate of about 8 percent. This economic problem will affect Nokia because it may have to lower the price of its products in order to maintain growth.

In addition to strong market demand, related industries are supportive and can help Nokia gain a competitive advantage. Nokia creates relationships with companies that are already established in Chinese industry. For example, it has contracted with Cellstar, a wholesaler and retailer of wireless phones and communications products, to distribute Nokia cellular phones and accessories. Cellstar is a wholly foreign owned entity with franchise stores throughout China. Nokia also creates relationships with domestic companies to manufacture infrastructure equipment and mobile phones and accessories.

The electricity industry also supports Nokia's telecommunications and information infrastructure. Electricity prices in China vary greatly depending on geographic location. Recently, however, the director of the State Development Planning Commission's Pricing Department stated that China will delete 560 different fees that local governments have been levying on electricity. This will increase demand for technology that relies on electricity such as the use of the Internet, e-mail, electric data interchange, and so on.

The government takes steps to protect its domestic companies. These include entry barriers, project ratification, and entry modes. The entry barriers set up by the Chinese government were high when Nokia entered the market. This contributed to low competition. Project ratification means that certain industrial groups or sectors are encouraged by the government while others are discouraged. Industries using high technology are greatly encouraged while those that cause pollution are prohibited. Some ventures are restricted, including those involving facsimiles, photocopying, video recording, and television. Nokia is in an industry that has been encouraged by the government despite initial high entry barriers. This business also enjoys the advantage of not being restricted to specific geographic locations.

Internal Environment

Financial

Nokia is in the growth stage of its life cycle. In 1996, its sales increased by 6.8 percent, in 1997 by 33.8 percent, and in 1998 by 62 percent. Its profits increased by 85 percent between the third quarter of 1997 and the third quarter of 1998.

Overall, its ratios (current assets divided by current liabilities) are similar to those of its competitors. This indicates that the company is fairly stable.

Nokia's current ratio is somewhat higher than those of similar companies, which may indicate inefficient management of current assets.

A debt ratio (total debt divided by total assets) indicates the percentage of total funds provided by creditors. Overly high ratios suggest more risk for creditors.

TABLE C1.1.   Current Ratio: Comparison among Nokia, Motorola, and Ericcson

Company	1997	1996	1995
Nokia	1.76	1.67	1.49
Motorola	1.46	1.42	1.35
Ericcson	2.03	1.54	1.60

TABLE C1.2.   Debt Ratio: Comparison among Nokia, Motorola, and Ericcson

Company	1997	1996	1995
Nokia	.11	.18	.20
Motorola	.13	.14	.16
Ericcson	.09	.08	.08

TABLE C1.3. Profit Margin: Comparison among Nokia, Motorola, and Ericcson

Company	1997	1996	1995
Nokia	.12	.08	.06
Motorola	.04	.04	.07
Ericcson	.07	.06	.05

TABLE C1.4. Inventory Turnover: Comparison among Nokia, Motorola, and Ericcson

Company	1997	1996	1995
Nokia	7.19	6.12	3.69
Motorola	7.27	8.69	7.66
Ericcson	7.10	6.42	5.15

The profit margin of sales (net income divided by net sales) is the return a company receives from sales.

The inventory turnover ratio (sales divided by inventory) estimates how many times a year an inventory is sold. If a company is not turning its inventory over fast enough, too much money may be tied up in inventory.

Organizational

Nokia is divided into four business units. The Nokia Research Center is a corporate research facility that interacts with the business units. Its goal is to enhance Nokia's technological competitiveness. The Nokia Telecommunications unit develops and manufactures infrastructure equipment and systems for mobile and fixed networks. Nokia Mobile Phones develops new types of mobile phones. The Nokia Communications Products unit is further divided into Nokia Multimedia Network Terminals and Nokia Industrial Electronics. Nokia Multimedia Network Terminals pioneers digital satellites, cable, and terrestrial network terminals for interactive multimedia applications. Nokia Industrial Electronics develops and manufactures computer and workstation monitors, including applications for professional desktop communications and new technology displays.

The Nokia Ventures Organization is a separate entity that runs parallel to the business groups. This organization expands the scope of new telecommunications and data communications. It includes three business units: Wireless Business Communications, Wireless Service Applications, and Wireless Software Solutions.

Operational

Nokia holds only one patent, for a strand accumulator with a rotatable drum and rolls. It currently has 36 research and development sites in 11 countries. It spends about 9 percent of its total sales revenue on research and development. In January 1998, Nokia opened an R&D center in Beijing to enable it to better adapt its products to the Chinese market. The center carries out research on mobile communications, mobile terminal technologies, wireless data systems, and fixed access systems. The center's first milestone was a third-generation mobile trial, which tested services that could come into demand in China.

On the Chinese market, the most popular Nokia phones are the analog 909, analog 232, and digital 2110. They are expensive at U.S. $350, $420, and $578, respectively. Older, less popular models are also available at lower prices. A total of 130 countries sell Nokia products. Major markets are in the United States, the United Kingdom, China, Germany, Finland, Italy, France, Sweden, Australia, and Denmark.

Nokia has five main products. First, its network infrastructure system, GSM, holds a global market share of 30 percent. It also produces about 30 different types of mobile phones and wireless data products such as integrated digital voice and data communications devices. The fourth major type is display technology products, that is, computer monitors. Finally, it produces multimedia network terminals that utilize satellite and digital technology.

Nokia once thought of itself simply as a technology provider. Now it realizes that it is a consumer products company that must market its goods. Its customer-oriented strategy is aimed at retaining leadership in the market. Nokia is building an image as a dynamic, flexible, market-driven company.

Competitive Strategy

Nokia relies on four building blocks to create a competitive edge through product differentiation. First, due to its horizontal organization, the company is able to make quick decisions and promptly apply new technologies. Such superior efficiency results in lower costs and higher prices.

Nokia achieves quality by concentrating on customer satisfaction and internal efficiency. To reach these goals, managers are expected to regularly evaluate the skills of team members. Superior product quality leads to a higher productivity, which results in lower costs and greater reliability, again resulting in higher retail prices for its products.

Superior innovation also can produce higher prices or lower costs. Nokia has four company values: customer satisfaction, respect for the individual, achievement, and continuous learning. To check internal performance, it uses regular employee opinion surveys. It also stresses continuous learning to adapt to changes in the industry. Employees are trained in management, leadership, specific skills, and technology.

Nokia also increases its value by using new services and technologies and increasing its capacity at the lowest possible lifetime cost for each product. It was the first company to acknowledge that different market segments have different needs and to begin offering a range of features to suit these needs. One example is the Nokia 3110, which has a Navi key that provides quick and easy access to phone functions. Another innovation is the Chinese character message service for mobile phones.

Nokia gives customer service a high priority. According to the three principles, its employees are expected to operate according to strict ethical ideals, to serve society, and to protect the environment.

An important element of Nokia's business strategy is the desire to augment its internal research and development by setting up alliances and cooperative arrangements with other leading industrial participants.

Entry Strategies

Entry Mode

Nokia established itself in China's telecommunications market in the early 1980s by delivering the first wireless network. Since then, it has established several joint ventures to supply mobile phones and mobile and fixed telecommunications networks.

One of the first joint ventures was established in 1994, when Nokia partnered with the Hang Xing Machinery Manufacturing Co. to form a new entity called Beijing Nokia Hang Xing Telecommunications Systems Ltd., or BNT. This equity joint venture produces DX200 fixed switching systems and manufactures mobile switching centers and base station controllers.

Beijing Nokia Mobile Telecommunications Ltd. was formed in 1995. This fifty-fifty joint venture between Nokia and Beijing Telecommunications Equipment Factory 506 manufactures digital cellular telecommunications products and distributes, markets, and services mobile telephones and network products. During the same year, Nokia and the Cable-Wire Group of Shanghai partnered to form Shanghai Nokia Optical Cables to produce optical cables. Nokia received a 65 percent equity share, and the Cable-Wire Group of Shanghai received 35 percent.

Nokia and the Fujian Post and Telecommunications Administration also signed an agreement to establish a joint venture in China. More recently, Nokia signed an agreement with the Chongqing Telecommunications Bureau and Chongqing Post and Telecommunications Administration Corp. (PTAC) to establish Chongqing Nokia Telecommunications, Ltd. This venture will provide a full range of services and manufacture and supply products for fixed networks.

In addition to forming partnerships with China's government, Nokia has formed strategic alliances with foreign distributors. One such alliance is with CellStar Corporation, a wholly owned foreign entity with extensive retail experience and distribution networks. It is the world's largest wholesaler and retailer of wireless phones and wireless communications products. Another strategic alliance was arranged with Brightpoint, Inc., a leading provider of distribution and value-added logistics services to the wireless communications industry. Both corporations were appointed as authorized distributors of Nokia phones and accessories in China.

Nokia selected the joint venture entry mode because it provided several advantages based on country, industry, firm, and project-specific factors. Equity joint ventures account for about 50 percent of the total amount of FDI in China. This mode is encouraged by the government because it provides more technological know-how to China. More preferential treatment is given to foreign companies such as Nokia that are technologically advanced or infrastructure oriented.

Equity joint ventures provide foreign companies with long-term connections to the local market. Nokia has superior relationships with various government officials who know about market conditions and can provide marketing and distribution channels.

Unlike cooperative joint ventures, equity joint ventures maintain consistency between profit share and percentage of ownership. In its partnership with the Cable-Wire Group of Shanghai, Nokia received a 65 percent share of equity, indicating that it will receive 65 percent of the profits. Likewise, in the fifty-fifty joint venture with Beijing Telecommunications Equipment Factory 506 Nokia receives a 50 percent share of any profits.

Joint ventures are necessary to offset structural uncertainty. Since China has only recently become an emerging economy, its government needs time to learn how to deal with foreign investors and regulate FDI.

It is also more advantageous for firms to work with local partners because of China's complex social, economic, and political systems. Local partners have knowledge of the market, established reputations, and market power.

Establishing a joint venture is a good choice when a firm's strategic objective is to escalate market power and improve its competitive position in a foreign country. The joint venture mode has enabled Nokia to obtain a substantial local market share. It has already captured about 30 percent of China's communications business. It has established a network of offices and several research and training telecommunications centers. Its success is partly due to superior relationships with government officials and partly due to the good use it has made of the market power, reputation, and customer loyalty of its partners.

Joint ventures also allow Nokia to share the high start-up costs of large projects such as network expansion into distant regions in China.

Entry Timing

Nokia established itself in China's telecommunications market in the early 1980s just as China opened its doors to foreign direct investment. As an early mover, Nokia was presented with many opportunities by the government and the market as a whole. It was able to acquire resources at lower cost due to the lack of competition, high entry barriers, and low technological standards of the time. These included human resources, natural and scarce resources, facilities, and information.

Nokia achieved high customer loyalty and brand advantage due to strategic alliances with CellStar and Brightpoint, the two leading distributors of wireless phones and telecommunications products in China. It was able to seize technological leadership over local firms and other foreign businesses.

Nokia thus achieved high performance in terms of foreign direct investment in China in the early period. Its high asset turnover of 1.26 reveals that more than enough volume of business was being generated given the total asset investment. Its annual sales in China alone now amount to $20 billion.

Location Selection

Nokia's technologically advanced projects are located in many parts of China. Agreements were made with the Post and Telecommunications Administration (PTA) in each region. Nokia supplies a GSM network, mobile phones, and other telecommunications services in various places in Fujian Province, including the provincial capital of Fuzhou, Quang-zhou, Xiamen, Putian, and Zhangzhou. It also services Zhejiang, Beijing, Shanghai, Jiangxi, Hunan, Henan, and Yunnan. Each of these cities is located in an open coastal economic region, an economic and technological development zone, or a special economic zone.

Depending upon the location, Nokia receives varying tax benefits and encounters different market conditions. Technologically advanced or infrastructurally oriented projects in open coastal economic areas such as Fuzhou, Xiamen, and Shanghai are given an income tax rate of 15 percent and are exempt from the industrial and commercial consolidation tax (ICCT). These areas enjoy better infrastructure (transportation, communications, production, and business services), are more economically developed, and have Western-style facilities and a cultural atmosphere that promotes international activities. In addition, these regions are given greater economic autonomy than others. For example, the central government has granted Shanghai a great deal of authority to approve FDI projects. Shanghai is home to the most profitable first-generation American joint ventures in China, with returns on investments reaching 16.2 percent.

Nokia has several projects in economic and technological development zones, particularly in Fuzhou, Guangzhou, and Beijing. In these zones, it enjoys an initial corporate income tax rate of 15 percent and a 50 percent reduction on taxes for the subsequent three years. It is exempted from the ICCT and tariffs and value-added taxes for imported materials, equipment, and parts and accessories used in production and operations.

Beijing is the second-largest city in China, after Shanghai, with an estimated population of 12 million people in 1994. The city is the political, financial, educational, and transportation center of the country. Guangzhou, one of the largest cities in China, is the capital of Guangdong Province in South China, with an estimated 1990 population of 3.8 million.

Xiamen city is one of five special economic zones that provide similar tax benefits to those of the ETDZs. It also has increased credit loans and favorable rates for land usage. The local government has provincial-level power to conduct economic affairs.

Cooperative Strategies

By forming joint ventures with domestic companies, Nokia was allowed to enter the Chinese market. Its partners have been governmentally owned and operated, including the Shanghai Post and Telecommunications Administration and the Beijing Telecommunications Equipment Factory. Nokia and the Chinese government have several things in common, which make them good partners.

First, the partners have compatible goals. Nokia's goals in China are to achieve market power and a long-term market share. The main goal of the Chinese government is to obtain leading-edge technology. By contributing advanced technology, Nokia has been able to increase its market power.

Second, each partner offers complementary skills to the venture. For example, Nokia has technological and product innovation skills. Its authorized distributors, CellStar and Brightpoint, have market knowledge and distribution channels. Its partners therefore make it possible to serve new market areas while Nokia develops products suited to the needs of different customers.

Nokia has also demonstrated that it is committed to remaining in China since it has continuously expanded its networks there. It has set up seven joint ventures, established a network of offices, and employs over 3,000 people.

In terms of commensurate risk, stakes are high for Nokia and its partners. For example, each partner shares equal risks in the equity distribution of the joint venture between Nokia and the Beijing Telecommunications Factory 506. However, Nokia has assumed greater risk in its joint venture with the Cable-Wire Group of Shanghai.

Capability also contributes to the success of joint ventures. The highly bureaucratic Chinese government is generally known to be inefficient and not very innovative, so it needs Nokia's technological skills. Nokia, on the other hand, has developed good relations with the officials who have the power to change FDI policies.

Nokia has a fifty-fifty equity position in the Beijing Nokia Mobile Telecommunications joint venture. The government provides land, buildings, and construction materials. In the Shanghai Nokia Optical Cables venture, Nokia has a dominant equity position. It needs to maintain a high degree of control over this venture because its partner is opportunistic and the company wants to protect its proprietary competencies. A dominant position is also better suited to long-term profitability.

Global Integration

Nokia's international global strategies include setting up units in various countries under the centralized control of corporate headquarters;

seeking standardized products suitable for a variety of markets; coordinating production centrally to create economies of scale; and entering countries such as China, which are stable enough to support technological market growth.

With this global strategy, Nokia standardizes its products in China while controlling its competitive advantage from its home office in Finland. The units operating in China are interdependent; the home office maintains integration among them. This international strategy allows Nokia to exploit experience-curve effects and location economics, but it lacks local responsiveness, which makes it difficult to coordinate strategies and operating decisions among its international ventures.

Nokia has addressed these disadvantages through cooperation, coordination, and sharing resources with China's industries. Its global strategy is to work to increase efficiency, quality, and innovation. A global product group structure was also adopted by Nokia to coordinate resource transfers between its corporate headquarters and Chinese divisions. Each division is responsible for its own area. Many of Nokia Group's international products are made overseas in several countries. Managers in Finland are responsible for organizing all aspects of product design and deciding in which countries to manufacture.

In conclusion, Nokia has shown a clear commitment to research and development as well as to promoting the visibility of its brand name. It has actively worked to strengthen its market position, streamline and increase the volume of production, and maintain quality throughout its operations. Customer orientation and competitive solutions are the top priorities of the company. It has taken major steps to improve customer responsiveness and its ability to foresee changes in the market. As a result, the company has grown significantly in several business segments, expanded into new markets, and strengthened its global position.

CASE 2

Hewlett Packard

Founded in 1939 by Bill Hewlett and Dave Packard, Hewlett Packard (HP) designs, manufactures, and services products and systems for measurement, computation, and communications. The company's purpose is to create information products that advance knowledge and improve the effectiveness of organizations and people. It currently provides products and services in industry, business, engineering, science, medicine, and education.

The current chairman of the board, president, and chief executive officer is Lewis E. Platt. He oversees 121,900 employees in more than 120 countries. Headquarters are in Palo Alto, California. Its main offices for each geographic area are located in Causeway Bay, Hong Kong (covering the Asia Pacific region), Geneva, Switzerland (for Europe, Africa, and the Middle East), and Cupertino, California (for the Americas).

Hewlett Packard's corporate culture came together in 1957 when key managers formalized its corporate objectives. These objectives, which were shaped by corporate values known as the "HP Way" of doing business, include integrity, trust in and respect for individuals, and high levels of achievement, teamwork, flexibility, and innovation. Hewlett Packard employees practice "management by wandering around," the phrase applied to informal and structured communications. Employee concerns and ideas are communicated through impromptu discussions with managers and networking across the organization during coffee breaks, lunch periods, and hallway conversations. "Management by objective" further incorporates all levels of employee contributions toward company goals with those of their managers and HP. For this to work, managers need to be open to alternative approaches. In addition, HP's "open door policy" enables people to share both positive and negative feelings in a constructive manner. These three practices are based on the belief that open communication, given the proper training, tools, and information, allows employees to contribute their best.

Hewlett Packard's goal is to be the most admired company in every country in which it operates. Its corporate objectives include

1. Financing growth with sustained profits and providing resources for other corporate objectives.
2. Providing products and services of the highest quality and value to its customers, enabling it to gain their respect and hold their loyalty.
3. Participating in various fields that build on its current technologies, competencies, and customer interests while offering opportunities for continued growth.
4. Allowing growth to be limited by profit levels and the firm's ability to develop and produce products that meet and satisfy customers needs.
5. Helping employees share in HP's success by providing employment security based on performance, maintaining a work environment that recognizes diversity, and allowing employees to gain a sense of satisfaction and accomplishment from their work.
6. Allowing managers the creativity and freedom to act in pursuit of HP's goals.
7. Being a good citizen by contributing intellectually and socially to the societies in which it operates.

For example, in the Asia Pacific region HP has focused on education, allocating 85 percent of its total grants budget for 1997 to educational institutions such as the Shanghai Jiao Tong University and the Ministry of Education of the People's Republic of China as well as contributing to the Indonesian Society for the Care of Disabled Children (YPAC) and rural schools in Thailand.

In August 1979, founder Dave Packard visited China to discuss development of the Chinese electronics sector. In November 1981, the Chinese Electronic Import and Export Corporation (CEIEC) began distributing HP products and services throughout the People's Republic of China. In 1983, a joint venture company between HP and Chinese partners led by the CEIEC was formed. It was established in Beijing two years later. Today 63.75 percent of the company is owned by HP and it has branches in Shanghai, Chengdu, Guangzhou, Xi'an, and Shenyang.

China Hewlett Packard has three ongoing objectives: to expand the distribution and service of HP products in the PRC, to establish PRC-based manufacturing for both domestic consumption and export, and to set up an R&D facility to focus on product localization and development. China Hewlett Packard has been ranked as one of the top ten best managed joint venture companies in China for six consecutive years. Its major business is the manufacturing of computers, medical systems products, and analytical chemical equipment.

Hewlett Packard and the Fluke Corp. signed an agreement in 1997 that allows Fluke to sell HP Basic Instrument products through two Chinese distributors, the China National Electronic Components and Equipment Corp. and the Beijing Oriental Integrated Machine and Electronic Equipment Co., Ltd. The company believes that this partnership will expand product sales across all of China.

The External Environment

The Industrial Environment

The global computer manufacturing industry has experienced an increasing growth rate since the early 1980s. One of the primary reasons for this expansion is the popularity of the personal computer. Industrial analysts predict that the electronic computer industry will continue to grow, although not as rapidly as in the late 1980s and early 1990s.

The computer industry involves many competitors ranging in size from large global corporations to small specialized companies. Recent trends have shifted production from large, expensive mainframes to smaller, cheaper, and more standardized personal computers (PCs). The capital requirements for entering this market depend on the extent to which a company wants to compete. A new company engaged in reconstructing computers requires little start-up capital. However, to compete with organizations like Hewlett Packard and IBM, a tremendous investment in technology, research and development, and operations must be made. Technology in this field is volatile and always advancing. The race to bring new technology to market quickly is a primary driver behind competition in the industry.

The threat of new entrants seems low because capital investments tend to be high. Another important factor is economies of scale. The most successful organizations are large manufacturers that gain cost advantages by producing computers for the mass market. Smaller companies cannot compete. Governmental policies also play an important role. Organizations that decide to set up operations globally face controls over many factors imposed by local governments.

Rivalry within this industry is high. Competition is fierce among many firms led by a few main competitors. Most notable is competition over price and product offerings. The threat of substitutes is also high. Switching costs from the customer's point of view are relatively low. Customers can easily choose different brands of PCs. From the retailer's point of view, switching costs are also low. A large retailer such as

Computer City can easily choose to sell various brands, although it does incur the cost of liquidating existing inventories.

The bargaining power of buyers is substantial because switching costs are so low. If a customer risks little when switching brands, firms are forced to compete to provide what customers demand. For example, Compaq gained a fair share of the PC market because it was able to lower production costs and in turn lower its selling price. This eventually forced other firms to follow its lead because customers were able to dictate the price they were willing to pay for PCs.

The bargaining power of suppliers is marginally high. Two of the important factors that make this force unfavorable are the number of suppliers and the product's importance to buyers. Many of today's personal computers run Microsoft software using Intel processors. This gives companies like Microsoft and Intel an advantage when they negotiate with computer manufacturers. Since customers want Microsoft Windows and Intel chips, manufacturers have to make deals with these companies to provide the necessary components.

Overall, the computer industry is fairly unfavorable to firms within the industry and nearly impossible for new entrants. However, this does not mean that computer companies cannot be successful. With the acceptance of the Internet as a basic communications necessity, businesses must use computers to compete globally. The reliance of consumers on computers means that the industry will continue to grow. The challenge lies in how each company in the computer industry will deal with the five forces outlined earlier.

The National Environment

A worldwide recession swamped producers in the early 1990s, decreasing profits and slowing demand. To combat both long- and short-term downward profit pressures, producers in industrialized regions cut costs, consolidated operations, increased research and development spending, and implemented cost-saving automation and information systems. As a result of these initiatives, many organizations have joined in partnerships to move manufacturing operations to developing nations. This worldwide trend has given China an opportunity to welcome foreign direct investment, making it a competitive location for manufacturing.

The lack of technological centers in China has limited the types of operations that can succeed there. For example, an organization will be less likely to move its research and development operations to China because of the lack of skilled labor and adequate facilities. Manufacturing firms are more likely to operate in China because technology can be transferred from headquarters and machine operators can be trained. The types of businesses that thrive in this environment are therefore mostly labor intensive. China has been able to lure investments with the promise of cheap labor, thereby expanding the capabilities of its citizens. As a result, sales of personal computers in China are expected to grow. By the year 2000, sales are expected to reach 8 to 10 million units. This indicates that foreign ventures in China are already affecting the technical know-how of the Chinese consumer. Typical PC customers in China are households that want to purchase computers for their children. With the recent growth in household income and one-child families, the primary users of the PC will soon be young adults. With this in mind, computer companies have the challenge of designing a basic computer that will satisfy consumer demand for high-tech programs at a reasonable price.

In late 1993, AST Research, Inc., set up China's first major joint venture PC assembly plant in Tianjin. Since then, Compaq, IBM, Hewlett Packard, NEC, Siemens-Nixdorf Information Systems, and others have established PC factories in China. Over the next few years, foreign and Chinese manufacturers will continue to invest in the growing computer market.

Usually, investments occur through joint ventures in which foreign manufacturers provide capital, technology, and managerial skills to the partnership and the Chinese partners provide land, factory space, and knowledge about government rules and the local market. The end products of these joint ventures are almost always exported. This has aided in the growth of China's economy.

The recent influx of foreign investment has allowed the computer industry to grow annually. Competitors such as IBM, HP, Compaq, and AST are able to produce computer equipment at a much lower cost than in the United States. As the industry matures, local companies such as the Legend Group have been able to use their experience with foreign firms to their own advantage. The Legend Group entered the market as the distribution partner of HP and adopted many elements of its corporate culture. Legend is now the leading overall domestic information technologies vendor in China and the largest vendor of home PCs. The Legend Group has proven that domestic companies in China can understand the consumer and will push a homemade product. Western companies such as Compaq and Dell, which make cheaper computers with applications and programs that appeal to Chinese customers, also have an advantage. These are the challenges faced by foreign companies in China.

The Internal Environment

Strengths

Hewlett Packard is well known for offering quality products and excellent customer service. With a clearly stated vision and a solid corporate culture, HP has won many awards as an excellent place to work and as a leader in measurement products. Its products range from handheld computers to life-saving medical devices, and it has won awards for each product line.

Based on information in Hewlett Packard's 1997 annual report, HP is doing very well financially. Net revenue and earnings have been rising steadily. Sales outside of the United States make up more than half the company's revenue. In 1997, U.S. sales amounted to $18.8 billion and international sales equaled $24.3 billion. This reflects HP's commitment to becoming a global leader.

Hewlett Packard has a strong, positive corporate culture. In 1998, *Fortune* rated HP number 10 among the 100 best companies to work for, number five among America's most admired companies, and number one in the "most admired computers, office equipment" category. A clear vision statement (the "HP Way") leads the organization. There is also a strong commitment by employees to make the company succeed.

Hewlett Packard is a leader in the development of computer equipment and technology. It holds the number 1 position for reliability for its notebooks, desktop PCs, and PC servers. This shows that HP has a wide range of computer component technology. Besides PCs, it manufactures test and measurement equipment, medical equipment, and desktop printers. This shows that it has a wide variety of electronics expertise. It is able to use its development skills to create products across a wide product range.

Weaknesses

In the past, HP has been able to turn its weaknesses into strengths, and this is what has put it in a leadership position. Nevertheless, there are areas in which it could improve. One is activity measurement. Its inventory and asset turnovers are lower than industrial averages. This could be a result of using third-party retailers versus direct retail sales. Companies such as Dell and Gateway sell directly to customers. Third-party retailing dramatically affects inventory turnover rates, which would increase industrial turnover. This is the only weakness that was apparent from HP's financial data, however.

One weakness that could have been avoided is that many of the company's key operational facilities are located near major earthquake faults. A major earthquake could devastate HP's headquarters in California, which would have a detrimental effect on global operations.

As technology advances, HP is sometimes forced to replace its own products. As the company develops, its computers become obsolete. This is a weakness because HP is ultimately competing with its own products as well as those of other companies. Another weakness is that short product life cycles require extensive expenditures on technology, although cutting back on spending would take HP out of the computer market.

Third-party distribution channels are an operational weakness for HP. The distribution logistics restrict it from selling and competing directly as Dell and Gateway do. Third-party distribution also relies a great deal on the retailer. If a large retailer is not able to sell its inventory, HP's inventory will also be affected. Another operational weakness is that HP relies on component parts from other companies. Should there be a major flaw in these parts, HP's equipment will be affected. The company has limited control over the internal processes of its suppliers.

Entry Strategies

Location Selection

Hewlett Packard wanted to invest in China because of its untapped market of 1.2 billion consumers. It felt it could attract the burgeoning middle class and capture a large portion of the Chinese market. Another reason was China's abundant pool of conscientious, talented, low-cost engineers, who could become employees. China also enticed HP with the special benefits directed at foreign companies. The country created some 200 laws and provisions aimed at attracting and securing foreign investment. These included (1) not having to pay customs duties on imported materials and a consolidated industrial and commercial tax on equipment; (2) a variety of ways to invest, including financially or with machinery and equipment, raw materials, transportation, trademarks, or technical know-how; and (3) no limitations on the percentage of shares owned by foreign investors in a joint venture.

Shanghai had its own foreign investment commission offering special benefits to foreign investors in order to develop its infrastructure and university. Incentives included tax and export advantages and full ownership of ventures. Hewlett Packard took advantage of the commission's FDI policies to establish a wholly owned factory in 1997.

Entry Timing

The company had the foresight to become the first foreign computer maker in China. As a first mover, it acquired market power and shares, developed brand loyalty, got access to the infrastructure, had first choice of partners in its equity joint ventures, and accessed marketing channels. It also faced little competition at first and therefore could purchase resources at lower costs. In 1992, after having become solidly established in China, HP's Asia Pacific sales were growing faster than its operations in any other part of the world.

Entry Mode Selection

HP has made a total of 12 investments in China. Eight of them (67 percent) are joint ventures. This was partly the result of government influence. China prefers joint ventures so that the country as a whole will profit from the introduction of new technology, knowledge, and industries. It also wants to keep out foreign investors who are only interested in increasing their profits. The Chinese government likes foreign companies to make long-term commitments to the welfare of the country. Joint ventures are the best insurance that these objectives will be met.

The company's first joint venture was with China Electronics Import and Export Corp., the China Great Wall Computer Group, and the Beijing Computer Industry Co. Together they formed the China Hewlett Packard Company Ltd. (CHP). Then HP formed a joint venture with the Putian Integration Co., Ltd. Next came the HP Medical Product Co., Ltd., venture, in cooperation with the China National Corporation of the Medical Equipment Industry. A subsidiary is the Hua Pu Information Technology Co. The HP Computer Products (Shanghai) venture was then formed, in which HP invested $29 million. It then invested $4.8 million in the Hewlett Packard Shanghai Analytical Products Co., Ltd. It holds a 70 percent share in this venture, while its partner, the Shanghai Analytical Instrument Factory (SAIF), holds 30 percent. Joint ventures with the government to support research and development are also pursued, as when HP joined the State Science and Technology Commission of China (SSTCC) to form the STC and HP Joint R&D Center. About $1 million in research funds was donated to SSTCC by HP. The R&D center provides professional services and support for HP's clients in China, especially the major fields of telecommunications, finance, manufacturing, and engineering design.

Approximately 10 years after HP first entered China, it launched its first wholly owned operation. It was able to do this because of its excellent relations with the Chinese government. It believes that its overseas ventures should be integral parts of China's marketing structures, manufacturing endeavors, and research programs. Moreover, it has shown a willingness to upgrade its overseas subsidiaries and let them play an increasingly large role in its corporate strategy. Companies such as IBM, which are only interested in infiltrating the local market or reducing their component production costs, have failed where HP has succeeded.

The company has now set up the wholly owned HP World '96 Technology Center, in which it has invested $6 to 7 million per year. It also has reached an agreement to set up a new wholly owned factory.

Project Selection

Because of Hewlett Packard's status as a leading global provider of computing, Internet, and intranet solutions and services, communications products, and measurement tools, it was only natural for it to enter the same industries in China.

Today CHP is responsible for the overall sales and support of HP products in China. It is a minicomputer assembly venture. Hewlett Packard also produces ink jet printers for export to Europe. Additionally, HP in China manufactures workstations and medical equipment such as cardiographs, patient monitors, and ultrasound imaging systems. The HP Medical Products Group was the official patient-monitoring and defibrillator supplier to the 1998 World Cup. The company is also producing analytical chemistry instrument products in China, including gas chromatograph, liquid chromatograph, ultraviolet/visible spectrophotometer, and atomic absorption instruments.

Cooperative Strategies

Usually, HP is the dominant partner in each venture. It possesses many advantages, which it brings to bear during negotiations. Which advantages it makes use of strategically depends on whether the potential partner is a supplier, customer, or competitor, the size of the potential partner, and HP's specific objectives (e.g., lower production costs, increased channels of distribution, or improved products).

For vertical joint ventures, Hewlett Packard has used the volume size of its purchases as an advantage over smaller suppliers. The advantages such a partnership provides to the smaller partner are the security of a long-term customer, the prestige of working with a well-defined and respected company, possible increases in technical experience and knowledge, financial contributions, managerial support and guidance, and tax incentives or special governmental treatment as a partner in a multinational joint venture.

For horizontal joint ventures, Hewlett Packard provides different advantages for its potential partners, including existing distribution channels, product features, name recognition and familiarity, research and development, production and marketing expertise, managerial and planning experience and knowledge, market share and existing facilities, equity, and other partnerships.

Distribution is one of Hewlett Packard's strongest contributions to a joint venture. Thanks to its reputation and involvement in many joint ventures, it possesses a wide variety of distribution routes. A joint venture can also take advantage of different economic conditions within the United States and China to minimize import and export costs.

Since the mid-1980s, HP has been successful in China. Today it reaps the benefits of established business relations and is opening up more sites there. Its transnational strategy has optimized two-way communications between the company and its Chinese subsidiaries. A global strategy would only permit one-way interaction between headquarters and subsidiaries, while a multidomestic strategy gives subsidiaries too much autonomy. The HP strategy successfully balances global integration with local responsiveness.

Operational Strategies

Developing human resources is critical to successful growth. Careful selection and retention of employees who embrace the company's culture provide powerful advantages for global integration. The "HP Way" is passed from one generation of employees to the next, not through a process of indoctrination but through selection and a subtle, gradual process of enculturation. As new employees are exposed to behaviors practiced by their managers and fellow employees, they gradually conform and adopt them as their own. There has also been a growing emphasis on providing managers with the special tools needed to succeed in difficult foreign assignments. Since HP has expatriates in about 40 countries, it puts approximately 1,200 employees and their entire families through an annual cross-cultural training program. During these sessions, employees and their families are taught about the historical, cultural, social, and business practices of the host countries. Chinese students attending college in the United States are aggressively recruited, under the assumption that they will be more compatible with HP's corporate culture than nationals hired in China.

Although divisional and purchasing managers act autonomously in daily operations, corporate procurement often intercedes in strategic issues that might affect the company as a whole. Procurement Strategy Boards (PSBs) have been established for key commodities used across the board or at least by several divisions. Every division is represented on the Procurement Council, which meets quarterly. According to its charter, the PSB is to (1) develop support and enforce procurement strategies; (2) enhance the R&D procurement link, with the goal of significantly reducing the materials cost of new designs; (3) focus on parts standardization, supplier improvement, and material cost reduction; and (4) influence HP's resource allocations. Thus, even though HP is highly decentralized, it acts as one big corporation on the purchasing front, using corporate contracts to leverage its buying power. Eventually, the company hopes to establish a common, global data warehouse of suppliers in order to uniformly secure the lowest possible prices in all of its locations around the world. It is attempting to create a directory of warehouse data that will provide a consistent view of corporate information.

Like many large, decentralized companies, weaving together its disparate warehouses into a coordinated whole has not been easy. Among the challenges it has had to face are building an enterprise warehouse from multiple functional or geographic warehouses, persuading operating units to participate in the creation of an enterprise data warehouse, avoiding collection of the same information from different operating units, and achieving consistent access to information that has been stored in a variety of formats.

Regional balance has become one of the overriding issues in HP's sourcing strategy. During the 1980s, it worked to set up a network of international procurement offices (IPOs) staffed by local agents familiar with the customs of the region. Acting as the eyes and ears of purchasing, these agents provide the latest scoop on potential new sources. The company has more than 60 purchasing agents stationed at eight IPOs around the world, four in Asia, two in Europe, and two in North America. Major benefits provided by the IPOs include (1) quick feedback to suppliers about HP's requirements, (2) transactions in local currency, (3) easier overseas buying as a single company despite its decentralization, and (4) a stronger network with the best foreign suppliers.

Integration of financial systems on a regional basis has provided cost savings due to economies of scale. In 1989, every sales and customer support office had its own accounting, payroll, and payments function. Each office (over 150 worldwide) maintained its own internal staff plus the requisite hardware and software. The local informational technology staff would modify the basic source code developed at headquarters and distribute it throughout the firm's local offices. Hewlett Packard is in the process of consolidating over 50 financial processing centers around the United States into a single, central unit in Colorado Springs. It is also establishing regional centers in Singapore and Brussels. The next step is the integration of manufacturing accounting and sales accounting with its treasury.

HP has been hedging for more than 25 years and reviews and adjusts its Asian translation exposures on a monthly basis. Cross-border transaction risks also have to be hedged because the company produces and sells in several Asian countries. Within the company's Singapore, Japanese, and Malaysian manufacturing operations, many transaction exposures net out, reducing HP's risks significantly. It sells in U.S. dollars or in local currency invoiced at the spot rate when the transaction occurs. If the latter is impossible, it builds a self-insurance buffer into the local currency price. In China and Taiwan, HP has adopted different hedging strategies that call for matching assets and liabilities as closely as possible. Additionally, when a hedge gain or loss occurs HP works to move it to Palo Alto. In California, it can be hedged by means of a basket approach. Corporation-wide, the unrealized gains and losses from hedging contracts deferred under the company's accounting policies amounted to $103 million and $86 million, respectively, in 1997.

In China, HP is working with the Sustainable Development Networking Program (SDNP) and the State Science and Technology Commission to spearhead various economic, social, and environmental development efforts. The goal of China's SDNP is to create a structure that will enable sustainable development throughout the country by simplifying access to information and encouraging information sharing at all levels. In a related effort to leverage technology for economic development, environmental protection, and related social issues, HP has also launched an initiative called the HP Sustainable Future Program.

The company adopted a global pricing initiative in November 1992. All businesses are entirely responsible for their own worldwide pricing. Each now has geographic outposts, called marketing centers, which advise it on the local marketplace and help formulate local prices. It seeks to justify prices on the basis of customer value instead of merely passing along incremental costs. Swings in exchange rates now directly affect each business's financial performance, and significant price differences leave them open to arbitrage and cross-border buying.

The company is developing a global theme in all its consumer advertising as part of an initiative to build a consumer franchise. The objective is to create a broad umbrella that all divisions can use to unify the entire organization. A major goal is for each consumer products group to develop a brand statement that can be used for decades. A consumer brand task force created "expanding possibilities" as the signature phrase embodying the company's spirit and new direction. It conveys the message that HP is a reliable, high-quality brand that can help consumers accomplish exciting things with easy to use, innovative technology.

In conclusion, HP's corporate structure, the HP Way, is one of its major strengths, allowing formal and informal communication between managers and employees and providing guidance in everyday decision making. The company is respected for its quality products and excellent customer service. It employs a transnational global strategy based on major product groups that seek to gain worldwide integration while maintaining local responsiveness. To do this, HP vertically integrates the company from inception to its final interface with the consumer. It is also able to achieve its objectives due to its intense focus on what the company does best. Overall, Hewlett Packard's investment in China has been highly successful. It now has 12 major investments there. As a leader in the industry, it has used its strengths in technology and service to set up joint ventures and wholly owned subsidiaries.

CASE 3

IBM

An industry giant, IBM creates, develops, and manufactures computer systems, software, networking systems, storage devices, and microelectronics. Its mission is to become a leader in the most advanced information technologies while providing value and expertise to its worldwide customers.

Founded in 1914, IBM is one of the largest international information technology companies in the world, with branches and subsidiaries in over 150 countries. Over 200,000 employees currently work for IBM. Its headquarters is in San Jose, California. Its current CEO is Louis V. Gerstner.

An early entrant into the Chinese market, IBM commenced operations in China by helping the Peking Union Hospital install a business machine in 1934. This operation was terminated due to the civil war. After the formation of the People's Republic of China, IBM returned. Two representative offices were opened in Beijing and Shanghai in the mid-1980s. In 1995, IBM hired more than 12,000 employees in China.

Like an umbrella company in China, IBM has a wide variety of operations mainly located in large cities such as Shanghai, Guangzhou, and Shenyang on the east coast. Besides a few wholly owned subsidiaries, IBM has many joint venture partners, including Tsinghua University, Shenzhen University, the China Great Wall Computer Group, and the Ji Tong Co. Although each joint venture company operates independently, all have agreed to work together in order to provide the best customer service. Over the last two decades, IBM has built up an image as one of the most reliable technological companies in China; its business has expanded and become integrated in almost every sector of the Chinese economy. This has been possible because of cooperation with the firm's Chinese partners.

IBM has set up the Greater China Group, replacing the traditional product-based business approach with a sector-based approach. Customer service network centers have been set up in dozens of Chinese cities, including Beijing, Shenyang, Shanghai, Nanjing, Guangzhou,

Shenzhen, Chengdu, Wuhan, and Xian. Shanghai itself is already the site of several leading IBM technology initiatives, including a software development center, information technology (IT) centers at several universities, and one of the world's most advanced networking installations at the Shanghai Post and Telecommunications Administration.

One of IBM's major goals in China is to adapt its information technologies to meet the needs of Chinese consumers, thereby enhancing its competitiveness. The success of the company in China has had a lot to do with these customization strategies. For example, IBM has developed software that uses Chinese characters, including Chinese versions of its operating systems. The company has also established many research centers and laboratories to test products and foster innovation. By providing the best technologies, products, and services, IBM has met many local customer needs and become a key IT company in China.

The External Environment

The Industrial Environment

The personal computer market has maintained solid growth. Worldwide PC factory shipments rose 14 percent over the fourth quarter of 1996 and 21 percent over the third quarter of 1997. In the United States, total PC shipments grew by a healthy 15 percent over the previous year and 6 percent subsequently. During 1997, worldwide PC factory shipments grew by 15 percent over 1996 and U.S. factory shipments increased by 19 percent. It is estimated that as much as 70 percent of the world's data reside on IBM servers, with most of those data on S/390 Enterprise Servers (mainframes). The vast majority of servers that run the world's economic infrastructure, including most of the world's largest corporations and banks, are IBM S/390s. The IBM Enterprise Servers use complementary metal oxide semiconductor (CMOS) technology. It is the most powerful mainframe processor technology on the computer market.

In 1997, China had a population of more than 1.2 billion, with about half under the age of 40. As the population increases, its average age gets younger and younger. This has generated an economic boom and a new consumer group. This is a good sign for IBM since young people tend to purchase more computer products than does the older generation.

To date, IBM has diversified its products and services into five areas. The most profitable area is hardware sales, which generated 46 percent of IBM's total revenue in 1997, while services accounted for 25 percent, software 16 percent, maintenance 8 percent, and rental and financing 5 percent. Since hardware sales is IBM's primary business, this analysis focuses on potential competitors that are PC vendors.

In 1997, IBM ranked as the number two PC vendor worldwide. It turned in strong performances in Western Europe and Asia. Commercial desktop computers and servers continued to drive worldwide growth. The introduction of the company's first low-cost consumer PC and a renewed focus on inventory management enabled IBM to post 42 percent sequential growth worldwide.

The company holds about 8 percent of the PC market in China, but it has many rivals (see table C2.1). Strong local competitors include the Legends Computer Co. and the Great Wall Corp., which together held over 20 percent of the total market in 1994. Foreign competitors are even stronger, with over 60 percent of the market held by companies such as Compaq, AST, Hewlett Packard, and DEC. AST is IBM's strongest overall foreign competitor, with 25 percent of the market share. Its main PC competitors are Compaq (ranked number one worldwide) and Hewlett Packard (number three).

The Internal Environment

The profitability of IBM in 1997 reflects its successful implementation of strategic priorities, including revenue growth, stable net income margins, and leveraged growth in earnings per share. The increase in revenue in the Asia Pacific region also reflects the continued shift toward

TABLE C2.1.   Market Shares of Major
PC Suppliers in China, 1994
(in percentages)

Company	Market Share
AST	25
Compaq	16
IBM	8
DEC	7
Great Wall	6
Legend	6
Acer	4
Langchao	3
Changjiang	2
Other importers	4
Other producers	19

high-growth businesses. Approximately 9 percent of IBM's revenues and 10 percent of its net earnings come from the Asia Pacific region. Revenues there were approximately $13.9 billion in 1995, $14.7 billion in 1996, and $15.2 billion in 1997. Net earnings were roughly $1.1 billion, $1.5 billion, and $1.8 billion, respectively, over the same years. Clearly, revenues and earnings from the region are rising.

With state of the art equipment in its classrooms, IBM's training programs in the United States are superb. Each new employee must attend a month-long training session related to his or her particular job. This is followed with on the job training. The company does not have as thorough a training program in China, however, although it employs over 1,200 local personnel. Unfortunately, the labor market in China is still underdeveloped and restricted by North American standards. China has many intelligent, hardworking, and trainable employees but not enough to meet IBM's demands at the present time. This is because China does not have many alternatives to job training and career development.

The company has attempted to rectify this lack by donating PCs, printers, software, storage systems, and magnetic tape subsystems to Chinese universities in order to upgrade the country's overall information technology capabilities. Donations of over $32 million represent one of the largest contributions IBM has ever made for educational purposes. It signed an agreement to develop a national computer science education curriculum and expand its partnership with China's national education network. The goal of the partnership program is to improve China's computing capabilities, advance it directly to the forefront of information technology, and help it prosper in the global business market. More than 30 institutions have participated in these educational partnerships, including 23 IBM technology centers. The technology centers conduct seminars for university faculty members, with training on new products, technology, and instructional techniques. More than 8,400 students have taken courses on IBM technology and more than 1,200 students and faculty members have been certified as product experts. The company also has sponsored 12 university professors to attend a training program at Northern Illinois University. The three-month course focuses on ways to incorporate instruction on IBM large servers into China's core curricula.

Henry Chow, IBM Greater China's chairman and CEO, as well as other company executives deliver presentations all over China on IBM's network computing model, new products, and services. The company also dispenses promotional gifts such as pens, calendars, key rings, T-shirts, and mouse pads stamped with its logo. Such strategies can be very effective. In a recent study, 63 percent of all consumers surveyed were either carrying or wearing an advertising specialty item. More than three-quarters of them were able to recall the advertiser's name or message.

To satisfy the special demands of the Chinese market, IBM has stepped up its efforts to develop Chinese-character software and applications, including Chinese versions of its various operating systems. In late 1996, it introduced two new products to the Chinese market, the POS machine and open network printers. The POS-4612 SurePoint is a wireless portable computer that uses advanced open industrial standards and IBM's PC technology with a touch screen and pen-input mode. It is light and stable; highly portable and flexible; suitable for data collection, inventory control, and sales support; and can be used as a managerial workstation. Warehouse personnel can use its bar code scanning function to check inventory, and supermarket clerks can use it to guide customers in selecting commodities. It can function as a cash register when it is connected to a keyboard, printer, cash box, and monitor. More than 1,000 sets were sold on the Chinese mainland in just three months, demonstrating that the product has been well received.

The IBM China Company also introduced a series of open-network workgroup laser printers in Beijing to meet the needs of businesses that want user-friendly, reliable, printing networks. The network-ready, low-cost printers include one color and three monochrome models. They are designed to support the evolving demands of both users and network administrators in shared or workgroup environments. Connectivity options, paper-handling options, print features, environmental features, two-sided printing, and document confidentiality boxes are all designed with network users and administrators in mind.

The company spent $4.88 billion in 1997, $4.65 billion in 1996, and $4.17 billion in 1995 on research and development, including product-related engineering, basic scientific research, and the application of scientific advances to the development of new and improved products. A large amount of these funds has been invested in China.

An IBM software development center in Shanghai has been set up to enhance cooperation with Chinese business partners. In 1995, IBM set up an information technology center and a Shanghai IBM coordination team to ensure that each project is launched and completed in the most effective manner. The China Research Laboratory was established to test IBM's latest technological innovations and provide a clear channel for building bridges between the company and researchers in Chinese universities, industries, the State Science and Technology Commission, and the Academy of Sciences. Research activities at the lab focus on software and applications products that are especially relevant to China. Examples include a digital library, speech recognition for Mandarin, Chinese-language processing, object-oriented technology, and parallel processing.

Entry Strategies

Location Selection

Expanding into China has definitely given IBM cost advantages. China's factor endowments include cheap resources for the production of computer components. Land and labor are also abundant and cheaper than in the United States. One problem that IBM had was China's below-standard computer technology. Initial materials and supply costs were high because they had to be imported. Related and support companies have sprung up in China, however, which has driven costs down. Many joint ventures with local suppliers have allowed IBM to obtain materials and supplies at discounted rates. Also, it does not maintain a large inventory since it can order materials directly from local suppliers.

Most of IBM's joint ventures are located on the east coast and in the major cities of China (see table C2.2). It has chosen larger cities because they usually have more economic development. Many other firms have their headquarters in these cities, and these are more likely to spend money on IBM's technology. The company has also been limited in its choice of location by its joint venture partners, most of which are

TABLE C2.2. Computer Industry Revenues by Province, 1992 (in millions of dollars)

Rank	Province	Revenue
1	Guangdong	446.3
2	Beijing	199.3
3	Shangdong	122.2
4	Fujian	58.4
5	Jiangsu	55.6
6	Liaoning	35.6
7	Sichuan	29.4
8	Shanghai	26.3
9	Tianjin	22.7
10	Yunnan	16.2
11	Hebei	14.8
12	Hunan	12.7
13	Zhejiang	11.5
14	Shanxi	9.8
15	Shannxi	7.2

state-owned enterprises located in major cities. Large cities have better infrastructure, transportation, and communications systems than do rural areas. This is very important for technological industries. Computer products depend on reliable telecommunications.

Another reason for setting up operations in big cities is because demand is higher in those areas. For example, Shanghai alone has a population of 7,830,000 and many industries are based there. Demand is high since companies that want to industrialize usually need computer products.

Most of China's computer companies are located in big cities such as Beijing, Shanghai, and Guangdong. These cities generate over 50 percent of the total revenue of the computer industry in China. As competition increases, however, operating costs will rise, so IBM should consider locating new production sites in smaller cities such as Hubei, Jiangsu, and Sichuan. Operations in these areas could have the benefits of lower costs and a large potential market.

Entry Timing

One of the earliest foreign companies to enter the information industry in China, IBM began by selling its 370/138 system to the Shenyang Turbine Factory in the late 1970s. In the mid-1980s, the State Planning Commission bought an IBM 38 mainframe. At that time, however, IBM was facing high start-up costs because supplies had to be imported. Also, there was a high risk of political and market instability. Nevertheless, having entered the market so early, IBM gained market power and created entry barriers for followers. It also developed a strong brand image and enjoyed the advantage of technological leadership.

Entry Mode Selection

The company has used a number of entry modes in China. At first, it was only able to open representative offices and involve itself in projects with the local government. Although it was barred from further involvement by government restrictions, it was able to test the market and gain experience and knowledge from local firms. By the mid-1980s, IBM had built up connections and *guanxi* with many local companies. It then changed modes and entered into many joint ventures. Recently it has started a few wholly owned companies.

The success of IBM is related to China's national computer industry projects. For example, the Golden Project focuses on promoting information technology and a nationwide public telecommunications network.

Industries such as banking, finance, foreign trade, and credit cards are becoming more important in China, and computer technology is necessary for these industries, too. In 1994, Jitong and IBM signed an agreement to jointly invest in a venture called the Beijing Jitong Information Network Development Co. (registration capital was $9 million), which focuses on telecommunications and computer systems for the Golden Bridge network. China's seventh and eighth five-year plans also called for the development of new businesses, which will require computers.

Altogether, IBM has three manufacturing, two software, and two information technology joint venture companies. In order to achieve international joint venture success, it looks for the four Cs (capacity, commitment, compatibility, and complementarity) in its partners. It tends to form alliances with companies with large manufacturing plants that can handle production for products in high demand. These partners tend to be committed to technological advances, innovation, and improvement of China's IT infrastructure. They are compatible when their managers have a shared vision and try to work toward the common goal of producing good products with IBM. Partners such as the Tianjin Advanced Information Products Corp. (TAIPC) in Tianjin and the GKI Electronics Co., Ltd., in Shenzhen also provide complementary products. The former is responsible for manufacturing banking peripherals and point of sale terminals for export and the domestic market, while GKI makes electronic cards and boards.

In 1994, IBM launched the International Information Products Corp. (IIPC), a JV in Shenzhen between IBM and the Great Wall Computer Group. IBM chose Great Wall because it is China's second-largest domestic PC manufacturer. The IIPC is tied into IBM's global purchasing network and is just hours from its most important supplier. It makes the IBM and Great Wall brands of PC, which have rapidly gained recognition for quality. In addition, IBM can source components in bulk for significant discounts, a key advantage over domestic competitors.

The company has formed two components JVs of its own, Shenzhen GKI Electronics and the Shenzhen Storage Product Corp. Casings, covers, frames, monitors, and power supplies are available locally, but hard drives, motherboards, and Pentium chips are imported from Taiwan via Hong Kong. The firm also joined forces with China Great Wall Computer Shenzhen and Shenzhen Kaifa Technology to build a hard drive component plant called Hailang Co., Ltd. These companies were chosen because of comparative advantages in their own niches.

The company has also formed two software JVs, the International Software Development Co., Ltd. (ISDC), in Shenzhen and the Advanced System Development Co., Ltd. (ASDC), in Beijing. Both of these companies have local universities as partners. The former customizes software from IBM, other vendors, and customers with Chinese requirements. It also develops and markets ISDC brand software for financial, hotel, point of sale, and production management uses and provides object-oriented software for IBM and its customers.

There are two information technology joint venture companies. Both are located in Beijing. These are the Blue Express Technical Service Co., Ltd. (BE), and the Xun Tong Information Networking Research Development Co., Ltd. Blue Express provides a low-end product support network across China. Xun Tong is a networking services company.

These joint ventures make strategic contributions to all parties involved by providing economies of scale, technological synergies, fulfillment of local content requirements, and vertical quasi-integration through access channels to major buyers. Although all the IBM joint venture companies are independent, together they form a complete network of coverage to assist IBM in serving its customers in China.

The sharing arrangements vary for each joint venture. In the partnership between IBM and the Great Wall Computer Group, IIPC, IBM owns 51 percent and IIPC 49 percent. This 2 percent advantage is crucial to IBM because it needs to own more of the company and have more control in order to succeed internationally.

In the deal between IBM, China Great Wall Computer Shenzhen, and Shenzhen Kaifa Technology, IBM has an 80 percent stake and the other two Chinese companies own 10 percent each. Once again, IBM likes to be in control of things.

Operational Strategies

Huge amounts of money have been invested by IBM to make products more innovative and better serve the Chinese market. The most important new products are a speech recognition system called ViaVoice (introduced in 1997) and an on-line booking system (1998). ViaVoice was the first Chinese speech recognition system implemented by the China Research Laboratory, and IBM is the only company in the world offering dictation products that use it. ViaVoice is user independent. This means it can recognize voices even if they have slightly different accents. It is a truly personalized intelligent system that can communicate with human beings. Thus, ViaVoice marks the beginning of an era of true human to machine dialogue, allowing people to use computers in a natural way. This product is especially helpful to customers who cannot type.

CAAC has successfully implemented IBM's on-line booking system, allowing its passengers to book flights through the Internet. With IBM's Airline Control System (ALCS) as the booking engine, ALCS is considered one of IBM's high-performance transactions processing solutions, allowing high transaction rates where fast response and maximum availability are paramount. Once the required information has been provided and processed, customers receive confirmation of their bookings. Airlines, banks, and organizations requiring credit card authorizations can also benefit from ALCS.

The IBM Research Laboratory in Beijing has a staff of 30 of the most talented scientists and researchers in the world. Some of their innovations include the Chinese ViaVoice Speech Recognition System, the Digital Library, Chinese-language processing, and parallel processing. The IBM China Digital Library was designed in cooperation with Fudan University, which hopes to use the system to research Chinese texts, generate abstracts for Chinese documents, study historical maps, and show the evolution of maps during China's different dynasties.

To succeed in the marketplace, technology must not only offer various useful features but it must be reliable, durable, and free of defects. For example, IBM's Solution Partnership Center in China provides performance tests, ports, and benchmarks applications. It facilitates the development of network-based commercial applications incorporating IBM systems and technologies. The tests are done at two offices in Beijing, the IBM China Research Lab and the China Computer Limited Information Technology Center.

An example of IBM's superior input efficiency is its Blue Logic Technology (BLT). The BLT program includes custom logic technology and services. Another example is its MQSeries, messaging software that links major computer systems with almost any network so that the links within a business's value chain can be maintained, improving efficiency and increased responsiveness. The MQSeries is being used by many of the world's most successful manufacturers to keep their value chains at peak efficiency.

The creation of the IBM Greater China Group, a consolidation of operations in Hong Kong, China, and Taiwan, has enabled IBM to be more efficient and exert greater leverage on its global resources. All the networks in the greater China region are now connected, including Shanghai, Guangzhou, Shenyang, Shenzhen, Nanjing, Chengdu, Wuhan, Xian, Fuzhou, Hong Kong, and Taiwan.

In addition, IBM customizes its products to meet the unique needs of its customers. It uses the Internet intensively to gain feedback from its customers and respond to queries. In China, it also relies on support centers to give Chinese customers service and support. It has established three regional support centers in Beijing, Shanghai, and Guangzhou. Its support system features phone-in and fax-back services, and it plans to offer electronic access soon.

The IBM China Research Laboratory has also put Hot Video on the Web as part of IBM's Alpha Works on-line virtual lab. The Hot Video application makes it possible for developers to insert hot links for multimedia video clips directly into Internet web pages. Other applications include electronic commerce, advertising, distance learning, games, and entertainment. Customers are able to download and experiment with new software technology months before it becomes part of IBM's standard products and services. This also gives IBM the opportunity to glean feedback from users of the new technology.

The company has faced some human resources problems in China. There is a scarcity of highly educated labor, especially in rural areas. Chinese managers are sometimes narrow-minded, doing things in prescribed ways to meet specific goals. The company also has to deal with personnel administrators who delegate work, record salaries, endorse job changes, and indoctrinate workers in party policies. There has been little job training, career development planning, or compensation linked to employee performance.

In response, IBM headquarters is trying to train its Chinese managers to think and analyze globally. Some attend American business schools to broaden their outlooks. IBM China also needs to focus on encouraging soft people skills. The incentive structure lags behind that of the United States. Furthermore, Chinese managers are not open to suggestions or criticism from their subordinates. Slowly, however, some Chinese are trying to imitate American managerial styles and create better reward systems.

CASE 4

Motorola

Motorola began as the Galvin Manufacturing Corp. in 1928 with five employees and $565. By the early 1990s, Motorola was ranked among the 25 largest companies in the world. At the start of 1998, it had approximately 139,000 employees in 45 countries with sales revenues of close to $30 billion.

Motorola is trying to position itself to capitalize on the Chinese market. It sells cellular phones, pagers, radio communications systems, and semiconductor products in China. It became the largest investor in China by committing more than $1.2 billion by the end of 1996. It has one wholly owned venture in Tianjin and a holding company registered in China and is involved in six equity joint ventures, five cooperative projects, and dozens of other major investments.

Motorola's fundamental objective, as stated in 1987 by its CEO, Bob Galvin, is "total customer satisfaction." The entire company structure and its daily activities are focused on meeting or exceeding every requirement of every customer. The company has a continuous improvement philosophy based on defect and cycle time reduction. In China, Motorola's stated goal is to serve as a model of cooperative development.

In 1986, Motorola opened a representative office in Beijing and leased a manufacturing facility in the city of Tianjin. It opened a sales and marketing office in China the next year but withdrew most of its personnel following the Tiananmen Square demonstrations in 1989. The company later reentered China with a wholly owned subsidiary rather than a joint venture. In March 1992, Motorola Electronics Ltd. (MEL), a wholly owned entity, was incorporated. Motorola pledged to develop as many as 5,000 new jobs and transfer to China the technology necessary to produce products for domestic and foreign consumption.

By 1993, China had become Motorola's largest cellular market outside of the United States. Sales of its products in China exceeded $1.2 billion for the year. Motorola (China) Ltd. was awarded the International Standard Organization (ISO) international quality certification, which ensures that products manufactured in China meet or exceed worldwide quality standards.

In 1995, Motorola cellular systems were operating in 23 of China's 27 provinces. Sales of Motorola products reached $3.3 billion. Motorola's first joint venture in the People's Republic of China was established with Leshan Radio Co., Ltd., to manufacture semiconductors. By the end of the year, cellular telephone networks covered the entire country. Five more joint ventures were established by March 1996. China adopted Motorola's technology as its national paging standard in the same year.

In 1995, Motorola entered into a joint venture with the Panda Electronics Group of Nanjing, China. Under the terms of the agreement, a new entity, Nanjing Power Computer Ltd., would have developed, produced, and sold computers based on PowerPC microprocessors and Macintosh Operating Systems (OS) under license. Motorola had a 60 percent equity investment and Panda held 40 percent equity in the joint venture. In September of 1997, Motorola announced that it would exit the MacOS clone business at the end of 1997 because it was unable to reach an acceptable licensing agreement with Apple Computer. Apple would not let licensees make Macs using a new hardware standard and was seeking higher fees for clones built with current technology. Motorola has said that it will try to push the PowerPC line of chips into embedded applications, selling the processors for use in portable products, automobiles, and network hardware. It has not released information regarding the future of Nanjing Power Computer and its facilities.

Motorola's prices have suffered from a deflated currency, industrial price competition, and slowdowns in the semiconductor industry. Currency devaluation has slowed Motorola's cellular infrastructure business in Asia, although sales and orders in Japan and the Americas are solid. Motorola's sales of cellular phones in China and Japan have remained relatively strong, but it has downgraded its expectation of a 12 percent increase to 5 percent in chip industry revenues due to the Asian financial crisis. Consumer confidence in Asia has not stabilized as a result of efforts by the International Monetary Fund. Company officials state that it will cut costs and spending in the short term since there is no indication of when the Asian economy will recover.

Motorola is driven by technology in that it pioneers new technologies and creates new markets for them. Currently active areas of technology include wireless semiconductors, and measurement and control. The applications that offer the most opportunity to Motorola in China for the next several years, as well as some problems, all are in the general area of wireless technology: cordless and cellular phones, paging, and wireless in local loop (WILL). Motorola's wireless technologies make possible such major consumer applications as cordless phones, cellular phones, pagers, mobile radio, WILL, global mobile satellite-based communications, and wireless computer networking. Without a doubt, wireless is Motorola's core competency as well as the most relevant technology in the Chinese context.

Motorola's key markets in terms of sales are the United States (42 percent of sales), Europe (19 percent), and China (11 percent), with the Asia Pacific region, Latin America, Japan, and other minor markets making up the balance.

Motorola products sold in China include cellular phones, pagers, radio communications systems, and semiconductor components. Its Tianjin plant is a large, integrated circuit wafer fabrication plant. The semiconductors manufactured at the plant supply the automotive, communications, personal computer peripherals, and digital products markets.

The External Environment

Opportunities

The proportion of Chinese living in urban areas increased from 26.2 percent in 1993 to about 52 percent in 1998. This leads to increasing demand for telecommunications, especially mobile cellular services. China should become the largest mobile cellular and fixed telephone market in the world by the year 2016. The untapped market potential of China represents a major opportunity for Motorola to further expand into the market.

From 1992 to 1995, the Chinese economy as a whole grew by an average of 12 percent per annum. China has been quite successful in achieving technological transfer by means of a strategy of trading market share for technology. If economic growth continues, China should be able to catch up with many Western countries in terms of purchasing power over the next 20 years. It ranked the highest in terms of its real GDP and real GDP per capita growth in 1996. The IMF estimates it will take China 16 years to close half the gap between its per capita income and the $16,790 annual income of richer nations based on China's 1990–95 growth rates. The number of mobile cellular subscribers will be further stimulated by real income growth among middle-income earners. In China, where less than 10 percent of the 1.2 billion people have yet to make their first phone call, wired and wireless customers should increase by about 20 million a year in the near future.

The telecommunications industry in China is therefore in a growth stage. In 1997, there were approximately 6.85 million mobile cellular subscribers, mainly businessmen. The Ministry of Posts and Telegraph's (MPT) estimate for the year 2000 was recently revised upward from 18 to 30 million. There are 30 to 40 million pagers operating in China, and it is estimated that pager usage will jump to 60 million by the year 2000. As recently as the mid to late 1980s, China had less than 10 million telephone lines. According to some estimates, it is currently adding about 15 million telephones, 6 million cellular subscribers, and 16 million pagers per year.

The telecommunications scene in China is somewhat chaotic, with more than one organization occasionally duplicating the services in some locations as well as different foreign suppliers providing a multiplicity of analog and digital equipment and standards. There are more than 30 private networks run by about 20 ministries and state enterprises. The State Council recently approved two public telecommunications carriers in addition to the MPT.

Mobile cellular systems are less likely to be subject to the capacity constraints created by the poor local infrastructure than are fixed telephones. Manufacturers of GSM such as Motorola, Ericsson, Nokia, Siemens, Nortel, and Philips will continue to enter into joint ventures, providing the technology and capital needed to develop infrastructure for these rapidly expanding networks.

Entry barriers are high not only because of large capital requirements but due to the rigorous regulations set by the Chinese government and limited access to distribution channels. The government has announced that it will no longer allow new entrants into the telecommunications industry and has thus further insulated existing firms from that threat. In addition, the product life cycles of the telecommunications industry have shortened; innovations are making older technologies obsolete at a quicker pace. Given the dynamic operating environment, companies have to have superior research and development expertise and the ability to adapt rapidly to technological change and product transitions.

There are two types of buyers: the final customer and the national telephone networks. Final customers make small purchases, while the national telephone networks purchase large infrastructure equipment from foreign investors. Thus, buyers still exert considerable bargaining power over suppliers. The major buyers are local governments and foreign manufacturers of telecommunications equipment. Buyer switching costs are high since different companies tend to use different standards.

There are many local suppliers for different types of components, including semiconductor devices, integrated circuit lead frames, micromotors, and liquid crystal displays. Components and parts are relatively standardized. There are approximately 130 local Chinese suppliers for direct materials and 600 for indirect materials across China. The local suppliers provide 35 different types of components to Motorola. In 1996, total annual purchases from local suppliers accounted for $473 million while the total value of exported, locally sourced components accounted for $80 million. It takes great time and effort to establish a relationship with new suppliers. On the other hand, local suppliers depend heavily on Motorola to facilitate the formation of joint ventures with appropriate foreign suppliers, to improve their technology, and to expand their exports. With the help of Motorola, Chinese local suppliers were able to export $18 million worth of their products in 1996. Since local suppliers have to rely heavily on the manufacturing and marketing expertise of foreign investors, the threat of forward integration is low.

Threats

The magnitude of the future market in China will depend heavily on the economic performance of the country as a whole. More importantly, Motorola's success will depend on the economic situation in Asia, which accounts for 26 percent of the company's business. Motorola's 1996 sales to China (including Hong Kong) totaled $3.1 billion or approximately 11 percent of the company's total worldwide revenues. Its exports to China from the United States totaled nearly $1 billion. Any economic problems in Asia will inhibit orders and intensify pricing pressures on Motorola.

Besides the large potential market, foreign investors are subject to high political risks. Any political setback will definitely affect the well-being of foreign companies. In 1992, per capita income in rural areas averaged $1,342 per annum, while in urban areas it amounted to $3,308. Economic disparities between provinces, rapid urbanization, and degradation of the countryside may lead to social unrest.

Since the telecommunications industry is considered vital by the Chinese government, it is subject to many rules. Foreign companies must strictly follow regulations and adhere to the terms set by their contracts.

At present, China still depends heavily on foreign companies in terms of telecommunications technology. Motorola has actively promoted technical, engineering, and production line skills in its branches and among suppliers. Local partners may try to consolidate the implicit knowledge gained during years of cooperation with Motorola and subsequently become less dependent on their foreign partner.

There is tremendous competition in the Chinese cellular phone market. Besides the three major competitors (Motorola, Ericsson, and Nokia), there are some smaller companies such as Siemens and Philips, which are trying to exploit the Chinese market. For instance, Philips has just set up a $60 million joint venture in Shenzhen to produce telecommunications equipment. It also envisions the company as becoming one of the big three cellular phone providers. Relatively high fixed costs in this market increase the tendency toward rivalry.

Although Motorola is still the leader in China, it continues to lose market share. It is dominant in analog cellular and strong in digital CDMA cellular but lags behind digital GSM cellular, which seems to be emerging as the standard for digital cellular in China. Digital GSM cellular is taking approximately 40 percent of the new phone market, and the Swedish company Ericsson is ahead of Motorola in selling it. On the other hand, digital cellular technologies is an area into which Motorola can diversify. The new digital technologies offer improved voice quality, longer battery life, superior security, and enhanced services such as e-mail, voice mail, and caller identification.

If foreign investors choose not to source their materials locally, they can import components from other countries. However, they still have to meet local content quotas imposed by the Chinese government. Therefore, the number of substitute products is moderately low. The favorable situation created by great reliance on suppliers is offset by a reciprocal relationship between local suppliers and foreign investors. The local suppliers have great influence over the quality of final products.

The Internal Environment

Strengths

Motorola has devoted its greatest efforts to management localization in China. It employs 9,300 people in China, and most of the midlevel management positions in its operations are held by Chinese. To attract and retain top employees in China, Motorola set up its own Employee Home Ownership Program (EHOP), which has been endorsed by the Chinese government. Motorola also plans to identify and recruit highly qualified Chinese students from overseas. It can achieve a greater degree of local responsiveness by deploying the local work force. In other words, it is in a better position to gain firsthand customer knowledge and adapt to changes in customer preferences.

Motorola provides intensive training to its employees. For example, it requires that every employee engage in at least five days (40 hours) of training each year. In 1996, it exceeded this goal and provided an average of 70 class hours of training per employee in China. A total of 19,000 student-days were taught in 1996, spread among 130 courses.

Motorola has proven to be a company with great employee relations. It has been actively fostering harmonious relationships with its employees, suppliers, and the Chinese government. It has gained tremendous support from the Chinese government because of the nature of its investments, its transfers of high technology, and its good corporate citizenship. In addition, it has management courses for Chinese government officials, including exchanges with Motorola operations overseas.

In 1995, Motorola received two certificates from the Chinese government: the Advanced Technology Enterprise Status Certificate and the High-Tech Enterprise Status Certificate. In 1996, it was second among the top 500 foreign-invested enterprises in China. These awards are strong evidence of the government's recognition of its long-term commitment to China. Motorola is also recognized by the Chinese government for its responsible corporate citizenship. It has participated actively in community service. For instance, it has been particularly active in the promotion of environmental protection and higher education and is the largest donor to China's Hope Project. From 1993 to 1996, Motorola provided an estimated 3,000 scholarships to Chinese students at major universities throughout the nation. Its relationship with the government is therefore reciprocal.

In 1996, China adopted Motorola technology as its national paging standard. Motorola has always been an important innovator in the communications equipment industry. Its FLEX technology has become the de facto world standard for one- and two-way high-speed messaging. Its Integrated Digital Enhanced Network (IDEN) has enabled specialized mobile radio (SMR) wireless technology to be used in a nationwide wireless network that competes with existing cellular technology. From 1969 to 1996, Motorola received 10,026 patents. It ranked fifteenth on the list of top patent recipients for 1969–96. In 1996, it received 1,064 patents and ranked third among other corporations in terms of the number of patents received.

In addition to being the largest American investor in China, Motorola is the leader in cellular phone, pager, two-way radio, and commercial CDMA technology. It has been cited specifically for its achievement in research, development, production, sales, and after-sales service in the PRC. Furthermore, it is widely recognized for product quality and innovation.

Meanwhile, Motorola works closely with the local Chinese suppliers to help them improve management, efficiency, and quality control systems. It provides training courses for distributors, suppliers, and business partners. By forming partnerships with Chinese suppliers, Motorola provides them with designs and new technology, helps them secure credit for capital improvements, and facilitates advantageous joint ventures with appropriate foreign firms. This approach has helped Motorola develop a pool of local suppliers across China that already numbers 130.

Motorola enjoys great cost advantages because it uses materials sourced directly from its suppliers in China. In 1996, it spent a total of $473 million on locally sourced components, materials, and services, double the amount for 1995 and a figure that represents 42 percent of total expenditures. Its manufacturing presence in China also provides strategic flexibility. Local sourcing will lessen the impact of expected lower economic growth and greater pricing pressures.

Weaknesses

The marketing skills of Motorola are less extensive than those of Ericsson. It seems that Motorola lags behind in technologies invented by other companies. For example, it excels in analog cellular phones and digital CDMA but not in digital cellular phones and digital GSM cellular. Nearly half of the phones Motorola sells are designed for analog networks, in which subscriber growth has flattened. While the company has begun the transition to products for the much faster growing digital networks, competitors such as Nokia and Ericsson are already introducing its second- and third-generation lines of digital phones.

Although Motorola's profitability ratios are comparable to the industrial average, they are lagging behind Nokia and Ericsson. Compared to Nokia, Ericsson, and the industrial average, Motorola's short-term obligations are not well secured by its short-term assets. In general, Motorola incurs less debt than its competitors in financing capital. In addition, the lesser use of long-term debt is reflected in its high-interest coverage ratio. In terms of activity ratios, Motorola is less tied up in inventory than its major competitors. Meanwhile, its asset turnover is very close to those of its competitors and the industrial average.

Entry Strategies

Entry Timing

In the late 1980s, there was essentially no consumer wireless market in China. Therefore, Motorola entered an arena where competition was close to zero. It began importing pagers and cellular phones into major cities to help China build a wireless infrastructure. The pagers were a hit. In a country with few phones, pagers were a cheap and easily acquired communications tool. Cellular phones, which could cost several months' salary, also took off. Motorola was such a force that cell phones became generically known as Motorolas. By popularizing the cellular phone in China, Motorola became a market leader. It derived revenues of $3.1 billion—11 percent of its 1996 earnings—from greater China, including Hong Kong and Taiwan. It still has incredible brand equity in cellular and dominates the Chinese market for analog handsets, with an estimated 40 to 50 percent share.

Given its early-mover position in the wireless market, Motorola also faced the difficulty of having to employ inexperienced workers. Massive and intensive training sessions lie ahead.

Political uncertainty was another disadvantage. As there was no precedent in wireless manufacturing, the road was full of uncertainty and risks, especially in the firm's dealings with the complicated Chinese bureaucracy.

Entry Mode

Motorola opened a representative office in Beijing in 1986 and has since experienced rapid growth as an active participant in China's transition to a market economy. Motorola (China) Electronics, a wholly owned Motorola entity, was incorporated in March 1992. In the same year, Motorola broke ground on its first major manufacturing facility in the Tianjin Economic Development Area (TEDA). The facility, which began operating in March 1993, produces pagers, cellular telephones, communications components, and semiconductors, mostly for sale in China and other markets in Asia.

In November 1995, Motorola began construction of a large integrated circuit wafer fabrication plant, also in the Tianjin area. The semiconductors manufactured at the plant supply the automotive, communications, personal computer, peripherals, and digital products markets. The building of the Tianjin manufacturing plant is a milestone in the long and mutually beneficial relationship between Motorola and the People's Republic of China. The wafer fabrication facility in Xiqing Tianjin is known as MOS17 (MOS is an abbreviation for metal oxide semiconductor).

Since March 1995, Motorola has formed six joint ventures with local partners in China to manufacture a range of high-tech products from pagers and multimedia computers to CDMA infrastructure and semiconductor products. These joint venture partnerships with China's strongest high-tech companies afford opportunities to manufacture advanced equipment using world-class technology. Motorola brings the latest technology and new technical and management skills to its partners in order to manufacture the highest quality products for the Chinese and export markets.

Ever committed to research and the development of new technology, Motorola has entered into five joint development projects to conduct research projects and develop communications and computer technology. Motorola has undertaken these projects together with prestigious research institutions such as Tsinghua University and the National Research Center for Intelligent Computing Systems as well as enterprises like Legend and the Xi'an Datang Telephone Corp.

In addition to production facilities in Tianjin, Motorola's investments in China include its headquarters in Beijing; branch offices in Shanghai, Guangzhou, Tianjin, Harbin, Nanjing, and Chengdu; and service shops and software centers in Beijing and Tianjin. Future plans call for opening sales and service offices in another 20 cities throughout China.

Location Selection

Tianjin

Tianjin is an international seaport and was one of the first Chinese cities opened to the outside world. It is the largest foreign trade port city in the northern part of China, the second-largest industrial city in China, and one of the largest commercial and trade centers in the north. The total population of Tianjin is 9.3 million, with urban dwellers accounting for 5.8 million. The level of expertise availability in Tianjin is relatively high. It has more than 300 scientific research facilities with various specialties. Engineering and technological workers exceed 340,000. Tianjin has a total of 28 universities and colleges, among which there are represented roughly 230 disciplines.

Joint ventures funded with Chinese and foreign investments were established in Tianjin as early as 1980. Before 1992, the average annual foreign investment was about $100 million. In 1992, the amount increased drastically to $1.2 billion. At present, the total amount of foreign investment in Tianjin is the fourth largest in China and the first in

North China, which makes it the hottest region attracting foreign investment today. There are now over 8,300 foreign-invested enterprises. Cumulative negotiated foreign investment exceeds $8.5 billion. More than 120 transnational corporations and consortiums have settled in Tianjin, including Motorola, Otis, and Mobil Oil from the United States and NEC, Honda, and Yamaha from Japan.

The Tianjin Economic and Technological Development Area was approved by the State Council in late 1984. Known as TEDA, this economic zone is located in the southeastern part of Tianjin, 50 kilometer from the center of the city and adjacent to Tanggu District, an important coastal town with a population of 400,000. It borders the port and the Tianjin Port Free Trade Zone. Transportation is convenient, and the prospect for development is promising. Its major economic indexes place it first among all development areas nationwide.

Along with these advantages, TEDA enjoys the favorable terms and flexible policies of China's special economic areas. Its main function is to establish equity joint ventures, contractual joint ventures, and exclusive foreign investment enterprises. The TEDA Management Committee exercises unified administration over TEDA on behalf of the People's Government of Tianjin Municipality. The committee examines, approves, and handles all administrative procedures and affairs relating to foreign-invested enterprises in TEDA, entertains complaints brought by such enterprises, and protects their lawful rights and interests according to the law.

Investors in TEDA are entitled to favorable taxation terms. After the expiration of a stipulated period of income tax exemption and reduction, enterprises whose exports exceed 70 percent of total output in value in the current year pay income tax at a rate of 12 percent. Enterprises located in the Xiqing Economic Development Zone pay a 10 percent income tax. For high-tech enterprises, the period of 50 percent reduction can be prolonged for another three years.

The total planned space within the TEDA jurisdiction is 33 square kilometers. The first 4.2 have been developed. The second phase is in full swing. Several years after its inauguration, TEDA has laid an excellent foundation for serving enterprises. It can provide steady supplies of water, power, and gas for production, and IDD lines for telephones, telexes, and facsimiles.

Pudong, Shanghai
Motorola has two joint venture projects in Pudong, the Shanghai Motorola Paging Products Co., Ltd., and Shanghai Motorola Automotive Electronics Co., Ltd. Pudong, symbolizing Shanghai's future promise, is

meant to be developed into a modern area that is outward looking and multifunctional. China plans to expand the boundaries of the Pudong New Area to encompass 100 square kilometers by the end of the year 2000. Development of such a vast area calls for global participation. Pudong has benefited from Deng Xiaoping's theory of socialist construction with Chinese characteristics, the strengthening of economic foundations as a result of more than a decade of economic reform, and the experience gained in several special economic zones in the south. Rmb 15 billion were invested in 10 infrastructure construction projects in the early 1990s in order to improve the investment environment.

To encourage both domestic and overseas firms to invest in the Pudong New Area, the central government and Shanghai Municipal People's Government have formulated preferential policies. These policies have granted more decision-making power to Shanghai with respect to approving manufacturing and other projects and granting import and export rights.

Since the beginning of 1994, Shanghai has implemented a series of reforms in the annual unified industrial and commercial, value-added, and consumption taxes to simplify the system and align it better with the international taxation system. However, the income tax preferential policy granted to foreign-invested and foreign enterprises in the Pudong New Area remains unchanged. Under the preferential income tax policy, foreign investors in industrial production pay income taxes at a rate of 15 percent. For those enterprises with an operating period of over 10 years, an exemption from income taxes for two consecutive years starting from the first profit-making year is granted and a 50 percent reduction is allowed from the third to the sixth years. High-tech enterprises may pay the enterprise income tax at a reduced rate of 10 percent for another three years when the current period of exemption and reduction expires.

The population of Pudong is 1.4 million. The work force is relatively well educated in accordance with the municipality's strong educational emphasis. There are about 400 primary and junior high schools within the New Area. There are also institutions of higher learning such as the Shanghai Maritime Institute and some university branches. Pudong is cooperating with 10 prestigious universities, including Fudan University, for the cultivation of advanced administrative and technical abilities at its Continuing Education Center.

Hangzhou

Motorola set up Hangzhou Motorola Cellular Systems Ltd. and Hangzhou Motorola Cellular Subscriber Ltd. in Zhejiang. Zhejiang enjoys a superior geographic location, advanced communications facilities, convenient transportation, and a well-educated and highly trained labor force. Since the beginning of the 1990s, many infrastructure and basic industrial projects have been completed there and many more are under construction. These have significantly improved Zhejiang's environment for investment. In terms of such economic norms as GDP and total volume of export trade, the province rose from twelfth or thirteenth to fifth or sixth place in China in the 1980s. In 1994, Zhejiang's economy was still growing rapidly.

Preferential control and taxation policies have been used to motivate foreign direct investment in Zhejiang. For production-oriented enterprises with foreign investment, the local income tax is computed and levied at a reduced rate of 1.5 percent. Production-oriented enterprises with foreign investments scheduled to operate for a period of 10 years or more are exempted from local income tax for five to 10 years commencing in the first profit-making year.

Nanjing

Motorola's joint venture in Jiangsu is called Nanjing Power Computer Ltd. Located at the eastern part of China, Nanjing is the capital of Jiangsu Province. It is also a major international commercial port, second only to Shanghai. Nanjing is a thriving city known for its rich resources and abundant products as well as its prominent people. It has been ranked one of the 40 cities with the best investment environment. Total retail sales of consumer goods there in 1995 amounted to Rmb 24 billion, a 27 percent increase over the previous year.

Nanjing is an important industrial base where electronics, automobiles, chemicals, and more than 2,000 categories of products are manufactured. The industrial output value of the whole city in 1995 amounted to Rmb 81,800 million, a 24.4 percent increase over the previous year, and the ratio of output to sales reached 96.4 percent, the best in the province. The government especially encourages foreign investors to set up export-oriented or technologically advanced enterprises and will give them preferential treatment with respect to taxation, credit, utilities, and telecommunications and transportation facilities.

Nanjing's work force is well educated, particularly in terms of technical training. In Nanjing, there are over 460 natural science research institutions with more than 320,000 technical personnel of different specialties and over 40 social science research institutions with more than 50,000 researchers. In scientific and technological expertise, it ranks third in the country.

Cooperative Strategies

Motorola's Chinese partners are usually state-owned enterprises. In three joint ventures, the Chinese partner is actually a subsidiary of the Ministry of Posts and Telegraphs (MPT), which has enormous regulatory power and industrial influence. All the Chinese partners are well-established, large firms that enjoy high market recognition and have good capabilities.

The Leshan-Phoenix Semiconductor Co., the largest of Motorola's joint ventures, was its first in China. It was started at a cost of $30 million, an investment that later expanded to $50 million. In 1997, Motorola announced plans to invest a further $200 million in this venture.

Motorola's Chinese partner in Nanjing Power Computer Ltd. is Nanjing Panda, one of China's largest and most competitive manufacturers of televisions and other consumer electronics products. Panda is one of the best-known brands in China. Nanjing Panda's 1996 turnover was about $400 million, with a profit of about $20 million. Nanjing Panda is also associated with Nanjing Ericsson and Nanjing ADC. Motorola has a 60 percent stake in Nanjing Power Computer, while Nanjing Panda holds the remaining 40 percent. Plans were to manufacture 20,000 computers in 1996, about 50,000 each in 1997 and 1998, and 100,000 computers in 1999 and beyond. The company planned originally to start with Macintosh clones and then expand to include Windows NT machines. Since Motorola has since made an exit from the Windows NT and the Macintosh clone businesses, the future of this company is unclear.

Shanghai Motorola Paging Products Co., Ltd., is a $12 million joint venture with Shanghai Radio Communication Equipment Manufacturing Co., Ltd. (SRCEMC), which is in turn majority owned by China National Posts and Telecommunications Industrial Corp. (CNPTIC), the largest enterprise of the MPT. SRCEMC was founded in 1993. It manufactures pagers and cellular phones. Its 1995 sales were about $37 million. Shanghai Motorola Paging was Motorola's first joint venture with CNPTIC. The general manager of Shanghai Motorola Paging Products is a Motorola employee, while the deputy general manager is from SRCEMC.

Motorola holds 52 percent of Hangzhou Motorola Cellular Systems Ltd., which has registered capital of $29.5 million. In January 1998, Motorola announced the signing of a contract worth $110 million to manufacture GSM infrastructure equipment in collaboration with Eastcom, one of the Chinese partners in this joint venture. It is not known whether this contract will be handled through this JV or in a separate venture.

In conclusion, Motorola's experience in China demonstrates that a good, long-term relationship with the government is valuable but that it shouldn't require compromise on essentials like quality or majority ownership. Motorola, like Boeing and a few other multinational companies, goes out of its way to express and demonstrate its commitment to China's economic and technological development. At the same time, employee education is essential to inculcating a corporate philosophy and satisfying Motorola's obsession with quality. Unusual employee benefits such as help with home ownership retain trained employees and reduce risk of know-how leakage.

Motorola may be trying to do too many things. Its exit from the computer business is a partial response to this problem, but now it is stuck with Nanjing Power Computer. Nanjing Panda is one of China's largest consumer electronics companies. Maybe Motorola can use its distribution channels and brand recognition to manufacture or market television Internet products, low-end consumer electronics such as cordless phones, or even GSM phones. It could enter into a strategic alliance with either Microsoft or Sun to include their software in Motorola's consumer products and make them "smarter." Another problem Motorola faces is the U.S. policy of not exporting sensitive technologies, including the latest semiconductor manufacturing processes and state of the art encryption for cellular phones. Motorola's European and Japanese rivals do not face this problem. Since China considers technology transfer crucial, Motorola's competitors may gain an advantage in this area.

Nike

The East Asian region holds tremendous potential for growth. It is no secret that East Asia's largely untapped human population, industrialization, and changing government attitude toward trade have made it the primary focus of many international companies. Nike, Inc., is no exception. With 1997 worldwide sales of over $9 billion, the athletic footwear and apparel maker has already made strides to conquer the East Asian market. Nike produced shoes in Japan until the mid-1970s. Between 1974 and 1985, it moved operations to South Korea and Taiwan. During the 1980s, the company moved into Vietnam, Thailand, Indonesia, and China. Currently, China and Indonesia produce two-thirds of Nike's footwear. Nike has contracted with several Chinese companies to assemble its products. For a small labor-processing fee, Chinese workers put together the world famous "Swoosh" shoe. By means of this arrangement, commonly known as subcontracting or compensation trade, the company utilizes one of China's greatest strengths, manpower, at a minimal cost. While this operation may work for now, company management acknowledges that with labor standards increasing and competition heating up it must look beyond subcontracting in order to maintain its position as the top athletic apparel and shoe manufacturer in the world.

Nike, headquartered in Eugene, Oregon, is currently under the command of Phillip H. Knight, its chairman, chief executive officer, and cofounder. The 1980s proved to be a decade of unsurpassed dominance. After Nike went public in 1980 with two million shares of stock and gained the endorsement of young basketball rookie Michael Jordan, nothing stood in the way of the company's success. In 1986, nearly 20 years after Knight received his first order for shoes from Japan, revenues hit the $1 billion mark. The success of the "Just Do It" campaign in 1988 and Nike's international presence were clear indicators that it was on its way to sports and fitness dominance. In the 1990s, it continued its fast-paced growth. Initiatives such as Reuse-a-Shoe, Participate in the Lives of America's Youth (PLAY), and the Nike Environmental Action Team (NEAT) gave it an opportunity to give something back to the community and the athletes who supported the company. With the successes of Michael Jordan, Carl Lewis, Gabby Reece, and, more recently, Tiger Woods, Nike continues to seek endorsements from inspirational athletes who exemplify that heart and soul that began at Blue Ribbon Sports.

"Just Do It" is one of the most recognized slogans in the world. Likewise, Nike's Swoosh logo is known internationally. Known for its humble beginnings and tremendous growth and popularity, Nike has become the world's leader in sports and fitness. Its momentum in the global marketplace has been highly publicized as the need to become globally competitive has increased in this industry. In order to accomplish its mission of maximizing profits through products and services that enrich people's lives, it has created five corporate objectives and a brand mission. The corporate objectives are to provide an environment that helps people maximize their contributions to Nike, identify consumer segments, provide quality and innovative services and products internally and externally, establish and nurture relevant emotional ties with consumer segments, and maximize profits. Nike's mission is to be the world's best sports and fitness brand by focusing on the customer, employee, product, environment, and shareholder.

The External Environment

Nike monitors the industry for changing trends and often leads it in product innovation. In this industry, technology has created fierce competition. The ability to innovate and provide products to fit the needs of a changing market is essential if Nike wants to stay on top. Technology is growing at a fast pace and therefore offers many opportunities for innovation. In the U.S. market, consumers are very aware of new technological improvements in footwear. Methods for increasing stability, support, comfort, and performance are constantly being integrated into new designs. In the United States, companies that produce athletic footwear and apparel have capitalized on the American trend toward a healthier lifestyle. People are becoming more active. In 1995, over $11.4 billion was spent on athletic shoes, amounting to nearly 81 million pairs of shoes. The athletic footwear industry is currently in the mature stage of the industry life cycle.

Major threats to established players in this industry include government regulation, economic downturns, and changes in fashion. Any addition or removal of legislative or regulatory constraints on, for example, the import and export of materials or finished goods can pose a major threat to or opportunity for these companies. The current Asian economic crisis and a recent slowdown in the U.S. footwear business has obviously hurt this industry. Plummeting currencies and other financial woes have made high-end shoes like Nike's an unaffordable luxury for many East Asian citizens. In shoe fashions, there has been a slight movement away from the athletic, "white shoe" look and toward the outdoor, "brown shoe" look. The outdoors look has been gaining popularity in Japan. In response to this trend, Nike has concentrated on its All Conditions Gear (ACG) line, specializing in outdoor footwear and apparel.

Right behind Nike, Reebok International Ltd. is second in worldwide sales of athletic shoes. Reebok is a global sports and fitness company that was founded in 1895. Under the administration of CEO Paul Fireman and chief financial officer (CFO) Kenneth I. Watchmaker, Reebok currently has endorsements from Shaquille O'Neal, Emitt Smith, Frank Thomas, Michael Chang, and Arantxa Sanchez-Vicario. Reebok's Internationals brands also includes Rockport, a maker of causal, walking, and dress shoes, Weebok for kids, and Greg Norman. Rockport contributes over $400 million a year in sales. Rockport and Polo Ralph Lauren have entered into a joint venture, and Reebok recently sold a subsidiary, Avia Group International. Reebok's strategy in the Asia Pacific region is quality, not quantity. It currently has two distribution networks in China. Reebok's operations in Guangdong Province are managed by its Hong Kong–based joint venture. Beijing and Shanghai operations are run by Reebok's China subsidiary, also a joint venture.

Former market leader Adidas is currently third in the race for worldwide sales of athletic footwear. Alfred "Adi" Dassler began Adidas in Germany in 1948. Many apparel manufacturers have created knockoff versions of Adidas's trademark triple-striped products. In 1997, Adidas's U.S. sales were $500 million and worldwide sales increased 92 percent over the previous year. It currently has endorsements from Kobe Bryant, Donovan Bailey, Denise Lewis, and other track athletes. This year, National Basketball Association (NBA) affiliates appointed Adidas Australia as a major apparel partner. Adidas enjoys sustainable market dominance in soccer. For these reasons, it continues to be a hot competitor. Within the Asia Pacific region, Adidas is picking up momentum with increasing international sales, but it currently does not have any specific strategies for this particular region.

There is a possibility of new entrants into the athletic footwear market. Barriers to entry are not significantly high, and established companies can easily extend their product lines to carry athletic footwear. For example, companies such as DKNY and Tommy Hilfiger represent brand names that are attempting to capitalize on the athletic footwear market in the United States. Their designs appear trendy but are questionable as far as meeting the demands of an athlete.

There are many reasons why Nike decided to establish a presence in China. China has 2.4 billion consumer feet that Nike dreams of covering. If it sells a pair of athletic shoes for every 11,812 people in China, it will make profits equivalent to what could be realized if it sold one pair to every fourth person in the United States. China is already the biggest shoe-manufacturing country in the world, producing over a third of the world's athletic shoes. Many shoe companies are attracted to China not only because of its cheap labor but because products manufactured there are well received in the United States for their quality. China hosted a total of 26.7 million overseas tourists during the first half of 1997, an increase of 8.67 percent compared to the same period of the previous year. A mounting tourism environment enhances conditions for Nike by creating a diverse customer base in developed cities where the company's retail distributors are located.

Many of Nike's retail stores are located in the developed cities of Shanghai, Beijing, and Guangzhou. It is important for any successful company to understand market structure and consumer profiles. The top five markets in China include the cities of Beijing and Shanghai as well as Guangdong, Jiangsu, and Zhejiang Provinces. Together these comprise 16.9 percent of the country's population and account for 33 percent of 1994 national retail sales. These prosperous coastal areas are considered the trendsetters and opinion leaders for the rest of China.

The basic character of the average Chinese consumer is generally pragmatic, price conscious, a careful planner, and patriotic. Those who work in China's coastal cities have plenty of spare change and spend freely. They do not buy Western products blindly. They have proven to be more sophisticated and discriminating than originally anticipated by MNCs. They prefer imported high-quality products sold at a good price.

China's consumers can be classified as nouveau riche, yuppies, salaried workers, and the working poor. The nouveau riche (*baofahu*) group includes entrepreneurs, celebrities, and government officials of various ranks between the ages of 30 and 65. They are known as China's superspenders, making over $5,000 a year. The nouveau riche are likely to use credit cards and own cellular phones and cars. They are eager to purchase products perceived as status symbols.

China's yuppies (*dushi yapishi*) are individuals who range in age from 25 to 45 and tend to have at least some college education or technical training. They reside in major metropolitan areas and work in China's new enterprises, joint ventures, and foreign companies for generous wages by Chinese standards. The annual household income of this group is between $1,800 and $5,000. These young, urban professionals are likely to be receptive to new ideas and products. The yuppies, together with the nouveau riche, can be considered China's emerging middle class. They are the primary consumers of foreign products because they reside in areas easily accessed by advertising campaigns and product distribution. A forecast by the State Information Center predicts that the gap in income between China's cities and the countryside will more than triple by 2005. The difference between average city and country annual incomes is expected to be Rmb 10,000 by 2005. This means an increase in disposable income for Nike's target customers.

Selling in China requires a more direct approach than in a developed market. Product focus is highly concentrated. Nike's strategic approach to marketing is to create an emotional tie with the consumer. Sponsoring basketball star Michael Jordan has been one of its most successful moves. A 1992 survey conducted in the PRC found that many Chinese schoolchildren believed that the two most famous men in all of world history were the revolutionary hero Zhou Enlai and Michael Jordan. To announce its presence in China, Nike held a gala dinner at which six women, scantily dressed in Nike clothing, performed aerobics to Madonna's song "Like a Virgin" and "New York, New York." Nike felt these songs perfectly fit the dawning of the age of the new Chinese consumer.

Nike does not appear worried that the price of its shoes may still be too high for the average Chinese consumer ($60 to $100). China's urban men are already interested in football and the NBA, so executives believe that more and more people will be willing to pay premium prices. Nike uses ads and sports sponsorships as well as deals with professional football and basketball teams at the national, provincial, and municipal levels. It claims to have sponsored more local sports teams and won higher domestic revenues than any other international brand.

Nike, like most companies, is susceptible to piracy. In China, fake Nike shoes are one-fifth the price of the genuine article. Since the real thing only holds a small percentage of the Chinese sports shoe market, counterfeits pose a real threat. In 1995, sales of foreign sports shoes and high-end Chinese brands in Beijing, Shanghai, and Guangzhou grew by less than 5 percent, compared to the 10 to 15 percent growth in overall retail sales. Although counterfeiting limits opportunities today, long-term possibilities excite international sports shoe companies like Nike. While fake Nikes may sport the Swoosh, the "Air" and "Zoom" make the shoe a true Nike. One counterfeit deterrent is importing its patented air cushions from the United States to China, where the shoes are assembled. Nike also investigates and brings legal action against counterfeiters either alone or in cooperation with international competitors like Reebok.

The Internal Environment

Nike can be classified as a technological innovator. Over the years, it has boasted many product innovations. One such breakthrough was Nike's patented Air-Sole technology. Another is "functional innovative technology" (FIT), which has yielded garments that are lighter, more durable, and better able to help an athlete's sweat evaporate than materials used in the past. Despite Nike's many product innovations, it is less innovative in its processes. With the recent adoption of Richter System's RAMS 2000 merchandising computer system, Nike has at least taken strides in becoming an innovator in this area as well. According to reports, this network will help coordinate Nike's inventory, distribution, and merchandising functions worldwide.

Through contracts with professional and collegiate athletes, Nike has been able to have its products endorsed and worn by charismatic superstars and famous sports teams. After securing contracts with these athletes and teams, Nike runs expensive television and magazine advertisements to showcase new products using selected athletes. These ads tend to focus on the emotional aspect of sports such as love for a particular sport or camaraderie between teammates.

Nike distributes its products through specialty stores that sell athletic apparel, such as Foot Locker, as well as through department stores such as J. C. Penney. More recently, however, it has opened NikeTowns across the United States to distribute and display its products directly. Through licensing agreements, strategic alliances, and acquisitions, Nike has built a stronger and more diversified company. These strategies have allowed Nike to enter and market itself in growing industries using existing industrial leaders and popular sports.

Nike vertically integrates by forming licensing agreements not only with individual teams but also with entire sports leagues. In 1996, it paid $200 million to the National Football League (NFL) to become an NFL Pro Line apparel licensee. It has also broken into the $500 million–plus snowboard market by entering into a partnership with Marker Snowboards. Plans are under way to launch a workout program, Athletic Total Conditioning (ATC), in health clubs in eight key markets. The program will incorporate the exercises used by athletes who endorse Nike. Some will even take part in workshops for health club instructors to help launch the program. This kind of diversification is related to Nike's main business and doubles as a marketing tool. By using diversification strategies such as these, Nike has become the market leader, capturing 47 percent of the world's sportswear market. Adidas and other competitors use the same strategy, but, while Adidas, for example, only licenses soccer sportswear, Nike licenses sportswear for football, hockey, baseball, and much more.

Nike also diversifies by acquiring companies that offer established know-how, expertise, and economies of scale. Examples include Tetra Plastics, the maker of Air-Sole materials; Canstar Sports, Inc. (Bauer), the largest manufacturer of hockey equipment; Cole-Haan, a dress shoe manufacturer; and Sports Specialty, a manufacturer of sports hats.

Nike is currently in the midst of restructuring due to a downturn in the retail economy. Because of the drop in business in Asia and declining demand in the United States, Nike is expecting to take a restructuring charge of $125 to $175 million in the fourth quarter of 1998. Approximately 7 percent of Nike's work force around the world will lose their jobs. One recent report announced that Nike had already laid off 250 people, most from the corporate office and the rest from offices abroad.

Nike's investment in research and development is crucial to its livelihood. In 1997, it spent an estimated $75 million on R&D. Its Air and Zoom technology, the catalysts for its more recent successes, are products of Nike's R&D team, the Advanced Product Engineering Group (APE). An innovation that has allowed Nike to remain ahead of the industry in China and abroad is its central merchandising system, RAMS 2000, which is licensed from Richter Systems. The system functions to meet the needs of its growing international business and to improve store-level services as well as to better manage inventory and boost profitability. The RAMS 2000 system features global multilingual, multiple currency, and tax and duty capabilities.

Entry Strategies

Entry Timing

Nike established itself in China as one of the early movers, along with Reebok and Adidas, in the early 1980s. The early timing of foreign direct investment has several advantages, including new markets, segmentation, distribution channels, and the lack of strong competition. Successful market pioneers usually hold higher market shares than late entrants do. Product advantages include new products, new product positioning, materials supply, and brand loyalty. New patent technology and technology leadership over local firms and other businesses are also benefits. Early entrants enjoy resource access advantages such as the pick of facilities, information, partner selection, scarce materials, human and natural resources, and other investment infrastructure. The early investor also may place its strength in businesses, industries, and markets in which competition from local firms is weak or where it has better technological and organizational expertise. The overall goal accomplished in this long-term process is superiority in sales growth.

Early movers face higher risks and uncertainty because they are less familiar with the local environment. Therefore, many firms consider joint ventures to be the preferred entry mode for foreign direct investment. When alliances are formed with local partners, however, the government may impose complicated rules and regulations. In most instances, the pursuit of self-interest rather than congruent goals between partners results in significant uncertainties for joint venture operations. Many times, these uncertainties extend beyond the scope of the foreign investor's control. Therefore, the early mover in a foreign market normally pays a high price in learning how to deal with the local environment. Early movers also have to pay higher switching and start-up costs.

Entry Mode

When Nike first entered China, it did so through contractual joint ventures. This proved to be an unsuccessful strategy for several key reasons. Nike tried to deal directly with state enterprises, but state-owned factories could not comprehend what Nike wanted in terms of price, quality, and delivery. Nike found itself making shoes to build up China's manufacturing capabilities rather than selling them under its own brand name. Its American managers faced problems in dealing with China's public sector. Its China operations posed a heavy financial burden when Reebok temporarily became the world's largest athletic firm and Nike experienced overwhelming inventory problems. Nike gradually wound down its relations with state-owned factories as the Chinese door opened to Taiwan-based investors. The last contract with a state firm ended in 1989, the year after Feng Tay, one of Nike's major agents, set up a Hong Kong unit to invest in Chinese footwear producers.

When Nike's first strategic choice failed, it looked to subcontracted labor as the answer to its problems. By subcontracting labor, production risks are shifted to the contractors. This strategic choice proved successful. Nike retains the advantages of firms that produce in-house such as a high degree of control over quality, the ability to respond rapidly to changing tastes, and the ability to focus on salesmanship and distribution. At the same time, it has built upon the lessons learned through its first entry mode selection.

The basic process in Nike's international operations is accomplished in four steps. First, designers collaborate with marketing people at the company's headquarters in Oregon to come up with the shape and feel of next season's athletic shoes. Next, blueprints are relayed by satellite to its contractors' computer design systems in Taiwan, where the plans are turned into prototype shoes that can be run off the line. When Nike units in South Korea receive the plans by fax, engineers in both countries work out how to manufacture the shoes dreamed up in the United States. Finally, the shoes are manufactured at contractors' factories throughout the region, particularly in China.

Nike manages its operations through Taiwanese businessmen who are established in Taiwan and South Korea. The Taiwanese businessmen contact affiliates located in Hong Kong, who oversee Nike's business in China. Although Nike manufactures its shoes with subcontracted labor, 610 of its 7,800 employees work at subcontractors' sites in China to ensure that the factories will produce shoes of the right quality and see to it that they meet delivery schedules.

Nike's three main suppliers are Yue Yuen, Xiefeng, and Sung Hwa. Yue Yuen is described as the world's largest footwear supplier. It is located in China's Pearl River delta and also produces athletic shoes for other companies. Xiefeng Footwear has a facility in Fuzhou and two factories in Fujian Province. Its rubber mill in Fujian Province produces synthetic soles, which are exported to its Taiwan affiliate, Feng Tay, for finishing. Xiefeng imports about 95 percent of its raw materials, mostly from Taiwan and South Korea. It only buys packaging and wrapping materials and some basic chemicals in China. Sung Hwa is a firm in South Korea.

One of the major reasons Nike converted its operations to subcontracted labor is that this enables it to shift production quickly in response to protectionist threats. For example, in the event that the United States withdraws the most favored nation status from China, Nike could ship its Chinese-made goods to Asia and Europe and send products made in Indonesia and other nations to the United States. Furthermore, if costs in a particular factory rise too much and productivity fails to compensate, Nike can go elsewhere. It is continuously looking for new manufacturing sites.

Location Selection

Nike operates 13 footwear and 14 apparel factories in cooperation with local companies in China, and it has more than 300 retail distributors and flagship stores within the country. The factories are located near

Hong Kong, mainly in the Pearl River delta provinces of Guangdong and Fujian. Most foreign investors' factories and distribution operations are located in China's attractive coastal regions, the source of nearly 40 percent of the country's rising gross domestic product.

Guangdong accounts for a high percentage of national GDP, 11 percent in 1992, the highest share of China's 30 provinces. Light industry in this area constituted 13 percent of the national total. Western companies see the Pearl River delta as a gateway for getting consumer goods into China and a region where economic reform has gone the furthest. It is best known as an export dynamo. Chinese and foreign companies have made the area a major source of shoes, garments, and toys destined for world markets.

In past years, Guangdong and Hong Kong formed what was called the economic "Cantonese Tiger." Hong Kong was known as the shop where everyone did their business, and Guangdong was the backyard where businesses from Hong Kong set up their factories. Now Guangdong is being challenged, as new sources of cheap labor and rival trading centers have opened up in other parts of China. These changes have forced Guangdong to improve its overburdened infrastructure and poor environmental conditions. Guangdong plans to spend $7 billion from 1996 to 2000 in solving these problems.

Lately, Nike has been accused by many U.S. activist groups of permitting its contractors to perpetrate labor abuses in their factories. Although Nike has imposed labor codes of conduct, factory workers may have not been informed of this. The company passes the buck to contractors and claims it has no control over what goes on in their factories. As a result, many U.S. consumers perceive Nike as a corporation that is more concerned about making a dollar than moral issues. Nike's labor strategy has proved tremendously profitable and successful. In the long run, however, as the standard of living of targeted Chinese consumers improves and the U.S. public becomes increasingly aware of the inhumane practices of Nike's contractors, these circumstances could have an adverse effect on the firm's stock. By setting up wholly foreign owned enterprises in China and promoting better working conditions, Nike could set an ethical example for the Chinese and at the same time encourage comparable practices in China among all U.S. companies.

CASE 6

General Motors

General Motors Corp. (GM) is the world's largest vehicle manufacturer, with 17.4 percent of the total vehicle market worldwide. It is a recognized world leader in new automotive technologies and safety and environmental initiatives. Its entrance into China's automotive market was a landmark decision that enabled it to secure a global position in the automotive industry. China's growing economy and General Motors' ability to capitalize on global business ventures imply a great future for GM in China. It has participated in many joint ventures to create excellent products with superior quality to meet the needs of the Chinese people. China is a large part of General Motors' global plan to become a major player in all the growth markets of the world.

General Motors is the largest industrial enterprise in the United States and the world's foremost manufacturer of cars and trucks. Based in Detroit, GM is investing heavily in both truck production and global expansion. In 1996, the company employed more than 647,000 people and partnered with more than 30,000 supplier companies worldwide. With about 40 percent of its automotive sales outside of North America, it is no wonder that General Motors leads the industry in the global marketplace.

In addition, GM provides financing, makes vehicle components, and produces autos for foreign car makers in which it has a stake, including Opel, Holden, Isuzu, and Saab. It also develops telecommunications networks, such as the digital satellite system, for direct television services.

General Motors' fundamental purpose is to provide products and services of such quality that its customers will receive superior value, its employees and business partners will share in its success, and its stockholders will receive sustained, superior returns on their investments.

The major international markets for GM are Europe, Latin America, Africa, the Middle East, Asia and the Pacific, Canada, and Mexico. A total of 1,798,000 vehicular units were delivered to Europe in

1996; 691,000 vehicles were delivered to locations in Latin America, Africa, and the Middle East in the same year. The Asia Pacific region received 629,000 vehicles, and about 470,000 were delivered to Canada and Mexico.

The External Environment

In 1994, the United States had 512,489 wholesale establishments. This industry employed 6.365 million people and had a payroll of $210 billion. Of this total, the automotive industry made up approximately 25 percent of total trade. In 1995, the automobile industry directly employed about 900,000 people, and about 2.3 million were employed indirectly through 18,000 automobile dealers and suppliers. The automobile industry ranks first in manufacturing and contributes $260 billion to the U.S. economy. This accounts for approximately 4 percent of the nation's gross domestic product. The automobile industry accounts for one-sixth of all shipments of durable goods, 30 percent of iron, 15 percent of steel, 25 percent of aluminum, and 75 percent of natural rubber.

The "Big Three" U.S. automakers are General Motors, Ford Motor Co., and Chrysler Corp. (before it merged with Daimler). Together they account for over 60 percent of the automobile market. In 1996, new car registrations in the United States totaled 8,548,068; GM accounted for 32.7 percent (2,795,218), Ford for 20.4 percent (1,743,806), and Chrysler for 9.8 percent (837,711).

Ford boosted its market share from a low of 16.3 percent in 1981 to 20.4 percent in 1996. This increase was due to improved quality, bold new styling, and major promotional efforts on behalf of the Ford Taurus. Ford is also preparing for the new millennium by implementing Ford 2000. This is intended to reduce costs by consolidating the company's design and engineering operations worldwide.

Chrysler's market share also improved in 1996. Its truck sales rose about 18 percent over 1995 levels, and its light truck and minivan sales increased from a low in 1992 of 21.1 percent to 23.3 percent in 1996. These increases were due to the success of its new minivans and the Jeep Cherokee and Grand Cherokee sport utility vehicles. Chrysler expects to continue its investment in China's Beijing Jeep Corp. after its 20-year contract expires in 2004. It plans to spend $230 million before then on research and development. It is developing a model to replace the military-style jeep, which should hit the streets of China in the year

2000. Beijing Jeep is the only manufacturer that did not cut prices during slumping sales. It sold 71,000 Jeeps in China in 1996.

Another of GM's competitors, Peugeot, is experiencing problems in Guangzhou. If attempts to salvage its unprofitable joint venture fail, managers may have to pull out of the Chinese market completely. In that case, an enormous bidding war will begin in which other automakers, possibly Daimler-Benz or Opel AG (a subsidiary of General Motors) will fight for this foothold in the expanding Chinese market. Peugeot's dilemma illustrates the difficulty of setting up large joint ventures in China.

Even Volkswagen is having problems. It is concerned that its partner lacks some of the business savvy to survive in the extremely competitive automobile industry. Its partners need to make better sales pitches and promote the quality and resale value of their cars. Although Volkswagen's sales have been rising by about 20 percent annually, it would like to open exclusive dealerships in China. It holds about 60 percent of China's market share and produced 239,000 cars in China in 1996, up by about 9 percent from the previous year.

For a company to succeed in the global market, it must work well with local governments. Shanghai GM (SGM) was designated as Shanghai's number one government project for 1998, and it received the full support of the Chinese government in launching its first vehicle. This was the first time in the history of the city that an industrial project was named the most significant project for the local government. According to Rudolph A. Schlais, chairman of the board of SGM, the company's future is dependent on the cooperation of the Shanghai government department. It wants to exceed the quality of GM's competitors domestically and internationally. Government policies can also have a negative effect, as when Beijing imposed a tight money policy. This in turn suppressed China's demand for cars.

General Motors has found that not many people in China can afford cars. The typical means of transportation is the bicycle. However, GM feels that China's rapid economic growth will double individual incomes every seven years and enable the people of China to purchase automobiles. There are four categories of potential GM customers in China: the newly rich, employees of foreign companies, artists and entertainers, and the offspring of high officials. Newly rich, self-employed entrepreneurs in the private sector comprise the largest consumer group for GM. These are the people who went from rags to riches, the most successful group in the country. They have a low average education and do not travel outside of China. Although they may have unsophisticated tastes, they usually buy the most expensive name brand products.

The Internal Environment

General Motors uses what it calls "simultaneous engineering," a strategy in which designers and engineers with various specialties team up in the vehicle design phase. Cross-functional cooperation is used to reduce or eliminate redesign during the later development stages. Designers and engineers use supercomputers to create three-dimensional designs of engines, interiors, and even the entire vehicle in a short period of time. These technological innovations save time and reduce development costs.

Another innovation is the use of a common chassis. General Motor's Shanghai plant can produce a Chinese version of the company's new minivan because the chassis of the American Buick sedan is the same as that used in China.

According to GM's CEO, John Smith, excellent organizational skills will help the new joint venture in China steer clear of the pitfalls that are plaguing some of its competitors. For example, its current joint venture only involves one partner, the Shangai Automotive Industry Corp. (SAIC). This contrasts with Mercedes, which had problems negotiating with two different partners that were located hundreds of miles apart.

In 1996, GM's current ratio (of current assets to current liability) of 6.91 was rather high, especially compared to Ford's 0.97 and Chrysler's 0.46. A high ratio is considered favorable to creditors because it means the company can pay its debts, but it may also indicate improper use of assets. If there is too much cash, it could be invested somewhere with a larger rate of return.

The Big Three seem to be operating at just about the same level in terms of return on sales and debt ratio. In 1996, GM's profit margin was 0.03, the same as Ford's, while Chrysler came in at 0.05. General Motor's debt ratio (relative to total assets) is 0.89, Ford's is 0.90, and Chrysler's is 0.81.

Entry Strategies

Entry Mode

In January 1992, GM joined forces with the Jinbei Automotive Co. This joint venture produces light commercial vehicles in Shenyang. General Motors contributes management personnel, training, and technology to the joint venture. In 1994, First Auto Works Jinbei became the joint venture partner. More recently, the partnership was reorganized, and a core team is currently working on the development of a new product. In July 1996, GM was ranked as the best-known foreign automotive company in China according to a survey of Beijing residents. In 1997, it entered into a joint venture with SAIC in China. The new vehicle will be a mid- to high-end luxury sedan.

The main office of General Motors China, Inc. (GM China) has coordinating responsibility for all GM operations there, including all vehicle projects and components. The company's presence in automotive divisions and operations includes General Motors China, Inc.; Opel China GMBH; the Jinbei General Motors Automotive Co., Ltd.; and the General Motors Shanghai Office. Opel China is a wholly owned subsidiary registered in Germany. It was established to facilitate potential Opel investment in China. It has a representative office in Guangzhou and Guangdong. The Guangzhou office is responsible for the development of potential Opel engine and vehicle projects in China.

The GM China–Shanghai Operations venture (GM Shanghai) includes a representative office that supports the GM and SAIC joint venture, which will consist of vehicle, engine, and transmission assembly operations as well as a marketing and administrative headquarters. The new company is 50 percent owned by GM and SAIC.

GM China has also been very active in the components sector of one of its major divisions, Delphi Automotive Systems. Delphi's presence in China has allowed it to establish 10 joint venture and five licensing agreements with various Chinese partners.

Much of GM's expansion takes place through joint ventures with other companies. These are managed independently but incorporate GM's ideas and technology on a global scale. For example, SGM in China is independently managed but uses GM's global resources and technology. In February 1995, GM's Automotive Components Group was renamed Delphi Automotive Systems to reflect its global customer focus. Delphi is the world's largest and most diversified supplier of automotive components and systems. It has its own joint venture in China, with the Shanghai Mechanical and Electrical Holding Co., to manufacture automotive batteries. Together they plan to build a $50 million, wholly owned plant in Shanghai, which will manufacture steering systems and other chassis components. Delphi's experience in numerous worldwide joint ventures was a key influence during GM's SAIC negotiations in 1997.

General Motors International Operations (GMIO) plays a large role in GM's international expansion. Its main goal is improving global profitability and market share. It has maintained its focus on high-volume core markets by leveraging a strong distribution infrastructure in

Western Europe, South America, and Australia and pursuing opportunities in the growth markets of Asia, the Pacific, Central Europe, Argentina, India, and the former Soviet Union. Recently, the company announced plans to begin manufacturing vehicles in Russia. Through its global growth initiatives, GMIO intends to secure GM's leadership position in the world automotive market. The move into China is a large part of General Motors' ongoing plan to gain a greater share of the overseas automobile manufacturing market.

Entry Timing

General Motors was an early mover in the Chinese automotive market, although Volkswagen entered even earlier. General Motors holds the advantage, however, because as the largest automobile manufacturer in the world it can pour much more capital into foreign expansion than can Volkswagen. This gives it leverage over Volkswagen and other competitors. Volkswagen's contract with SAIC is expiring next year and SAIC does not intend to continue with that joint venture.

General Motors and Ford were in fierce competition to become SAIC's U.S. partner. They both knew that the deal with SAIC would determine who would be the market leader in China. This battle provided much delay for GM's entrance into the Chinese market. The GM-SAIC joint venture was initially agreed upon in October 1995, but operations did not start until the end of 1998. For any major joint venture project, approvals from various government agencies and bodies are required, including the final approval of the Ministry of Foreign Trade and Economic Cooperation. Although there was a delay while approval was pending, establishing a business contract with the largest automobile manufacturer in China was worth the wait.

Equity Sharing

After a long and competitive selection process, GM received approval for a joint venture with SAIC. It chose GM for its advanced automotive engineering capabilities. This joint venture alone gives General Motors a sizable advantage over its competitors. It named the newly established joint venture Shanghai General Motors. By bringing together world-class manufacturing processes and systems, SGM will benefit from GM's ability to leverage global resources.

China's largest automotive manufacturing plant, SAIC was founded in 1956. It now employs 57,000 people, producing over 150,000 passenger cars, 1,000 heavy-duty trucks, 300,000 motorcycles, and 12,000 tractors annually. It has established an initial scale of economy in sedan manufacturing and component supply systems and is one of the most profitable automotive companies in China.

The equity distribution between the partners is fifty-fifty. The Chinese government does not allow foreign companies to hold majority ownership in a local company. The president of SAIC, Chen Xiang-Lin, is the main partner, along with the president and chief financial officer of GM, John F. Smith Jr. General Motors' willingness to partner with SAIC shows its long-term commitment to the Chinese automotive market.

Both local and U.S. employees manage the joint venture with SAIC. General Motors offers Chinese employees the opportunity for advancement both locally and globally. In addition, it offers an excellent training program. These types of incentives attract many Chinese professionals.

It was expected that SGM would begin building Buick motor cars in late 1998 with an annual capacity of around 100,000 units. The cars will be based on a new car group platform and will feature a 2.98-liter V6 coupe with a new automatic electronic transmission. The all-new 160,000 square-meter assembly plant will feature the latest in automotive manufacturing technology, including flexible tooling and lean manufacturing processes.

Location Selection

The government recognizes that China's unorthodox brand of market-driven socialism needs to be radically overhauled. Its goal is to build a complete market system that will allow China to grow at an average 6.5 percent annually for 25 years and emerge as a $5 trillion modern industrial superpower. These goals will profoundly affect the future of foreign investments in China. Positive changes in the social, legal, political, and governmental environments will decrease the potential risks for foreign investors who strive to enter China's vast market. If China opens its markets to more foreign goods and services and joins the World Trade Organization, it could become an enormous market and a valuable partner in the global supply chains of U.S. companies such as Motorola, General Motors, and Hewlett Packard. The degree to which China carries out its reforms will have a profound impact on the shape of the global economy in the twenty-first century. The automotive industry in China has doubled in size by 2000. Accordingly, the Chinese government has assigned high priority to the development of the auto industry.

China not only represents a potential market in its own right, but it is also a vehicle-manufacturing base for the rest of Asia. A key factor in building the automotive sector into one of the pillars of Chinese industry and meeting rapidly growing consumer demand is the ability to manufacture in large quantities so as to achieve economies of scale. General Motors entered the Chinese market with the intention of realizing China's potential growth in the automobile industry.

It has established offices predominately on the east coast of China. Beijing, Shanghai, and the surrounding provinces of Hubei and Zhejiang are among the areas that have been targeted by General Motors because of their population densities and high standards of living. SGM is based in Pudong, a new industrial area in Shanghai. General Motors has had great success with these tactics. According to a local poll of Beijing residents in 1996, General Motors was the best-known foreign-owned automobile company in China.

Operational Strategies

A key factor in GM's selection by the Chinese was the agreement to exchange world-class automotive knowledge as part of the joint venture. Technological institutes have been set up in China in conjunction with the vehicles program, and GM's Technical Center is serving as the technology integrator for the program. Through joint ventures with Chinese educational institutions, GM will gain valuable information about China's culture and the expectations of its consumers.

The development of human resources is one of the key principles of GM's success in China. It is working hard to train local managers and establish highly skilled teams at all levels of operations. To attract, develop, and retain local employees, General Motors offers competitive pay and benefits and provides substantial training and development opportunities, including overseas training and the ability to grow with the organization. General Motors is making a significant investment in training to familiarize Chinese employees with the skills and technologies required for success in a market economy. Topics range from English comprehension and computer literacy to the enhancement of professional skills. The development of local employees is an important way to gain perspective on what works and what does not in the Chinese automotive market.

In conclusion, by competing globally, understanding its customers, building quality products, and hitting its financial targets, GM feels that it can build itself into a worldwide leader. It is a prime example of how foreign direct investment companies can expand globally through joint ventures to incorporate the ideas of local companies and maximize its leverage in target markets. Its continued dedication to research and development, shared technologies, and huge capital investments have met with great success. In addition, GM believes that progress has always come about through cooperation and the sharing of knowledge. This strategy played an important role in obtaining the approval of the Planning Council of China to build mid-sized sedans in its venture with SAIC. Through the power of technology, GM communicates and shares its knowledge.

CASE 7

Procter & Gamble

The Procter & Gamble Co. (P&G), a Cincinnati-based manufacturer of household and personal care products, has emerged as a multi-billion-dollar global enterprise. The success of this business empire hinges on its strategic focus on global growth and its ability to capitalize on the business opportunities in emerging markets such as those of China and India. Since its debut in China in 1986, Procter & Gamble has become the market leader in hair care products. It is the largest detergent manufacturer in China. The company's future goal is to increase its international growth opportunities in China, Russia, and other undeveloped markets. The key to this success is to maintain high standards of quality and remain competitive by entering the market on the local level.

Procter & Gamble's more than 300 brands are sold in over 140 countries. The company operates in five main product categories: laundry and cleaning, paper goods, beauty care, food and beverages, and health care. Besides household products, Procter & Gamble also produces a number of popular American soap operas, including *As the World Turns, Another World,* and *Guiding Light.*

Procter & Gamble has been reaching out to consumers around the world for the last six decades. Faced with a mature domestic market, U.S. consumer product manufacturers have long looked to international markets to expand their operations. The North American market accounts for 50 percent of worldwide sales. Procter & Gamble first entered the European market, its second largest, in 1930 with a subsidiary in the United Kingdom. After decades of effort, it has expanded to cover virtually all of the countries in Europe.

In 1961, it established its first European headquarters in Brussels, which now coordinates Procter & Gamble's business in Europe, the Middle East, and Africa. Throughout the years, Procter & Gamble has introduced more than 100 different brands in this market and expects to increase this number in the near future with the joint effort of 31,400 employees in its European operation. This region has become the major international market for the company, accounting for over 30 percent of worldwide sales. In 1995, sales in the Europe/Middle East/Africa region were $11,019 million, a 13 percent increase over 1994. Unit volume grew by 15 percent during the year, including 5 percent due to acquisitions. Net earnings increased by 22 percent to $687 million. This reflects a net profit margin of 6.2 percent compared to 5.8 percent in 1994.

Latin America, including the Caribbean, accounts for over 8 percent of Procter & Gamble's worldwide sales. The company established a subsidiary in Mexico in 1948 and opened its first Latin American headquarters in 1987. Since then, the company has introduced over 60 brands of products to the market with the effort of 11,525 employees. In 1995, the unit volume in this region grew by 6 percent. Net earnings for the region were $215 million, a 48 percent increase over 1994. The net profit margin increased to 9.8 from 6.4 percent.

The next major international market for Procter & Gamble is Asia, which contributes over 10 percent of worldwide sales. Procter & Gamble entered the Asian market in the Philippines in 1935. The company's success in the region grew significantly in 1985 when it acquired the Richardson Vicks Co. The current Asian headquarters was established in Japan in 1987. There are 19,200 employees in the Asian operation, which markets more than 40 different brands. In 1995, net sales in Asia were $3.6 billion, up 15 percent from 1994. Unit volume grew by 24 percent. Net earnings increased by 40 percent to $203 million. Net profit margins have grown from 4.6 percent in the prior year to 5.6 percent in 1995.

Procter & Gamble entered the Chinese market in 1988 with Hutchison Whampoa Ltd., a major Hong Kong company. An agreement was reached with the Guangzhou Cosmetic Plant and the Guangzhou Economic and Technological Development District's Construction and Development Corp. to form a joint venture making shampoo and skin care products. Since then, Procter & Gamble has formed several joint ventures in China in the areas of paper, laundry and cleaning products, personal cleansing products, and oral hygiene. In May 1996, the company invested in a major manufacturing facility in the Xiqing Economic Development Zone in Tianjin, which became the largest Procter & Gamble plant in China.

The External Environment

The Industrial Environment

Before Procter & Gamble entered China, the degree of existing competition in the daily-use chemical products industry was marginal. The daily-use chemical products sector was at the growth stage, characterized by growing demand and inadequate supply. At that time, there were few foreign companies manufacturing shampoos and detergents in China. Locally manufactured products did not pose a big threat to Procter & Gamble because they were of poor quality. The raw materials for shampoos and detergents were organic chemical products, which were in abundant supply in China. The bargaining power of suppliers was low because the growth rate in the number of new firms in the organic chemical products sector was 8.51 percent (between 1988 and 1991), well above the cross-industry growth rate of 2.49 percent. This huge increase in the number of new firms implied that the government had relinquished control over the industry.

This meant that Procter & Gamble would be able to acquire raw materials locally and at a relatively low cost. The daily-use chemicals manufacturing industry was neither prohibited nor encouraged by China. There were no stringent restrictions on entry mode, partner selection, location, or sharing/equity arrangements. Foreign indirect investments were welcomed by the government.

Market demand for daily-use chemical products was huge due to the rise in living standards of most of the Chinese people. As people in developing nations gain more disposable income, they initially tend to spend it on products that will enhance their personal appearance. Chinese consumers did not care much about packaging and design, however.

The bargaining power of end users in this industry is high because they can easily obtain similar products in the market. However, most of Procter & Gamble's products are distributed through grocery stores and other retail outlets. The buying power of retail stores will be lower than that of end users when strong brands are involved. Their customers demand that well-known brands produced by Procter & Gamble be made available for purchase. While consolidated retailers like Wal-Mart have increased their buying power, Procter & Gamble's brand loyalty tempers their power.

The bargaining power of suppliers is not a major factor in this industry. Most of the raw materials are produced by several suppliers. Procter & Gamble uses many suppliers. Moreover, Procter & Gamble and its Hong Kong partner, Hutchison Whampoa, produce some of their own materials, primarily chemicals. Because no single supplier is crucial to the success of Procter & Gamble, the threat from suppliers is low.

A significant number of substitute products is available for all product categories in this industry. Heavy investment in advertising, trademarks, and brand names create brand loyalty and somewhat reduce the impact of substitutes. Nevertheless, the availability of substitutes is a serious external threat to companies like Procter & Gamble. Fortunately, in China many local products are of lower quality.

Well-established brands continue to do well, even when low-priced generic substitutes are introduced.

While the market is fragmented, a few large companies share dominance. Uniliver and Procter & Gamble, for example, dominate the soap and detergent market. This oligopoly helps keep margins relatively high and aids in making this a profitable industry. But, since most of the major foreign competitors in China are able to produce the same quality as Procter & Gamble, they are direct competitors. Currently, Britain's Unilever, Japan's Kao, Switzerland's Nestle, and Johnson & Johnson are major competitors in China.

The mean of the number of new firms in the daily-use chemical products industry from 1990 to 1993 was 2.83. Compared to the cross-industry mean (5.64), the growth rate of the daily-use chemical products industry has been slow in the past few years. In addition, the industry's pretax profit mean was 3.75. It was growing at a slower rate than the mean of cross-industry pretax profit (26.02). Therefore, competition was rather intense.

The National Environment

The steady growth of the Chinese population will profoundly affect the overall demand for nondurable household products. The population in China is also aging. The number of people 65 or older was about 90 million by the year 2000. The aging population will force manufacturers such as Procter & Gamble to address the needs of older customers with more health care products.

China's population is also becoming more urbanized as economic development in the big cities is attracting people from rural areas in search of jobs. As the proportion of urban residents is rising every year, the demand for household products is expected to increase rapidly because the average urban resident consumes more than three times as much as the typical rural resident does.

Since the late 1970s, China's annual GDP growth has averaged nearly 10 percent. Despite a recent slowdown, it is predicted that China will have GDP equal to that of the United States by 2015. In the meantime, China's 1996 per capita income was around $3,000 (based on purchasing power parity). Many Chinese people, but not all, can afford color televisions, washing machines, and imported clothing. However, most of them can easily afford foreign-made toothpaste, shampoo, and other nondurable household goods. China's saving rate is huge, around 30 to 40 percent of its GDP, which enables it to finance most development from internal sources.

The Internal Environment

Procter & Gamble's human resource management focuses on diversity. Its upper management believes that all people are different, advantages can be created from these differences, and a diverse organization is essential to achieving Procter & Gamble's business objectives. Further, its strategy is to hire the best young people and encourage their development over their entire careers, promoting people from within to motivate them to work hard.

The latest innovation at Procter & Gamble is a standardized set of processes and technologies known as distributor business systems (DBS), an integrated ordering, shipping, billing, inventory management, and financial system based on off the shelf DOS systems. More than half of Procter & Gamble's Asian business was previously handled by 1,500 third-party distributors, many of them tiny, family-run shops processing orders, billing, and handling inventory manually. With no distribution data trail, sales information about shampoo and detergents was minimal. Since that time, DBS has transformed Procter & Gamble's inefficient overseas distribution channels into a real competitive advantage in the emerging markets of Asia.

Procter & Gamble has 17 research centers all over the world. Its goal is not more innovation but better ones. To that end, it has spent more than $1.5 billion on R&D. For example, it is launching a new fat-free potato chip, which uses the new Olean brand of cooking oil.

Procter & Gamble's sheer size has allowed it to reap the benefits of enormous economies of scale. In 1996, it spent $3.2 billion on advertising and marketing. In China, it spends much of its advertising budget on buying TV air time. Billboards, radio, and buses are also popular ways to advertise. In 1998, Procter & Gamble gave a $400,000 grant to Yale University to help develop a new public health training program in China. In this way, Procter & Gamble not only helps Yale and China but also gains publicity.

Entry Strategies

Entry Mode

Currently, Procter & Gamble has 11 joint ventures and wholly owned subsidiaries in China (see table C7.1). Its first joint venture was established in 1988 to manufacture detergents and skin care products. There were three parties to the joint venture: the Guangzhou Economic and

TABLE C7.1. Procter & Gamble's Joint Ventures in China, 1988–97

Year	Location	Name of Project	Chinese Partner	Foreign Partner	Business Scope
1988	Guangzhou	GZ Baojie Co.	GETDZ Trading	P&G Hutchison	Shampoo/skin care products
			GZ Cosmetics Plant		
1990	Guangzhou	GZ Baojie Paper Co.	GZ Baojie Co.	P&G Hutchison	Sanitary towels
1990	Guangzhou	GZ Baojie Detergents	GZ Baojie Co.	P&G Hutchison	Detergent
1993	Sichuan	Chengdu Baojie	Chengdu Synthetic Detergent Factory	P&G Hutchison	Detergent
1993	Beijing	Beijing Baojie	Beijing Daily Use Chemical Plant Number 2	P&G Hutchison	Detergent
1993	Tianjin	Tianjin Baojie	Tianjin Perfumed Soap Plant	Hutchison	Soap
1997	Guangzhou	GZ Baojie Oral Care			Toothpaste

Note: GZ = Guangzhou.

Technological Development District's Construction and Development Corporation (GETDZ Trading Corp.), the Guangzhou Cosmetics Plant, and Procter & Gamble–Hutchison Ltd. of Hong Kong.

Joint ventures with state-owned firms can strengthen P&G's commitment with the market power that has been established by the local partners. An existing obstacle for foreign companies doing business in China is the cultural distance between Western and Chinese business styles. A local partner can be an asset in dealing with these kinds of problems, guiding companies through uncertain situations and giving them the opportunity to learn. A good relationship with the Chinese government is also a critical element in the success of a foreign firm. A state-owned partner can assist a firm in building good *guanxi* with various governmental institutions, reducing political risk and uncertainty for the firm. In the case of joint ventures, Procter & Gamble did not have to expend a large amount of resources in studying the soap or paper goods industry in order to be competitive since it could rely on the experience of its local partners, some of which had been in the market for over 15 years. More experience also means an extensive marketing and distribution network that a foreign firm can use to increase its market share in China.

Since China has a weak market structure, the government has great regulatory power. Having a state-owned firm as a partner is an asset for foreign companies because they gain access to scarce resources, materials, capital, information, investment infrastructure, and distribution channels. The market power of state-owned firms enables a foreign company to relieve some industrywide output restrictions and offers the advantages of economies of scale.

There are some disadvantages to entering into joint ventures with state-owned firms. Enterprises owned privately or by a collective have fewer principal agent conflicts and more strategic flexibility than do state-owned firms. They operate with simple structures that give them the ability to react quickly to opportunities in the business environment. The tight budgets of private and collective enterprises and their lack of government funding gives them more self-motivation and operational autonomy. Because of the lack of self-motivation, state-owned firms often show losses, whereas private and collective enterprises have been showing continuous profits.

Entry Timing

Procter & Gamble is considered one of the early movers in the Chinese market, having entered in 1988. Before 1988, Procter & Gamble was already well established and very successful in the Hong Kong market. Since Hong Kong TV commercials could be seen in China, consumers had already been exposed to Procter & Gamble's brands and products. It saw a golden opportunity to enter the Chinese market.

A number of competitors entered the market a few years before Procter & Gamble, but they had not been successful. Procter & Gamble intended to create even greater demand in the consumer product market with the quality of its products. As an early mover, it had the advantages of preemption of scarce resources and local marketing. The status of its partners as state-owned firms put it in a better position in the market, setting barriers for its followers. However, as an early mover, Procter & Gamble risked dealing with a weak market structure and political uncertainty. Fortunately, it overcame many of these problems by choosing the right state-owned firms as partners.

There are several indications that Procter & Gamble's strategy was successsful. It currently has over 50 percent of the shampoo market nationwide and is the market leader in hair care products. It is also the largest detergent manufacturer in China. In 1991, it ranked twenty-fourth among the top 300 most productive foreign-funded enterprises.

Location Selection

Procter & Gamble selected Guangzhou for its base office and four major manufacturing plants. Guangzhou is located near Hong Kong, in the southeastern province of Guangdong. The most attractive reason for choosing Guangzhou was the establishment in the area of a special economic zone and within it an economic and technical development zone. These territories are designed to attract foreign investment to the area by offering tax incentives. It is a double benefit for a foreign firm to locate in an ETDZ because the firm enjoys the benefits of both zones.

In order for Procter & Gamble to operate in the ETDZ, it must export at least some of its products. Procter & Gamble's operations in China are largely oriented to the domestic market, but a low percentage of products are manufactured for export in order to meet this requirement.

Another reason for choosing Guangzhou is its proximity to Hong Kong, which facilitates the recruiting of expatriate managers and other talented employees from its Hong Kong office. Recruiting in Hong Kong is substantially less expensive than bringing a team of expatriate managers from the United States.

In addition, Guangzhou has an economic growth rate of 13 percent and is one of the most developed cities in China. The residents have more disposable income to spend on consumer goods and they are much more inclined to consume foreign products. Guangzhou also has a well-developed infrastructure system, with a highway network linking to all provinces in the country.

Cooperative Strategies

Partner Selection

The GETDZ Trading Corp. was the local government's profit-making agent, which engaged in the import and export of various commodities. As a state-owned organization, it had privileged access to scarce resources, materials, capital, and information. It also had a strong relationship with various government institutions. Most importantly, it had access to state-instituted distribution channels, which play a dominant role in product distribution in the Chinese market.

As an import and export corporation, the GETDZ Trading Corp. had accumulated some international experience. Thus, it was already receptive to modern management styles, quality standards, and customer responsiveness. Contact with foreign companies had exposed it to foreign values, so the firm was able to effectively communicate with its foreign partner. It hoped to gain both profit and managerial skills from the joint venture.

The Guangzhou Cosmetics Plant, established in 1957, was a medium-sized factory with 438 employees. It originally manufactured cosmetics and synthetic detergents, products closely related to the skin care products and shampoos that the joint venture was established to produce. For this reason, Procter & Gamble was able to use the distribution channels, product image, customer loyalty, and production facilities it had already established domestically.

Like GETDZ Trading, the Guangzhou Cosmetics Plant was state owned and enjoyed preferential treatment from the government. Although it was just a medium-sized factory, it enjoyed some economies of scale and market power. It also had some bargaining power with local authorities. The plant sought export facilitation, know-how, and market power from the joint venture.

Sharing Ownership

In most of its joint ventures in China, Procter & Gamble has opted to hold majority equity within the range of 70 to 80 percent so that it will have more say in the management of projects, board composition, and the nomination of managers. It also believed it could not entrust the management of its projects to partners who lacked its experience and skills.

In 1998, Procter & Gamble restructured its Chinese joint venture with its partner, Hutchison Whampoa Ltd. Under the terms of this agreement, Procter & Gamble will pay $650 million to Hutchison Whampoa Ltd., increase its ownership in the joint venture from 69 to 80 percent, and assume total management control of the business. Procter & Gamble's stake could increase to 100 percent by 2017 through the exercise of options. The price of future options will be based on a formula using the current market value of the business at that time.

Procter & Gamble's stronger bargaining power allowed it to assume more control over the venture. This power stemmed from its contribution of know-how and capital, managerial and marketing skills, and global brand image.

Operational Strategies

Procter & Gamble entered China with a strong competitive position as the world's leading provider of household and personal products. It decided to employ a product differentiation strategy, which would offer Chinese consumers high-quality, foreign-made products. It did not pursue a cost-leadership strategy because competition in China prior to its entry was not vigorous and it wanted to compete with other firms on quality rather than price.

The first way Procter & Gamble differentiated its product offerings from those of its competitors was by superior quality. High-quality products had a huge market in China at that time due to the rise in the living standard of the general public and the decentralization of the daily-use chemical product sector. Products offered by many formerly state owned domestic enterprises were unable to catch up with P&G's quality standard and could not compete.

Another means of implementing the product differentiation strategy was superior customer responsiveness. Knowing that local shampoos did not treat dandruff, Procter & Gamble introduced its Head & Shoulders dandruff shampoo, which is designed to help relieve the dryness, itch, and flaking caused by dry scalp. Procter & Gamble also successfully introduced Head & Shoulders Menthol, a shampoo that provides a cool sensation and appeals to consumers in hot, humid climates. In response to the local preference for lustrous hair, it invented the Pantene Pro-V formula, which helps restore shininess.

The last tool Procter & Gamble used to achieve a competitive edge was superior input efficiency. It adopted a local sourcing strategy and has been striving to localize production and take advantage of low-cost raw materials and labor.

Ninety-five percent of Procter & Gamble's employees have been recruited locally. Procter & Gamble is also training local management to replace the expatriates to whom it has been paying annual salaries and benefits of more than $20 million. Local college graduates provide a steady stream of candidates for managerial positions. When Procter & Gamble implemented the DBS system, local college graduates were trained to work on the Center of Expertise team.

Procter & Gamble is using a global structure in which its international operations are divided into four main regions, each with its own functional units. The functional units are directly accountable to their regional headquarters but do not necessarily report directly to U.S. headquarters. For example, in the Asian Division there is one regional headquarters in Kobe, Japan, and two major technical research centers. Hence, the regional headquarters in Japan is responsible for research and development. Another regional headquarters of the Asian Division is located in Hong Kong. One of its major functions is to help Procter & Gamble distribute its products. The advantage of this structure is that the regional headquarters enjoys a great degree of flexibility in dealing with local markets.

Procter & Gamble's global distribution system, DBS, facilitates efficient consumer response and reduces inventory interest expenses. Its competitive advantage is in the increased communications efficiency of third-party distributors and greater control over products in the developing markets of Asia and Europe. In Asia, Procter & Gamble has invested $10 million and realized a net profit of $120.5 million by using the standardized regional system. The company is now implementing DBS globally.

In conclusion, Procter & Gamble's operations in China have been successful because it had strong bargaining power and has chosen the right country, industry, time, and partners. The case of Procter & Gamble demonstrates several lessons that may be helpful to foreign companies planning to enter the Chinese market. First, one must thoroughly research the host country's market before taking initial action. Second, joint ventures with state-owned firms are preferred for companies aiming to increase their market power, competitive edge, and consumer reach. Finally, it is advisable to locate manufacturing plants in special economic zones, economic and technical development zones, or cities where the infrastructure is already highly developed.

CASE 8

Johnson & Johnson

Johnson & Johnson, with more than 180 subsidiaries operating in 51 countries and products marketed in more than 175 countries, is the fifth-largest pharmaceutical company and the third-largest medical diagnostic company in the world. It is headquartered in New Jersey but is expanding internationally. In 1985, Janssen Pharmaceutica of Belgium, a subsidiary of Johnson & Johnson, entered Xian, China, where Western medicine accounts for 55 percent of the pharmaceutical market. For more than a decade, Janssen, with its Chinese partner the State Pharmaceutical Administration of China (SPAC), has been heralded as one of the most successful joint ventures in China.

Johnson & Johnson's corporate culture is rooted in "Our Credo," a full-page mission statement written by Gen. Robert Wood Johnson in 1943. It outlines Johnson & Johnson's commitment to its consumers, employees, communities, and stockholders. The company always puts consumers first. Johnson believed that by providing quality products to its consumers, a good working environment to its employee, and reliable commitment to its communities the company would make reasonable profits and stockholders would receive a fair return on their investments. Johnson & Johnson aims to establish itself as the leading pharmaceutical manufacturing company in China.

Johnson & Johnson is one of the world's largest, most comprehensive, and most diversified health care product makers. Its 92,000 employees serve consumer, pharmaceutical, and professional markets with a focus on research-based, technology-driven products.

The consumer segment produces personal care and hygienic products, including oral and baby care products, first aid products, non-prescription drugs, sanitary protection products, and adult skin and hair care products. Some of the major brands are Johnson & Johnson Baby Oil and Shampoo, Band-Aids, Tylenol, Reach toothbrushes, and Acuvue contact lenses. These products are distributed both to wholesalers and directly to independent and chain retail outlets, but they are marketed principally to the general public. Johnson & Johnson's sales of consumer products have increased significantly in recent years, from $5.8 million in 1995, to nearly $6.5 million in 1997. However, consumer products as a percentage of total sales have dropped due to even more rapid growth in the pharmaceutical and professional segments.

The pharmaceutical segment represented only 34 percent of sales but 55.87 percent of the company's operating profits in 1997. Principal brand name products include Duragesic (an analgesic), Eprex (anti-anemia agent), Ergamisol (cancer treatment), Floxin (antibacterial), Ortho-Novum (birth control), and Retin-A (acne cream). These products are distributed both directly and through wholesalers for use by health care professionals and the general public.

Products in the professional segment are used by physicians, nurses, therapists, hospitals, diagnostic laboratories, and clinics. Principal products include suture and mechanical wound closure products, minimally invasive surgical instruments, diagnostic products, cardiology products, medical equipment and devices, surgical instruments, joint replacements, and products for wound management and infection prevention. These products are distributed both directly and through surgical suppliers and other dealers. Sales in the professional segment grew from $6.7 million in 1995 to $8.4 million just two years later. This is the largest of Johnson & Johnson's three segments, accounting for over a third of total sales.

Johnson & Johnson expands its production through acquisitions and partnerships with smaller firms. Rather than merging with other major health care companies, Johnson & Johnson prefers to grow by forging partnerships with small firms capable of developing innovative new products. By the end of 1997, Johnson & Johnson had more than 180 operating companies in 51 countries selling products in more than 175 countries. In the Asia Pacific region, Johnson & Johnson's operating units can be found in China, Taiwan, Hong Kong, Japan, Korea, the Philippines, Thailand, Malaysia, Singapore, Indonesia, India, Pakistan, and Australia.

The External Environment

The Industrial Environment

Fifteen of the world's top pharmaceuticals joint ventures are in China, including that between Procter & Gamble and the Shanghai Pharmaceutical Factory. In September 1982, Sino-American Shang Squibb Pharmaceutical Ltd. became the third pharmaceutical joint venture in the PRC. Another of Johnson & Johnson's competitors, Tianjin Smith Kline and

French Laboratories Ltd. (SKF) invested in China in October 1982. The U.S.-based Pharmaceutical Technology Corp. (PTC), which entered in 1992, had sales volume in China of $70 million in 1995.

The ability of China's medical and pharmaceutical products to compete in the international market is also being gradually enhanced. The total pharmaceutical sales volume in China had reached Rmb 25.1 billion ($3.02 billion) in 1994. China's medical device industry has developed rapidly in past years, with industrial output growing at an average annual rate of more than 20 percent. The output value of China's medical device industry topped Rmb 10 billion ($1.2 billion), with 2 billion's worth ($240 million) exported in 1996. With the industrial restructuring of the international community, export of China's medical and pharmaceutical products will be facilitated. At present, China exports only 15 percent of its medical and pharmaceutical products. This will increase steadily in the future.

China's population will reach 1.4 billion by 2010. Lifestyles in China are expected to become more comfortable. As demand for quality of life increases, so will demand for protective and health-enhancing medicines. According to a 1994 survey, 90 percent of urban consumers interviewed had used a cold medication during the previous six months and 50 percent had taken painkillers. As another example, over the course of the past decade China has focused on improving nutrition for infants and small children. Although China's overall pharmaceutical market was sized at $7.5 billion in retail sales in 1992, there have been virtually no nonprescription supplements to fill this need.

Until recently, most medical charges were reimbursed by a patient's work unit. Since an increasing number of workers are no longer part of the "iron rice bowl," and China's work-unit health system does not cover self-employed people or those working for private enterprises, more patients are buying medicine at local drugstores. Purchasing over the counter (OTC) medicine is also seen as a more appealing option than seeing a doctor to get a prescription. China's OTC sector will be the main trend of the Chinese pharmaceutical industry at this stage in its life cycle. Demand for more efficient curative medical and diagnostic equipment is also expected to increase. The number of hospitals increased by 4,000 to a total of 67,000 between 1976 and 1994. The number of specialized hospitals and scientific research institutes doubled during the same period.

The bargaining power of suppliers is low because China has become the second-largest producer of pharmaceutical raw materials in the world. Also, China has more than 3,000 medical device firms, which are capable of producing 3,564 types of products in 48 categories.

Threats from substitutes are high because traditional Chinese medicine is often preferred. Most Chinese believe that traditional medicine works far better than Western medicine. Chinese herbal remedies are also being increasingly exported.

The National Environment

China's Law on Drug Management is intended to protect the medical and pharmaceutical industry. All commercial pharmaceutical distributors must have three licenses. The first qualifies them to sell drugs as enterprises. This is approved and issued by the supervisory Department of Pharmaceutical Production and Trade. A second permit is issued by the Public Health Administrative Department. The third is an operational license issued by the Industrial and Commerce Administrative Department.

Foreign firms must display their latest developments in pharmaceutical manufacturing and packaging, medical examination, and laboratory products in China. For example, PTC scheduled technical seminars to instruct Chinese companies about advanced pharmaceutical technology.

In the rural areas, a shortage of doctors and medicine has been overcome. A total of 89.1 percent of all villages have set up clinics, and doctors and nurses in rural areas numbered 1.32 million in 1996. Epidemic diseases such as smallpox have been entirely eliminated, and endemic diseases such as schistosomiasis have been controlled. The health of both urban and rural citizens has greatly improved. The average life expectancy in China has increased from 35 in 1949 to 70 at present. At the same time, the weight and height of the children have shown a marked increase.

Buying power in the Asia Pacific region (excluding Japan) has reached the level of the United States. It is increasing at an annual rate of 8.1 percent, while the U.S. rate of increase is only about 4.2 percent per year. China, of course, holds a big portion of the purchasing power of the Asia Pacific region.

China maintains favorable rules for foreign-invested enterprises. In 1997, the Peoples Bank of China began implementing a new policy to allow Chinese enterprises earning more than $10 million a year in foreign exchange to keep up to 15 percent of their receipts. Since January 1996, the renminbi exchange rate has appreciated slightly against the U.S. dollar to just under 8.3 to 1.0. China still lacks market interest rates and a market where foreign exchange dealers can interact directly with international markets.

China is slightly larger in total area than the continental United States. Its 1.2 billion people, the greatest population of any country on earth, have the potential to become the world's largest consumer market. China's population density is relatively high. Distribution, however, is uneven. The coastal areas in the east are densely populated, with more than 400 people per square kilometer, while the plateau areas in the west are sparsely populated, with fewer than 10 people per square kilometer. China is a united, multinational country of 56 ethnic groups.

China absorbed $11.7 billion worth of imports from the United States in 1995, up 27 percent from 1994. The average consumption rate for every citizen was Rmb 2,675 in 1996, with rural residents at about Rmb 1,718 and urban residents at 5,736.

The International Environment

American pharmaceutical companies are growing faster than those of any other country. Because of tight accounting standards and the United States' political stability, they are also safe companies in which to invest. At 45 percent, the United States holds the largest share of the international pharmaceutical industry, with the United Kingdom at 14 percent, Switzerland and Germany each at 9 percent, Japan at 7 percent, and all others at 6 percent. In the meantime, Johnson & Johnson's market share in the United States was almost 30 percent of the 45 percent total share.

Although Johnson & Johnson's pharmaceutical market share was high, it still faces huge competitors. There are many private brand names besides Johnson & Johnson's in the United States, including Long's, K-mart, and other supermarket chains. These competitors provided their own pharmaceutical brands in their own stores or pharmacies at very competitive prices. This competitive environment pushed Johnson & Johnson to invest in China.

The Internal Environment

Financial Aspects

Johnson & Johnson's sales increased from $8 billion in 1987 to $23 billion in 1997. Its key financial ratios show that its financial performance is very solid with respect to profitability, liquidity, leverage, and asset management. Its gross profit margin, net profit margin, and return on assets are all higher than the health care industry's averages. While the average industrywide increase in return on investment is 5 percent, Johnson & Johnson's has increased by 22 percent from 1996 to 1997. In the health care industry, the average current ratio only increased from 1.5 in 1994 to 1.6 in 1997 while Johnson & Johnson's current ratio has increased from 1.6 to 2.0. The decreasing and below-average inventory to net working capital ratio shows that Johnson & Johnson's inventory is highly liquid and indicates no inventory overstock problems.

When compared to the industrial figures, Johnson & Johnson has a relatively low percentage of debt with respect to its total assets and equity. Debt as a percentage of assets and equity is much lower than industrial averages and still decreasing. Its activity ratios are also good. Inventory turnover increased by 23.5 percent between 1994 and 1997, while the industrial increase was only 15.5 percent. Johnson & Johnson's average collection period also improved from about 60 days in 1994 to 53 in 1997.

Technological Aspects

The drug industry is one of the most highly research oriented sectors of the U.S. economy. Johnson & Johnson understands that research and development are the force behind continued growth. Spending both in dollar amounts and as a percentage of total sales has increased over the past several years. These expenditures relate to the development, improvement, and technical support of new and existing products. In 1997, 35 percent of Johnson & Johnson's annual sales were generated from products introduced within the past five years. The company also spent more than $1.9 billion in 1998 on research and development to further advance its medical and technology research.

Full-time occupational ergonomics engineers are employed by Johnson & Johnson in the Industrial Engineering Department. The objectives of the program are to eliminate high-risk work practices on the job, redesign jobs at manufacturing centers, and follow up medical cases. Since these programs were launched, there has been a 10 to 12 percent increase in productivity and a dramatic decrease in new medical problems among employees.

To meet new challenges and stay competitive, Johnson & Johnson has adopted productivity-enhancing modern technologies to enable better and faster control of information. An electronic data interchange (EDI) service called Traderoute was implemented to facilitate electronic links with customers and suppliers. The program involves personnel from various departments in the company. The benefits of EDI include computerized records of purchases, error reduction, and time and cost savings.

Information management is now of great concern at Johnson & Johnson. According to Edward Parrish, vice president of information management, information technology is designed to achieve at least one of the following three goals: reduce costs, increase information, and improve quality or productivity. Parrish has linked use of information technology to Johnson & Johnson's value chain. The four major links in the chain are infrastructure, transaction processing, information management, and revenue growth. Each of Johnson & Johnson's 172 operating units develops its own IT budget and makes its own investments. In 1997, these units began to structure their budgets according to the value chain.

Operational Aspects

The medical industry is much more product focused than other industries. Consumers are very concerned about the quality of products. Other than quality and price, consumer choices depend on how much they know and like the company. Recognizing this new trend in consumer behavior, Johnson & Johnson has focused its marketing efforts on building positive perceptions among customers. In the last decade, it has promoted its products as reliable and trustworthy.

Part of the aggressive promotion drive at Johnson & Johnson is cause-related marketing. Johnson & Johnson uses this to enhance its community relationships, create a public association between the company and various worthy causes, and find further opportunities to express its corporate values in the public arena. In the early 1990s, it ran a successful cause-related promotional campaign known as the Shelter-Aid Program, conceived by its Personal Products Co., which markets feminine protection products. According to Mava Heffler, the spokesperson for the scheme, domestic violence is the target of the program. Although this issue was controversial, it helped differentiate Johnson & Johnson's feminine products from the rest of the crowd. In addition, the Shelter-Aid Program used a variety of marketing tools with a clear focus on women, including coupons, counter displays, and local and national advertising. The program also had a local angle. Part of the money it generated was passed along to provide shelters across the country. Such promotional programs help the company build a better public image and position itself as a community-friendly company.

Organizational Aspects

Johnson & Johnson has been named one of America's 10 most admired companies by *Fortune* magazine because of its superior financial performance, reputation, and leadership. The 1943 credo written by Robert Johnson has been translated into 36 languages and is shared throughout Johnson & Johnson's subsidiaries. Periodically, company employees participate in a survey and evaluation of how well the company meets the responsibilities laid out in this credo. Appropriate steps are promptly taken to rectify any shortcomings.

Leadership is critical for controlling Johnson & Johnson's decentralized family of businesses. Ortho Biotech, Inc., a subsidiary of Johnson & Johnson, experienced and overcame challenges at its uppermost levels when its leaders began questioning the values, attitudes, and habits of everyone from the top to the bottom of the managerial ladder. They succeeded in transforming the organizational culture to harmonize with the diversity of the workplace and its customers.

Since 1990, Johnson & Johnson has evaluated its common processes across company lines. Programs are designed to eliminate duplicate processes. The most dramatic changes have taken place within the Human Resources Department. Johnson & Johnson of Puerto Rico, for example, is concentrating on developing a work force with greater flexibility. With the use of advanced technology, its employees are more empowered and better trained to be competent and skilled. In 1992, Johnson & Johnson instituted its Signature of Quality Program. More than 700 top executives from operating units around the world participate in a regular series of executive conferences to evaluate the company's competitive strengths and weaknesses. The cross-functional programs focus on three general goals: improved customer satisfaction, cost efficiency, and bringing new products to market more quickly.

A solid relationship with employees is heavily emphasized at Johnson & Johnson. Top management believes that employees are the first ambassadors of the company. To attract and retain talented employees, Johnson & Johnson provides a family-friendly work environment. It has on-site child care centers in various locations. It also offers flexible work schedules, such as flextime, part-time work, telecommuting, and job sharing. It extends its employee benefits to provide long-term care programs to employees and their spouses, parents, and even grandparents. According to a study by the Families and Work Institute, Johnson & Johnson is one of the most progressive, family-friendly American businesses. Johnson & Johnson and three other companies are the only organizations to have successfully linked their strategic concerns with work-family issues and then made effective cultural changes in the workplace.

Entry Strategies

Entry Mode

The first reason why Johnson & Johnson invested in China was because it has the third-largest economy in the world. Economists predict that

China will become the world's largest economy as early as the year 2010. With expansion at a very early stage in the growth cycle, the stage is set for rapid growth in stocks. China has one of the lowest correlations with the U.S. stock market. By offering superior diversification benefits, China allows investors to participate in its growth potential at a lower level of overall portfolio risk than is possible in other emerging markets.

Moreover, although the practice of traditional Chinese medicine has been promoted by Chinese leaders and remains a major component of health care, Western medicine gained increasing acceptance in the 1970s and 1980s. The China International Medical and Pharmaceutical Equipment Design and Manufacturing Technology Exhibition, held in Shanghai in 1998, aimed at speeding up the advancement of China's medical and pharmaceutical equipment manufacturing technology. China is already able to produce enough medical equipment and pharmaceuticals to meet its basic health needs, but the backwardness of its techniques and the poor quality of China's medical devices hinder further development of medical products. Johnson & Johnson realized if it entered the Chinese market it could help the country reach its medical goals.

Johnson & Johnson China Ltd. manufactures health care products serving the consumer (Acuvue contact lenses, Reach toothbrushes, baby products, and Band-Aid bandages), pharmaceutical (Tylenol pain reliever), and professional (surgical instruments) markets. Medical devices, packaging materials, and hospital services are related forms of diversification that will also take place as China's medical market becomes increasingly standardized and legally constrained.

In 1961, Johnson & Johnson purchased Janssen Pharmaceutica of Belgium. Janssen entered the Chinese market in 1985. It located in Xian and selected an equity joint venture as its entry mode. Its Chinese partner was the State Pharmaceutical Administration Committee. The joint venture split was 52 to 48 percent, with Janssen holding the majority share of a total investment of $48 million. This joint venture was the biggest pharmaceutical company in China.

In 1990, Johnson & Johnson Shanghai Ltd. was established to produce Band-Aid brand adhesive bandages. One year later, Johnson & Johnson China Ltd. was opened to manufacture and market Johnson & Johnson's consumer products.

Johnson & Johnson's entry into China is part of a strategic goal of international expansion. The company's objectives are long term. By forming a joint venture with SPAC, Johnson & Johnson established an attitude of commitment to the Chinese market. Since the parent company allows a certain degree of autonomous power to its subsidiaries, Janssen was able to better respond to the dynamics of the joint venture.

China requires that all foreign investment enterprises and projects have prior government approval. It was easy for Janssen to obtain approval by forming a joint venture with SPAC, a government agency. The joint venture also helps Janssen work its way through the complex Chinese legal system. For example, China's Ministry of Health tries to outdo the U.S. Food and Drug Administration (FDA) by requiring more clinical data. Another example is the prohibition of "umbrella branding," which is a common practice in the United States. Umbrella branding means having a range of products, with slightly varying formulas, marketed under the same brand. For instance, there are both Tylenol and Extra Strength Tylenol in the United States. In China, if the active ingredients are altered to produce Extra Strength Tylenol, the name must also be changed to an unconnected Chinese name, that is, one without the word *Tylenol* in it. Janssen's Chinese partner has been very helpful in understanding and dealing with these laws and regulations as well as in differences between the American and Chinese cultures.

Competition was not intense in the late 1980s. The three largest joint ventures were Janssen, Smith Kline French, and Bristol-Myers Squibb. Many early joint ventures shared similar characteristics: a fifty-fifty split, a 20-year commitment, and a location in or near Shanghai.

The long-term commitment and huge start-up costs of the pharmaceuticals business serve as entry barriers to other companies. Meanwhile, the joint venture mode can lessen the financial burden and risk of investment for foreign investors.

Besides high start-up costs, each subsequent project involves millions of dollars. For instance, Janssen's joint venture with the Shaanxi Pharmaceutical Industrial Co., established in 1988 to produce a large range of Janssen's medicinal products, required $10 million from Janssen. Janssen was rated by the Chinese government as the country's top joint venture in 1992 and 1993. The company consistently ranks in the top 10 among China's foreign-invested enterprises based on per employee sales revenue, tax payments, profits, exports, trading expenses, and investment in research and development.

Entry Timing

Johnson & Johnson entered China as a first mover. One benefit of being the first mover is low competition, which helps a company earn a higher market share. In the late 1980s, there were less than a dozen foreign-invested pharmaceutical companies in China. Early entrants like Janssen, SKF, and Squibb enjoyed sales growth in excess of 40 percent a year. By the end of 1995, however, there were more than 1,500 such companies and another 3,000 state factories producing local brands that cost 30 to 50 percent less.

First movers can establish brand loyalty since there are fewer brands around for consumers to remember. As mentioned earlier, China prohibits umbrella branding, so there are many different brand names for one type of drug like a headache relief product. Several large companies respond to this rule and distinguish their products from those of their competitors by associating products with their corporate names.

Preemption of resources is also a major advantage. Foreign-invested companies usually pay higher wages, including bonuses and allowances, than local competitors do. This attracts a skilled work force. However, as local government wages keep increasing and as China has become involved in the General Agreement on Tariffs and Trade (GATT) the wage gap has narrowed. This implies that late entrants may have to provide more incentives to obtain a skilled work force.

During the early years, several unique characteristics of the Chinese economic system contributed special benefits to first movers in the pharmaceutical industry. The first was China's health care reimbursement system, which provided free health care to 30 million government employees, including military personnel, students, and teachers, and to 140 million employees or dependents of state-owned enterprises. These consumers demanded more expensive, higher quality Western drugs. Furthermore, there was a lack of legal distinction between prescription and OTC drugs, so even the purchase of Band-Aids at a hospital was reimbursed.

A second characteristic is that pharmaceuticals accounted for 60 percent of health care expenditures in China. This may be compared to the United States at 8 percent and Germany at 12 percent. This was because 60 to 70 percent of the revenue of Chinese hospitals came from drug sales. Hospitals were required to be economically self-sufficient, so doctors were willing to prescribe as many expensive drugs as possible. Realizing the defects in this system, the Chinese government took two approaches to end the reimbursement program in 1995. First, it compiled a national Essential Drug List; only drugs on this list would be reimbursed. Meanwhile, price caps were imposed on prescription drugs. Sales growth of the foreign-invested companies began to decline as firms found themselves competing more intensely for a piece of a smaller pie.

Another final characteristic was the "administrative pipeline protection" clause in the Chinese Patent Law, which extended 7.5 years of patent protection to drugs patented between 1986 and 1993 in countries that have bilateral trade relations with China. This means that late entrants (after 1993) are more likely to have their products counterfeited.

All this evidence suggests that being a first mover was appropriate and profitable in this dynamic market.

Location Selection

Western medicine accounts for about 55 percent of China's $6 billion annual market. China's annual sales are about $15 billion in the year 2000 and will be $60 billion by 2010. In addition, many Chinese doctors and consumers prefer Western to traditional Chinese medicines because of their high quality.

Johnson & Johnson had nine offices in China as of early 1998. One was in Xian, one in Beijing, and the rest in Shanghai. Xian is in the Shaanxi Province, where Johnson & Johnson's Belgian subsidiary, Janssen, had previous experience. Janssen had earlier set up a compensation trade agreement with the Hanjiang Pharmaceutical Plant in Shaanxi. It selected Xian because of its potential as a centrally located city to become a gateway to China's northwest provinces. Xian has more than 500 scientific and technological research institutes as well as 42 institutes of higher learning, providing it with one of the best-educated populations in China.

Janssen has the only joint venture in Xian. This means there is less direct competition for resources, both human and material. This monopoly status has allowed Janssen to nurture a close relationship with the biggest state pharmaceutical distributors. Xian's labor and land costs are lower than those in other highly invested cities. Average salaries for managers and technicians range from Rmb 500 to 1,500 per month. In comparison, salaries of supervisors and professionals in Shanghai range from Rmb 1,167 to 4,167 per month. Cheap labor has meant that the company can afford to help its employees purchase homes, thereby retaining their loyalty and keeping them in the area.

After entering Xian, Johnson & Johnson turned to Minhang in Shanghai. Recently, much emphasis has been put on the development of the Pudong New Area in Shanghai to attract foreign investment. In fact, most of the invested enterprises are still found in the older zones of Minhang, Honggiao, and Caohejing. These are national-level zones (which have more protection than country-level zones). The zones have received approval from Beijing to operate as economic and development zones, which have tax breaks and other incentives similar to those of special economic zones.

Shanghai's attraction lies in its industrialization, skilled work force, and wealth. Although Shanghai has only 1 percent of China's population, it supplies 10 percent of the country's revenue. Great purchasing power was a substantial motivation for Johnson & Johnson to locate in Shanghai, where it can market its relatively expensive consumer products.

Cooperative Strategies

Partner Selection

Johnson & Johnson's international growth has been accomplished through the creation of new companies and the acquisition of existing ones, as in its purchase of Janssen. It enters into joint ventures with Chinese pharmaceutical companies because they will give it connections to the market and help it adapt to the Chinese business culture. It tends to form alliances with companies that have large manufacturing plants in China so that they can handle production for high-demand products. It chooses local partners that share a commitment to technological advancement and innovation and the improvement of family medical resources. Compatibility is ensured when managers of both companies share the same vision and are willing to work toward the common goal of producing good products.

The State Pharmaceutical Administration of China leads current efforts to upgrade domestic production capabilities as part of its responsibility to oversee manufacturing, distribution, and marketing activities of all the domestic and foreign pharmaceutical operations in China. Unfortunately, both SPAC and the Ministry of Health (MOH) encourage policies that favor the growth of state companies and discriminate against foreign joint ventures. Johnson & Johnson has circumvented this problem by forming joint ventures with SPAC's approval.

One of these is Xian-Janssen, which was set up between Janssen and four partners from SPAC. The sharing arrangements vary among Johnson & Johnson's joint ventures, but the company prefers to have majority control in order to maintain a strong presence in the foreign market. Fifty-two percent of Xian-Janssen is owned by Johnson & Johnson. The enterprise is the largest pharmaceutical joint venture in China. It is run by a team of more than 50 Chinese managers and a handful of expatriates, who together oversee a staff of about 600.

In 1990, Johnson & Johnson Shanghai Ltd., a joint venture producing Band-Aid adhesive bandages, was opened in China, followed the next year by Johnson & Johnson China Ltd. Furthermore, a new joint venture between Johnson & Johnson and the Shanghai Number One Biochemical and Pharmaceutical Co. has set its sights on becoming the leading nonprescription pharmaceuticals company in China. Shanghai

Johnson & Johnson Pharmaceuticals Ltd. is 95 percent owned by Johnson & Johnson. It already markets six Tylenol acetaminophen products.

Johnson & Johnson chose SPAC because it shares the same goals. Johnson & Johnson is committed to philanthropic environmental strategies in human health, education, and conservation. It seeks to build relationships with governments, nongovernmental organizations, industrial counterparts, academic institutions, and communities to encourage sustainable practices. Such an approach appeals to large, state run organizations such as State Pharmaceutical.

Johnson & Johnson is also funding a multiyear program with the World Wildlife Fund to deter the trade in parts from endangered species, such as tiger bone and rhinoceros horn, which are used in traditional medicines in China. This project has the support of the Chinese government.

The company has also supported medical education in China. Johnson & Johnson China Ltd. has sponsored a professional educational project for more than 200 doctors and nurses in conjunction with the China Medical Association (CMA) in the cities of Beijing, Shanghai, and Guangzhou. In another program, 18 physicians from prominent hospitals in China were trained in diabetes management through a grant from LifeScan, Inc. The goal was to enhance the quality of life for diabetic patients in China by improving the expertise of physicians involved in diabetes management.

Operational Strategies

Johnson & Johnson has six companies operating in the People's Republic of China and three in Hong Kong. It is oriented toward the local market. In order to establish secure, long-term market power in the Chinese health care market, the company has been adopting strategies to differentiate its products from those of its competitors. It has invested heavily in R&D as well as the expansion of its manufacturing capacity in China. The marketing leaders at Johnson & Johnson China have carefully studied the demography of the population in order to target customers with the right products.

Johnson & Johnson's strength in establishing a positive public image has been transferred to its wholly owned subsidiary, which has been marketing itself as a giant health care products maker with excellent quality. In addition, Johnson & Johnson China strives to reduce its manufacturing and operational costs in order to maintain affordable prices.

Improving the health and welfare of children around the world is an integral part of the company's credo. There are 250 million children under the age of 12 in China. Until a few years ago, there were no non-prescription medicines available for this large, high-potential market segment. Colds and fever are common ailments of young children. However, many families could not afford even the fees to consult doctors, so children were simply given half of an adult-strength pain and fever medication. Johnson & Johnson responded to this unique market by providing more products to satisfy children's needs. It set up its wholly owned subsidiary as a leading nonprescription pharmaceuticals company. Similarly, the joint venture known as Shanghai Johnson & Johnson Pharmaceutical Ltd., formed between Johnson & Johnson and Shanghai Number One Biochemical and Pharmaceutical Company in 1996, emphasizes serving the health care needs of children. During its first year of operation, it marketed six nonprescription Tylenol acetaminophen products for relieving pain and cold symptoms. Four were for children.

Johnson & Johnson China Ltd. also works closely with hospitals. Most local hospitals are not fully equipped with the latest pharmaceutical facilities. Johnson & Johnson has focused its R&D and manufacturing on satisfying hospital needs as it has strengthened local ties. For example, because sterilization systems, dialdehyde solutions, and disinfectants are in high demand, R&D facilities and technologies were transferred to a new manufacturing plant in Shanghai to produce exactly the right products.

Johnson & Johnson China Ltd. also has special products for women and diabetic patients. In September 1996, it sponsored the Johnson & Johnson Speakers Program in Beijing, Shanghai, and Guangzhou to help educate more than 200 doctors and nurses. The main topics were early infant care and diabetes management. In addition, the new Johnson & Johnson facility in Shanghai began to manufacture and market its popular feminine personal care products such as Carefree sanitary napkins.

Johnson & Johnson China has maintained lower costs and achieved greater efficiency by producing products that are in high demand. Pharmaceutical sales of drugs on the national Essential Drug List are subsidized by China's health care reimbursement system. For instance, 30 million government employees and 140 million state-owned-enterprise employees get free medical care. The government in each major city has established its own drug reimbursement list, outlining approximately 1,200 drugs eligible for government reimbursement. These drugs are in high demand by both patients and doctors. In order to fill this unique market segment, Johnson & Johnson China has linked its development and manufacture of drugs to match the government lists.

Two of Johnson & Johnson's most important competitive advantages are the quality of its employees and its organizational ability. The company is well known for its decentralized organizational structure, which has been transferred to its operations in China. Employee participation is encouraged. The company trains its employees in the use of various technologies and encourages them to become more sensitized to customer needs.

Xian-Janssen, Johnson & Johnson's joint venture with four local partners, recognizes the advantage of the effective management of local personnel. Its unique recruitment and management training techniques have been keys to the venture's success. All new employees attend a standard training program and spend three to six months on probation before joining the permanent staff. The objectives of the program are to foster a strong set of corporate values and reinforce the importance of initiative. Continuous on the job training, through seminars, coaching, and lectures, is also provided to educate employees in specific technical and managerial skills. Once or twice a year, the company runs a 10-day camp to bring employees and managers together. Workshops, lectures, and management games help develop analytical skills and locate managerial weaknesses. Participants are awarded points, and further training is provided to improve the weaknesses uncovered at the camp.

Johnson & Johnson maintains a decentralized organizational structure that combines the advantages found in smaller companies with the resources available to the larger organization. It provides multiple functional growth opportunities. In line with its policy of decentralization, each international subsidiary is managed by citizens of the country in which it is located.

Johnson & Johnson's international business structure contributes to its success. For example, both Johnson & Johnson Shanghai and Janssen Pharmaceutica have research labs and information technology centers so they can communicate with each other quickly and easily.

Johnson & Johnson uses a hybrid strategy to balance global integration and localization. Units coordinate their activities with headquarters and with one another. Each unit in China adapts its procedures to fit its own circumstances while drawing on corporate resources as necessary. This is because Johnson & Johnson wants the technological advances of global integration but the decentralization of localization. It also wants to cater specifically to the Chinese people and their preferences by fitting marketing strategies to the people and the provinces in which they live. The hybrid strategy gives Johnson & Johnson a lot of flexibility in dealing with problems as they arise since all of its headquarters around the world share information and assistance.

In conclusion, as a multinational company marketing products in more than 175 countries, Johnson & Johnson is considered successful. Some of the lessons it has learned in expanding into China may be useful to other companies. For example, before entering China a company should conduct thorough research, especially into the current legal system. For instance, where copyright-, patent-, or trademark-sensitive industries are concerned, foreigners must be careful. Johnson & Johnson was wise to link its products to its corporate name because there are many similar products within the pharmaceutical sector. In addition, remaining innovative through the use of technology has definitely given it a competitive edge and prevented its products from being imitated.

CASE 9

General Electric

General Electric is America's third most profitable company. *Fortune* magazine has described it as America's most admired company and "first in wealth creation." If ranked independently, eight of GE's businesses would be on the Fortune 500 list. Not only has GE created a booming business in the United States, but it also operates in more than 100 countries around the world. It has 250 manufacturing plants in 26 nations and employs 276,000 people worldwide, of which 165,000 are in the United States. Revenues in 1997 totaled $90.8 billion, of which $38.5 billion came from international operations.

April 15, 1892, marked the birth of a new corporate enterprise, the General Electric Co., formed by consolidating the Edison General Electric Co. and the Thomson-Houston Co. Foreseeing the advent of global competition, GE undertook a dramatic restructuring in the 1980s. Businesses that weren't first or second in their global markets were fixed, closed, or sold. It divested $10 billion worth of marginal businesses and made $19 billion worth of acquisitions to lead it into the 1990s. In addition to these changes, GE also set out to instill in its people the spirit and soul of a small company. Self-confidence, simplicity, and speed were emphasized and rewarded, and steps were taken to eliminate excess bureaucracy.

In 1997, GE became the first company in the world to exceed a market value of $200 billion. In Asia, it has continued to invest for growth. For example, Hitachi GE Lighting Ltd. consolidated all its marketing and sales into one business, resulting in increased sales and, more importantly, a simpler approach to dealing with its customers. This action positioned GE for strong growth in Japan, the world's second-largest lighting market. Throughout Asia, it has introduced more than 80 new products, increased sales by 25 percent, developed a better market share in GE branded lighting products, and achieved 10 percent factory productivity.

General Electric is a highly diversified corporation involved in appliances, capital services, electrical distribution and control, industrial control systems, information services, lighting, medical systems, broad-casting, plastics, power systems, and transportation systems. The divisions most active in China are appliances and lighting.

General Electric Appliances is one of the largest manufacturers of major appliances in the world, producing the Monogram, Profile, GE, RCA, and Hotpoint brands as well as several private label brands. Its products include refrigerators, freezers, electric and gas ranges, microwave ovens, washers, dryers, dishwashers, disposals, compactors, room air conditioners, and water purification systems. During 1997, GE Appliances introduced several new products, including the GE SmartWater filtration and softening systems. It also broadened its capabilities and expanded its global presence in service management. It serves the world's fastest-growing markets, including those of India, China, Asia, Mexico, and South America.

General Electric is a leading supplier of lighting products for global consumer, commercial, and industrial markets. Products in this sector include incandescent, fluorescent, high-intensity discharge, halogen, and holiday lamps, along with portable lighting fixtures, lamp components, and quartz products. It also manufactures outdoor lighting fixtures, residential wiring devices, and commercial lighting controls.

The External Environment

The company faces threats from new competitors entering the industry each year. This industry is highly competitive because it is one of the fastest-growing sectors in Asia, with appliance sales growing at a 12 percent annual rate. One reason for the growth of the appliance industry is local producers' export aspirations, which motivate them to spend more on R&D and quality control to meet international standards. The localization of parts and components has also driven down the cost of production and enhanced cost leadership. Finally, multinational corporations have brought innovation, technological skills, capital resources, international channels, and managerial expertise to China. These facilitate the competitive edge of the industry in the global market. Maytag, which experienced major losses in the past, invested $35 million in a joint venture with China's leading washing machine company and plans to invest another $35 million to expand the joint venture's operation into refrigerators.

To combat this fierce competition, GE implemented a "smart bomb" strategy in which it targets only those Asian markets in which it can earn more than 20 percent on its investment. It examines each country's idiosyncrasies, then tailors a mix of products, brands, manufacturing facilities, marketing, and retail approaches to wring the best performance from each. It measures factors such as the quality and strength of local competitors, the market's growth potential, and the availability of skilled labor. Its goal is to generate the handsomest returns from the smallest possible investment. By zeroing in on each market, or "smart bombing," GE's appliance division has been profitable in Asia since its first week of operations in January 1994.

In the United States, GE has a 32 percent share of the appliance market, but Whirlpool is leading with a 35 percent share. In Asia, GE made $320 million in profit between 1995 and 1997, while Whirlpool experienced $142 million in losses during the same period. Maytag and Electrolux also experienced losses. Asian appliance competitors are Matsushita, Sanyo, and Samsung, all of which are also involved in joint ventures in China. Domestic competition comes from Chinese manufacturers such as Haier, Xiaoya, Wanbao, and Zhongshan Weili.

Currently, these players are producing more appliances than the market can absorb. Saturation levels in most cities are peaking. Customs duties on appliances are falling, attracting more imports, and companies are struggling for market share. The main beneficiary is the consumer, who has turned out to be a rather quick study. Gone are the days when demand exceeded supply and the mere availability of home appliances ensured they would be snapped up quickly. Chinese consumers today know exactly what they want, what is available on international markets, and what standards are being achieved. Their expectations are specific and demanding, so the industry has found itself shifting strategies, perhaps a bit sooner than it had planned. The strongest Chinese firms have also vaporized the quality gap that once existed between their products and imported appliances. A growing nationalistic consumer segment is increasingly predisposed to buy Chinese brands.

The Internal Environment

General Electric is a technologically innovative company. In 1996, its research and development expenditures exceeded $1.9 billion. Its technology organization, which manages projects around the globe, now has more than half its engineers outside the United States, most notably in Hungary and China. Its sourcing organization continues to capitalize on GE Lighting's worldwide presence to attain the best products, price, and service available.

Six sigma is a statistical term that means the virtual elimination of defects from every process, product, and transaction. This is GE's goal. Using a disciplined, scientific methodology of measuring, analyzing, improving, and controlling every process, GE intends to attain a quality level of only 3.4 defects per million opportunities. To meet that bold objective and make six sigma an integral part of its corporate culture, GE invested $200 million in training and projects in 1996 and an additional $300 million in 1997. Progress toward achieving six sigma quality is an important factor in determining managerial bonuses at GE.

General Electric is also a financially solid company. As table C9.1 shows, its various profit ratios were significantly higher than Whirlpool's in 1997. The net profit margin of GE reached 48.93 in 1997, more than 10 times as much as that of Whirlpool. This profitability ratio was fundamentally higher than the average in the industry. Nonetheless, the capital structure of GE showed its reliance on external debt. The current ratio of GE was much lower than that of Whirlpool, while GE's various debt ratios were much higher than those of Whirlpool.

Entry Strategies

Entry Mode

Prior to the Second World War, GE manufactured lamps and table fans in Shanghai. It went back to China in 1973 to negotiate a technical assistance agreement for the manufacture of gas turbines, but this project was shelved in 1975 when China severed ties with all U.S. companies with close business links to Taiwan. Ties were reestablished in 1979, and

TABLE C9.1.   General Electric's Financial Ratios, 1997

Ratios	General Electric (1997)	Whirlpool (1997)
Liquidity ratios		
Current ratio	0.76	1.16
Quick ratio	0.71	0.58
Leverage ratios		
Debt/assets	47.59	30.16
Debt/equity	420.11	137.10
LT debt/equity	135.32	60.64
Profitability ratios		
Gross profit margin	57.25	22.97
Net profit margin	48.93	4.11
Return on asset	5.04	1.34
Return on equity	26.36	−.78

GE registered its first representative office in Beijing in 1981. Nothing came of GE's exploration of opportunities to source lighting and major appliances in 1984 and 1985, but that was GE's first real introduction to China. In 1986, the international corporate executive office began funding operations for the first three to five years to enable GE's businesses to explore opportunities and establish themselves in China.

The establishment of representative offices in Beijing, Shanghai, and Guangzhou was a simple way for GE to become acquainted with the Chinese market. It had representative offices in China for 15 years before it formed joint ventures in the appliance and lighting industries. Representative offices gave GE a formal presence in China and allowed it to become familiar with the business environment without the complications of an unfamiliar local partner or a major financial commitment. The establishment of representative offices also gave GE a position from which it could convince government officials to open other sectors to foreign businesses such as GE Capital. The disadvantages of its representative offices included high regulatory and start-up costs as well as high labor costs and rents in major cities, where office space was in short supply. The company continued to use its three representative offices even after it established other types of ventures in China.

In 1994, GE selected equity joint ventures as its mode of entry into China's lighting industry. There are several advantages to forming an equity joint venture. Chinese partners can provide essential business contacts and market knowledge. They can smooth things over with the government if necessary. The foreign investor's business risks are reduced, as the Chinese partner has to provide direct equity in the venture. Each partner's liability is limited to its share of paid-up capital. An equity joint venture enjoys preferential tax treatment in comparison with other forms of business.

Of course, there are also several disadvantages. Equity joint ventures are subject to a well-developed regulatory framework, and there is little room for maneuver. The distribution of profits or losses is not flexible, as it is usually made in accordance with each partner's capital contribution. The foreign investor's equity contribution must not be less than 25 percent.

General Electric has formed joint ventures with local companies that have a grip on national and regional markets with the idea of cutting costs and gaining the expertise needed to target markets precisely. It is to GE's advantage to enter into equity joint ventures in China because of new cultural, political, and economic systems. Indigenous firms have also developed unique country-, industry-, and firm-specific skills and advantages that would be costly, if not impossible, to duplicate.

Entry Timing

General Electric entered the Chinese appliance and lighting industries in 1994, around the same time as Samsung, Electrolux, and Whirlpool. These companies are all considered late movers. In the early 1990s, foreign entrants such as the Matsushita Electrical Industrial Co., Letsum Development, and the Sanyo Electric Co. had already entered into joint ventures in China. Daehan Jungsok entered in the mid-1990s. There is a long list of Chinese firms established in China prior to GE. Major local firms are the China Great Wall Industrial Corp., established in 1980, and the Shanghai Electrical Machinery Manufacture Works, established in 1949.

While early movers have better relationships with government authorities and the business community and an established organizational reputation and product image, late movers can learn from early foreign investors in a host country. They can reduce risks and operational uncertainty by studying early investor behavior in dealing with the local government, suppliers, customers, and other stakeholders in the value chain.

GE could examine its competitors' performances and then measure factors such as the quality and strength of local competition, market growth potential, and the availability of skilled labor. Its appliance division has been profitable since its first week of Asian operations because it zeroed in on its market.

Location Selection

In its involvement in the Chinese lighting industry, GE did not get to select its region. Rather, the Chinese government instructed Shanghai Jiabao to engage in a joint venture with GE in 1994. Shanghai is a coastal city and open economic region that is best developed economically and contains good infrastructure for transportation, communications, and production. Shanghai has Western-style business facilities, a cultural atmosphere conducive to international activities, support at the highest levels in Beijing, and a skilled labor force. These advantages are exemplified in a 350 square kilometer site called Pudong, the home of GE's joint venture with Shanghai Jiabao.

In April 1990, the State Council opened the Pudong New Area in eastern Shanghai. Foreign investment enterprises in the Pudong area are granted many privileges, chiefly breaks on corporate income taxes, tariffs, and value-added taxes. Moreover, land use rights can be transferred within the area with up to a 70 year grace period, and the government's income in the area will all be reinvested in further development and improvement of its infrastructure.

Special incentives for foreign, export, and high-tech enterprises in the Pudong area include priority in obtaining water, electricity, gas, transportation services, and telecommunications facilities and help with loans and other credit services. Pudong's infrastructure is good. More than $3 billion is being spent on public transportation, computerized utilities, and fiber optic telecommunications. When completed, this infrastructure is expected to support an export-processing zone, a free-trade area, and a scientific industrial park. Project proposals by foreign enterprises receive official replies within 30 days of submission.

Cooperative Strategies

Shanghai Jiabao, GE's major partner in China, was founded in 1970. By the time it went public in 1992, it had become China's largest manufacturer of lighting products, with an annual net profit of Rmb 27 million. Shanghai Jiabao's status as a state-owned enterprise was also an asset for GE, since such enterprises often have advantages in gaining access to materials, information, and investment infrastructure. Their market power, production, and innovation facilities are usually better than those of other firms, and they often have privileged access to distribution channels. Shanghai Jiabao's marketing and distribution channels were already well established when it entered into the joint venture with GE.

One of several reasons why the GE Lighting and Shanghai Jiabao joint venture has not been successful is that the quality of domestic lighting components was not as high as GE anticipated and it had to import components from India. Shanghai Jiabao claims that GE managers, in their ignorance of the Chinese lighting market, raised prices at the wrong time, cutting into prospective sales. Shanghai Jiabao also resented the excessive amounts of money that GE spent on items such as cars for expatriate managers in China. Jiabao claims six visiting technicians spent Rmb 12 million on living expenses during a one-month stay in China.

General Electric doesn't see things in the same light. It claims the venture is producing world-class quality products and is now able to export lamps to South Korea. It has introduced new products and advanced the GE brand in China. Therefore, it believes that the funds expended in meeting these objectives was money well spent.

In addition, GE claims that it met resistance from Shanghai Jiabao over its strategy of investing heavily to improve quality. The two firms had different approaches to running the business. General Electric was in for the long haul and wanted to reinvest profits to build market share. Shanghai Jiabao wanted to pocket the profits straightaway. Shanghai Jiabao eventually sold most of its 35 percent stake to GE, keeping just 11.5 percent.

General Electric Appliances' joint venture with the Shanghai Communications and Electrical Appliances Commercial Group, a seasoned distributor, proved more beneficial. The Shanghai Group understood the territory and could help identify factories scattered around the country that were capable of producing GE products. To make sure that its standards were met at each factory, the joint venture flew in teams of experts in quality, technology, service, manufacturing, billing, collecting, and other skills on what it calls "bubble" assignments. Each member of the bubble spent as much time as it took to bring the suppliers in line with GE's standards.

Operational Strategies

GE Lighting has continued to increase its global presence in the market. A key element in GE Lighting's philosophy has been the training of distributors, users, and designers. This project was a huge success, but it suffered some setbacks due to cultural differences, which resulted in bad communications and poor decisions. The venture got off to a bad start when the GE-led management team discovered that the quality of domestic lighting components was not as high as anticipated. Differences over pricing strategy followed. This resulted with at least two production stoppages. China was disappointed with the venture's financial performance, which GE expects to improve.

General Electric, with more than 20 projects in China today, prefers to start joint ventures from scratch, but it decided to build its lighting business through an existing operation because of the huge capacity available in China. In the end, GE decided that it would streamline the operation and cut its labor force of 8,000 employees, which has been reduced to 5,500. The venture is now introducing a broad range of products in China and learning which products sell best.

Aside from its success in selling equipment in China, GE is also recognized for its management training program. Under this program, about 30 mid- to upper-level Chinese managers receive eight months of English-language training in China, followed by a month of business education at GE's management institute in New York.

The chief smart bomb strategist at GE Appliances is CEO David

Cote. He stresses rigorous rules for capital outlays because the industry does not reward investment alone. A major reason for his tightfisted approach is that GE has no wiggle room on the pricing side. Indeed, appliance prices are lower today than they were a few years ago, even without adjusting for inflation. Refrigerators that not long ago cost $800 now run about $750.

General Electric implements a global strategy in which standardized products are offered in international markets and competitive strategy is dictated by the firm's home office. This international strategy seeks and emphasizes international economies of scale. The global strategy also offers GE greater opportunities to utilize the innovations developed in the individual units.

To implement its global strategy, GE uses a worldwide product divisional structure, an organizational form in which decision-making authority is centralized in the worldwide division headquarters, which coordinates and integrates decisions and actions among disparate divisional units. This form is the organizational structure of choice for rapidly growing firms seeking to manage their diversified product lines effectively. Integrating mechanisms also create effective coordination through mutual adjustments of personal interactions. Such integrating mechanisms include direct contact between managers, liaison roles between departments, temporary task forces or permanent teams, and the integration of roles. As managers participate in cross-country transfers, they are socialized in the philosophy of managing an integrated strategy through a worldwide product divisional structure. A shared vision of the firm's strategy and structure is developed through standardized policies and procedures that facilitate implementation of this organizational form.

Its global strategy allows GE to coordinate tasks across the region. One of its most valuable functions is managing human resources. For example, the company finds that executives from a GE company in one Asian country can easily be transferred to another location. They usually speak English and share the experience of having worked in relatively small markets. A regional focus helps GE form a critical mass of capable executives who can easily be shuffled as new opportunities arise.

This strategy will help GE in its latest shift away from capital-intensive manufacturing and toward human-intensive services. To make this leap, GE will have to transfer technology and put the right people in place. Transplanting technology is not a problem because the company already has a policy of transferring as much knowledge as possible to its overseas subsidiaries.

General Electric has many ways of maintaining and controlling global integration. First, it dispatches managers globally. Expatriate manager responsibilities include licensing, divestiture, global sourcing, and venturing. The company employs a team of globe-trotting managers who search for joint venture opportunities, coproduction candidates, and the technologies that are most in demand in countries with primitive infrastructures. This strategy seeks to penetrate fresh markets rather than hunting for cheap labor. According to GE, being national doesn't pay. Its strategy is to transform its management ranks, moving managers to front-line positions in the field and attempting to create "global brains" that can manage operations in Third World cultures. Dispatching managers globally is one way in which GE achieves global coordination and integration. The company invests about $500 million annually on training and educational programs around the world, from assembly lines to corporate classrooms to boardrooms.

General Electric's pay system gets people working faster and smarter. One secret is giving workers bonuses only if they meet tough goals. It awards stock options to all kinds of employees so that they will perform even better in the future. The key principle of compensation is to link it to performance rather than power. General Electric has tried to get away from the idea that an employee has to move up to make more. It cut the number of salary grades from 29 to six, a technique known as broadbanding. It also invites employees to assess and reward their peers on the spot in a program called Quick Thanks!

In conclusion, General Electric is an example of a global company that can provide technological and managerial skills that China urgently needs. In China's markets, political and economic risks loom, but GE reckons that placing many small investments of a few tens of millions of dollars each will cushion the company as it taps this gigantic market.

McDonald's

Since the founding of the McDonald's Corp. in 1954, it has grown at a staggering rate. Originally, there was one store located in Des Plaines, Illinois. Today, McDonald's is the largest and best-known global food service retailer, with more than 23,000 restaurants in 110 countries. In 1997, sales hit a new high of $33.6 billion. McDonald's places great emphasis on four important values: quality, service, cleanliness, and value. These values, combined with powerful and creative marketing strategies that include the endorsement of athletes from all over the world, Ronald McDonald, and Disney characters, make McDonald's a very competitive force. It is very careful in its choice of franchisees as well as in choosing its joint venture partners.

The mission of the McDonald's Corp. is to dominate the global food service industry. It considers global dominance dependent on setting the performance standard for customer satisfaction and increasing market share and profitability by successfully implementing its convenience, value, and execution strategies. According to its chairman and chief executive officer, Michael R. Quinlan, its international strategies are simple. Its aim is to make customers happy with low prices and outstanding restaurant operations. In addition, it looks to increase its market share by attracting more customers with greater frequency. Finally, it hopes to increase profitability by means of efficiency and economies of scale.

The history of McDonald's in China begins in the mid-1980s, when company personnel traveled to China to lay the foundations of an enterprise that would serve the huge Chinese population. McDonald's believes in controlling supply and distribution and developing strong local contacts. This desire for control led to five years of planning in order to get the supplies just the way it wanted them. The first Chinese McDonald's restaurant opened in Shenzhen, just across the border from Hong Kong, in October 1990. The opening in Beijing on April 23, 1992, shattered the Moscow opening day record, when more than 30,000 people were served. In Beijing in 1992, McDonald's served some 40,000 customers. In 1992, there were three restaurants in China. At the end of 2000, McDonald's has about 300 restaurants in China.

Major international markets in which McDonald's operates include the United States (12,380 restaurants as of December 31, 1997), Europe (3,886), the Asia Pacific region (4,456), Latin America (1,091), and others (1,319). Countries in the European region include Austria (103), England (746), France (629), Germany (850), and the Netherlands (176). Countries in the Asia Pacific region include Australia (642), China (184), Hong Kong (140), Japan (2,437), and Taiwan (233). Latin American countries include Argentina (131), Brazil (480), and Mexico (131). Other countries include Canada (1,050), Egypt (20), Saudi Arabia (27), and South Africa (35).

Systemwide sales in 1997, which include sales by all restaurants, whether operated by McDonald's, franchisees, or affiliates, totaled $33.6 billion, an increase from $31.8 billion in 1996. Sales increases in 1997 were primarily due to restaurant expansion worldwide, partly offset by weaker foreign currencies and 1996's negative comparable sales on a constant currency basis. In the Asia Pacific region, the Philippines and Taiwan had strong sales increases, which were driven by Extra Value Meal marketing campaigns and restaurant expansion despite difficult economic conditions in the latter part of the year.

Total revenues accrued by McDonald's include sales by company-operated restaurants and fees from restaurants operated by franchisees and affiliates. These fees include rent, service fees, and royalties that are based on a percentage of sales with specified minimum payments along with initial fees. Fees vary by type of site, investment by the company, and local business conditions. Revenues increased at a faster rate than sales in 1996 and 1997. This was primarily due to the weakening Japanese yen, which negatively affected sales more than revenues due to the economic structure of Japan and the higher growth rate in company-operated versus franchised restaurants. Revenues from the Asia Pacific region grew to $250 million and $262 million in 1996 and 1997, respectively. In 1997, the consolidation of Singapore's restaurants due to increased ownership, along with continued strong results in Taiwan, helped increase revenues, but these were somewhat mitigated in the second half of 1997 by the Asian financial crisis.

The External Environment

The Industrial Environment

In China's market, McDonald's has many competitors. Not only does it have to worry about Pizza Hut, KFC, and Kenny Rogers, but it also has to be concerned about competitor expansion. For example, Subway currently operates a total of three stores in Beijing, but it plans to open 55 new stores by 2005.

Another worry for McDonald's is Dunkin Donuts, which has so successfully penetrated the Chinese market that its doughnuts and coffee have become a regular part of the average Chinese diet. Internationally franchised through the British company, Allied Domecq, Dunkin Donuts started with one store in Beijing in 1995 and has grown to seven stores in the city. It has plans for future expansion into Shanghai. Because there are few places where youths can gather in Beijing, Dunkin Donuts has wisely carved out a niche in the fast food market by targeting young adults rather than children.

While McDonald's is fighting for market share with its fellow foreign competitors in China, local fast food chains are creeping up on their Western counterparts. After improving their decor, hygiene, and service, many local fast food restaurants have become nearly as crowded as McDonald's sites. Many Chinese entrepreneurs are diving into the market by offering noodles and traditional Chinese dishes as fast foods. Chinese fast food excels in taste; after sampling foreign flavors, many older people still prefer traditional Cantonese fast food restaurants. Chinese children, however, are very excited about eating at McDonald's because of its Western ties.

The Chinese fast food industry has tremendous potential for growth. According to statistics from the Ministry of Internal Trade, 400 Chinese fast food companies were operating 280,000 restaurants nationwide by the end of 1995. Their total annual sales were estimated to be Rmb 30 billion, one-fourth of the total in the catering trade.

However, all is not lost for McDonald's. The domestic fast food industry still lags behind its foreign counterparts. Most domestic restaurants are small scale and of limited profitability. It is difficult for them to purchase expensive machines and dismiss their employees. On the other hand, foreign fast food chains have standardized operations that ensure reliable quality and a unique consistency of cuisine, qualities often sought by consumers.

American affiliates and subsidiaries do not supply restaurants outside of the United States. In China, McDonald's relies upon independent suppliers, who are required to meet and maintain the company's standards and specifications. One McDonald's supplier is Bama Foods. Located in Beijing, it supplies apple, pineapple, and bean curd pies to various McDonald's restaurants in China. Another supplier is a joint venture named McKey Food Services Ltd., which is located in Shenzen city. The Chinese partner is the China Livestock Co. It produces meat for McDonald's in China. These suppliers have relatively high bargaining power because of the lack of suppliers that are able to meet McDonald's high standards of quality.

In the fast food industry there are many options for consumers, including pizza, chicken, and frozen foods. The biggest competitor in China is probably cold and hot noodles. Noodles have been around much longer than hamburgers. The majority of the older population is more accustomed to eating them, and many Chinese prefer their taste to hamburgers. They are also less expensive. This could be a definite weakness for McDonald's.

There is a constant threat of new entrants in the fast food industry because of low entry barriers. The greatest new entrant threat comes from local companies because they know the Chinese culture better than any foreign firm. The threat is prevalent due to low capital requirements and start-up costs and the lack of managerial complexity involved in running small restaurants.

The National Environment

Millions of people each year eat hamburgers under the "golden arches" of McDonald's in China. Since McDonald's is primarily identified by its trademark and name, protection of intellectual property rights is one of the most important legal considerations. These laws help protect McDonald's and its products in China. China adopted its trademark and trade name laws in 1982. An exclusive right to use a trademark can only be acquired by registration. A trademark character or figure must be distinctive enough to distinguish the goods of one enterprise from those of another, and it must not be misleading or deceptive. Article 8 of the Trademark Law provides a list of characters and figures that cannot be used as a trademark, including national flags and emblems, foreign flags and emblems, the red cross and red crescent, marks that discriminate against any nationality, and those detrimental to socialism, morals, and customs. A foreigner or foreign enterprise may file a trademark application in China provided its country of nationality has reciprocal trademark relations with China. The duration of a registered trademark is 10 years from the date of approval. The trademark may be extended for an unlimited number of 10-year periods by submitting an application within six months of the expiration date.

With an average annual per capita income of $547 and a growth rate of 10.5 percent for 1997, China represents a market worth exploring. The Chinese in the larger cities have higher incomes ($893 in Shanghai, $858 in Guangdong Province, and $787 in Beijing in 1997).

A number of recent trends in the cities will ensure a strong demand for American products. In Fujian and Guangdong Provinces, 41.1 and

92.3 percent of women are employed, respectively. Assuming that men are at least that highly employed, time for couples to shop for and prepare food has become limited. At the same time, employment of the female population tends to raise average household incomes. This in turn generates greater demand for a variety of convenience foods.

The rapid expansion of quick service restaurants such as McDonald's and KFC has provided another outlet for American suppliers, as local restaurants are adding Western-style dishes to their regular menus in order to satisfy the demands of newly affluent customers and increasing numbers of tourists.

The policy of one child per family has had the effect of turning single children into fussy little emperors, the center of attention of parents and relatives. High-quality food and beverage products provided by companies such as McDonald's are often targeted at children, where they find a ready market.

Nevertheless, Chinese government policies are perhaps an area where McDonald's could encounter some difficulty. First, the Chinese Ministry of Trade gives special, preferential treatment to Chinese fast food enterprises that have the potential to be successful. These businesses receive benefits such as prime locations in large Chinese cities. Even worse, in 1994 the McDonald's restaurant in central Beijing was ordered to vacate its prime location after signing a 20-year lease to make way for a project known as the Oriental Plaza, which was being developed by a Hong Kong businessman. Policies such as these show that foreign fast food companies are at the mercy of the government and its policies. These two examples also show that the Chinese government values *guanxi,* or close personal relationships, very highly. Because the government has closer ties to the Chinese people, it will likely give them preferential treatment.

The Internal Environment

The net profit margin of McDonald's was 14.32 for 1997, with the industrial average at 9.61 and the sector average at 6.87. The company's return on assets is rather high at 9.28, while the industry and sector averages are 7.52 and 4.96, respectively. McDonald's return on equity, 18.9, is wedged between the Standard & Poors average of 22.39 and the industrial average of 14.67. McDonald's debt to asset ratio is .51. Its debt to equity ratio is .71, while the industrial average is performing at .61 and the sector average is 1.02. The McDonald's inventory turnover ratio was at 115.06 in 1997, while the industrial average was 41.69. Finally, McDonald's had an average collection period of 15.26 days. These indicators suggest that its financial position is strong.

McDonald's achieves this through training and incentive programs. It conducts crew-level training at 25 workstations in addition to using step by step manuals and videotapes. Due to its international scope, translators and electronic equipment are provided, which enables professors to teach and communicate in 14 languages at one time. In addition to training, its Hamburger Universities provide a variety of advanced business management courses, which allows aspiring managers to earn college credit.

One McDonald's incentive program is McDonald's Employee Stock Option Program (McDESOP), which allows employees to make contributions on a pretax basis. The company matches half of the contributions, up to 6 percent of a worker's salary. McSave is another incentive program in which after tax contributions are deposited into a taxable money market mutual fund via payroll deductions.

McDonald's is recognized as one of the best marketers in the world today, spending hundreds of millions of dollars annually on advertising and promotion of its brand image. Ronald McDonald and the golden arches are symbols recognized by consumers throughout the world. The company's basic strategies are (1) to maintain a global image of quality, service, cleanliness, and value via heavy media advertising and in-store merchandising promotions; (2) to use value pricing and Extra Value Meals to build customer traffic; and (3) to use Ronald McDonald to create greater brand awareness among children and the *Mc* prefix to reinforce the connection between menu items and McDonald's.

McDonald's uses special interest marketing because of its diverse customer base. To target children, it created the Happy Meal and the McDonaldland characters: Hamburgler, Grimace, Birdie the Early Bird, Mayor McCheese, and the McNugget buddies. It put the characters in the Happy Meals, and children have been collecting these special toys ever since.

Sports marketing is another key part of the company's special interest marketing. By sponsoring such worldwide events as the Olympics and World Cup soccer, the company gains international visibility. McDonald's is also active in women's gymnastics, auto racing, the National Football League (NFL), and the NBA.

Entry Strategies

Entry Mode

McDonald's only enters countries that it believes will bring the firm success and increased profits. Demand in China is very high. In 1996,

China's GDP per capita was at an all-time high of Rmb 5,634. The average Chinese person spends 49 percent of his or her disposable income on food. Related and support industries are present in China and have been developed successfully to meet the specific needs of McDonald's. The firm believes in local sourcing, through which it creates strong relationships with local suppliers. For example, the McDonald's in Shanghai purchases 90 percent of its products from local suppliers. Local sourcing of raw materials has been made possible in two ways. McDonald's has worked very hard teaching Chinese farmers to grow potatoes in a certain manner so they can be used to make McDonald's signature style fries. Additionally, McDonald's uses other MNCs located in China. Finally, China's factor endowments have the potential to be very beneficial to McDonald's. Labor costs are low compared to those in Western countries such as the United States. With such a large population and so much agricultural land, almost all the raw materials McDonald's needs for its products can be found in China. With costs also kept to a minimum by using local suppliers, profit margins will most likely continue to be high.

Although McDonald's usually franchises its fast food operations outside of the United States, it has chosen to utilize the equity joint venture strategy in China. The main reason for this choice is the issue of quality control. Although franchising provides an easy way to expand quickly, McDonald's realized the importance of carefully considering applicants before venturing into any kind of business arrangement. Applicants must be able to mount a clean and efficient operation. McDonald's realized that franchising would be problematic if it expanded too fast and had only limited control over its Chinese affiliates.

The joint venture strategy gives McDonald's access to local distribution channels, supplier relationships, and the knowledge of its partners. It also has overcome entry barriers placed by the Chinese government on foreign companies, acquired natural resources within the country, and increased its market power. However, one of the drawbacks it faces is that joint ventures are a temporary mode. Once the life of the contract is over and the partner has fulfilled its goal, the joint venture will be terminated. This contradicts McDonald's long-term commitment to staying in China.

The equity ownership strategy between McDonald's and the Beijing Department of Agriculture is a fifty-fifty arrangement, with McDonald's investing $2.4 million. McDonald's has 85 percent equity with the China Livestock Joint Co. in Shenzhen.

In Beijing, McDonald's consciously presents itself as a Chinese company on the grounds that the Chinese partner owns 50 percent of the business. The company also emphasizes that 95 percent of the food used by the Beijing McDonald's is locally produced. While McDonald's remains essentially American in terms of menu, services, and management, the company has made serious efforts to adapt to the Chinese cultural setting. To present itself as a local company, all the restaurants in Beijing actively participate in community projects with local schools and neighborhoods.

Entry Timing

McDonald's is a late entrant into the foreign fast food industry in China. PepsiCo opened its first Kentucky Fried Chicken in Beijing in 1987, followed by Pizza Hut. In less than 10 years, KFC expanded to 33 cities and established over 100 restaurants in China. By 1995, its sales were almost $90 million.

In 1990, McDonald's opened its first restaurant in Shenzhen. Today it is located in over 10 cities and has approximately 184 restaurants. Despite its late entrance, it still has an advantage over its competitors because people all over the world recognize its name and trademark as symbols of America. As a late entrant, McDonald's was able to research what the Chinese consumers really wanted and provide these services. Its highly efficient service and management, spotless dining environment, and fresh ingredients have been featured repeatedly in the Chinese media as exemplars of modernity.

However, one drawback of entering the Chinese market late is the "garbage can" effect, in which earlier entrants are able to utilize more resources, thereby limiting those available to later entrants. For example, the Chinese government regulates the number of joint ventures in each province and closes the door when the limit is reached.

Location Selection

The primary McDonald's strategy in selecting locations outside of the United States is to target central cities first, establish a presence there, and then branch out to peripheral areas. McDonald's did not, however, immediately follow this strategy when it entered China. The first McDonald's restaurant was opened in Shenzhen city, a small city near Hong Kong. Shenzhen was declared a special economic zone in 1979. It was the first region to be opened to foreigners. McDonald's realized that Shenzhen would be a wise location for the following reasons: low taxes, more governmental support, adequate infrastructure, less interference from the government, and convenience.

After McDonald's initial entrance, it began utilizing its location

strategy of targeting busy central cities. On April 23, 1992, it opened its largest restaurant in the world in Wangfujing, Beijing. This two-story, 28,000 square foot facility seats more than 700 and employs 1,000. Prior to the opening in Beijing, the company's name was already popular among trendy consumers. On the day of its grand opening, thousands lined up for hours just to be a part of the experience of eating there.

McDonald's selected this location for many reasons. Beijing is highly populated. A great many foreigners pass through this city, so the American dollar is accepted there. McDonald's realized that foreigners as well as locals would make up its customer base in Beijing. Furthermore, average purchasing power is greater in Beijing than in many other areas. Consumers who are able to afford imported food and beverages tend to be concentrated in Beijing and Shanghai.

McDonald's also chose to enter Shanghai. Consumers in Shanghai and Beijing are considered middle class, earning somewhere between $10,000 to $40,000 annually. Currently, the middle class consists of 100 million people in China's coastal, urbanized provinces. By the year 2000, China's middle class numbered 445 to 580 million. McDonald's wanted to target areas where the middle class was growing since these are the people most likely to frequent its restaurants. It then expanded to other cities, including Guangzhou, Xiamen (which was the second special economic zone), Fuzhou, Dongguan, Foshan, and several others.

Cooperative Strategies

The entrance of McDonald's into Beijing was accomplished through an equity joint venture with the Beijing General Corp. of the Agriculture Industry and Commerce United Co. (in other words, the Beijing Department of Agriculture). The joint venture is located in Beijing city and began in 1991. The duration of the investment is 20 years, and the total investment is $4.8 million. The main reason why McDonald's chose this partner is that the Department of Agriculture is controlled by the government of China. In order to receive agricultural supplies (e.g., wheat, rice, barley, oats, apples, and even tea), McDonald's must go through the department for approval. Therefore, McDonald's wants to have a good relationship with it in order to get all the supplies it needs. McDonald's definitely needed the support of the government. Its partner not only utilizes the Department of Agriculture's connections in dealing with barriers concerning agricultural products but is also able to offer supplier relationships and distribution channels.

This agreement was made because the government saw that

McDonald's would be able to promote the development of China's economy and raise its scientific and technological levels for the benefit of modernization. Its efficient and consistent operations methods met the qualifications required for approval by the Chinese authorities.

The China Livestock Joint Co. is another partner in an equity joint venture with McDonald's. This venture commenced in 1990 in Shenzhen city. The name of the project is McKey Food Services Ltd. The joint venture agreement has a 50-year term. With a total investment of $15 million, this joint venture alone gives McDonald's a sizable advantage over its competitors. The business produces meat and other food products for McDonald's.

McDonald's selected China Livestock because it had compatible goals. Both companies want a long-term relationship, as is shown by the 50-year agreement. McDonald's uses China Livestock to get meat, and China Livestock obtains Western technology from McDonald's.

McDonald's joint ventures are managed by both local and U.S. employees. This cooperative strategy of placing locals in management positions allows McDonald's to capitalize on its vision of what will make McDonald's work in China. It offers Chinese employees great opportunities for advancement both locally and globally. In addition, it offers an excellent training program. These incentives attract many Chinese professionals.

Operational Strategies

McDonald's has focused heavily on differentiating itself from other fast food chains in order to make its products and image immediately distinguishable to its customers. More importantly, the differentiation strategy fits its long-term goal of keeping and attracting lifelong customers. By keeping its customers satisfied and listening to their needs, McDonald's helps to ensure that its customers will remain loyal. It focuses some of its efforts on cost leadership, but this goal is secondary to product differentiation.

According to its 1994 annual report, McDonald's firmly believes that there should be "quality in all we do." This statement has been supported by the creation of the McDonald's Quality Management process (MQM), which focuses directly on the ideas and processes that comprise what McDonald's considers quality, including customer satisfaction. In addition to MQM, McDonald's has founded the Center for Corporate Training and Education (CCTE), which trains managers in areas such as benchmarking, effective management, and process reengineering, all of which can help increase the quality of its restaurants. Finally, McDonald's ensures that the food it serves is of the best quality by enforcing high product and health standards. Regardless of whether it is potatoes or apples pies, it will purchase only the best raw materials from suppliers.

McDonald's has used superior customer responsiveness to distinguish itself from the competition. It alters its menu slightly depending on what country it is in so that it will offer something that is directly in line with local tastes. For example, pork sandwiches and beer are sold in Germany, wine is sold in French restaurants, fish and rice are sold in Japanese restaurants, and bean curd pies are sold in China. Additionally, McDonald's provides nutritional information about its products to the public. Nutritional information is usually found on either the paper used to cover trays or on a large board at the cash registers.

Finally, McDonald's is very quick to respond to its customers' wants and needs. For example, when it found that it was losing a large portion of its adult customers because they felt the restaurant was catering too much to children, the company introduced the Arch Deluxe, which is marketed as a burger for an older, more mature customer. Regardless of whether this attempt was successful, McDonald's is responsive.

One of the reasons why McDonald's has remained the number one fast food retailer in the world is its excellent corporate culture and value system. The values the company believes has made it successful for years have remained the same from the time of Ray Kroc: quality, service, cleanliness, and value.

McDonald's high standards of quality ensure that customers receive food that is the result of good ingredients, strict standards, and proven preparation procedures. The quality concept has been extended throughout the corporation as MQM, which instills the principles of customer responsiveness, managing with facts, valuing people, and continuous improvement.

In conclusion, McDonald's will continue to face favorable and unfavorable situations in China. There is great competition from foreign franchises and local fast food restaurants. In addition, both buyers and suppliers in China have great bargaining power since there are so many fast food restaurants to choose from and so few suppliers that can meet the company's high standards. Finally, the government has a great deal of control and at any time can implement strict measures over foreign investment.

However, there are ways that McDonald's can cope with minor setbacks. First, with innovative marketing it has achieved high brand recognition. By sourcing locally, it keeps its costs at a minimum, which in turn helps increase its profit margin. The government can be dealt with by selecting good joint venture partners. Joint ventures are a good choice of entry mode because they give McDonald's a direct interest in the restaurants. Finally, McDonald's has followed a good entry strategy in China by commencing operations in special economic zones and coastal cities.

When looking toward the future of the fast food industry in China, it would appear that McDonald's will continue to expand. The Chinese economy is primed to become the world's largest in the near future. There will also be more Western influence as more MNCs enter this alluring market. With Chinese people having more money and being subject to more influence from Western sources, the demand for McDonald's food could very well increase, especially if television becomes popular in China and Western stations provide services to the Asian superpower. The Chinese people will still eat noodles in great abundance, but McDonald's will become a daily part of their lives sometime in the future.

CASE 11

Ford

The Ford Motor Co. was established in 1903. Over the years, it has become the second-largest producer of cars and trucks in the world. Its major businesses include selling or renting cars and trucks, selling auto parts, and financial services. Feeling that the North American and European markets are saturated, Ford has its gaze set on the Asian market, China in particular. This market is difficult, with many rivals, high entry barriers, scarce suppliers, many similar products, and knowledgeable buyers. On the whole, however, China has a huge potential due to its embryonic market. Ford decided to enter the Chinese market through an equity joint venture with Jiangling Motors. The inland location of Jiangxi Province allows Ford to capitalize on cheap labor, access to western China, and isolation from its competitors. A 30 percent equity stake in Jiangling allowed for this globally strategic company to team up with a firm with compatible goals and visions.

In order for Ford to succeed, it must change its strategy to accommodate the Chinese environment. Under its Ford 2000 plan, it hopes to achieve cost leadership as well as some product differentiation. Through efficiency, innovation, quality, and customer responsiveness, Ford plans to win customer loyalty. It must keep in mind that its managers dispatched overseas are valuable links between the home office and China, while Chinese managers provide links between the government and Ford. Preparedness for the long term and maintaining good relations with the government will be necessary for Ford to succeed in the highly competitive Chinese market.

The Ford Motor Company's mission statement includes a commitment to value and sharing a vision of success with its customers, shareholders, and employees. In China, Ford sponsors 40 research and development projects with 28 universities and institutes to promote collaboration in science and technology.

The company is divided into five major parts: Ford, Ford Credit, Hertz, The Associates, and Visteon. Ford Credit specializes in providing auto loans. Hertz provides quality cars for sale and rent across the United

States. The Associates specializes in mortgages and personal loans. Visteon produces parts for many automakers around the world. This case study focuses mainly on Ford the automobile manufacturer. Its divisions include Ford, Mercury, Lincoln, Jaguar, and Mazda. Ford is also concerned with repairs of its cars and sets strict guidelines for its dealers to follow. Major competitors include BMW, Chrysler (now Daimler Chrysler), Fiat, General Motors, Honda, Nissan, Toyota, and Volkswagen.

Ford's major international markets are in North America, South America, Latin America, Europe, and Asia. Currently, two-thirds of Ford's sales are in the United States. It is the world's largest producer of trucks and the second-largest producer of cars. Its operations in 38 countries include 111 plants employing 225,900 people. There are 15,800 Ford dealerships in over 200 countries.

The External Environment

The Industrial Environment

Currently, the industrial outlook varies from region to region. Within the North American and European markets, automobile sales are rather stagnant. Projected growth between 2000 and 2005 is expected to be 0.5 percent at best. On the other hand, sales in Asia are projected to be 10 million units over the next few years. In Asia, 3.6 million cars were sold in 1996, about 25 percent of the U.S. figure. Fewer than 1.5 million cars were sold in China in 1997, only 10 percent of the number sold in the United States.

The entire industry is now focusing its attention on capitalizing on future automobile sales in Asia. General Motors is working toward integrated production of parts and vehicles through its ties with Isuzu and Suzuki. Daimler Chrysler plans to manufacture in Asian countries to take advantage of lower labor costs and export the majority of its products. Ford is taking what is called the "reasoned approach," forming alliances and joint ventures with local vendors.

Currently, Japanese manufacturers control 80 percent of the Chinese auto market, including imported autos. Daimler Chrysler has about a 2 percent share. Ford and GM each control only 1 percent of the market. If Ford and GM are to achieve the 10 percent market share they each desire, they will have to take market share from the Japanese and alter their vehicles to suit Chinese tastes.

The Asian market favors small, less profitable cars. Since the end of the Vietnam War, demand for large V8 engines has dwindled. While American corporations concentrated their efforts on selling high-profit

cars to the American and European markets, the Japanese stepped in to fill other needs. American manufacturers must be able to produce small autos in the $4,000 range rather than cars in the $15,000 to $20,000 range.

Although China and India are the largest potential markets in the world, the payoff on investment is still far away. Of the five million autos to be produced over the next few years, 30 percent will go unsold. This means that there will be intense rivalry between manufacturers. The excess supply of vehicles will cause price slashing and smaller profit margins as manufacturers try to sell their inventories. In addition, buyers will have great bargaining power since they will have a wide variety of choices while remaining relatively few in number.

The power of new entrants in China is weak due to high start-up costs and limitations on the number of new companies imposed by the Chinese government. Ford should not have to worry about abundant new entrants, as has been the case in Thailand.

The National Environment

Since most individuals cannot afford vehicles (given China's roughly $513 per capita income), 80 percent of the vehicles go to the government and 19 percent to businesses. The remaining measly 1 percent is made up of individual buyers. This is quite different than the United States, where the majority of vehicles are purchased by individuals within a more evenly distributed market.

Legally, the Chinese government is very strict. In addition to having stringent entry procedures, China chooses the partners and locations for joint ventures with American auto companies. The government may also impose production restrictions, price limits, and buyer constraints.

One of the greatest boosts for American businesses hoping to enter China is that it is expected to join the World Trade Organization soon. As a result, the Chinese government has seemingly been more lenient than before. International competition is still very fierce, however. Korean auto companies are a new force to be reckoned with. They have competent technology and produce quality products. They are also very aggressive in the marketplace.

Another aspect to consider is the culture that American auto manufacturers encounter in China. Japanese managers are considered better able to adapt with their flexible management style. American managers are more set in their ways and do not adjust readily to different cultures. As a result, they are unable to motivate or manage foreign employees as effectively as their Japanese counterparts do. If Ford is to increase its 1 percent market share to 10 percent, it must learn to communicate more effectively with its Chinese employees.

The Internal Environment

Ford's performance from 1995 to 1997 can be compared to those of GM and Daimler Chrysler. Ford's figures are consistent and not excessively out of place, as the other two companies' figures seem to be. Ford seems to be more conservative. It has better current and quick ratios than the other two, demonstrating a better ability to meet its short-term obligations without liquidating inventories.

Further examination shows that the industry as a whole is highly leveraged with debt. The implications are that shareholders' returns are greatly affected by every change in net income and loss. These companies need to continually turn their inventory over to ensure their ability to meet short-term obligations. Also, these companies are unable to undertake long-term projects that will pay off in the long run, decreasing the likelihood of consistent, long-range gains for shareholders.

In 1995, CEO Alex Trotman announced the Ford 2000 plan. This plan was designed to incorporate North American and European operations under one central facility located in the United States. The Latin American and Asian divisions are to be consolidated at a later date. In addition, Ford plans to use the same platforms and power trains for all its vehicles. This means that the same frames, bodies, engines, and transmissions will be used for all markets with only a few cosmetic changes. This would result in huge cost savings, but there are some major drawbacks to the plan. Globally similar cars are often viewed as boring and inadequately adapted to the needs of different societies and the tastes of different cultures.

Ford is one of the biggest users of computer systems. It recently installed one of the largest enterprise systems in the United States. It is designed to track all aspects of Ford's business cycle and connect it with all its suppliers, retailers, and customers. Since all the business processes are automated, this makes the operations much more efficient.

Entry Strategies

Entry Mode

Ford chose China as one of the most significant markets for the future of the company. By 1996, it had already invested $250 million in China. By the end of 1998, its investment will be over $500 million. The officers of Ford believe that China is a market with huge potential due to its large population.

The auto market in China is especially large because it has a very low auto per capita ratio. Recent research shows that there is only one auto for every 100 people compared to 75 cars per 100 people in the overcrowded U.S. market. China already produces a total of 1.5 million cars per year, and this number is expected to double by the year 2010.

Among all the potential markets in Asia, car sales in China have performed the best. Ford is still losing money, however, because its initial investment was so huge. In addition, the auto market in China is at the beginning stage, where profits have not yet been realized. Furthermore, current demand is low. Therefore, most foreign car manufacturers in China are not making a profit. Instead, they have invested for the long run since China has a car sales growth rate of 8 percent per year. A cheap labor force, access to abundant raw materials, and supportive governmental policies are three more important factors that attract foreign automakers to China.

After Henry Ford II's meeting with the late Deng Xiaoping in 1978, the company decided to enter China through a procedure known as the reasoned approach, which relies on alliances with local partners in selected markets. Ford formed five joint ventures to produce such automotive components as climate control products, radiators, glass, plastic, and electronics. By forming such small joint ventures, Ford believed that it could develop a favorable relationship with Chinese officials without posing a threat to the indigenous automobile industry. Smaller Chinese producers were struggling, and Beijing was careful to keep big foreign manufacturers from swamping the domestic market. Contrary to Ford's expectations, the reasoned approach led it nowhere. It became the only U.S. automobile manufacturer without a joint venture that would have allowed it to produce vehicles.

Ford encountered its most cataclysmic loss in late 1995 when GM won a bid to form a joint venture with the Shanghai Automotive Industry Corp., China's largest car maker. This occurred after Ford had spent two years and millions of dollars on its parts joint ventures and licensing agreements in an attempt to procure this partnership.

Following this defeat, Ford took a more cautious approach and decided to form a joint venture to produce vehicles through an acquisition. After only two months of talks, Sun Min, chairman of the Jiangling Motor Corp., convinced Gerald Kania, vice president of Ford China, to invest in his company. In 1995, Ford spent $40 million to purchase 80 percent of the state-owned enterprise's B shares, which are reserved for foreign investors. Due to the success of the venture, in 1997 Ford purchased another 120 million shares for an additional $55 million. Now it is finally able to assemble vehicles in China, although not in the hoped-for

category of small family sedans priced under $10,000. If the jointly built Transit minibus prevails, Chinese officials, who have a tight grip on the car market, may allow Ford to become the next foreign manufacturer to join the revered group of passenger sedan assemblers.

In 1995, Ford obtained a 20 percent equity stake in Jiangling through the purchase of 80 percent of the state-owned enterprise's B shares. This purchase made Ford the second-largest shareholder in Jiangling. Jiangling has the largest share, with a 51 percent equity stake, entitling it to place three representatives on the board. As a minority shareholder, Ford entered the joint venture with less risk and lower start-up costs. However, it wanted more control over the relationship. That is why it bought 120 million more shares, raising its stake to 30 percent. This purchase left few B shares to Jiangling Motors. While a 30 percent equity stake may seem to have put Ford in an inferior position, circumstances have proven otherwise.

Ford's superior marketing power raised its 30 percent stake to a higher number, giving it equal or better control than Jiangling. As the world's second-largest automobile manufacturer, Ford has the resources and ability to expand Jiangling to a size it could never aim for alone. Ford has transferred a great deal of equipment to Jiangling to modernize its assembly plant. It has also trained Chinese engineers and manufacturers abroad. These factors have allowed it to control many aspects of the joint venture that it otherwise could not.

Entry Timing

In China, constraints on the automobile industry have reduced first-mover benefits. It is true that once an automotive firm establishes itself in a province, no other car manufacturer is allowed to form a joint venture there. First movers are therefore able to limit competition. On the other hand, only two joint ventures are allowed by each foreign manufacturer. Once a joint venture is formed, no other partnerships can be made with non-state-owned firms. This has resulted in the problem Volkswagen faces, in which there is no hope of expanding into different provinces or taking advantage of other local firms because it has already filled its quota. Finally, first movers face high anti-imitation costs.

Ford made its first impression in China in 1913 when the Model T first appeared on China's roads. After much political instability and a lack of demand for automobiles, Ford reentered the market in 1978, when Henry Ford II expressed an interest in China. Ford has had 80 years of experience dealing with China, so in that sense it is a first mover. However, in terms of FDI, this is not so. Chrysler has been

assembling Jeep Cherokees in Beijing since the mid-1980s, General Motors formed a joint venture before Ford, and Japanese car manufacturers were in China even earlier than Chrysler. With Chrysler in Beijing and General Motors in Shanghai, Ford will never be given the opportunity to situate itself in these two important, highly developed cities.

Ford is a late mover because of the numerous roadblocks set up by the political structure. The remnants of a centrally planned economy, expanding market forces, increasingly decentralized decision making, low demand for vehicles, overproduction, and tight government controls have all led to serious delays. The types of automobiles that will be assembled are selected by government officials; a firm can easily lose a joint venture deal if its bid is not considered beneficial enough. Ford could not compete with General Motors' $1 billion bid to become the foreign partner in a joint venture with the Shanghai Automotive Industry Corp. General Motors also offered technical workshops, technology-sharing projects, and research grants. Ford fell short of this offer and lost the joint venture to General Motors.

As a late mover, Ford has been able to capitalize on some issues. It learned a valuable lesson from its nemesis, General Motors. In 1991, GM teamed up with Zhao Xiyou, who promised that a small truck venture would eventually lead to bigger and better things. By 1995, barely a dozen pickups had been sold. On the verge of collapse, Beijing forced the operation to merge with one of China's largest government-approved automobile assemblers, First Auto Works, without informing General Motors ahead of time. Ford has watched such developments and taken a more cautious approach.

Location Selection

Jiangxi, at first glance, hardly seems to be an ideal location for any automobile manufacturer, but it may turn out to be exceptional. While Chrysler and General Motors are located north of Jiangxi Province toward the eastern border, Ford is located in the center of the country. Although the east coast is more modern, it is difficult to gain access to the central and southern regions where development will more likely expand in the future. Ford is therefore isolated from its competitors and has access to regions Chrysler and General Motors do not.

Jiangxi Province is quite large, with an area of 166,900 square kilometers and a population of a mere 36.95 million. It boasts a unique landscape and rich agricultural resources. It also has a well-established, comprehensive, industrial system. The Jiangxi Tractor Factory's "harvest-180" tractors have been well received in dozens of countries around the world.

Military aircraft and the Silkworm Missile were developed in the Nanchang Airplane Manufacturing Plant. The nation's largest copper producer, the Jiangxi Guixi Smeltery, the first of its kind in China, is equipped with advanced, computer-controlled, flash-smelting technology imported from abroad.

Jiangxi also has convenient transport. Just downstream from Jiujiang Harbor is the East China Sea. The province also has rail and air links with most of the big cities in China. Nanchang, the capital of Jiangxi, is a major stop on the Beijing to Hong Kong railway line, and one can fly from Nanchang to Beijing in only two hours.

Most important to Ford, however, is the fact that Jiangling Motors is located in this province. In 1997, Ford invested $54.5 million in Jiangxi to establish a production base because Jiangxi is one of China's major manufacturers of light trucks and pickups. In addition, since the late 1980s, the provincial authorities have adopted a number of measures and policies to improve the investment environment, which has brought some obvious benefits to this province.

Finally, because this province is located in the southern part of China, where labor and land are much less expensive, costs are up to 50 percent cheaper than in other parts of the country. This makes Ford's costs much lower than those of its competitors, which are located where the prices of land and labor are comparable to those in developed nations.

Cooperative Strategies

A company located in the developing world looks for a few specific things in its American partners. First and foremost would be financial backing. One of the goals Sun wanted when the joint venture mode was established was regular infusions of cash. Jiangling Motors also needs technology and expertise to convert the company into a successful manufacturer. With Ford's help, Sun is optimistically waiting to see Jiangling's operations improve and become more competitive.

Ford, on the other hand, has less materialistic goals. It hopes to somehow pave the way for entry into the Chinese passenger car market. Though the Ford Transit line only consists of trucks, vans, and buses, company officials are hoping that the success of the Transit will allow them to begin producing passenger vehicles.

Since it has been producing trucks since the 1940s, Jiangling possesses many skills that have enabled Ford, at least for now, to reach the difficult goal of producing any kind of vehicle in China. The transition from military trucks to vans, buses, and pickups has not been too difficult for Jiangling, since it has quickly implemented much of the technology Ford offered. The product relatedness between Ford and Jiangling has allowed both to take advantage of economies of scale and scope and efficiencies of transaction costs.

Jiangling has proved its ability to absorb the knowledge and skills acquired from Ford. Ford has been able to save time and money by jointly producing buses with Jiangling, which not only supplies parts for the vehicles but also uses Ford's machinery, plans, and designs to assemble them. As a state-owned firm, Jiangling offers more skills to Ford than a privately or collectively owned enterprise could. In terms of industrial experience, market power, and production and innovation facilities, a state-owned firm is quite advantageous. Moreover, state-owned firms have access to state-instituted distribution channels. Relationships with various government institutions are also valuable, since state-owned firms are given preferential treatment when selecting market segments. For Ford, therefore, Jiangling is an ideal partner for market expansion.

Aside from being state owned, Jiangling has other beneficial traits. It has a large number of employees (currently 6,100 workers), so it is able to reduce risks and mitigate uncertainty by exercising more bargaining power when dealing with local authorities. Jiangling also has some international experience. In 1996, it began exporting some of its trucks to Egypt and the Middle East. Its long existence has allowed it to develop not only a reputable image but stable supply relationships. For example, while Jiangling supplies the engine, transmission, axles, and drive shafts for the Transit, 60 percent of the parts on the vehicles (soon to be 85 percent) are supplied by outside domestic sources with which Jiangling already has relations.

At the beginning of the joint venture, a lot of time was spent on basic communications, and some problems were encountered in bridging the cultural divide. Both companies are committed to the long haul, however, and both have worked to build a good relationship.

Operational Strategies

Ford uses cost leadership plus product differentiation as its generic competitive strategy. In order to develop a car market for individual users and cater to people's current purchasing power, Ford plans to produce cars with a price range between Rmb 50,000 and 70,000 by lowering its costs through technological innovation.

In addition, Ford has increased the company's competitive power in the market by designing products that meet Chinese people's needs. The

Transit minibus, with its diesel engine, was specially designed for China's narrow, busy roads. According to Chinese law, foreign investors need to buy some resources from local suppliers. Over 60 percent of the parts on the Transit come from local suppliers, and this percentage is expected to increase to 85 percent within a few years.

The automobile industry in China is still embryonic, which means that there is a great opportunity for investors to make a profit. Even though Ford entered the Chinese market later than other auto manufacturers, its competitive position is considered strong because it has chosen good partners and superior locations in which to operate.

In order to produce products in China efficiently and maintain good quality, Ford upgrades employee skills through training programs in foreign countries. Recently, 15 Chinese engineers were sent to London to work on bus design for a year. Another six manufacturing engineers went to one of Ford's factories in Portugal to study how the Transit is built. Ford also reduces its customer defection rate by improving the technology at its partner companies. It brought in equipment to modernize its partner's outdated technology when the company began manufacturing the Transit in 1995. For Ford, quality is a priority, so the company is willing to spend money to maintain high-quality products.

Ford hired Automotive Resources Asia Ltd. of Bangkok to evaluate its investments in Asian countries, including China. Also, it reengineers those of its vehicles that sell worldwide. After reengineering, vehicles produced by Ford require less scheduled maintenance and can be driven as far as 100,000 miles before they need their first tuneup. Product improvements give customers confidence that Ford's products are built to higher standards than is normal in the Chinese market.

Customer satisfaction and responsiveness are very important to Ford. It redesigns the size and body shape of its vehicles to serve different customers. Ford will also offer high-quality service contracts to customers at 225 sales outlets run by 40 different dealers in China by the year 2000.

Ford has not had much success in producing a world car. It faces high costs in time and money that could swamp potential savings. It feels it is worth the risk, however, because the strength of the Ford 2000 plan is that it fully utilizes the company's depth of human diversity. Ford believes that diversity will be the engine that drives the creative energy of the corporation in the twenty-first century. It believes that the most successful companies will draw on this diversity to stay on the innovative and competitive edge.

Ford's marketing and industrial characteristics are more globally integrated than locally responsive. Product standardization is a major factor in this since Ford will use almost identical basic platforms and manufacturing systems. For example, Ford's European operations will make smaller, front wheel drive cars because Europe is mainly a small car market. But the same platform, manufacturing, and design processes will be used to build small cars for the U.S. market.

Some Lessons

Since the payoffs for projects in China are set far in the future, American managers of automotive manufacturing companies must change their mind-sets. They are often concerned with short-term profits due to the American system of quarterly and yearly reporting. In order to be successful, American managers must let their projects in China mature and either maintain other facilities that can support the Chinese projects or inform their shareholders of each project's long-term value.

American auto manufacturers must also be wary of their expatriate managers and Chinese managers. Managers from overseas must possess strong communications skills and a love of China. Without good communications skills, the language barrier could be devastating. In addition, they must enjoy living in China since they will be there for a long time. Furthermore, American manufacturers should have a strict plan for phasing out such individuals in middle management if they want to build loyalty and trust among their Chinese managers. The expatriates should also understand that they are there to guide the Chinese, not command them. Without the freedom to make decisions, the Chinese will be unable to adapt the company to local conditions. Chinese managers should also hold positions of power so that valuable connections with the government may be made.

Finally, the companies should be prepared to encounter a government unlike any other. Not only is the Chinese government strict about which company enters the market, but, because of the size of automotive companies, it restricts the number of new entrants. It also controls who their partners are and where joint ventures may be set up. Furthermore, it can set prices and output levels and control other aspects of production. Without proper *guanxi,* companies must resort to bribery to ensure smooth production. The result is a government with which American companies are very uncomfortable.

Realistically, the China market will be a dominant force in the future. The question is how far in the future. American companies prepared to deal with China's unusual environment may reap high rewards. Without doing the proper homework, ventures have failed in the past and will in the future. Merely entering the Chinese market is no guarantee of success, but with careful planning joint ventures can be profitable.

References and Further Reading

Agarwal, S., and S. N. Ramaswami. 1992. Choice of foreign market entry mode: Impact of ownership, location, and internalization factors. *Journal of International Business Studies* 23 (1): 1–27.

Almanac of China's Foreign Economic Relations and Trade (1996/1997). Hong Kong: China Resources Advertising.

Anderson, E., and H. Gatignon. 1986. Modes of foreign entry: A transaction cost analysis and propositions. *Journal of International Business Studies* 17 (3): 1–26.

Baliga, B. R., and A. M. Jaeger. 1984. Multinational corporations: Control systems and delegation issues. *Journal of International Business Studies* (3): 25–40.

Baum, A. C., and J. V. Singh. 1994. *The Evolutionary Dynamics of Organizations.* New York: Oxford University Press.

Beamish, P. W. 1993. The characteristics of joint ventures in the People's Republic of China. *Journal of International Marketing* 1 (2): 29–48.

Beamish, P. W., and J. C. Banks. 1987. Equity joint ventures and the theory of the multinational enterprise. *Journal of International Business Studies* 18: 1–16.

Benito, G. R. G., and G. Gripsrud. 1992. The expansion of foreign direct investments: Discrete rational location choices or a cultural learning process? *Journal of International Business Studies* 23:461–76.

Bleeke, J., and D. Ernst. 1991. The way to win in cross-border alliances. *Harvard Business Review* 69 (November–December): 127–35.

Blodgett, L. L. 1991. Partner contributions as predictors of equity share in international joint ventures. *Journal of International Business Studies* 22 (1): 63–77.

Boddewyn, J., and T. L. Brewer. 1994. International business political behavior: New theoretical directions. *Academy of Management Review* 19 (1): 119–43.

Buckley, P. J. 1983. New theories of international business: Some unresolved issues. In M. Casson, ed., *The Growth of International Business.* London: Macmillan.

Bulletin of MOFTEC. 1997. No. 1, 1–45. Bulletin of the Ministry of Foreign Trade and Economic Cooperation, People's Republic of China.

Butler, R. 1995. Time in organizations: Its experience, explanations and effects. *Organization Studies* 16 (6): 925–50.

Casson, M., and Zheng, R. 1991. Western joint ventures in China. *Journal of International Development* 3:293–323.

Caves, R. 1971. International corporations: The industrial economics of foreign investment. *Economica* 38:1–27.

Chang, S. J. 1995. International expansion strategy of Japanese firms: Capability building through sequential entry. *Academy of Management Journal* 38: 383–407.

Chen, M. 1996. Technological transfer to China: Major rules and issues. *International Journal of Technology Management* 10:747–56.

Child, J. 1994. *Managing in China during the Age of Reform.* Cambridge: Cambridge University Press.

Child, J., and L. Markoczy. 1993. Host-country managerial behavior and learning in Chinese and Hungarian joint ventures. *Journal of Management Studies* 30:611–31.

Chow, G., and Y. Kwan. 1996. Estimating economic effects of the political movements in China. *Journal of Comparative Economics* 23:192–208.

Clark, P. 1985. A review of the theories of time and structure for organizational sociology. In S. B. Bacharach and S. M. Mitchell, eds., *Research in the Sociology of Organizations.* Greenwich, CT: JAI Press.

Cohen, W. M., and D. A. Levinthal. 1990. Absorptive capacity: A new perspective on learning and innovation. *Administrative Science Quarterly* 35: 128–52.

Contractor, F. J. 1984. Choosing between direct investment and licensing: Theoretical considerations and empirical tests. *Journal of International Business Studies* 15:166–88.

Contractor, F., and P. Lorange. 1988. The strategy and economics basis for cooperative venture. In F. Contractor and P. Lorange, eds., *Cooperative Strategies in International Business.* Toronto: Lexington Books.

Dang, T. 1977. Ownership, control, and performance of the multinational corporations: A study of U.S. wholly owned subsidiaries and joint ventures in the Philippines and Taiwan. Ph.D. diss., University of California, Los Angeles.

Davidson, W. H. 1980. The location of foreign direct investment activity: Country characteristics and experience effects. *Journal of International Business Studies* 11 (2): 9–22.

Davidson, W. H. 1987. Creating and managing joint ventures in China. *California Management Review* 29:77–94.

Davidson, W. H., and D. G. McFetridge. 1985. Key characteristics in the choice of international technology transfer mode. *Journal of International Business Studies* 16 (2): 5–21.

Day, R. H., and P. Chen. 1993. *Nonlinear Dynamics and Evolutionary Economics.* New York: Oxford University Press.

Dong, J. L., and J. Hu. 1995. Mergers and acquisitions in China. *Federal Reserve Bank of Atlanta Economic Review,* November–December, 15–29.

Doz, Y. L., and C. K. Prahalad. 1991. Managing DMNCs: A search for a new paradigm. *Strategic Management Journal* 12:145–64.

Dunning, J. H. 1980. Toward an eclectic theory of international production: Some empirical tests. *Journal of International Business Studies* 11 (1): 9–31.

Dunning, J. H. 1988. The eclectic paradigm of international production: A restatement and some possible extensions. *Journal of International Business Studies* 19 (1): 1–31.

Erramilli, M. K. 1991. The experience factor in foreign market entry behavior of service firms. *Journal of International Business Studies* 22 (3): 479–501.

Fagre, N., and L. T. Wells. 1982. Bargaining power of multinationals and host governments. *Journal of International Business Studies* 12 (3): 9–23.

Franko, L. G. 1989. Use of minority and 50–50 joint ventures by United States multinationals during the 1970s: The interaction of host country policies and corporate strategies. *Journal of International Business Studies* 20 (1): 19–40.

Freeman, J., G. R. Carroll, and M. T. Hannan. 1983. The liabilities of newness: Age dependence in organizational death rates. *American Sociological Review* 48: 692–710.

Gatignon, H., and Anderson, E. 1988. The multinational corporation's degree of control over foreign subsidiaries: An empirical test of a transaction cost explanation. *Journal of Law, Economics, and Organization* 4:305–36.

Geringer, J. M., and L. Hebert. 1989. Control and performance of international joint ventures. *Journal of International Business Studies* 20:235–54.

Glaser, R., and M. Bassok. 1989. Learning theory and the study of introduction. *Annual Review of Psychology* 40: 631–66.

Gomes-Casseres, B. 1990. Firm ownership presences and host government restrictions: An integrated approach. *Journal of International Business Studies* 21 (1): 1–21.

Hamel, G. 1991. Competition for competence and inter-partner learning within international strategic alliances. *Strategic Management Journal* 12: 83–103.

Harrigan, K .R. 1985. *Strategies for Joint Ventures.* Lexington, MA: Heath.

Hennart, J. F. 1982. *The Theory of the Multinational Enterprise.* Ann Arbor: University of Michigan Press.

Hennart, J. F. 1988. A transaction costs theory of equity joint ventures. *Strategic Management Journal* 9:361–74.

Hennart, J. F. 1989. Can the "new forms of investment" substitute for the "old forms"? A transaction costs perspective. *Journal of International Business Studies* 20 (2): 211–34.

Hennart, J. F., and Y. Park. 1994. Location, governance, and strategic determinants of Japanese manufacturing investment in the United States. *Strategic Management Journal* 15:419–36.

Hill, C. W. L., P. Hwang, and W. C. Kim. 1990. An eclectic theory of the choice of international entry mode. *Strategic Management Journal* 11:117–28.

Hill, R. C., and D. Hellriegel. 1994. Critical contingencies in joint venture management: Some lessons from managers. *Organization Science* 5:594–607.

Hymer, S. H. 1976. *The International Operations of National Firms: A Study of Direct Foreign Investment.* Cambridge: MIT Press.

Inkpen, A. C., and P. W. Beamish. 1997. Knowledge, bargaining power, and the instability of international joint ventures. *Academy of Management Review* 22:177–202.

Jefferson, G. H., and T. G. Rawski. 1993. A theory of economic reform. University of Pittsburgh, Department of Economics, Working Papers, no. 273.

Johanson, J., and J. Vahlne. 1977. The internationalization process of the firm: A model of knowledge development and increasing foreign market commitment. *Journal of International Business Studies* 8 (1): 23–32.

Johanson, J., and J. Vahlne. 1990. The mechanism of internationalization. *International Marketing Review* 7:11–24.

Kelley, L., and Y. Luo. 1998. *China 2000: Emerging Business Issues.* Thousand Oaks, CA: Sage.

Killing, J. P. 1983. *Strategies for Joint Venture Success.* New York: Praeger.

Kogut, B. 1988. Joint ventures: Theoretical and empirical perspectives. *Strategic Management Journal* 9:319–32.

Kim, W. C., and P. Hwang. 1992. Global strategy and multinationals' entry mode choice. *Journal of International Business Studies* 23 (1): 29–53.

Kogut, B. 1983. Foreign direct investment as a sequential process. In C. P. Kingleberger and D. Audretsch, eds., *The Multinational Corporation in the 1980s.* Cambridge: MIT Press.

Kogut, B., and S. J. Chang. 1991. Technological capabilities and Japanese foreign direct investment in the United States. *Review of Economics and Statistics* 73:401–13.

Kumar, V., and V. Subramian. 1997. A contingency framework for the entry mode decision. *Journal of World Business* 32 (1): 53–72.

Kwon, Y., and L. Konopa. 1993. Impact of host country market characteristics on the choice of foreign market entry mode. *International Marketing Review* 10 (2): 60–76.

Lecraw, D. J. 1984. Bargaining power, ownership, and profitability of transnational corporations in developing countries. *Journal of International Business Studies* 15 (2): 27–43.

Levinthal, D. A. 1991. Organizational adaptation and environmental selection-interrelated processes of change. *Organization Science* 2:140–45.

Levinthal, D. A., and J. G. March. 1993. The myopia of learning. *Strategic Management Journal* 14 (winter): 95–112. Special issue.

Levitt, B., and J. G. March. 1988. Organizational learning. *Annual Review of Sociology* 14:319–40.

Li, J. 1994. Experience effects and international expansion: Strategies of service MNCs in the Asia-Pacific region. *Management International Review* 34:217–34.

Lin, J. Y. 1992. Rural reforms and agricultural growth in China. *American Economic Review* 82:34–51.

Luo, Y. 1998. *International Investment Strategies in the People's Republic of China.* Aldershot, U.K.: Ashgate.

Luo, Y. 1999. *Entry and Cooperative Strategies in International Expansion.* Westport, CT: Quorum.

Luo, Y., and M. W. Peng. 1999. Learning to compete in a transition economy: Experience, environment, and performance. *Journal of International Business Studies* 30 (2): 278–307.

Luostarinen, R. 1980. *Internationalization of the Firm.* Helsinki: Helsinki School of Economics.

Madhok, A. 1997. Cost, value, and foreign market entry mode: The transaction and the firm. *Strategic Management Journal* 18:39–61.

March, J. G. 1991. Exploration and exploitation in organizational learning. *Organization Science* 2:71–87.

Markoczy, L. 1993. Managerial and organizational learning in Hungarian-Western mixed management organizations. *International Journal of Human Resource Management* 9:210–20.

McCarthy, D., S. Puffer, and P. Simmonds. 1993. Riding the Russian roller coaster: U.S. firms' recent experience and future plans in the former USSR. *California Management Review* 36 (1): 99–115.

McClain, D. 1983. Foreign direct investment in the United States: Old currents, new waves, and the theory of direct foreign investment. In C. Kingleberger and D. Audretsch, eds., *The Multinational Corporations of the 1980s.* Cambridge: MIT Press.

McGrath, J. E., and J. R. Kelly. 1986. *Time and Human Interaction: Toward a Social Psychology of Time.* New York: Guilford.

Nelson, R. R., and S. G. Winter. 1982. *An Evolutionary Theory of Economic Change.* Cambridge: Harvard University Press.

Mjoen, H., and S. Tallman. 1997. Control and performance in international joint ventures. *Organization Science* 8 (3): 257–74.

National Council for U.S.-China Trade. 1991. *Special Report on U.S. Investment in China.* Washington, DC: Department of Commerce.

Naughton, B. 1995. *Growing Out of the Plan: Chinese Economic Reform, 1978–1993.* New York: Cambridge University Press.

Osborn, R. N., and C. C. Baughn. 1990. Forms of interorganizational governance for multinational alliances. *Academy of Management Journal* 33 (3): 503–19.

Osland, G. E., and S. T. Cavusgil. 1996. Performance issues in U.S.-China joint ventures. *California Management Review* 38:106–30.

Ouchi, W. G. 1977. The relationship between organizational structure and organizational control. *Administrative Science Quarterly* 22:95–112.

Pan, Y. 1996. Influences on foreign equity ownership level in joint ventures in China. *Journal of International Business Studies* 27(1): 1–26.

Park, S.-H. 1996. Managing an interorganizational network: A framework of the institutional mechanism for network control. *Organization Studies* 17: 795–824.

Parkhe, A. 1993. Strategic alliance structuring: A game theoretic and transaction cost examination of interfirm cooperation. *Academy of Management Journal* 36:794–829.

Peng, M. W., Y. Luo, and L. Sun. 1998. Firm growth via mergers and acquisitions in China. In L. Kelley and Y. Luo, eds., *Towards the Year 2000: Emerging Business Issues in China.* Thousand Oaks, CA: Sage.

Pennings, J. M., H. G. Barkema, and S. M. Douma. 1994. Organizational learning and diversification. *Academy of Management Journal* 37:608–40.

Perkins, F., and M. Raiser. 1996. Productivity performance and priorities for the reform of China's state owned enterprises. *Journal of Development Studies* 32:414–44.

Pfeffer, J., and G. Salancik. 1978. *The External Control of Organizations: A Resource Dependence Perspective.* New York: Harper and Row.

Prahalad, C. K., and G. Hamel. 1990. The core competence of the corporation. *Harvard Business Review* 68:79–91.

Randall, D., and P. Telesio. 1995. Planning ahead. *China Business Review* (January–February):14–18.

Raswki, T. G. 1999. Reforming China's economy: What have we learned? *China Journal* 41:139–56.

Root, F. R. 1994. *Entry Strategies for International Markets.* Washington, DC: Lexington.

Rothstein, J. 1996. Easing your way into China. *China Business Review* 23 (January–February): 30–32.

Sarkar, M., and S. T. Cavusgil. 1996. Trends in international business thought and literature: A review of international market entry mode research — integration and synthesis. *International Executive* 38 (6): 825–48.

Schaan, J. L. 1983. Partner control and joint venture success: The case of Mexico. Ph.D. diss., University of Western Ontario.

Schaan, J. L. 1988. How to control a joint venture even as a minority partner. *Journal of General Management* 14 (1): 4–16.

Shan, W. 1991. Environment risks and joint venture sharing arrangements. *Journal of International Business Studies* 22 (4): 555–78.

Shane, S. 1994. The effect of national culture on the choice between licensing and foreign direct investment. *Strategic Management Journal* 15:627–42.

Sharma, A. 1995. Entry strategies of U.S. firms to the newly independent states, Baltic states, and Eastern European countries. *California Management Review* 37 (3): 90–109.

Shaw, S. M., and J. Meier. 1993. Second generation MNCs in China. *McKinsey Quarterly* 4:3–16.

Shaw, S. M., and J. Meier. 1994. Second-generation MNCs in China. *China Business Review* 2 (September–October): 10–15.

Shenkar, O. 1990. International joint ventures' problems in China: Risks and remedies. *Long Range Planning* 23:82–90.

Shenkar, O., and M. Nyaw. 1995. Yin and yang: The interplay of human resources in Chinese-foreign ventures. In *Global Perspective on Human Resource Management.* Engelwood Cliffs, NJ: Prentice-Hall.

Singh, J. V., D. J. Tucker, and R. J. House. 1986. Organizational legitimacy and the liability of newness. *Administrative Science Quarterly* 31:171–93.

Stopford, J. M., and L. T. Wells. 1972. *Managing the Multinational Enterprise.* New York: Basic Books.

Sun, H. 1998. Macroeconomic impact of direct foreign investment in China, 1979–1996. *World Economy* 21:675–94.

Tallman, S. B., and O. Shenkar. 1994. A managerial decision model of international cooperative venture formation. *Journal of International Business Studies* 25 (1): 91–114.

Tan, J. J., and J. Litschert. 1994. Environment-strategy relationship and its performance implications: An empirical study of the Chinese electronics industry. *Strategic Management Journal* 15:1–20.

Tateisi, N. 1996. How to invest in China. *Columbia Journal of World Business* 3 (summer): 66–75.

Teagarden, M. B. 1990. Sino-U.S. joint venture effectiveness. Ph.D. diss., University of Southern California, Los Angeles.

Teece, D. J. 1983. Multinational enterprise, internal governance, and industrial organization. *American Economic Review* 75 (2): 233–38.

Teece, D. J., G. Pisano, and A. Shuen. 1990. Firm capabilities, resources, and the concept of strategy. Working Papers, no. 90–8, Center for Research in Management, University of California, Berkeley.

UNCTAD (United Nations Conference on Trade and Development). 1998. *World Investment Report, 1998.* New York: United Nations.

Vanhonacker, W. 1997. Entering China: An unconventional approach. *Harvard Business Review* (March–April): 130–40.

Walder, A. G. 1995. China's transitional economy: Interpreting its significance. *China Quarterly* (4): 963–79.

Welch, L. S., and R. Luostarinen. 1988. Internationalization: Evolution of a concept. *Journal of General Management* 14 (2): 34–55.

Wilson, B. D. 1980. The propensity of multinationals to expand through acquisitions. *Journal of International Business Studies* 11 (1): 59–65.

Williamson, O. E. 1985. *The Economic Institutions of Capitalism.* New York: Free Press.

World Bank. 1995. *China: Reform of State-Owned Enterprises.* Washington, DC: China and Mongolia Department, World Bank.

World Bank. 1996. *The Chinese Economy: Fighting Inflation, Deepening Reforms.* Washington, DC: World Bank.

World Bank. 1997. *China 2020.* Washington, DC: World Bank.

World Bank. 1998. *China 2020: China Engaged.* Washington, DC: World Bank.

World Bank. 1999. *Global Economic Prospects and the Developing Countries.* Washington, DC: World Bank.

Yan, A., and B. Gray. 1994. Bargaining power, management control, and performance in United States–China joint ventures: A comparative case study. *Academy of Management Journal* 37 (6): 1478–1517.

Yan, Y., J. Child, and Y. Lu. 1995. Ownership and control in international business: An examination of Sino-foreign international joint ventures. Working Papers, no. 6, University of Cambridge.

Yu, C. J. 1991. The experience effect and foreign direct investment. *Weltwirt-schaftliches Archiv* 126:560–79.

Yusuf, S. 1994. China's macroeconomic performance and management during transition. *Journal of Economic Perspectives* 8:71–92.

Zaheer, S. 1995. Overcoming the liability of foreignness. *Academy of Management Journal* 38:341–63.

Index

Page numbers in bold indicate tables.